Ernest B. Bax

A Handbook of the History of Philosophy

for the use of students

Ernest B. Bax

A Handbook of the History of Philosophy
for the use of students

ISBN/EAN: 9783337238445

Printed in Europe, USA, Canada, Australia, Japan

Cover: Foto ©Thomas Meinert / pixelio.de

More available books at **www.hansebooks.com**

BOHN'S PHILOSOPHICAL LIBRARY.

A HANDBOOK

OF THE

HISTORY OF PHILOSOPHY.

A HANDBOOK

OF THE

ISTORY OF PHILOSOPHY

FOR THE USE OF STUDENTS.

BY

ERNEST BELFORT BAX.

EDITOR OF 'KANT'S PROLEGOMENA,' ETC.;

HOR OF 'JEAN PAUL MARAT, A HISTORICO-BIOGRAPHICAL SKETCH,' ETC.

)NDON: GEORGE BELL AND SONS, YORK STREET,

COVENT GARDEN.

1886.

LONDON:
PRINTED BY WILLIAM CLOWES AND SONS, LIMITED,
STAMFORD STREET AND CHARING CROSS.

PREFACE.

When I was requested to undertake the editing and revision for Bohn's Philosophical Library, of a new edition of 'Tennemann's Manual of the History of Philosophy,' a very brief examination sufficed to make it evident to me that the amount of correction and alteration required to bring the latter only approximately up to date would be such, that the last state of that manual would bid fair to resemble the condition of a certain relic associated with the Thirty Years War, respecting which we are told, the "head, neck, legs and part of the body have been renewed, all the rest is the real horse." It was therefore decided that I should undertake an entirely new volume on the subject.

The plan adopted has been to give a more or less detailed account of those philosophers who either constitute epochs in the history of speculation, or at least have contributed something of their own toward its subsequent development, without filling the work unnecessarily with a mere crowd of names. Of course in the case of thinkers of subordinate importance, a selection made on this principle must always be open to criticism, but that there are no flagrant cases of partiality or carelessness is my conscientious belief.

It will be observed that there is a progressive expansion in the treatment as modern times are approached. A bibliography has been appended where it has been considered necessary, especially in the case of those earlier periods of which the exposition has been more condensed. As regards later writers, the view taken is that the primary need of the student is to study the original works themselves rather than what other people have written about them, desirable as this may be as a supplementary aid. Works, moreover, treating of these thinkers are numerous, and their titles readily accessible to the student. I must, in conclusion, beg the reader to remember, as some extenuation of any short-comings he may find, that this little work only professes to be a "handbook" to the study of the subject, and not an exhaustive treatment of it.

It should also be stated that I have been ably assisted by Mr. Davison's compilation of the excellent index which concludes the work.

HANDBOOK

TO THE

HISTORY OF PHILOSOPHY.

GENERAL INTRODUCTION.

I. What is Philosophy?

Man finds himself conscious of being in a ready-made world, of which he forms part and parcel. He apprehends this fact long before the impulse arises in him to comprehend it. He is aware, that is to say, of this world in its *concrete actuality*, long before he feels himself driven to try and become aware of it in its *abstract possibility*. But this impulse nevertheless arises at a certain stage of man's development, and the result is philosophy, which may be described as the offspring of the conscious endeavour to reconstruct the given world of perceptive experience—the world found constructed in *actuality*—according to its *possibility*. This enormous and all-embracing problem, as a matter of course, exhibits a variety of aspects, and has naturally been approached by many paths. The History of Philosophy shows us these aspects as they progressively unfold themselves to the human mind, and the various paths that have been struck out for their investigation, one or two proving highways, many byways, and not a few blind roads.

The first aspect under which the problem presented itself in ancient Greece, whose philosophical development may be taken as typical, was that of *Being* or existence; the statement was—to discover the ultimate constituent of the physical universe. In the next stage, the problem became refined. It was no longer an ultimate

B

cosmical principle that was sought for, but the ultimate form of existence was conceived as one of which the world of sense was a mere mode, if it were not indeed opposed to it. The problem of philosophy continued to be attacked on the side of *being* from these two points, the concrete and the abstract, until the Sophistic Revolution which issued in Socrates, when the standing-ground was radically changed. It was now seen for the first time that inasmuch as the possibility of formulating, much more of solving the problem of the *Being* of the sensible world, presupposed the capacity of *Knowing*, the first step in philosophy must be an investigation of the conditions under which this knowledge comes to pass, in other words, an examination of the capacity of knowing, itself. The philosophical labours of the two typical thinkers of antiquity, Plato and Aristotle, were mainly occupied with this problem.

Philosophy distinguishes itself from mythology and theology, by being essentially a conscious and reasoned effort to explain the universe, while mythology and theology are, at least in their genesis, essentially the unconscious and spontaneous results of a primitive imagination, which employs the notion of volition and personality as the basis of causal condition. The fact of their being at a later stage refined and presented in a quasi-philosophised guise, or supported by philosophical arguments, does not alter their intrinsic character.

The radical distinction between philosophy and special science lies in that while the latter is concerned either with the classification and description of certain isolated groups of phenomena, or with formulating the real or causal conditions of the possibility of these groups considered *per se*, the former is occupied with the totality of all phenomena, either as concerns its *real conditions* in time (cosmology and psychology), or its *elemental conditions*, i.e. the conditions of its possibility (metaphysic proper).* Science is concerned with a part for itself alone, while philosophy, if it concerns itself with any part or isolated group of phenomena at all, only regards it in its relation

* Of the distinction between *real* and *elemental* conditions, we shall have occasion to treat more at length in a subsequent division of the present work.

to the whole, or as a necessary propædeutic to a coherent view of the whole.

The word philosophy tradition states to have been first used by Pythagoras. This semi-mythical personage, according to the well-known legend, when asked by Leon, the tyrant of Phlœus, what vocation he followed, replied that he had none, but that he was a philosopher. On being interrogated as to the meaning of the word, he replied, that as in the Olympic Games some sought glory, others gain, while others, more noble, came to enjoy the spectacle; so in life, while there were many prepared to work for honour, many for riches, there were yet a few who, despising all these things, found their occupation in the contemplation and knowledge of nature and man, and that these were the philosophers.

In the dialogue Euthydemus, Plato defines philosophy ατίσις ἐνιστήμης. It is concerned alone with the *ideal*, and is identical with *wisdom*, as opposed to *opinion*, the subject-matter of which is the *sensible*. Aristotle sometimes employs the term in a general sense, so as to include all science, but retains its narrower signification for what would now be termed Ontology, namely, the science of Being, in itself, as opposed to the subject-matter of the special sciences. The Stoics defined wisdom (σοφία), as the science of divine and human things, but philosophy (φιλοσοφία),* as the endeavour after perfection, theoretic and practical, in the three departments of Logic, Physic, and Ethic. Philosophy, with the Stoics, thus comprehended the whole range of human interests, active no less than speculative, but only as a disposition of character, not a body of doctrine, for which the former term was reserved, which hence corresponds properly to 'philosophy.' Epicurus,† in a similar way, calls philosophy *the rational endeavour* after happiness.

The above were the leading definitions of the term in antiquity. Turning to modern times, we find Christian Wolff enunciating the following, in his 'Philosophia Rationalis,' as an original definition of philosophical knowledge: *Cognitio rationis eorum, quæ sunt vel fiant unde*

* Plutarch, 'De plac. philosop.' i.
† 'Empir. adv. Math.' xi. 169.

intelligatur cur sint vel fiant. (A knowledge of the reason of those things which are or come to pass, by which it is understood why they are or come to pass.) Kant divided all knowledge into historical, *cognitio ex datis* (knowledge through facts), and rational, *cognitio ex principiis* (knowledge through principles). The last was again divided into mathematical knowledge, through the construction of conceptions, and philosophical knowledge, through conceptions as such. The post-Kantian definitions of philosophy in Germany have been in most instances based on special systems. Thus Herbart defines philosophy as the working-out of conceptions, this working-out consisting in definition, classification, &c. He divides philosophy into three main departments: logic, metaphysic, and æsthetic, the last-named including ethic. Schelling defines philosophy as the science of the absolute identity of subject and object; Hegel, as the science of the absolute, as dialectical movement, or, again, as the science of the self-comprehending reason. As independent definitions may be cited, Professor Zeller's ('Pre-Socratic Philosophy,' vol. i. p. 8, of the English translation): "Thought that is methodical, and directed in a conscious manner to the cognition of things in their interdependence." In Schopenhauer (*Parerga und Paralipomena*, vol. ii. p. 19), we find the following: "Philosophy, it is true, has experience for its subject-matter, yet not like the other sciences, this or that particular experience; but rather experience itself in general, as such, according to its possibility, its range, its essential content, its internal and external elements, its form and matter." For Auguste Comte, philosophy consists in the methodical filiation of the special sciences, according to a unifying conception; for Herbert Spencer, it is similarly the "unification of knowledge."

It may not be out of place, in an English Manual of the History of Philosophy to add a few words respecting the perversion, and in some cases the degradation the word has suffered until recently in this country.

It will be seen that all the definitions of "Philosophy" we have cited have this in common, that they involve the universal, as opposed to the particular, as the subject of investigation; they all imply the conditions of the sum of things as the subject-matter of inquiry, either directly or indirectly. The remarks offered at the commencement of this section on the scope of philosophy are sufficiently comprehensive to cover all these definitions, while abstracting from anything in them which would narrow the term to any particular philosophical theory.

The Englishman, however, has until recently indulged his fancy for garnishing his conversation with high-sounding words by vulgarising the term philosophy into meaning any kind of reasoning on any subject whatever. Till within the last quarter of a century the expression "natural philosophy" figured, even in the syllabuses of academic and learned bodies, as a designation for the department of scientific research known as Physics, while to the common man, chemistry, astronomy, physiology, were no less "philosophy."

We have had, besides, philosophy of manufactures, of love, of cookery! There is a sense, of course, in which the expressions "philosophy of history," or "philosophy of nature," may be justifiably employed, where, namely, history or nature, as wholes, are treated deductively in the light of a philosophic theory or conception, as part of a system; but it is needless to say that it was not in this sense that such phrases were formerly employed among the English-speaking race. The salutary change which has taken place in this respect within the last few years is one more indication of the opening up of English culture to continental, and especially German influences, as well as of the philosophic revival visible throughout English-speaking communities.

The ancient division of philosophy was into Logic, Physic (including Metaphysic), and Ethic. It is said that this division had its origin with the Stoics. It was certainly first definitely formulated by them. But marked indications of it are to be found in both Plato and Aristotle. By Logic, or organon, was understood not merely formal logic, but the doctrine of method in general, including theory of knowledge (or what answered as such in the ancient world), and to some extent psychology; under physic was embraced cosmical theory, as well as ontology, in short, all that pertained to the existence of things as such; while Ethic covered the whole range of active human interests, including politics, although its chief problem was, in accordance with the later Greek attitude of mind in such matters, the discovery of the ideal of life for the individual. In the Middle Ages, when philosophy was subordinated to the dogmas of Christian theology, no systematic division was made. In modern times philosophy proper has been generally taken to include logic, metaphysic, psychology, and ethic, the "practical philosophy" of the Germans. The usual ill-fate that has befallen the word in Great Britain, has not been wanting, however, in this connection. Owing to the special line philosophical development took in this island, to the influence, that is, of Locke and the Scotch psychologists, the word showed a tendency even where legitimately employed to become narrowed to psychology and ethic, or, as these departments were usually designated, "mental and moral philosophy."

A not unnatural reaction against this view of the scope of philosophy has been recently exhibited in a desire to exclude psychology altogether from the sphere of philosophical studies. It has been argued that mental phenomena being amenable in all essential repects to the inductive method employed in the study of material phenomena, and only differing in being the object of internal rather than external observation (to use the current phrase), there is no reason for regarding their treatment in any other light than as constituting one of the special sciences. To this it is replied, that psychological investigation has a special, although indirect bearing on "theory of knowledge," and *à fortiori* on the whole subject-matter of philosophy; a bearing which cannot be alleged of any objective science; that only within certain limits do the methods of the objective sciences apply to psychology; that "there is something in Mind, as the subject-matter of Psychology, unlike anything else," and that "the events or states (however they are called) which psychology investigates" being "apprehended only in the peculiar attitude of introspection, makes a profound difference,"&c.*

* Professor Croom Robertson in 'Mind,' vol. viii. p. 9.

It must be admitted, I think, that a good case is made out in these, and similar arguments—in addition to anything that might be urged from the universal practice of history—for retaining Psychology as a department of Philosophy. But conceding this, it must be none the less recognised as holding a position quite subordinate to the higher departments, and the greater care must be taken to avoid introducing psychological material into them, and thus obscuring the main issue, one of the most fruitful sources of fallacy and confusion. The leading problem of philosophy is undoubtedly "Theory of Knowledge," to discover the conditions under which knowledge, or experience, is possible, in order to re-construct in the forms of abstract thought according to its elements, the world given as constructed in concrete intuition.

The advances made by science during the latter half of the present century have resulted in a striking rehabilitation of cosmology, *i.e.* the systematic doctrine of nature, or the object-world, as a leading philosophical discipline. The doctrines of the Conservation of Energy and of Evolution have given to cosmology definite guiding principles for the abstract explanation of the world according to its causal conditions, which can never be taken from it, however their application may be modified by subsequent research.

The main departments of philosophic investigation are these:—(1.) "*Theory of knowledge;*" (2.) *Ontology* (if such be admitted; and (3.) *Cosmology*. To these must be added as a pendent to cosmology, or the systematic doctrine of objective or material nature, *Psychology*, or the systematic doctrine of subjective or mental nature; the phenomenology of the *moral* consciousness falling to be dealt with by cosmology and psychology at their point of contact in sociology. But inasmuch as all these departments are simply aspects of one reality to be explained—to wit, the *totality of knowledge*—the great and ultimate task of philosophy is to bridge over the chasms which apparently divide them, to show their interconnection as an organic whole, and their ultimate root in the conditions of knowledge itself.

II. THE HISTORY OF PHILOSOPHY.

As we remarked at the commencement of the last section, the History of Philosophy is the history of the unfolding to the Human Mind of the various problems involved in experience, and the struggles of the reason to resolve them. This has been sometimes attempted in their entirety, but more frequently the necessity has been felt of dealing with them separately, and it has indeed not seldom happened that in the course of their isolated treatment the view of the whole as the end of philosophy has been left out of sight.

An objection has been raised to the history of philosophy as an introduction to philosophic study, that in the necessarily condensed expositions of systems which are given, the true spirit of the founders is lost; that the love of research and devotion to truth which actuated them, and the steps by which the systems reached their ultimate form, as well as the conflict of tendencies of which they may be the issue, can be at best but indicated in a dry and cursory manner. It must be admitted that an amount of truth underlies this criticism, especially as regards the greater number of actually extant histories, and even the ideal history, whenever it shall appear, we can scarcely expect will deprive it altogether of its point; but it must we think also be admitted that though no mere reading of compilations will suffice for a serious philosophic culture, yet that such compilations are a necessary aid to the student, and further, that it is possible for a history of philosophy to be presented in a way in which the inherent drawback complained of may be reduced to the *minimum*. "The events which it is most important to comprehend," says Dühring truly, "do not stare one in the face." "He who will give account of the spiritual working of the greatest minds must himself be capable of descending into the depths." * A history of philosophy, to be of real use, must not merely be an abstract of doctrines, but afford an insight into the historical and psychological genesis of those doctrines; and although no history of philosophy

* Dühring, 'Kritische Geschichte der Philosophie,' p. 4.

can approach the first-hand study of the works of philosophers,* yet inasmuch as it is impossible for any but a very small number of students to construct for themselves even the history of a single period from original sources, a surrogate is requisite, and need not of necessity be an altogether inadequate one.

The history of philosophy has been written mainly on three different plans. There is the compilation-history, which consists in a collection of undigested anecdotes, facts, and bald, and for the most part loose, statements of opinion. Then there is the tendency-history, which reads into the ideas of the past, the doctrines of a modern system or code of ideas; and, in addition, seeks for conformity with the method of this system in the course of historical development. Lastly, there is the critical-history, in which a spirit of scientific acumen and a comparative criticism is brought to bear at once upon the authorities used, the doctrines treated, and the filiation of those doctrines.

Of these several plans, the first is the most utterly execrable, and the last, it need scarcely be said, the only one capable of furnishing a uniformly reliable history. It must not be supposed, however, that in denying this character of any tendency-history as such, we imply that the history has no tendency; for just as general history exhibits a certain determinate course of development, so does the history of philosophy. But the duty of the historian, as historian, is to maintain strictly an objective attitude, merely pointing out that element in systems which perpetually recurs—which in various guises is unmistakably present—in all the more important thinkers, from those elements which are traceable to the personality and the age or the country, while being cautious with apparently striking anticipations of modern thought. It is perhaps a failing in most existing histories, that the evolution of philosophy is too much isolated. It is not sufficiently brought into connection with the history of civilisation or with historic evolution generally. It surely cannot but lie within the province of the historian of

* This does not, of course, apply to the fragmentary works of ancient authors, which require special research and critical treatment.

philosophy to trace the action and reaction of speculative thought upon its surroundings, intellectual and material. Although we cannot expect to carry out this principle to its full extent in a volume like the present, an effort will be made to indicate the leading points of contact between the philosophy and the general intellectual conditions of the several epochs.

The earliest, and the only ancient history of philosophy, in the proper sense of the word, which has come down to us, is that of Diogenes Laertius, who wrote probably about the third century. It is a bad specimen of a bad class, the compilation-history, but being one of the most copious sources of information respecting the lives and characters of the ancient philosophers, has been extensively utilised by all subsequent writers. The work of Diogenes is, however, so utterly uncritical, and in many respects childish, that it requires to be used with the utmost caution.

The first modern history is that of the Englishman, Thomas Stanley, which was originally published in 1655, and passed through three editions, being re-issued in 1687 and 1701. The work is confined to ancient philosophy, and is a mere compilation from Laertius and other classical writers. Contemporaneously with Stanley, a certain Jacobus Thomasius published an ecclesiastical and philosophical history combined, in Latin, at Leipsic. This was succeeded in 1697 by the great *Dictionnaire historique et critique* of Bayle, which, although not strictly-speaking a history, nor concerning itself exclusively with philosophical matters, is entitled to mention, on account of the dimensions and importance of its articles on the Greek philosophers.

The first history in which modern philosophy was treated of appears to have been the *Histoire Critique de la Philosophie*, in 3 vols., by Deslandes. (Paris, 1730–6.) More important than the last-mentioned was the *Historia Critica Philosophiæ à mundo incunabulis ad nostram usque ætatem deducta* Johann Jakob Brucker (5 vols.; Leipsic, 1742). Brucker's work, although by no means critical in the modern sense of the word, is an undoubted advance upon its predecessors, at once in scope, in method and in style. The historical point of view is certainly absent, but where not clouded by prejudice (for Brucker was a tendency-writer of the most pronounced type), Brucker exhibits an amount of discernment, to be looked for in vain in previous writers. The standpoint is Leibnitzian. Brucker's work was condensed into English, by Enfield, and published in a single volume in 1791.

It was succeeded after the lapse of a few years by an Italian History of Philosophy, by one Cromaziano, subsequently translated into German. Next came Tiedemann's *Geist der Speculativen Philosophie* (Strasburg, 1791–7). This work extends from Thales to Berkeley—the standpoint is Leibnitz-Wolfian. Tiedemann was the first to attempt an objective handling of the history of philosophy. The method and style of the work is a marked advance on Brucker's, in fact Tiedemann may be looked upon as in many respects the founder of the modern critical history of philosophy. From this time forward, histories of philosophy, and works on the history of philosophy, form a leading feature in the literature of Germany. It will be only necessary to mention and characterise the most important of these treatises. The great Kantian movement produced several works of the kind, partly of a tendency, and partly of a critical nature. First in order comes Johann Gottlieb Buhle's *Lehrbuch der Geschichte der Philosophie* (8 vols.; Göttingen, 1796–1804). The work is Kantian, leaning to the mystical tendencies of Jacobi and his school. The most meritorious of the pure Kantian histories is that of Tennemann, an unfinished work in eleven volumes, an abridgment of which in English has formed one of the volumes in Bohn's library. From the standpoint of Schelling, we have Rixner's *Handbuch der Geschichte der Philosophie* (3 vols.; Salzbach, 1822–23). Ernst Reinhold's *Handbuch der Allgemeinen Geschichte der Philosophie* (3 vols.; Gotha, 1828–30,) which passed through two or three editions, is spoken of as meritorious. But the history which until recently has been unanimously regarded as the standard authority, not only in Germany, but throughout Europe, is Ritter's *Geschichte der Philosophie* (12 vols; Hamburg, 1829–30: 2nd ed. 1836–38). Ritter's accurate scholarship combined with his impartiality to give his work a value likely to endure, in spite of recent advances in research.

In 1833, two years after Hegel's death, his disciple Karl Ludwig Michelet* published his master's Lectures on the History of Philosophy, in the collected edition of Hegel's works. Hegel's history is the most perfect representative of the tendency-history we possess. It is based on the positions that, though every form of historical reality has its relative justification, there exists beside these justifiable systems their negations, which are not even relatively justifiable; that the Hegelian system forms, so far as essentials reach, an absolute conclusion to the course of historical development; and that the historical sequence of philosophical standpoints must coincide with the logical sequence of categories. These principles are carried out in the course of the exposition with the rigour of logic, and the clever manipulation of data characteristic of Hegel.

By far the most popular history of philosophy is that of Albert Schwegler, in one volume. Since its first publication in 1848 it has passed through nearly a dozen editions in Germany. It has also been twice translated into English by J. H. Seelye, in America, and with annotations by Mr. Hutchison Stirling, the last-mentioned rendering being now in its eighth edition. Schwegler's work is rigorously impartial, and contains a mass of closely-packed information; but his presentation is somewhat arid and unappreciative. Of more recent treatises, for the combination of exhaustive research and fulness of detail, with critical appreciation, Ueberweg's History, the English translation of which is well known, occupies the foremost rank. The work of Johann Eduard Erdmann, though not so well known in England, is almost as much read in Germany at the present time. Erdmann's literary faculty is much greater than Ueberweg's. Among those treatises whose renown is as much literary as philosophical, may be mentioned Lange's 'History of Materialism,' translated into all the more important European languages, and in Germany become almost a classic, and the small

* K. L. Michelet must not be confounded with Jules Michelet, the eminent French historian and essayist.

Geschichte der Philosophie kritisch dargestellt of Dühring. The latter, although so far as we are aware untranslated at present, is as remarkable for the brilliancy and clearness of its style as for its strongly marked tendency-character.

The Latin nations, not excepting France, have failed in achieving great original research in the history of philosophy. Among the principal modern French treatises on the subject may be mentioned Dégérando's *Histoire comparée des Systèmes de la Philosophie* (4 vols.; Paris, 1822–3). J. F. Nourrisson's *Tableau des progrès de la pensée humaine de Thales jusqu'à Hegel* (Paris, 1858). Laforet's *Histoire de la Philosophie* (Brussels and Paris, 1867). Alfred Weber's *Histoire de la Philosophie Européenne*; Alfred Fouillée's *Histoire de la Philosophie* (Paris, 1874). The best-known French history is Victor Cousin's *Histoire Générale de la Philosophie depuis les temps les plus reculés jusqu'à la fin du* XVIIIe *siècle* (5th ed.; Paris, 1863). The few Italian and Spanish treatises do not call for any special notice.

The first English history of philosophy, after Stanley's, was the execrable compilation from Brucker by William Enfield, first published towards the close of the last century. This was followed by Johnson's translation of Tennemann's small manual (subsequently reprinted, with additions and annotations, in Bohn's Philosophical Library). Robert Blakey's 'History of the Philosophy of Mind' appeared in 1848; and shortly after the late F. D. Maurice's, so far as style is concerned, cleverly written 'History of Moral and Metaphysical Philosophy.' But more widely read than any of these was the 'Biographical History of Philosophy' of the late George Henry Lewes, first published in 1845, in four pocket volumes, and expanded in 1867 (2nd ed., revised 1871) into 'The History of Philosophy from Thales to Comte,' in two thick volumes (crown 8vo.). Lewes, who writes more particularly from the standpoint of the *Philosophie positive*, but generally from that of English empiricism, furnishes an example of a probably unique development of the tendency-history, to wit, the didactic-history. There is no positive reading of the author's own position into the systems of older thinkers, or distortion of those systems in the course of their development, as in the tendency-history proper, but they one and all serve as foils to the superior wisdom of the empirical philosophy in general, and the positive philosophy in particular. This is their only purpose save in so far as they, here and there, show weak and faltering adumbrations of the "one true method."

To Mr. Hutchison Stirling's highly successful translation of Schwegler reference has already been made. The latest, and perhaps most important contribution to works in English on the general history of philosophy is the translation of Ueberweg's work, published a few years since by Messrs. Hodder & Stoughton. The present work, although limited in point of size, it is our aim to render as complete as possible in all points essential to the student, while omitting unimportant details.

THE ORIENTALS.

At the outset of the history of philosophy, as of other departments of culture, we are confronted with the prehistoric region occupied by the primitive theocratic civilisations of the Oriental world, of Egypt and Asia. The view largely prevalent, at the end of the last and beginning of the present century, was that these social organisations were the surviving monuments of a high primitive culture. In the light of the scientific conception of history, to which modern research and criticism has accustomed us, they are seen to be cases of arrested development, or of premature decay. The evolutionary principle in them, so to speak, their capacity for spontaneous development and progress, exhausted itself before the birth of that great world-evolution constituting the history of Humanity proper, and of which ancient Greece and modern Europe, with its colonies, are the extreme terms. The sixth century before Christ, or thereabouts, the age of Gautama, Confucius, Zoroaster and Thales, is the dawn of history in the latter sense. The history of the modern world is closely and definitely knitted to that of the Middle Ages, and this again to the history of ancient Greece and Rome, the whole forming an organised system. But the direct influence upon the classical civilisations of those of Assyria, Babylonia, Palestine, China, India, or even Egypt, is at best obscure. For this reason we do not purpose dwelling at any length on the quasi-philosophies, or more properly theosophies, of the East.

It is probable that a considerable body of theosophic lore was enshrined in the Egyptian temples; but encased as it was in mythological language, and coming to us as most of it does through Greek sources, it is impossible to give anything approaching a coherent and correct view of its general features. The Semitic race, on the other hand, has never in any of its branches produced an original philosophic or even theosophic system of its own. The Semitic mind is, in its pure state, anti-philosophical. Though it has given to the world no less than three important ethical religions, we search in vain through the whole body of pure Semitic literature, that is, such as reflects the Semitic intellect unaffected by non-Semitic culture (*e.g.* the Hebrew Scriptures and the Koran), for a single trace even of a philosophic thought, much less a system, unless indeed we choose, as some have done, to read a metaphysical meaning into the old Hebrew formula, "I am that I am"—the general character and isolated position of which, however, would give colour to the hypothesis of an Egyptian origin. The fragments of reputed Assyrian and Akkadian literature are likewise entirely destitute of a philosophical side. In the Medo-Persian literature, as that of an Aryan race, we might naturally expect to find something like a philosophy, and, in fact, the latter portions of the Zend-Avesta show attempts to render the theological doctrine of the dual principle philosophic. But there is even here no sign of an independent and original philosophical movement. In China the only ancient writing possessing any speculative interest is that of Lao-tse, born B.C. 604, and the main position of which is practically identical with that of Indian Metaphysic, though alleged to have been uninfluenced by it; but there is much in the treatise of a purely theological character, and devoid of all philosophic interest.

It is in India, that we first find a distinct and unmistakable philosophic development. In the sixth century before Christ, when the non-Aryan monarchies of Egypt, Phœnicia, Babylonia, and Assyria, were sinking into decay, and their empires fast becoming disintegrated by foreign influences, the Hindoos felt the thrill of that mighty wave of energy heralding the birth of the new human consciousness—moral, intellectual, and religious —which was consequent on the decline of the earliest forms of civilisation. But the philosophic development of India is deprived of the interest which would otherwise attach to it, owing to its separation from that of the main trunk of the historic races, and its consequent crudity and limitation in scope.

The sacred philosophy (so-called) of India is contained in the Upanischads, or third section of the Vedic scriptures. Their main thesis consists of the monistic idea of the one true existent Absolute, spoken of variously under the names of *Paramathman*, *Brahman*, as opposed to the world of falsity and appearance, or the *Maya*. The *Maya* is the negation of *Brahman*. In itself, *Brahman* is unthinkable and undifferentiated in-ness of Being; only through the illusion, or the *Maya*, does it become conscious, mutable, undividualised. "As the colours in the flame or the red-hot iron proceed therefrom a thousandfold, so do all beings proceed from the Unchangeable, and return again to it." "As the web issues from the spider, as little sparks proceed from fire, so from the one soul proceed all living animals, all worlds, all the gods and all beings." "Two birds (the *Paramathman*, the universal soul, and *Jivathman*, the individual soul) inhabit the same tree (abide in the same body), &c."

"As from a blazing fire substantial sparks proceed in a thousand ways, so from the imperishable various souls are produced, and they return to him." These, and numberless other passages of similar purport, are to be found scattered throughout the Upanischads. The one theme is varied in a hundred different ways, but its substance is the same. This Metaphysic of the Upanischads, as will be readily seen, is, to the last degree, abstract. No *modus vivendi* exists between the Absolute One and the world of "many-hued reality"—between the real and the non-real. The practical consequence of this is an Ethic of Asceticism, which has absolute indifference and passivity for its ideal of life.

A little later than the Upanischads, which are for the most part poetic in character—and rather semi-conscious attempts to picture the mystery vaguely felt, than conscious efforts to explain it—come the six philosophical systems—properly so-called. Their dates are supposed to lie between the fourth and fifth centuries before Christ. The first in order is the *Nyaya*, founded by Gotama; the second, the *Vaisĕhika* of Kanada; the third, the *Sānkhya* of Kapila; the fourth, the *Yoga* of Patanjali; the fifth, the *Mīmānsā* of Jaimini; and the sixth, the *Vedānta* of Bādarāyana or Vyāsa. These systems are given in the form of Sutras or Aphorisms. The *Nyaya* is essentially a system of Logic. It deals at length with the proposition, the syllogism, the category, the predicable, &c. The *Vaiseshika* is a supplementary development of the *Nyaya*, but in addition to its elaboration of the categories furnished in the former, it contains a definite cosmology of an atomistic character. The resemblance of this to the Greek atomism, and even in some respects to that of modern science, is striking. The foundation of the *Sankhya* philosophy is a Monism, which in the course of the system issues in a species of Dualism. The distinction between matter and spirit is insisted upon; it being laid down as an axiom that the production of mind from matter, as of something from nothing, is an absurdity. The *Sankhya* also contains a systematic theory of Emanation. The *Yoga* is a kind of pendant to the *Sankhya*. Its bearing is mainly practical. It treats of the means by which the individual soul may attain union with the universal soul, these means being asceticism of the most drastic description. In the *Mimansa* we have no properly philosophical doctrine taught, and indeed its claim to rank among the philosophical systems rests solely on its logical method. Its central idea is the deification of the Veda and Vedic ritual. It is opposed to both rationalism and theism, the Veda being the supreme authority. The *Vedanta* is really little more than an expansion of the doctrines of the Upanischads of the one Substance Brahma *realised* in the world, or more accurately the one *really* existent Brahma *manifested* in the world of illusion and plurality, to which, at most, a *practical* existence can be ascribed. The personal soul—the *Jivathman*—through ignorance mistakes itself and the world for real things. Once it is set free from this ignorance, and arrives at a proper understanding of the truth, the illusion vanishes, and it sees the identity of itself and the world with the universal soul, the one *Paramathman*. As will be apparent, wellnigh the whole theosophy and philosophy of India turns upon a more or less poetically expressed Monism. Its drawback consists in the fact that it is abstract, and incapable of furnishing a coherent and logically determined view of conscious reality as a whole, and also from its vague and mystical character, which precludes scientific deduction of the *data* of consciousness from the outset. Besides the six dogmatic systems we have noticed, the Hindoos possess an empirical, sceptical, and materialist school in that of *Carvaka* and his followers, whose doctrines and even their mode of statement bear a close resemblance to those of La Mettrie, and the French rationalism of the last century. Some also reckon the eclectic Pantheistic doctrine contained in the Bhagavadgita, as forming a distinct system.

In reviewing the prehistoric civilisations, that is, such as are found complete in all essentials at the dawn of history, and even then laying claim to a remote antiquity, we find that the great awakening of the sixth century (*circa*) passed over some of them without response. Of this class are the Egyptian, Assyrian, Chaldean, and Phœnician, with probably the Lydian and other civilisations of Asia Minor. Others again, such as the Aryan civilisations of Hindoostan and Persia, and to a lesser extent that of China, responded to the impulse of the new movement; but the results of the awakening sooner or later became crystallised, thus resolving themselves into mere accretions on the previously existing culture, which hence speedily relapsed into its former state of stagnation. The first had lost their independent vitality ere history dawned. The second had enough vitality to respond to the impulse agitating the world around them, but were too old and set for its influence to be more than very partial.

In contrast to these ancient Oriental civilisations already "in the sere and yellow leaf," we find the Greek civilisation bursting into life, and forming the focus of the newly awakened individual consciousness. Here there was a culture forming, and not fixed into a more or less rigid groove. Hence with the Greece of the sixth century and its colonies, we enter on the history of the main stream of human development. There is no longer the tendency to universal crystallisation, discoverable in all the prehistoric civilisations of the East. Henceforth the ever-widening stream never becomes completely frozen over. There is always a channel left for the currents of progress. For this reason, it is only in so far as the ancient civilisations acted or were reacted upon by the European civilisation of the classical nations, or that of their successors, that they have any real *historical* as distinguished from *anthropological* significance. In concluding the present section, we may observe that philosophy, as the product of a *conscious* effort to explain the world, cannot be said to have existed prior to the awakening of the human mind to definite consciousness of itself. Not until man *deliberately* formulated to himself *for their own sake*, and not to subserve religious or other ends, the problems, What am I? What is my relation to the world? What is the principle of the world? can he be said to have begun to philosophise. Hence we may fairly deny the title philosophy to any such theories of the world, as the theogonies, cosmogonies, and theosophies which obtained previously to this epoch. In no ancient country do we find an original movement of a philosophic character outside Greece with, as we have seen, the solitary exception of India. But in India the movement was but of short duration, and has exercised comparatively little influence on history. We pass on, therefore, to a consideration of the first period of Greek philosophy.

As among the best authorities for Oriental thought, apart from the ancient books themselves in their various translations, may be mentioned, for the Egyptians, Gardner Wilkinson's 'Ancient Egyptians,' and Bunsen's 'Egypt's Place in Universal History.' For the Chinese, Pauthier's *Esquisse d'une histoire de la Philosophie chinoise*, and Plath's *Religion und Cultus der alten Chinesen*. Among the numerous works on the Indians, Monier Williams's 'Indian Wisdom,' contains a good account of Indian thought; also Colebrooke's 'Essays on the Philosophy of the Hindoos,' in his 'Miscellaneous Essays'; various translations of the Royal Asiatic Society; and Barth's 'Religions of India,' which gives an excellent general view of the subject; for Buddhism, may be cited the various Review and other articles of Mr. Rhys Davids; Burnouf's *Introduction à l'histoire du Bouddhisme indien*; and Spencer Hardy's 'Legends and Theories of the Buddhists.'

GREEK PHILOSOPHY.

INTRODUCTION.

In Greek philosophy there are six well-marked periods. (I.) that of the Pre-Socratic Schools; (II.) the period of Socrates and what are commonly termed the imperfect Socratists; (III.) the culminating epoch of Greek thought in Plato and Aristotle; (IV.) the commencement of its specialisation, and decline with the Stoics, Epicureans and the various Sceptical schools; (V.) the period subsequent to the Roman conquest characterised by the recrudescence of the earlier pre-Socratic doctrines, or what may be termed the anti-quarian period; and (VI.) the period of Neo-Platonism. with which ancient philosophy closes. Respecting this arrangement, it may be desirable to remark that I have filiated the imperfect Socratic schools directly on to Socrates, in preference to placing them after Plato and Aristotle, for the reason that they seem more immediately the outcome of the actual Socratic teaching, so far as it has come down to us. With the Cyrenaics, the Cynics, the Megarics, the chief, where not the sole subject-matter of philosophy, remains, as with Socrates, ethical; the teaching was mainly oral, while, generally speaking, the doctrines themselves are directly traceable to utterances or actions of the historical Socrates. Plato and Aristotle, on the other hand, cannot be said to have received more than an impulse from Socrates. It is next to certain that they could not have obtained a single speculative doctrine from their master, while the extent to which the dialectical method of Plato's dialogues is attributable to Socrates or Plato himself, is, and will probably remain, a matter of dispute. In both Plato and Aristotle, philosophy, which Socrates had expressly subordinated to practical issues, is extended to the widest speculative questions—questions which, so far as we know, never even occurred to Socrates, as they had certainly not occurred to his predecessors.

After the great original achievements of these two giant thinkers, Greek thought ceased to be productive, and confined itself to the reproduction and development of pre-Socratic, Socratic, Platonic, or Aristotelian doctrines; in the end absorbing Oriental theosophy. The pre-Socratic philosophy falls under two sections; the first comprising what are usually known as the Ionian, the Italian, and the Eleatic schools; and the second taking in Herakleitos, Empedokles, the Atomists (Demokritos and Leukippus), and Anaxagoras.

In considering these early stages in the history of philosophy, we must guard ourselves from reading into systems ideas pertaining to later phases in the evolution of thought. There is a difficulty for many of us, accustomed as we are to modern rules of philosophising, in realising the *naïve* and crude fashion in which great problems presented themselves to the early thinkers, and the still more crude attempts at solution which satisfied them. It is essential to bear in mind, especially in the schools of our first section, that distinctions and modes of statement, familiar to us now as household words, were with them non-existent—such, for instance, as Materialism and Idealism, Theism and Atheism, Subjective and Objective, Knowing and Being, Mind and Matter. Hence, for example, it is impossible to label Thales as materialist or immaterialist, theist or atheist, and the attempt to do so only shows an utter lack of historical insight. The problems, or the aspects of problems, of which these expressions connote the supposed solution, had not as yet appeared above the horizon of speculation, and hence this terminology is altogether devoid of meaning. The Ionians were merely *naïve* Hylozoists, that is, they simply took the world as they found it; to them the object of external perception (as existent), being the all, the only thing standing in need of explanation. Accordingly, the problem was to find the ultimate form of that object, a particular form from which all other forms were derivative. Thales pronounced this to be Water; Anaximenes, Air; and Anaximander, a formless chaos. They might, and it is likely enough did, believe in the gods of their age and country; but these gods, like the souls of men and demons, were conceived, no less than the other objects of the world, as entities constituted of this same primitive matter. The attitude of mind represented by the early Ionian speculators was that of a simple childlike questioning, which readily accepts the first answer that offers itself, and with this rests satisfied, without waiting to test its consistency even with itself, much less with fact.

For Greek philosophy in general, the best work is Professor Eduard Zeller's *Philosophie der Griechen*, some of the volumes of which have been published separately in English; that on the pre-Socratic philosophy is translated by S. F. Alleyne: also Dyk's *Versokratische Philosophie*. Of the ordinary histories of Philosophy, Ritter's may be mentioned as particularly full on the pre-Socratic schools as on ancient philosophy generally. An English translation of this portion of Ritter (in 4 vols.) exists, but is now out of print and scarce. Ritter and Preller's 'Selection of Fragments' is also a standard work. Brandis' *Handbuch der Geschischte der Griechisch-Römische Philosophie* has considerable value. No good English work specially devoted to ancient philosophy exists, with the exception of Ferrier's 'Pre-Socratic Philosophy.' Of the numerous critical and antiquarian essays in Latin and German on individual philosophers and special questions of scholarship, only those of interest to the general student will be mentioned.

EPOCH I.—THE PRE-SOCRATIC SCHOOLS.

I. THE IONIAN SCHOOLS.

THALES.

THALES, one of the seven sages, is the reputed founder of Greek philosophy. He was born about B.C. 624, but the exact date is uncertain, at Miletus, whence his ancestors are said to have migrated from Bœotia. Of the numerous saws attributed to him, and his knowledge of Mathematics and Astronomy, it is not necessary to speak at length. It is sufficient to observe that Thales was one of the most famous mathematicians and astronomers of ancient times, is alleged to have introduced geometry to the Greeks, and to have been the first to foretell eclipses. Some doubt exists as to the authenticity of the story of his Egyptian journey, and still more as to his having acquired his learning from Egyptian sources. Little or nothing is known with certainty as to his life, though there are numerous legends respecting it.

The claim of Thales to be the founder of philosophy rests on his having been the first to attempt to explain the world on a non-mythological and non-theological principle. He propounded the question, What is the ultimate substance to which all things are reducible? and answered it by asserting the primitive substance to be *water*. How he arrived at this conclusion is not known, nor indeed the manner in which he conceived the world to be evolved, though, judging from the analogy of kindred systems, this was by a process of *condensation and rarefaction*. There have been plenty of theories as to how Thales was led to his central doctrine (*e.g.* Aristotle's, that it was by observing that the seeds of all things are moist), but they are one and all purely conjectural. Various cosmological speculations were attributed to Thales in ancient times, among others, that the earth was a flat disc floating upon water; that the heavenly bodies were glowing masses; also theories respecting the nature of demons, heroes, &c.

All the reports concerning the doctrines of Thales are, however, of so doubtful and contradictory a nature, that it is impossible to assert anything with certainty respecting them, except as concerns the cardinal thesis of water being the principle of all things. If we are to believe some of these reports, he seems to have been hardly, if at all, emancipated from the animistic or fetischistic attitude of mind peculiar to the early stages of human culture; but this would appear scarcely compatible with those which credit him with a comparatively high degree of scientific attainment.

Anaximandros.

Anaximandros, or, as it is usually Anglicised, Anaximander, was also a native of Miletus, and a younger contemporary, and some say pupil of Thales. The date of his birth is given as B.C. 611. Nothing is known of his life. Report states that he was also proficient in geography and astronomy; that he designed the first map and celestial globe; and, according to some, invented the sun-dial, though others attribute this to Thales or Pherekydes. He undoubtedly wrote the first philosophical treatise, its main thesis being that into that whence things arise, they must return; that this primal substance, which he is the first to designate by the word principle (ἀρχη), is a formless and infinite matter, incorruptible and eternal, and that of its own inherent force things arise from it and pass into it again, or perhaps we might say it determines itself in forms which either give way to other forms or lose all form whatever, *i.e.* return again to the primal indefiniteness. The first determination of primitive substance was heat and cold, a fiery sphere arising surrounded by cold air. From fire and air were formed the stars (Anaximandros regarded the stars as animated beings or divinities, according to the view prevalent in ancient times, and subscribed to by no less a thinker than Plato), in the midst of which floats the cylindrically-shaped earth, immovable, owing to its equidistance from all points of the surrounding heavens, which were apparently conceived as a circumscribed space like the interior of a hollow globe. The earth was originally fluid. Through the co-operation of heat and moisture organic life originated, passing successively into higher and higher forms. All land animals were primarily marine organizations, becoming modified, and gradually assuming their present characters as the conditions of their environment changed. As the earth began to dry, the fins gave place, among those inhabiting the dry portion of its surface, to members more adapted to life under the new conditions. This development from preexistent forms applied no less to man than to other animals.

A moot-point as regards Anaximandros has been the nature of his primitive essence. That it was conceived as material substance, few scholars of any eminence have doubted, but some, like Ritter, have been found to maintain that its differentiation existed in it from the beginning, in other words, that it was an infinite aggregate of determinate elements like the *homœomeriæ* of Anaxagoras. That such an assumption is not only unsupported by evidence, but is foreign to the whole nature of the speculation, has been conclusively shown by Zeller. All the accounts respecting the primitive substance of Anaximandros emphasise the fact of its absolute formlessness.

The advance made by Anaximandros upon Thales will be apparent to the most superficial student. There is little doubt that Anaximandros was a speculative genius of the first order. Prompted, in all probability, merely by the crude and disconnected *dicta* of Thales, he constructed a coherent system on the hylozoistic basis, a system, considering the then state of knowledge, possessing considerable plausibility, and containing one of the most remarkable anticipations of the great cosmological truth of modern times which history can offer. The wonderful guess of Anaximandros on the subject of Evolution must ever maintain his name as memorable in the annals of human thought. It is noteworthy that this idea, if not consciously deduced from his cardinal doctrine of a universal substance, infinite in quantity and indefinite in quality *per se*, yet possessing the inherent capacity for infinite modification, nevertheless, logically follows from it. The forecast of Anaximandros has slept for two thousand years. It first began to awaken at the end of the last century, and when in the fulness of time it burst into that richness of life which has so profoundly influenced the thought of our age, it was no longer on the shores of the Ægean, deserted by the genius of speculation for many a long century, but in the little village of Down in Kent. It is a remarkable circumstance, as the late Dr. Thirlwall observed ('History of Greece,' vol. ii. pp. 134–5), that the speculations of Anaximandros were so little followed up by later thinkers of antiquity, though it may be accounted for in more ways than one.

ANAXIMENES.

The date of Anaximenes' birth is uncertain; but he was probably a younger contemporary of Thales and Anaximander, being by some asserted to have been a pupil of the latter. He was, also, a native of Miletus.

Anaximenes re-affirmed the qualitative character of the primal substance, but instead of identifying it, as Thales had done, with water, asserted it to be air. The working out of the system accorded with this alteration. As Thales had conceived the earth to be a flat disc, floating upon water, so Anaximenes described it as a flat disc, floating upon air. The latter, however, definitely worked out the notion of the production of the real world through the condensation and rarefaction of the primitive element. Heat and cold appear to have corresponded to this process —heat representing rarefaction, and cold condensation. Anaximenes is reported as maintaining the production of clouds from air, of water from clouds, and of earth from water. The earth was the centre of the universe, the heavenly bodies, which consisted of a mixture of earth and fire, circulating round it. All things were destined to be ultimately resolved into air.

The work of Anaximenes in which these doctrines were propounded, was known to Aristotle and his pupil Theophrastus, but appears to have been lost soon after their time.

Diogenes of Apollonia.

A hiatus exists in the line of the Ionic physicists between Anaximenes and the present philosopher, the last of the school, only broken by one or two obscure personages, who are little more than names, such as Hippo, a follower of Thales and Idæus, who seems to have been influenced by Anaximenes.

Diogenes is generally supposed to have flourished about the time of Anaxagoras. Very little is known of his life, and even the identity of his birthplace, Apollonia, is not settled, but it is generally referred to the place of that name in Crete, though the fact that he wrote in the Ionic dialect, and belonged to the Ionic school, tends to militate against this supposition. With Diogenes we undoubtedly reach the highwater-mark of Ionic speculation. To Diogenes, as to Anaximenes, the circumambient air, which seems to interpenetrate all things, was the essence of which all things consist, the primitive form of matter of which all other forms are modifications, and into which they must ultimately be resolved. The great philosophic merit of Diogenes consists in his being the first to explicitly enunciate the principle of Monism. His predecessors had, one and all, assumed this principle implicitly at the outset, but Diogenes seeks to demonstrate it. He urges the inexplicability of mutual action and reaction, otherwise than on a monistic basis. He shows that the facts of nature and the real world all point to one primitive substance as their substratum. This explicit Monism denotes a considerable advance in speculation. Another distinctive feature of the philosophy of Diogenes, which some would maintain, though perhaps without sufficient reason, to be not so much a development on older lines as a change of front, was the attribution of intelligence to his 'air.' The soul, the intelligent element in man, was of course nothing but breath or air. Hence the question may have arisen, Why should not the air-matter manifested as intelligent in us, be so in its essential nature? Diogenes, in his attempts to prove this, gives us the earliest sample we possess of the design argument. At the same time, we have in the doctrine itself the first distinct expression of the theory of an *anima mundi*, which has played such an important part in subsequent speculation.

In Diogenes the Ionian Physicism finds its culmination and conclusion. The school had doubtless, in his time, fallen into disrepute, and the plausibility and more recent form its fundamental principles assumed under his auspices failed to rehabilitate it. Such was the condition of philosophy at the time of Anaxagoras. But as most of these early schools overlap each other, so to speak, it is impossible to deal with them chronologically, and hence we are compelled to retrace our steps, in order to follow another line of speculation, viz. the Pythagorean or Italian.

II. THE ITALIAN SCHOOL.

Pythagoras.

"Among all the schools of philosophy known to us," says Zeller, "there is none of which the history is so overgrown, we may almost say so concealed by myths and fictions, and the doctrines of which have been so replaced in the course of tradition by such a mass of later constituents, as the Pythagorean." It is indeed impossible now to disentangle the doctrines of Pythagoras himself with any certainty from those of members of his school. A still greater mystery overhangs the life of Pythagoras, the three biographies that have survived from antiquity being altogether unreliable. That Pythagoras was the son of a stone-cutter, named Innesarchus, and was born at Samos, as well as that he was of Phœnician descent, all are agreed; while his birth is generally fixed at between B.C. 580 and 590. In his fortieth year he is said to have left his home and started on his travels, extending over twelve years, in the course of which he visited Ionia, Phœnicia, and Egypt, finally settling down in the Greek city of Crotona in Southern Italy. There are, however, various conflicting reports on the age at which he left Samos, and also on the duration of his stay in the East, the only unanimity being as to his ultimate place of residence. In ancient times Pythagoras was commonly regarded as the main original channel for the introduction of Oriental, and especially Egyptian, ideas into Europe.

Pythagoras, soon after his arrival in Crotona, became a political and religious as well as a philosophical power throughout the Greek colonies of Italy. There is every indication of a desire on his part to establish a cult and polity on the model of the Eastern theocracies. Thus, we have the division of doctrine into esoteric and exoteric, with a corresponding distinction among its hearers, of the introduction of mysteries, the prohibition of sundry articles of diet, the institution of a special *régime* of life for the elect and such as aspired to be so, and above all, the attempt, for a time more than partially successful, to acquire a political authority for himself and his followers, amounting to the complete control of the state.

The circumstances of the death of Pythagoras are variously related. According to some accounts he was killed in one of the civil tumults which ended in the destruction of the whole faction, and the massacre or dispersion of its members; according to others, he died of starvation at Metapontum (about B.C. 500), whither he was compelled to fly to escape the vengeance of the popular party. As it is practically impossible to furnish a reliable account of the philosophy of Pythagoras himself, we shall confine ourselves to giving a sketch of the Pythagorean system as it has come down to us, without attempting to enter into moot points of scholarship as to the relative antiquity of its reputed doctrines.

The Pythagorean System.

With the Pythagorean philosophy we enter upon a new and more advanced phase of Greek thought than that of the Hylozoists of Miletus. The Pythagoreans were evidently capable of a high degree of abstraction. The principle and essence of all things was now no longer conceived as concrete, but as abstract.

The fundamental doctrine attributed to Pythagoras, that "All is number," must be taken as meaning not merely that everything can be treated numerically, but that number is that by which the constitution of things is determined. In other words, the *matter* as well as the *form* of the real was deemed to consist in number, although the antithesis of matter and form had not as yet become explicit in thought. The Pythagoreans were probably led to this theory by perceiving that all mathematical conceptions are reducible to terms of number. It was most likely to an attentive study of the mathematical aspects of astronomy and music, sciences which the Pythagoreans especially cultivated, that the doctrine of numbers is more immediately traceable. There is no doubt that the ideas of proportion and harmony pervaded the whole Pythagorean system. The world was conceived as a harmoniously articulated whole; the doctrine of numbers was merely the ultimate expression of this conception, an expression which will appear natural enough when one considers that the, to us, familiar distinction of abstract and concrete had not been made. This hypostasis, then, of numbers naturally gave rise to an emanation-theory. That whence all numbers are derivable, their source or generative parent, as it is termed, is the One or Unity. From the One, as their common root, all numbers proceed, and inasmuch as all numbers are contained therein, it is often designated as "*the* number." From the One, there issues the antithesis which plays so great a part in the system, of the Indefinite and Definite,* or the unlimited and the limiting, in which perhaps, we may see a faint adumbration of the later antithesis of matter and form. Thence proceeds the odd and the even; the even being identified with the indefinite, and the odd with the definite, because the odd sets a limit to bi-partition which the even does not. The definite or limiting is throughout regarded as the higher principle, but is equally with its correlate subordinated to Unity or the One.

From these main pairs (viz. the Indefinite and the Definite, the Even and the Odd) proceed eight subordinate couples, which, with the two primary, make up the sacred number ten; the complete Pythagorean categories being as follows: (1) Definite and Indefinite; (2) Odd and Even; (3) One† and Many; (4) Right and Left; (5) Male and Female; (6) Resting and Moving; (7) Straight and Curved; (8) Light and Darkness; (9) Good and Evil; (10) Square and Oblong. In so far as these contradictions, immanent in the original unity, appear in opposition to each other outside this unity, arises the system of numbers or things.

The application of this theory to the detailed explanation of the concrete world could not be effected otherwise than by a series of arbitrary combinations, as that one is the point, two the line, three the plane, that virtue is a harmony of certain numbers, &c.

* Erdmann remarks as characteristic that in place of the physical opposition of *heat* and *cold* as with the hylozoists, we have here a logical opposition. (Erdmann, vol. i. p. 26.)

† This antithetical unity was distinguished from the unconditioned unity at the basis of the system.

In the Pythagorean cosmology, the universe was divided into ten spheres, which were regarded as revolving round the central fire. The soul was of course conceived as in essence number; and cognition as arising in and through number. That which could not be expressed mathematically was therefore incognisable and nothing.

The above is of course only a brief sketch of the leading positions of a system which exercised a vast influence upon ancient speculation, but which nevertheless suffered more variations in the hands of its individual adherents than any other, for the reason that its founder committed nothing to writing. Add to this, that the earliest Pythagorean fragments probably date from a century after Pythagoras's time, and the difficulty of arriving at true Pythagoreanism with certainty, at present, will be sufficiently apparent.

It will be seen, however, from what we have said that the Pythagorean system (so-called) contains all the later philosophical disciplines in germ. Thus in addition to an ontology proper, we have the first attempt on the basis of this to solve the problems of Theory of Knowledge, Psychology, Cosmology and Ethics. These attempts, it is true, are confined to a few merely arbitrary and childish dicta, but still they are significant as showing a recognition of the existence of these problems, and of the duty of philosophy to explain them on its fundamental principles.

But it is of the utmost importance to bear in mind that Pythagoreanism was primarily a religion and a polity, and that to this its philosophy was supposed to lead up as its end and goal. It is in the character of hierophant, rather than that of philosopher, that the majestic and semi-mythical figure of Pythagoras stands forth so conspicuously in classical history. The remembrance of the personality of the great Samian as a religious leader lingered with the world till the last ray of the afterglow of ancient culture had died away.

The most interesting ancient sources for Pythagoreanism are the "Golden verses," with the commentary by Hierokles.

THE ELEATIC SCHOOL.

Xenophanes.

The reputed founder of the Eleatic school was born at Kolophon, in Ionia. The date of his birth is uncertain, but he is said to have flourished about B.C. 530. He spent the greater part of his life in travelling, in the manner of an ancient bard, through the chief cities of Sicily and Magna Græcia, finally settling in Elea, a town of Southern Italy.

The burden of the poems which Xenophanes, sung, was that the All or the One, as it was variously termed, was God. As a pendant to this we have a polemic against the current polytheism, and the immorality of the narratives of the poets. Some of the fragments preserved would seem to imply a theistic tendency,* but others distinctly identify "God" with the spacial universe. Thus the statement that the shape of the deity was spherical is plainly an inference from the apparent figure formed by the sky and horizon. Passionless, without motion, neither limited nor unlimited, "all eye, all ear, all thought," such was the God, Being, or ·All, of Xenophanes. It is the enunciation of unity and changelessness as the attributes of true Being against the multiplicity and change of the world of appearance, which gives Xenophanes his place in the history of philosophy. Otherwise he would have been no more than a religious reformer. As it was, the religious element in the teachings of Xenophanes remained almost still-born. The philosophical alone has left a mark on history.

Parmenides.

Parmenides, of Elea, probably a pupil of Xenophanes in his old age, and much esteemed in his native city for

* "There is one God alone, the greatest among gods and men, resembling mortals neither in body nor in thought." Apud Clem. Alex. i. I.

In the Pand statesmanship, embodied his philosophy in into ten sp?m of which considerable fragments remain. the central besides an introduction, of two main divisions, ess first treating of the doctrine of the true, and the second containing a cosmical theory of illusory appearance. In Parmenides, the theological terminology of Xenophanes is abandoned. Being, as distinguished from Non-being, is the subject-matter of philosophy. True knowledge, the knowledge of Being, is only to be obtained through intellect; the senses serve only to delude us with an apparent reality, which is in truth non-existent. Being is one, unchangeable, unbecome, infinite, and eternal. The appearance of change, multiplicity, limitation, etc., in the sense world, is illusory. Parmenides enunciated for the first time, in history, the doctrine of abstract Monism, and an abstract Monism it is, of the crudest and most uncompromising description.

MELISSOS AND ZENO.

The distinguished Samian General Melissos, also belongs to the Eleatic school. His subject-matter is the Ens, or being, which, like Parmenides, he regarded as an immovable, indivisible unity. Like Parmenides, Melissos has a polemic against the conception of a void, which is declared impossible. His work is mainly directed against the Ionian Physicists.

The *Eleatic* Zeno is stated to have been an adopted son of Parmenides, whose doctrines he embraced in their entirety. He was regarded as a man of heroic character, and numerous stories of his fortitude are related. There is no new doctrine taught by Zeno. His philosophical work consisted of an attempt to fortify the positions of Parmenides, and to clinch his arguments and demonstrations. This he effected or sought to effect by means of Dialectic, or the *reductio ad absurdum*, a method of proof which he was the first to employ. Numerous instances illustrative of his skill in this kind of argumentation are transmitted, of which the most noted is the so-called Achilles-puzzle. The object was to prove the impossibility of motion. If Achilles and the tortoise run a race, and

Achilles do but give the tortoise a start, however slight, he will never overtake the tortoise.—Proof as follows: If Achilles is to overtake the tortoise, he must first reach the point where the tortoise was when he started; next the point it has attained in the interval; next the point arrived at, while he is making this second advance; and so on *ad infinitum*, which is obviously impossible in a finite time.*

This is one of four arguments employed by Zeno to prove the impossibility of motion. Arguments of an analogous kind are brought forward to demonstrate the impossibility of plurality. In Zeno the opposition of the Eleatic philosophy to common sense is brought out into the most prominent relief. Multiplicity and motion are not encountered with general arguments, as with Parmenides, but their impossibility is sought to be drawn from their very conception. In this way Zeno's dialectic started problems which philosophy has never since been able to evade.

Soon after Melissos and Zeno, the Eleatic school seems to have died out, its dialectic being absorbed by the Sophists. It should be observed that several of the Eleatics included a cosmology (not very consistently perhaps) in their philosophy, of which, since it is destitute of value or importance, either intrinsically or as bearing on the system proper, no account has been given. One point only is worthy of notice, namely, that the Eleatics invariably assumed two elements as primal instead of the one element of the Ionian Hylozoists. In this we may perhaps see a transition to the four elements of Empedokles. The way in which the Eleatic system, starting from a polemic in the person of the founder against the current theology, became purely philosophic, has already been noticed.

* "The infinity of space in this race of subdivision is artfully run against a *finite* time; whereas if the one infinite were pitted, as in reason it ought to be, against the other infinite, the endless divisibility of time against the endless divisibility of space, there would arise a reciprocal exhaustion and neutralisation that would swallow up the astounding consequences, very much as the two Kilkenny cats ate up each other." De Quincey's works, Vol. XVI., p. 154.

THE METAPHYSICAL-PHYSICISTS.

HERAKLEITOS.

We have now reached a group of thinkers who combined the Hylozoism of the Ionians with the metaphysical methods of the Pythagoreans and Xenophanes.* The metaphysic of the Eleatics was purely abstract. It admitted of no *modus vivendi* with the material world. One unchangeable, immovable and eternal being alone existed as the essence of the real, all else was absolute illusion. The negation of the possibility of motion and change was now met by their affirmation as the inseparable attribute of real being. Physics, or cosmology, ceasing to be separated by an impassable gulf from philosophy proper, as with the Eleatics, was absorbed into its central doctrine. The leading names in this group are Herakleitos, Anaxagoras, Empedocles, and Leukippus and Demokritos.

Herakleitos sprang from an ancient family of Ephesus, claiming descent from the Homeric Nestor. He was an arch-aristocrat, and a bitter hater of the democracy of his native town. The date of his birth was probably about B.C. 532. On account of the mystical language in which his doctrines were couched, he obtained the cognomen of the "Obscure."

The cardinal doctrine of Herakleitos: "All things flow," was an aphorism for the great principle of "becoming;" of the identity in contradiction of all things, which it is the undoubted glory of the Ephesian thinker to have for the first time definitely enunciated. Everything is and is not at the same moment; it exists only in transition. The inherent opposition of all things, the strain of contradiction running through them, he describes as "the harmony of the world like that of the lyre and the bow."

Physically expressed, the ultimate essence of the real

* The work of Parmenides was subsequent to that of Herakleitos.

was "fire," that element being symbolical of non-stability, of ceaseless change. "The one world of all things, has not been made either by a god or a man; but it was, and is, and will be, an everliving fire, kindling itself according to measure and extinguishing itself according to measure." From the upper regions where the fire was purest it descended to the middle regions where it became water, less pure, less living; till finally it reached the lowest region of all, the region of least life, least change, and least motion, viz. the earth. At this point the reverse process commenced, the fire gradually ascending to the sphere of its original purity. From fire all things come, and into fire they must return. The "fire" of Herakleitos must be understood rather as an incandescent vapour than as actual flame. The processes of the evolution and dissolution of the world out of and into this fiery vapour are eternally alternating.

Herakleitos employed various illustrations to bring home to the mind the eternal flux of things; as that one could not step twice into the same river, etc. To illustrate that everything existed in combination with its opposite, he instanced sleep and waking, life and death, youth and age.

It is a manifest historical misapprehension to describe Herakleitos, as is done by Ueberweg, as a "Hylozoist to the backbone," * since the slightest acquaintance with his doctrines suffices to show us that their salient point is not so much the theory of a primitive fire, which is rather inferential and illustrative, as the doctrine of the eternal flux and reflux of things, and of contradiction and strife as essential to existence.

The Herakleitan school continued to possess numerous adherents, especially in Ephesus and the Greek cities of Asia Minor, till the time of Sokrates. One of Plato's teachers, Kratylos, was an Herakleitan.

The work of Herakleitos which bore the title, common to most of the pre-Sokratic treatises, *περι φυσεως*, was extant and much read by the Christians of the second and

* "Vom hause aus Hylozoist," Ueberweg, Vol. I., p. 46.

third centuries,—but fragments only have reached modern times.

There are several monographs on Herakleitos, by different German scholars, the most celebrated being Ferdinand Lassalle's great work, *Die Philosophie Herakleitos' des Dunkeln von Ephesos*, 2 *Bde.*, *Berlin*, 1858, the critical value of which, however, is impaired by its strong Hegelian tendency.

EMPEDOKLES.

Empedokles was born at Akragas, in Sicily, B.C. 490. His history is overlaid with legends, of which the well-known story of his suicide on Mount Etna is a specimen. Empedokles, like Parmenides, embodied his philosophical views in an epic poem.

The four elements (so-called), fire, water, earth and air,* were to Empedokles the ultimate forms of the real, but they were not like the Ionic primitive substance capable of qualitative change. All things were composed of these four elements, but by a *mixture* in various proportions. In themselves they were absolutely statical, possessing no inherent principle of determination, such as condensation and rarefaction, as with the Hylozoists and Herakleitos. The change and multiplicity of things is brought about by mechanical principles foreign to their essential nature. Those principles were love and hate, a uniting and a separating principle. By this dualistic conception Empedokles found the *modus vivendi* between the Absolute Being of Parmenides, which excluded all becoming, and therefore all reality, and the absolute flux of Herakleitos, which seemed to exclude all self-existent Being.

Empedokles conceived of absolute existence, like Xenophanes, as originally one unchanging all-encompassing sphere, which the opposing influences of love and hate first reduced to the world of change, motion, and plurality by the combination and separation of the four "roots," as Empedokles terms them, which it implicitly contained. Each of the two forces prevails alternately in the process

* We perhaps ought rathar to say, the solid, the liquid, the gaseous, and the ethereal, *i.e.* the four forms of matter.

of the world-formation. Originally, absolute love (*i.e.* union) obtained. Hate gained an entrance and severed the elements from one another, in which way individual beings arose. But the power of hate reaching its extremest point, individual things cease to exist. Every particle of matter is separated from every other particle. The combining influence of love then enters again, and new individual beings arise, till with the complete re-establishment of the power of love all reverts to the primal state of absolute quiescence and unity.

Empedokles' philosophy also contained a theory of the order in time and the manner of the origin of plants and animals. Sense-perception it explained by the out-flowing of particles from external bodies, and their impingement upon the organs of sense, every element in bodies being perceived by us through a corresponding element in ourselves.

Anaxagoras.

Anaxagoras, who was born at Klazomenœ about B.C. 500, of a noble family, subsequently migrated to Athens, and became the friend of Perikles. Owing to an accusation of atheism, he was compelled to leave the city, and fly to Lampsakos, where he died at the age of seventy-two.

Like Empedokles and the Atomists, Anaxagoras postulated qualitatively unchangeable substance, by the combination and separation of which, individual things arose. This substance consisted of an infinite interpenetration of elements, an infinite chaos. It was neither increased nor diminished, but suffered only combination and resolution into infinitely varying forms. The primitive aggregate was termed by subsequent exponents of the system *Homoiomeroi.* The union of these ultimate elements with each other was so complete, that they were divisible to infinity, there being no ultimate and irresolvable atoms at their basis. This formless mass was subjected not to a necessary law, but to νοῦς, or mind, an omnipotent and omniscient power that produced order and harmony out of the chaos. The separation is conceived as going out successively from a middle point in ever-widening circles. As with most of the ancients, Anaxagoras regarded the earth as the centre of the universe. His theory of the origin of organic beings strongly resembled that of Anaximandros.

The two most noteworthy points in the philosophy of Anaxagoras are the introduction of the notion of mind into philosophic speculation, and the assertion of the infinite divisibility of matter, or, as it is termed, *Dynamism.* A great deal has been made of the first of these points, as might naturally be expected, but so far from its supposing any advance in conception, we may rather consider it as philosophically a reaction to anthropomorphism. The appearance of the problem of the ultimate constitution of matter upon the arena of speculation, on the other hand, undoubtedly marks an epoch in the history of thought, and had immediate results.

THE ATOMISTS.

The reputed founder of Atomism in Greece was Leukippus, respecting whom scarcely anything is known, not even whether he committed his doctrines to writing or not. According to Aristotle, he originally belonged to the Eleatic school. The real literary founder of the school, Demokritos, who is described as a pupil of Leukippus, flourished about half a century later than Anaxagoras. He was born at Abdera, and is stated to have employed the large fortune he possessed in travelling throughout Egypt and the East. He died at an advanced age, much respected, in his native town. Demokritos composed a large number of works, all of which, with the exception of fragments preserved by later writers, have perished.

The Atomistic system connects itself by opposition, in an unmistakable manner, with that of Anaxagoras. The latter philosopher had assumed a chaotic aggregate divisible to infinity as the primal substance of all things. Demokritos postulates a *plenum* and a *void*, the former of which he also terms existent, and the latter non-existent. The existent consists of an infinite plurality of atoms, each of which is indivisible. Between the atoms is the *void* or non-existent. The connection and distinction between this system and that of Anaxagoras is obvious. With Anaxagoras the *plenum* was practically a continuous substance, for the plural designation can only have a qualitative application, the notion of the "*void*" or empty space being excluded. The atoms of Demokritos, on the contrary, were conditioned in their existence by the void, in other words they were discrete substances. The *Homoiomerioi* of Anaxagoras, again, were infinitely divisible, the atoms of Demokritos absolutely indivisible.

The action of the atoms was conditioned in a triple way, by their *order*, their *position* and their *form*. Their size was various, but upon it depended their weight, that is, their tendency to move downwards. The atoms, like the void, were eternal. Their motion was also original and eternal. The weight of the atoms being unequal, some falling with a greater velocity than others, gave rise, according to Demokritos, to lateral motions, which again with the original motion, constituted a circular or vortex motion, which was ever extending itself, and which was the proximate cause of the world-formation. In this theory, we have a distinct reminiscence of Anaxagoras. These positions, the Atomists thought, sufficed to explain the variety of phenomena.

The super-sensible atoms and the void alone existed *in themselves*, the real world existed *for us* only. Perception was explained by the efflux of atoms from bodies producing images on our mind through the medium of the organs of sense. Demokritos was the last of the Metaphysical-Physicists, and of the older Greek speculators. The crisis produced by the Sophists had already begun; the attention of philosophy was already being drawn away from the contemplation of Being to Knowing, from the object to the subject, and Greek thought was fast becoming ripe for the magical and renovating touch of Demokritos' younger contemporary Sokrates.

TRANSITION TO SOKRATES.

The Sophists.

The founder of the negative and sceptical school of the Sophists or "wise men" is usually designated as Protagoras. This brilliant philosophical free-lance was born at Abdera, the city of Demokritos, in a humble sphere of life, out of which his abilities soon carried him. After travelling in Sicily, he settled at Athens, where he made much money and fame by his teaching, for which he was the first to demand payment. Led, it is stated, by the Herakleitan doctrines to a sceptical attitude, his fundamental thesis gradually acquired shape. It consisted, to put it in modern language, in the denial of all objectivity and the restriction of all knowledge to mere impressions of the individual subject. Protagoras maintained that to every assertion a contrary assertion could be opposed with equal right. His favourite aphorism was: "Man is the measure of all things." As a result, probability took the place of truth, and immediate utility, of goodness.

Prodikos, born in the island of Chios, also came to Athens while a young man, and adopted the calling of Sophist. His chief merit lies in his having contributed to fix the definitions of words, thus preparing the way for the Sokratic dialectic. His lectures were so much in request as to enable him to make a charge of fifty drachmas a person.

Another eminent name in the Sophist school was Gorgias, who, evidently influenced by the Eleatics, maintained that neither being or non-being, one or many, become or unbecome, had any reality or meaning. His orations, in which a similar dialectical mode of argument to that of Zeno was employed, were delivered publicly on any given subject. Extemporaneous oratory and oral disputation he attached much importance to, and became eminent throughout Greece and the colonies for his skill in these arts. Two orations, of doubtful genuineness, have come down to us under his name.

Among other eminent Sophists may be mentioned Hippias, Polos, Thrasymachos, etc.

The Sophists practically dealt a death-blow at the earlier philosophies considered as independent systems, by opposing them to each other and showing the one-sidedness of each, while the plausibility of the several doctrines taken by themselves, combined with their mutually exclusive character to produce a spirit of universal scepticism throughout the philosophic world, even apart from the arguments more especially directed to this end. The individualist and utilitarian nature of the Sophistic ethics naturally procured for the doctrine wide acceptation at a time when the old civic feeling was beginning to wane. The "gilded youth" of the Greek cities flocked to the lectures of its professors, more to learn the art of skilful disputation, for the profitable exercise of which the public life of the Hellenic race afforded such a wide field at this period, than from any intrinsic interest in philosophical questions. As a natural consequence, the whole Sophistic teaching ultimately came to have mere rhetorical display for its end, by which those proficient therein might make the worse appear the better reason, as occasion required.

It was this empty dialectical art that reigned almost supreme in Greece under the name of philosophy, when the "Silenus figure" appeared in the Agora at Athens, with a dialectic similar indeed in kind, but employed for another purpose; a dialectic which was destined to make an end of Sophism, as Sophism had made an end of previous dogmatism. It has been often remarked, and with justice, that the Sophistic movement was never strictly philosophical, but was rather a popular rationalistic outburst, having its springs in the entire religious, political and social life of Greece shortly before the Peloponnesian war. As such it is difficult to fix upon any individual as the actual founder of the movement, which, so far as names are concerned, was rather consentaneous than successive. The sudden appearance of the Sophistic orators throughout the Greek world is one of those phenomena in the history of culture, for which not more than general causes can be assigned in the absence of exhaustive historical data.

SECOND EPOCH.

SOKRATES.

We have now arrived at the first great land-mark in Greek speculation. The personality of the son of Sophroniskos is one of the few world-personalities whose name and fame have found an echo amid all races, whereever human culture has existed.

The date of Sokrates' birth is approximately fixed at from B. C. 471 to 469. He was the first philosopher born in Athens, where his father was a sculptor, a calling he himself followed during the early portion of his career. After receiving the education prescribed by law, Sokrates appears to have taken up the studies of astronomy and geometry. The story of his having been a pupil of Anaxagoras or Archelaus, is generally regarded as a fabrication, though there is no doubt that he attended the lectures of the Sophists, notably Prodikos. It is also probable that he read most of the extant philosophical literature; he was certainly familiar with the treatise of Anaxagoras. Plato relates that he came personally into contact with Parmenides while a boy—a statement which Ueberweg credits, though generally considered doubtful.

Sokrates took part in three campaigns during the Peloponnesian war, in which he signalised himself by his courage and endurance. Otherwise he held aloof from public affairs, only once in his life occupying an official position. Seldom leaving his beloved Athens, he daily mixed with the crowds that thronged the Agora, willing to converse with all who wished to do so. Young men were especially attracted by him, and presently the world-famous group, comprising among others, Plato, Xenophon, Eschines, Euripides, Krito, etc., came to be formed. Meanwhile, Sokrates had acquired a celebrity which eclipsed that of his Sophist teachers, and which led the comic poet Aristophanes, who hated philosophy, to satirise it in his person in the 'Clouds.' It is a noticeable fact that Aristophanes appears to have been about as ignorant of the thing he was satirising as many popular writers in our own day, who, without his genius, attempt to make fun of new truths and their advocates, for, like them, he seemed to consider it immaterial, so long as he was attacking philosophy, what distinctions of stand-point he confounded. Thus Sokrates is represented in the character of a Sophist, Aristophanes being apparently oblivious of the fact that Sokrates led a polemic against the Sophists.

The main, and we may perhaps say, only, thesis in Sokrates' philosophy was the assertion of the identity of knowledge and virtue. No man was willingly bad, but only from ignorance and confusion. As a corollary from this we have the assumption that virtue is teachable, and that as all knowledge is essentially one, so is virtue. The revolution effected by Sokrates has been well described by Cicero as consisting in the bringing down of philosophy from heaven to earth. Had Sokrates written a treatise, it would not have borne the traditional title of those of his predecessors, "On Nature," but rather "On Man." The immediate object of his teaching was the attainment of clear ideas or concepts, the highest of all being that of the good, or the *Summum Bonum;* in order through this knowledge to attain the perfect life. Referring to his mother, the midwife Phanarete, he used to say that as her calling in life was to deliver children into the world from the womb, so it was his calling to watch over mental parturition, and deliver ideas from the mind. The method he used to effect this, was that of irony, or pretended ignorance. He would ask questions on any subject, as though for information. The oftentimes confident answers received would lead to further questions, till in the end the luckless victim of confused ideas and loose thought, would be brought to silence, if not to an admission of the victory of the Sokratic dialectic. Aristotle declares Sokrates to have been the founder of the inductive method, though this could only have been as applied to ethical subjects and the definition of words; but here again it would seem only fair to credit his master Prodikos with the foundation of this logical art.

The Sophists had identified truth with individual opinion or conception. Sokrates distinguished between individual conceptions as such, and those that, purified by Dialectic, were of universal application, *i.e.*, true. All learning was recollection; all teaching the bringing to light and clearness of ideas already existing, although confusedly, in the mind of the taught. The result of Sokrates' Dialectic was often simply to demonstrate the reciprocal untenability of rival theories, without reaching any positive conclusion. Much has been written respecting the *δαιμόνιον* of Sokrates. There seems every reason for thinking that in accordance with the prevalent beliefs he really regarded himself as under the supervision of a tutelary supernatural agent, which warned him of the danger attending certain courses of action.

The story of Sokrates' condemnation and death is too well known to need repeating at length in a work of the present scope. Having excited the enmity of the pietists, by his refusal to be initiated into the Eleusinian mysteries, and the hostility of the democratic party by his former friendship with Kritias, one of the worst of the thirty tyrants, for which the subsequent breach between them had not atoned; also probably by the fact of his having remained unmolested in Athens throughout the worst period of the tyranny; he was impeached by Meletos, an inferior poet, Lykon, a Rhetorician, and Anytos, a leather-dealer, on three counts, charging him respectively, with "introducing strange Gods," with corrupting youth, and with having moulded the character of tyrants. He was convicted and condemned to death, at first by a majority of six, but subsequently on appeal, of eighty votes. The circumstance that the sacred vessel bearing the Athenian offerings had just sailed for Delos, allowed him nearly a month's respite—during which he refused the means of escape offered him—before, in April B.C. 399, he drank the hemlock in the presence of his sorrowing disciples.

Much exaggerated blame has been bestowed on the Athenians for the condemnation of Sokrates. There is strong evidence that in its early stages at least he favoured the Lacedemonian policy, while his known intimacy with Kritias naturally threw grave suspicion on his teaching. As Thirlwall remarks, the strangeness consists not in the fact of the conviction, but in the smallness of the majority by which the philosopher was at first convicted. But, though even the external circumstances of the case are sufficient to account for the action of the Athenians, there is, we believe, a deeper significance in the attitude of all that was conservative in the Athenian state towards Sokrates. It was not zeal for the gods, *quâ* gods, as we take it, that formed the underlying ground of suspicion, but zeal for the old civic spirit. The citizens of Athens felt vaguely that the "Know thyself" of Sokrates was the expression of a religion and an ethic, radically incompatible with the old spirit of solidarity—an ethic of individualism and introspection, which, if pushed to its logical conclusions, must sap the ancient traditional ethic of duty to the state as an organised whole at its very root. This introspection was the "strange god" of which the Athenians felt an uneasy dread, as destructive of the old state religion and morality. It is somewhat of an irony on the almost servile respect with which Sokrates generally treated the established cultus, and his excessive care to avoid any imputation of impiety, that this should have constituted one of the main charges against him in the capital indictment.

The revolution in thought inaugurated by Sokrates consisted, (I.), in the retrospective method he employed, the change in the subject-matter of philosophy, from things to ideas, from being to knowing, and (II.), in the ethical and individualist tendency of all his work. Henceforward ethics, and the ethical sciences, occupy, if not as with Sokrates, an exclusive, at least a foremost, place in every system.

The Sokratic Schools.

In the nature of the case, it was impossible for Sokrates to leave behind him a school of pure Sokratists. His philosophy was rather a method than a doctrine. Sokrates had said that the only sense in which he could interpret the Delphic oracle's words, that he was the wisest man in Greece, was, that while others thought they knew something, he knew that he knew nothing, and thus in his person fulfilled the Delphic maxim "Know thyself." Thus the Sokratic method of philosophy, of the search after clear ideas and virtue, or the "perfect life," was pursued in various directions, and led with different temperaments to different results; for all of which, however, it was possible to find some justification in the many-sided utterances of the master. There were naturally, among the disciples of Sokrates, personalities, like Xenophon, mere men of the world, who had been generally influenced and attracted by the conversation of Sokrates, but had no independent interest in philosophy.

On the other hand, there were those who had a real interest in the philosophical side of Sokrates, who sought to derive some definite result from the life and teaching of their master, to formulate for themselves and their followers what his aims were, and what his teaching really led to, when logically carried out.

These were the founders of the minor or "imperfect" (because one-sided) Sokratic schools, as they are termed, of which there are three, the *Megaric*, the *Cyrenaic* and the *Cynic*. The originator of the first of these was Euklid, of Megara. Before he became a disciple of Sokrates, Euklid had embraced the Eleatic philosophy, which he never subsequently abandoned, interweavin the Sokratic Ethics in an ingenious manner with th One-Being doctrine of Parmenides. As with Sokrates, th proper subject-matter of philosophy was the Good; bu Euklid identified this ideal Good of Sokrates with t ontological One of the Eleatics. To him virtue, kno ledge, God, &c., were only diverse names for this absolu fact. There was certainly little more than a formal carrying out of the Sokratic doctrine in Euklid's system, since Ethics, *per se*, appear to have been neglected by him and his school, whose main interest centred in dialectical polemic, after the manner of Zeno.

Aristippus, the founder of the *Cyrenaic* school, was the son of a wealthy merchant of the gay and voluptuous city of Cyrene. Attracted by the fame of Sokrates, he came to Athens, and remained in close intimacy with him till his death. Aristippus was much more of a Sokratist than Euklid. He despised all speculation not having an immediate bearing on practice. The life of man alone had an interest for him. He diverged, however, from

Sokrates on the opposite side to Euklid, in the value he placed on Dialectics and reasoning generally; maintaining that all knowledge was in essence merely that of our own individual states of feeling. Hence the consideration of these and their causes make up the whole subject-matter of the theoretical side of his philosophy. All states of consciousness are reducible to violent motion, moderate motion, and the lack of all motion. The first is pain, the second is pleasure, and the third is apathy. Pleasure, Aristippus boldly proclaimed as the only good. The practical side of philosophy was the attainment of pleasure, the great art of life that of avoiding pain and apathy. With Aristippus, it was the immediate pleasure of the moment that was to be sought, and which the "wise man" was to seize. He was not, however, to be governed or controlled by it, but, as it were, to ride it, as a horseman rides his steed. On the other hand, the Cyrenaic "wise man" would not embrace a present pain even with a view to future pleasure.

It was this point which mainly distinguished the hedonism of Aristippus from that of Epicurus, of whose ethical system he was otherwise the forerunner, and in whose school the Cyrenaics became subsequently merged. Numerous writings are attributed to Aristippus, as to Euklid, but they have completely perished in both cases.

The creator of the *Cynic* school, or rather sect, was the Athenian Antisthenes, who, after an education at the hands of Gorgias the Sophist, came to Sokrates. What specially charmed him in the latter, was his independence of external "goods" and what to others were the necessities of life; his superhuman hardihood in adversity. He subsequently set up as a teacher in the gymnasium of the Kynosarges, whence the name of the sect. Antisthenes became enamoured of the notion of the pride of virtue, upon which he heard Sokrates dilate, and it was this that he and his followers caricatured in their own persons. With Antisthenes, as with Sokrates, virtue was the one thing worth living for, but his ideal virtue Antisthenes placed in deprivation and asceticism. Absolute indifference to circumstances was the first and the last demand of wisdom, which stood in no need of elabo rate argumentation, but only of strength of character. Its sole end consisted in the avoidance of the pleasures and desires that so readily gain the mastery over us, and *a fortiori* of all that bears the impress of luxury or even refinement. Accordingly the Cynics (of whom the best known is not so much the founder of the system, as his successor, the famous Diogenes of Sinope, but whose lives were all cast in one mould) were content with at most a wallet and a staff, ate anything they could obtain, slept in the first place that presented itself, and performed all the offices of life in public. The Cynics committed nothing to writing, and all that has been handed down from them consists of personal anecdotes, miscellaneous maxims and, to modern ears, somewhat feeble witticisms.

THIRD EPOCH.

PLATO AND ARISTOTLE.

THIS third epoch in Greek philosophy is a landmark not merely in the history of philosophy but in the history of human thought and culture generally. In these two great typical thinkers the thought of all preceding ages converged as in a focus, while from them have diverged rays, which have more or less guided all later inquirers directly or indirectly, and influenced all the more important currents of thought in the world's subsequent history. Plato and Aristotle are frequently regarded as antithetic and mutually exclusive; they are really complementary. Plato is occupied mainly with an inquiry as to the necessary and universal element in experience. Aristotle supplements this inquiry, by one respecting the contingent and particular element in the real, the empirical laws to which special departments of phenomena are subordinated. In this way, he became the founder of the inductive method of physical science. Before commencing our analysis of the systems of Plato and Aristotle it will be desirable to take a rapid survey of the ground we have been traversing, and which has led up to them. In this way we shall better be able to judge what is their special individual contribution to human thought, and what is merely the welding together into an organic whole of the more or less fragmentary doctrines of their predecessors.

The Ionian Physicists contented themselves with a search after some primitive corporeal substance. In this they implicitly assumed unity as the basis of the real world. The last important member of the school, Diogenes of Apollonia, explicitly formulated the monistic doctrine, and endeavoured to show that the world must be so to speak "cut out of one block," that there *must be* one principle immanent in its multiplicity. This, the Pythagoreans had already accentuated in their doctrine of the Noetic one, or unity, in which all numbers, and, *a fortiori*, all things were immanent. But the Pythagoreans, besides this, removed the inquiry from the ground of concrete substance to that of abstract mathematical relations. These were of course hypostasized, and made the essences of which the real world was the manifestation, and which were in their turn the manifestation of the original unity. Thus at the same time that an addition to the range of philosophic inquiry was made by this introduction of abstract notions, the monistic principle was raised to an integral place in philosophy. The Eleatics, by pushing this principle to its extreme limits, forced into relief the opposition of the abstract and the concrete, the one and the many, an opposition which they made absolute.

They were thus compelled by their fundamental principle to deny the sense-world, an issue which led to the introduction of a Dialectic, based on an examination of its fundamental notions. But the one-sided Monism of the Southern Italians was encountered in Asia Minor by a Monism embodied in perhaps the most brilliant of all the pre-Sokratic systems, that of Herakleitos. This Monism took its stand on the fusion of the very contraries whose opposition the Eleatics would have made absolute. The other philosophers of the Metaphysical-Physicist group attempted the solution of the same problem—namely, to find a *modus vivendi* between abstract absolute Being and the multiplicity of the sense-world—but they failed to formulate anything satisfactory. They all sacrificed the one to the many at starting; their systems are pluralistic; in other words, the knot is cut but not untied. Then came the Sophists, who placed all these various systems on a level, by declaring man to be the measure of all things, thereby practically denying the possibility of truth in a higher sense. Following the hint given by them, though despising their pedantry, Sokrates abandoned the search for physical or metaphysical truth, and applied himself to the search for logical truth, to the definition and formulation of concepts, and the attainment of "virtue" which necessarily followed from a knowledge of the ideal "good." Sokrates was emphatically the philosopher and the apostle of inwardness.

"Know thyself," was the beginning and end of his teaching. But this self-knowledge involved the transformation of the confused and haphazard thought of the multitude, which the least criticism could involve in hopeless contradiction, into clear, well-defined notions, capable of universal application.

A development of three hundred years thus culminated in Plato. Plato represents the synthesis of Sokratism and Pre-Sokratism. In Plato the essence of the whole pre-Sokratic philosophy is to be found transfused and transformed by the Dialectic of Sokrates. The element which is most prominent in the constructive portion of his work is Pythagoreanism, but he owes scarcely less a debt to the Eleatics, to Herakleitos, and even to the sceptical theories of the Sophists.

Aristotle, while starting from the synthesis of Plato, brought the power of his mighty intellect to bear upon it with the result that he effected a more complete fusion of the pre-Sokratic thought than even Plato had done; that is, he seized more completely the meaning and the essential in those systems. He more thoroughly separated the ore, which they severally contained, from the accidental dross with which it was combined. For instance, how many a clumsily expressed doctrine and distinction of Pythagorean and Eleatic lay hidden under the cardinal antithesis of *form and matter*. What a light was cast on the problems of philosophy by the at once definite and comprehensive expression (an expression covering neither too much nor too little), of a principle which preceding thinkers had been vainly groping after in the dark, now grasping it for an instant, now blindly clutching at some other, quite unessential fact in mistake for it. But Aristotle's more popular, though not greater title to fame, lay in his foundation of the inductive method, and of natural science itself in the modern sense of the word. Observation and experiment, the collection, sifting and comparison of facts, with a view of through them arriving at general principles, has its origin in the thinker of Stagira.

PLATO.

PLATO, or to give him his correct appellation, Aristokles, was born at Athens about B.C. 429, his father's name being Ariston, and his mother's Periktione. His youth was passed amid the artistic splendours which the age of Perikles had left behind it. Born of an aristocratic family, he hated the democracy of Athens no less than his master, Sokrates. As a youth, he appears to have occupied himself with poetic attempts, which he committed to the flames, when in his twentieth year, he decided to devote himself to philosophy. Previously to his acquaintance with Sokrates, which occurred at this time, he received instruction in philosophy from Kratylos the Herakleitan, and probably from Epicharmos the Pythagorean. He also seems to have been conversant with the philosophy of the Ionian school, as well as with that of Anaxagoras. Of his long and close intimacy with Sokrates, in the course of which his own system gradually took shape, it is only necessary to make mention.

After the execution of his master, he repaired to Megara, remaining some time in companionship with Euklid, doubtless devoting himself with ardour to the Eleatic philosophy, of which Euklid was the great post-Sokratic exponent. He subsequently entered upon a prolonged period of travel, visiting first Ionia, and then Cyrene and Egypt, and occupying himself with mathematical and other studies. Of more influence on his subsequent intellectual development was his journey to Italy, where he became more intimately acquainted with the Pythagorean system, and more thoroughly assimilated its doctrines, than previously. Possibly this influence induced him to intermeddle with the political affairs of Syrakuse. It was on his way home thence to Athens, that he was (under circumstances variously related) captured and sold into slavery; a state in which he might have remained but for the interposition of his friend, Annikeris, the Cyrenaic, who ransomed him. On his arrival at Athens, about forty years of age, he founded his school in the groves of Akademos, subsequently purchasing the garden on the hill Kolonos, as its perpetual possession. With the exception of two further fruitless expeditions to Sicily, he remained in Athens, devoting himself to teaching and writing for the remainder of his life, which terminated B.C. 347.

Plato's Philosophy.

Plato is the first ancient thinker of whom we possess anything more than fragments. All Plato's works are exoteric, that is, suited not only for the school, but for cultured readers generally. Critics, ancient and modern, have exercised their wits in determining which of the writings that have come down as Plato's are genuine, and which are the works of disciples. Even in Antiquity attempts were made to fix the order of the Platonic Dialogues in a systematic manner. In connexion with modern Platonic exegesis, it is sufficient to cite the names of Schleiermacher (*Plato's Leben und Schriften*), Socher (*Ueber Plato's Schriften*), Stallbaum (in his critical edition of Plato's works), Hermann (*Geschichte der Platonischen Philosophie*, Zeller (*Philosophie der Griechen*), Grote (*Plato and the other companions of Sokrates*), and Jowett (*Plato's works translated into English*).

The content of Plato's philosophy naturally falls into the well-known division of Dialectics, Physics, and Ethics, although it is doubtful if he himself so formulated it. The positive doctrines have to be sought out in the various dialogues, each of which is, generally speaking, devoted to the elucidation of some one point, but all of which possess a merely negative and preparatory in addition to their positive side. Plato, like any modern philosophic writer, always pre-supposes in his readers a knowledge of the chief philosophical literature of his time. His polemic, in common with that of his master Sokrates, is mainly directed against prevalent conceptions, and the doctrines of the Sophists; though there were not wanting sly shafts aimed at the Sokratic teaching itself.

In the *Theatætus* and the *Parmenides*, "common sense" is attacked; its object is shown to possess no stability, and its existence to be, at the best, probability or opinion merely. The goal of all these discussions is to produce scepticism of ordinary notions and the dictates of unreflective perception; and is thus identical with the conviction of ignorance, which it was the aim of the Sokratic Dialectic to bring about. But this is with Plato only the recoil previous to the philosophic spring about to be made. All philosophy begins with the *reductio ad absurdum* of common notions. There is no true knowledge; wisdom, or even morality, but that attained through philosophic reflection. The virtue of the common man is the effect of chance and custom. The success even of a Perikles, is merely due to a happy concurrence of character and circumstances. In the ordinary sense the man is termed brave, even though he fights from fear; but no action is really virtuous which does not spring from a full consciousness of its grounds. It is not, as with the Sophists, the *individual* perception or opinion that sums up the truth for man, but that which is divine and *universal* in him, namely, the reflective, self-comprehending Reason. Plato draws the distinction between impulse and rational will, and shows that where pleasure is made of set purpose the sole principle of action, the reverse of pleasure is attained. (*Gorgias.*)

The subjective condition of true knowledge is philosophical yearning or desire. Neither the all-knowing (σοφός) nor the wholly ignorant (ἀμαθὴς) is concerned therewith, but only the lover of wisdom (φιλόσοφος), he, namely, who represents the mean between perfect knowledge and absolute ignorance. The philosophical impulse is the germ from which art, morality and science proceed, but it needs training and nourishment. The learning which is the nourishment of the impulse, is the study of the beautiful. Hence music* is named as the introduction to philosophy. Mathematics is another stage midway between sense-perception and intellectual intuition. But the highest of all is the dialectical art. (*Phædo, Republic.*) Dialectics stands in opposition to the Rhetoric of the Sophists, which only teaches the art of expression. It is in dialogue, that by the sifting and opposition of common

* "Music," it must be borne in mind, with the ancients meant general culture, excluding mathematics and philosophy.

opinions, the true, the universal is evolved. Antithetic procedure is best for clear conceiving, as the consequences of a conception and its opposite are then drawn from its definition. But while the ironic method of Sokrates, the Sophists, and of Zeno, is commended as a means, yet viewed as an end in itself it is no less condemned. The ascent to a correctly defined conception does not exhaust the process. When it is reached, its grounds and its relations to other concepts have further to be determined. Plato, in his most subtle analyses, never loses sight of the fact that philosophy is and must be a unity or nothing. Thus the desire or love of knowledge (*eros*) is not sufficient to make the philosopher. He must understand and practise the dialectical art. In the Symposium Sokrates is treated as the incarnation of the Eros or love of wisdom. Plato, it should be observed, speaks somewhat differently in different places of Dialectics. Sometimes he identifies it with truth or philosophy itself, while at others, he more consistently speaks of it as the ante-chamber to knowledge, philosophy or truth.

Most of the more specifically *dialectical* among Plato's dialogues (*e.g.*, the Theætetus, the Sophists, the Parmenides, the Kratylos) are occupied with the attempt to discover a *via media* between Eleaticism and Herakleitism, between the conception of Being as one, self-existent, immovable, unchangeable, and the manifold, independent, moving, changeful world of sense-perception. Plato saw a half-truth in both of these doctrines; he also saw their seemingly contradictory nature. Hence his aim was to resolve this contradiction in a higher unity. This could only be effected on Platonic principles by their mutual trituration, so to speak. In the Parmenides,* Plato seeks to show that Eleaticism is destroyed by its own arguments, since its negation of the manifold, &c., leads to fully as great contradictions as the opposite doctrine. The *One* in and above the *Many*, *Being* in *Becoming*, *Identity* in *Difference*, and that which, existent, cannot be thought of, except as limited by non-existence is variously designated by Plato as ὄντως ὄν, as λόγος (a word first employed in a philosophical sense

* The genuineness of the Parmenides has been more than once disputed, but to all appearance on ground scarcely adequate.

by Herakleitos, whose subsequent history is both curious and important as regards speculative thought), as οὐσία, as γένος, as εἶδος νοητόν, or finally as ἰδέα. The last term is the one with which Plato's system is most characteristically associated. What Plato understood by Ideas is at once seen when we remember that he says there are as many Ideas as general names. The synthesis of qualities *con*noted in a universal term constitute the archetypal form or *Idea* of the concrete individuals which are *de*noted by it. Thus the general names "house," "bed," "animal," stand for the self-existent archetypal ideas of all the particulars and singulars falling severally under them, that is at once for all particular kinds of houses, beds or animals, and for every individual house, bed or animal. Plato's *via media* between the Eleatic changeless one and the Herakleitan flux of the many consisted in the system of Ideas, which showed a hierarchical order of gradation from the highest and most abstract concept to the concrete real of experience. Thus with Plato the inchoate "non-existent" world of pure sense was no less an element in the reality of consciousness than the self-existent world of pure intelligibility. The properly non-existent world of sense acquired a pseudo-existence through its participation in the world of ideas, the synthesis being our *real* world. But the essence of the Platonic ideas is not exhausted in their being the self-existent basis of the class they cover; they must also be regarded as potences positing their own ends. With this notion of *end* we get into the region of ethics and ontology or teleology. In the *Phædo*, we are expressly warned against conceiving the causal conditions of things as their true basis (*αἰτία*), for this latter can only lie in their end or purpose. The teleological aspect of individual things or of classes of things is indicated by the comparatives better, best, which presuppose their relation to an *absolute universal ideal good*, as the ultimate end, that in which all other ends, and, *a fortiori*, all ideas, are, so to speak, gathered up and concentrated. When we consider the ontological system of ideas as also a teleological system of ends, it is evident that this system must culminate in an Idea which presents itself as the highest end, that to which all other Ideas as ends tend to approach in varying degrees.

Thus with Plato the highest Idea or ultimate end-in-itself was manifested in a multitude of subordinate ideas or "ends;" and thus the problem of Pythagorean and Eleatic, the problem of the One and the Many was solved, the νοῦς of Anaxagoras, and the "good" of Sokrates being embraced in the solution. Hence, too, Plato achieved what his friend Euklid the Megaric had attempted, namely, an ethical Monism on the Sokratic lines. By Plato's highest and comprehensive principle of the Good is to be understood the universal *world-order*, natural no less than moral. The absolute end or purpose as the "ον οντως" is the object of Dialectics, inasmuch as this science leads from the lower ideas, which are the determinations of things, to that which is the determination of all determinations themselves. But the dialectician must not be satisfied merely with ascending from the lowest to the highest, he must also be able to deduce all lower ideas and all particular things from this highest principle. In his later life Plato seems to have more and more tended to Pythagoreanism, or at least to a Pythagorean mode of statement. This appears most prominently in the *Philebos*. The mathematical treatment of the doctrine of ideas which is there attempted leads to results almost identical with the Pythagorean theories. The idea of the good is identified with the Deity or divine Reason as well as with the Pythagorean Noetic One. The high estimation of the mathematical sciences, which is noticeable in the later writings, is not discoverable in the *Republic* and other of the more important dialogues, where they are spoken of merely as one of the preparatory stages from mere "opinion" to the higher philosophical insights obtained through the dialectical faculty, superior indeed to the first but inferior to the second, inasmuch as their subject-matter is still within the region of sense.

Plato's doctrine of reminiscence, as presented in the *Meno*, the *Phædrus* and elsewhere, is founded on the notion of the ultimate identity of the divine and human minds. The soul in its union with a material body enters on a period of degradation in which it has fallen from its high estate as a pure existent intelligible or formal essence, and become contaminated with the non-existent world of sense. But, however low it has sunk, it never entirely loses traces of its origin. The possibility of its regaining its lost birthright, nay, even the possibility of philosophy itself lies in this fact, in that it has a remembrance of the higher realities it was wont to contemplate, and which it is the object of the philosopher to disentangle from the confusion of sense, and rehabilitate as far as may be in their purity. This, which is the end of the philosopher's life, can only be proximately attained in this sphere of existence; yet the soul illumined by the philosophic contemplation may rise in proportion to its light the more speedily to be reabsorbed into that divine essence, in which the material, the sensible, has vanished, and the formal, and the intelligible, alone remains. How much of this as of other portions of Plato's doctrine was merely poetry or allegory, it is impossible to decide with certainty, but there is no serious reason for doubting that it was really held by Plato.

Plato's physical speculations are contained almost in their entirety in the *Timæus*. Inasmuch as the material universe is only the object of perception and not of pure intellection, no such strict deduction of principles can be expected in dealing with it, as in subjects capable of the application of pure Dialectic. The most that can be furnished is a body of probable opinion. The question immediately arises, what is that which must be added to the system or complex of Ideas in order that it may appear as Nature, or in other words, as the *Good* in the harmonious order of the sensible universe. The answer is, that, in the first place, the superadded principle must be foreign to the system of ideas itself; the one being *per se* the totality of absolute Being, the other must be that of absolute non-Being; since the one is the principle of all-embracing and eternal unity, the other must be that of self-contradictory, evanescent multiplicity.* This principle must in short be none other than that unqualified, formless, inconceivable matter which is the object of pure sense. *Pure sense* must not be confounded with conscious perception which involves a participation in the ideal or logical;

* It may be observed in passing, that this is simply a roundabout mode of stating the Aristotelian distinction of form and matter, which all the dialogues of Plato are struggling to express.

it is rather mere inchoate sub-conscious *feeling* (the *blinde Anschauung* of Kant). This is the properly non-existent element in the real world, and this it is which added to, or rather limiting, and, so to speak, blurring the ideal world transforms it into Nature or the world of actual experience. The purely sensible or non-existent as opposed to the purely intelligble or existent object seems to be identified by Plato as by Aristotle, with pure extension or space. Plato may have well seen in space the medium by which the self-contained ideas were confounded with one another and with their negation, in the form of concrete objects.

The foregoing doctrine, though not expressed in so many words by Plato, is implied more or less throughout his writings, and is the only consistent mode of stating in a few words his position. It is introduced here as assisting the student to understand the transition from the dialectical to the physical side of his philosophy. In the *Timæus* the universe is conceived as an animated being, "a blessed God," created by a Demiurge or divine artificer, a conception, however, difficult to reconcile with the other side of the system, and illustrating the looseness and essentially unsystematic character of Plato's exposition where it is so often hard to distinguish between philosophy and poetry. But it seems that Plato identified his creator with the supreme "Idea" or the "Good." The soul of the world which pervades its every part, manifesting itself in the numbers and harmony of the spheres no less than in the laws regulating mundane phenomena—was created prior to the body or material of the universe. Time is coincident with its formation. The universe represents the best possible of worlds. As the chaotic matter took form and shape it assumed determinate mathematical figures and relations. Thus the elementary constituents of fire are of pyramidal figure, those of water, icosahedral, those of air octahedral, and those of earth cubical. The spheres once constituted the deity proceeds to the creation of living beings. First in order come the heavenly gods (which are identified in part at best with the stars and other celestial bodies); secondly, the creatures inhabiting the air; thirdly, those living in water; and finally, those whose dwelling-place is the earth. Plato then gives a mythical description of the origin of those inferior species of animals which the supreme deity himself has not formed, but whose creation is delegated to the lower gods, with the exception of whatsoever is immortal in their constitution. Man is the analogue of the universe, in so far as, like the world, he consists of body and soul in mysterious unity. His soul is of a dual or indeed triple nature. In the head is lodged the divine and immortal part; in the breast the mortal and human part, consisting of the passions; while the liver and spleen were constructed and placed where they are for the purpose of divination and prediction of the future. The later chapters of the *Timæus* show that Plato, like most of his contemporaries, was a believer in metempsychosis, and contain some curious and fanciful applications of that widespread and time-honoured doctrine. Such is a brief outline of Plato's cosmical theory.

The essence of the Platonic metaphysic we have seen to consist in the doctrine, that to every concept or general name, there corresponds an eternal, *self-existent essence or idea;* that the system of *ideas* thence arising has at once as its basis and completion, the idea of the *Good* which is the common principle alike of being and knowing, and from which therefore all subordinate concepts and ideas are deducible (according to the *Philebos* on mathematical principles). This "good," it will have been apparent, is æsthetic and teleological as well as specially ethical. But inasmuch as it is the object of all philosophy, it is of course none the less so of Ethics. In this connection we have to regard it as constituting the content of the human will. Plato in the *Theætetus* expresses himself vehemently against the Cyrenaic Hedonists who would make pleasure the chief good. In the *Philebos* (as in the *Republic* and elsewhere, though at less length) he develops the thesis that only in the *Beautiful* and, *a fortiori*, in the *Proportionate* (since to Plato beauty consisted in nothing but symmetry, proportion, and harmony) does the good lie, and hence that all excess either on the side of asceticism or indulgence is evil, a position in consonance with his general attitude. Intemperate and exaggerated tendencies and conduct he regards as diseases of the soul, since they imply the ascendency of the merely human and animal over the divine portions, in other words a lack of the regulating power of insight and reason, and a consequent blind irrational play of impulses, indicating a disturbance of normal functions, corresponding to that observable in bodily disease. We have seen how Plato identifies the ethical with the æsthetic chief good which was at the same time the highest end. We shall, therefore, not be surprised at his teleological definition of Virtue as the adaptability of the life to its end—a definition which embraces all particular virtues and is coincident with Justice. Virtue is to be pursued as an end in itself, and on no account for subsidiary ends, such as pleasure and pain, reward and punishment. To do evil is always worse than to suffer evil.

In the *Republic* we have a presentation of the "good" in the form of perfect virtue or justice as embodied in the social order of a commonwealth, in the same way that in the *Timæus* we had a presentation of the manner in which this same idea embodied itself as harmony in the natural order of the cosmos. The state is nothing but a magnified individual. The highest function of the state is the training of its citizens to be virtuous. The orders in the state must correspond to the virtues of the human soul, consisting of the rulers, whose specific virtue is wisdom, corresponding to the divine part; the guardians or warriors whose virtue is courage, corresponding to the emotional, active, or human part; and the traders and labourers whose virtue is self-control and obedience, corresponding to the part of the soul concerned with nutrition and the organic functions.* There are to be no private interests or wealth, but all things are to be in common. Neither is marriage, or the family relation to be recognised. The condition of the realization of this ideal state lies in the assumption of the helm of affairs by statesmen who are at the same time philosophers. This platonic Utopia, though based on the then actually existing Lacedemonian polity,

* The ancients knew nothing of any hard and fast distinction between the "soul" and the life of the organism; the one was a part of the other.

Plato supplemented in his later years by a modified version elaborated in the *Laws* which was put forward as more easy of attainment.

Plato can hardly be said to have formulated a system proper. He retained too much of the Sokratic spirit and method of pretended ignorance ever to permit himself the expression of a decided judgment. The form, moreover, which he adopted for his writings rendered this impossible. His views on the various departments of philosophy are not grouped in any way, and even those on any one subject, often conflicting, have generally to be gathered together from several different dialogues. Under these circumstances the difficulty of furnishing a condensed account of true Platonism is sufficiently obvious. Plato may be considered as the founder of what is now known as "Theory of Knowledge." The pre-Sokratic thinkers had inquired for the principles of *Being;* Sokrates opposed to their inquiry that as to the principle of *Knowing;* Plato, while starting from the standpoint of Sokrates, sought to show that the two inquiries were identical, that Being involved Knowing, as Knowing involved Being. Plato was thus the first consistent Idealist. The only existence to him was the logical, the Ideal; which was limited and confounded by the non-existent Sensible.

Surprise has sometimes been expressed at Plato's including, besides abstract concepts proper, *i.e.*, such as express qualities, "natural kinds" or "class names" among his eternal self-existent ideas. To us it seems that it was in these latter that he believed himself to have found the bridge between the sense-manifold of experience and the intelligibles of Dialectics. "Natural Kinds," in other words, universals connoting a ready-made synthesis and only awaiting the "here" and "now" of sense for their concrete realisation, were plainly the link between the empirical and the intelligible worlds, between the world of change and multiplicity given in ordinary consciousness, and that world of abstract ideas, to the contemplation of which the philosopher aspired. The objects of the real world bore, doubtless, to Plato, much the same relation to the natural kinds which denoted them, as the system of ideas itself bore to the Supreme Idea.

There are some students who may be inclined to wonder at Plato's deification of the concept-form or universal; at what seems to be mere logical subtlety being constituted "our being's aim and end." Such persons forget the fact that education and culture itself is nothing other than self-universalisation. Every advance the individual makes in the higher life of thought means a breaking down of the limits which confine him to the "here," the "this," and the "now;" in short, in a sense a suspension, or at least, an ignoring of those space-and-time relations which rule supreme in the every-day world of his and his neighbours' "concerns." Listen to the conversation of a company of tradesmen, or women; of what does it consist, but of gossip immediately bearing on concrete personalities and their surroundings; everything turns on this. Listen, on the other hand, to the conversation of a company of thinkers, and it will in all probability be found to consist of discussion concerning, not the interests of any concrete person or persons, leastways *quâ* concrete, but of things and places or events probably far distant in time or space, but at all events in their abstract and general relations and altogether apart from personalities as such and their interests. It may be permitted us to regard this at least as one of the side-truths shadowed forth in the work of Plato. With this concluding observation, we pass on to Plato's great pupil and successor, Aristotle.

ARISTOTLE.

The birth of Aristotle was cast in one of the most critical periods of Grecian history. The old independent political life of the Greek cities was being extinguished by the monarch of a state that had hitherto taken little or no part in the affairs of Greece. It was at Stageiros, or Stagira—a city of this rising state, destined within the next half-century to become the master of the greater part of the then known world—that Aristotle was born (B.C. 385). His father, Nikomachos, and grandfather,

Machaon, were both physicians, an interesting circumstance to the student of heredity. Losing his father when a boy, Aristotle was early thrown on his own resources, and at seventeen years of age, came to seek his fortune in Athens, where Plato, then in the prime of life, was attracting to his lectures the philosophically-disposed among his fellow citizens. Aristotle seems to have found the leisure, in spite of his own professional avocations as apothecary, to become a regular attendant at the Academy. Some years later he set up as a professor of Rhetoric, but after Plato's death, left Athens, and repaired with his fellow-pupil, Xenokrates, to Hermeias, the tyrant of Atarneus, whose brother's daughter he subsequently married. On the death of Hermeias, he went to reside in the island of Mytilene, till called away by the offer of Philip of Macedon, to entrust him with the education of his son Alexander, then thirteen years old. Aristotle remained at the court of Macedon four years, and did not quit the country for a further period of four years, when he returned to Athens and established himself as teacher of philosophy in the Lyceum, a building deriving its name from the circumstance of its standing opposite the temple of Apollo Lykeios. The name "peripatetic," which clung to Aristotle's school, arose from his habit of pacing its halls while lecturing. His activity as lecturer only lasted thirteen years, after which, in consequence of a political accusation, he left Athens for Chalkis, where he died, B.C. 322, just one year after his pupil, Alexander the Great.

ARISTOTLE'S PHILOSOPHY.

The features mainly distinguishing the writings of Aristotle from those of Plato, are their strictly philosophical character, there being no trace in them of any artistic purpose. A legend relates that though Aristotle began his literary career by the composition of dialogues after the manner of Plato, he soon abandoned that form in despair of ever approaching the master. In addition to these dialogues, he wrote other popular pieces, to which allusions are made by many ancient writers, besides Aristotle himself, but these have all perished with the exception of one or two fragments. Aristotle's writings have reached us in a state of great confusion, and in some cases corruption, while several treatises (*e.g.*, the Eudemean and the "great" Ethics) handed down as the Stagirite's, are now universally recognised as the compilations of disciples. Several complete editions of Aristotle have appeared since the Aldine, published at Florence, in five folio volumes, in the 15th century. The best is generally considered to be that of Bekker and Brandis, issued under the auspices of the Berlin Academy of Sciences (4 vols., 1831–35).

In the Aristotelian philosophy, the departments of Logic, Physics, and Ethics become even more definitely pronounced than in the Platonic. Recognising, with Plato, the indwelling yearning for knowledge as the basis of philosophy, Aristotle maintains that philosophy is nothing but the extension and methodisation of common experience; that it does not, as Plato contended, involve a complete break with the sense-manifold, but that on the contrary it has its origin in common perception, or in other words, in particular objects. Experience is merely constituted out of the successive recognition of likeness in perceptions. Common sense thus involves a universal element no less than philosophy itself, although its relation to philosophy is that of a particular. The whole of knowledge is a scale or ladder in which there is no break, but a continuous progressive ascent from the singular sense-perception to the highest generalisation of speculative thought.

The occupation with mere logical forms, the universals of Plato, abstracts from an essential element in all existence, the higher no less than the lower—namely, the *material* element. The grounds of the reason can never, according to Aristotle, attain to the accuracy of sense-perception. Nevertheless, Aristotle assumes the fundamental position of speculative thought. Ontology, or the "first philosophy" of Aristotle, inasmuch as it professes to deduce the existent from principles, presupposes the question, what is a principle? The answer to this question is to be found in the four different senses of the words *αἰτία* and *ἀρχή*. The first book of the Metaphysics, which is the earliest attempt at a systematic

F 2

history of philosophy, is an endeavour to illustrate these four different senses by the various systems of philosophy. With the Ionians the principle or cause was *matter;* with the Pythagoreans, *form;* with Empedokles, *efficient cause;* with Anaxagoras, *end* or *final cause.* By *matter* (ὕλη) Aristotle understands the warp or basis, so to speak, to be operated on, or which *becomes.* Thus bronze is the matter of the statue, the acorn of the oak, the premisses of the conclusion, the instrument of the music it produces, the component sounds of the octave, the letters of which it consists of the word, etc., etc. *Matter* is in short the *undetermined* real. In the instances given it is of course only *relatively* undetermined, but, employed in an ontological sense, the term means the *absolutely* undetermined, corresponding to the unqualified *Infinite* of Anaximandros, or the non-existent sense-object of Plato. *Matter* considered *per se*, that is, abstracted from all determination, coincides with the *potential.* It is the mere *possibility* of the Real; the *incomplete*, the *unbecome* factor therein.

The second and opposite principle, that of *form* (μορφή, λόγος), denotes pure determination, the Platonic *Idea.* This second principle is related to the first, as activity to passivity, as actuality to potentiality. It is the figure into which the bronze is fashioned, to constitute it a statue; the melody which is produced by the notes of the flute; the relation of the sounds which give the octave; the particular conjunction of letters which make the word; the articulate whole into which the parts are gathered up, or the mass is moulded, etc. In an ontological sense it is of course pure, absolute determination as distinguished from the merely relative determination of the instances given. In short, the *form* of Aristotle corresponds as nearly as possible to the self-existent intelligible world of Plato, just as the *matter* of Aristotle corresponds to the non-existent sense-world of Plato. But with Aristotle there was no such thing as pure *form* (ideas) existing *per se* and apart from *matter. Form* only existed in and for *matter*, as a specific modification of matter. Aristotle is vehement in his polemic against the Platonic Ideas, the *universalia ante res.* But, while to assume as Plato did, the existence of pure forms apart from the matter of which they are the form, is inadmissible; it is equally plain that pure unqualified matter can never be an object of experience. Hence, to Aristotle, the two elements in question were equally essential to experience, and to all reality whatever, as much to "true" as to empirical being. This Aristotelian distinction of itself marks an epoch, most momentous in the history of thought, and at once clears the ground of a mass of extraneous material.

As regards the third sense of the word *principle* (to indicate which Aristotle makes use of a variety of expressions, but all of which are summed up with tolerable accuracy in the well-known scholastic phrase *causa efficiens*) it is enough to remark that it refers to the immediate empirical cause, or antecedent condition, (efficient cause) of anything, and is antithetical to τέλος, or the fourth sense of the word, which is that of *final cause* or purpose. The τέλος, it is important to remember, is the ultimate and highest form of the reality of a thing, to the attainment of which all the other forms are subservient, and with reference to which they may be regarded as *means* merely.

The four factors above enumerated furnish the data of ontology. Foremost comes the negative result before mentioned, that neither mere matter, nor mere form constitute the existent Real, but the union or synthesis of matter and form. This is insisted upon as regards *matter* against the Hylozoists, as regards *form* against the Eleatics and Plato. Matter is the *becoming*—neither being nor non-being, but, as Ferrier would have put it, more than *O* and less than *I*. There is no passage from non-Being to Being, but only from the not-yet-existent to the at-present existent. The οὐσία (essence), though sometimes employed as coincident with form, is generally used for the synthesis itself. The whole essence or synthesis, the real existent, is also said to be constituted out of the two momenta, the *genus* and the *differentia*—the first corresponding to *matter*, and the second to *form*. Thus Sokrates may be described as made up of the *matter* (*genus*) of *man* and the *form* (*differentia*) of *Sokratity*. But the synthesis is not to be regarded as a fixed or static entity. For Aristotle, all reality is expressed in the logical passage from matter to form; that is, from a lower, to a higher, from the less complex to the more complex—the lower stage being related as *matter* to the incoming element, the *form*, which denotes the higher stage. To take the above instance, Sokrates plus the differentia of Sokratity, that is, Sokrates *quâ* Sokrates, involves a formal element, over and above his material basis, Athenian. The Athenian again *quâ* Athenian is a formal modification of *his* material basis, Greek, which as Athenian he presupposes. Once more, the Greek *quâ* Greek is a formal modification of the material basis, Man; as Greek he involves an element of *form* additional to the *human* material (the common humanity) of which he consists, &c., &c. The final *terminus a quo* of the scale is thus pure undifferentiated *matter*.

We now turn to the third and fourth data in the Aristotelian ontology, the efficient and the final cause. Here the element of determinate agency comes into play. The first of these, the *conditio sine qua non* of the existence of a thing, may be regarded as its *material* cause; the second, the *end* or *purpose* of its existence, its *formal* cause. In the force or self-activity or actualisation (ἐντελέχεια) which is part of the essence of *reality*, the two elements of mover and moved, the passive and the active are to be distinguished. The first is the formal, the second the material. The one is the agent, the other the patient. But this formative activity, or subordinate motive, itself presupposes an end or purpose which it is to accomplish, and this leads us to the final cause or the ultimate principle of motion, that which moves but is not moved—pure energy. But Aristotle does not deny substantiality to this pure energy. On the contrary, just as matter *per se* is potentiality, always becoming but never become, so this ultimate formal principle is its counterpart, actuality, eternal self-subexistence. Thus Aristotle finds in this teleological conception of intelligent purpose the *terminus ad quem* of the scale of being, which the notion of mere *form*, *per se*, could not give him. It is needless to remind the reader that this ἀκινητόν of Aristotle is the representative, in his system of the supreme idea of Plato. It is not difficult to see how the Neo-Platonic harmonists of a later time might, with some show of reason, maintain the essential identity of the systems of Aristotle and Plato when they found so many cardinal features in common.

Aristotle is the first to distinctly apply the so-called cosmological argument. As every individual object presupposes a moving cause for all its changes, so the universe itself presupposes an absolute first mover, a primal determiner of its as yet undetermined matter. But Aristotle soon leaves this mechanical theistic conception. This principle (*πρῶτον κινοῦν*) must be essentially pure energy and form, untrammelled by matter, pure actuality, in which the shadow of potentiality is not; a conception which, it need scarcely be said, is hard to reconcile with Aristotle's assertions of the inseparability of matter and form, or with his bitter polemic against the Platonic system of ideal ends, which is its prototype. The ultimate self-thinking and active principle, or God of Aristotle, is not to be conceived as the creator of the world in time (like the demiurge of Plato), but rather as the immanent actuality of the world, the eternally complete ideal purpose to which the real is ever approximating, and which is at the same time its ultimate motive principle.*

Nature, according to Aristotle, is the totality of material and moving objects. Change, or motion, may be divided into origination (change or motion from the relatively non-existent to the relatively existent) and destruction (change or motion from the relatively existent to the relatively non-existent), which is again divided into the species quantitative, qualitative and spacial motion; or increase and decrease, change of quality and change of place. The conditions of motion are place or space and time. Place (*τόπος*) is the bounding of the encompassing body. Time is the measure or numerical aspect of motion or change. Time is endless, but space bounded. The world is eternal. The spheres in which the fixed stars inhere, possess the most perfect of all motions—the circular. The motions of the planets are explained by the hypothesis of immaterial essences or subordinate deities inhering in them. The spherical earth is fixed in the centre of the universe. The five elementary natural substances, ether, fire, water, air and earth have respectively their determi-

* I may point out here how nearly identical is Aristotle's conception with the *Idea* of Hegel.

nate places in the cosmic whole. The place of the ether is the celestial regions. Out of ether are formed the spheres and celestial bodies. The other (traditional) four elements belong to the terrestrial regions, but are distinguished by their heaviness and lightness, heat and cold, dryness and moisture, and are all found in various proportions in all bodies. The matter of earth is continually passing into higher and higher forms in the shape of a progressive scale (as it were) of living beings. Every stage in this formal determination of course embraces the whole of those below it, in addition to its own special and distinctive character. The force or formative energy of living beings in the widest sense, is, with Aristotle, identical with their souls, or ψυχή. Thus the capacity or soul of the plant is limited to nutrition and growth according to a certain figure; the animal possesses in addition to this the capacities of feeling, desire, and locomotion; the man again unites with all these capacities that of reason (νοῦς), the manifestation of which is partly theoretical (scientific) and partly practical (moral). The Reason is separable into two elements or sides, the receptive, determined and temporal, and the creative, determining and eternal. The first of these elements is the material, the second the formal side of the Reason. The synthesis of these two elements, the natural and the divine, constitutes the human soul or life of the man as man. The discussion of these subjects will be found in Aristotle's Physics and in the *De anima.*

The goal of all human activity, the highest human good, is happiness, which consists in the rational and virtuous activity of the soul, while this activity has, as its natural completion, pleasure. It will be seen by this that Aristotle does not posit, like Plato, an abstract ideal Good, Harmony or Proportion, as the object of Ethics. but is satisfied with the highest attainable good to Man; that which all men implicitly or explicitly recognise as such, however much they may differ as to the nature of its content. But in so far as this goal (happiness) is human, it must consist not merely in vegetating or living, but in rational activity, as such. In accordance with the animal and rational nature of man, there arise two classes of virtues; on the one side, the practical virtues proper, *i.e.* such as consist in the mastery of the Reason over the sensuous impulses; on the other side the dianoetic or logical virtues. Aristotle shows that the true mean—that rational happiness—consists in the art of bringing the *formal* or determining λόγος to bear on the *material* of impulses, passions and desires, of which the merely natural man consists. The capacity of doing this is not natural but human, inasmuch as it involves action following upon reflection.

Aristotle is a pronounced upholder of the doctrine of free-will, and polemicises in this character against both Sokrates and Plato. In addition to the Platonic virtues of courage and moderation, Aristotle enumerates liberality, magnanimity, love of honour, mildness, openness, &c., &c., and these are not as with Plato opposed to one only, but to two extremes. Justice is treated separately in the fifth book of the Ethics, as the foundation not only of all virtues, but of all social life whatever. It is indeed regarded by Aristotle as as much pertaining to the sphere of Politics as of Ethics. In the sixth book Wisdom is proclaimed identical with the highest happiness of man, being the satisfaction of the highest within him, namely, the νοῦς, or Reason, though in practical life, prudence and reflection are the more important, since they are concerned with the singular.

The *Nikomachæan Ethics* close with a chapter which serves as a transition to the *Politics*, a science which Aristotle regards merely as the continuation of Ethics. The first book of the Politics deals with domestic government, and affords some interesting glimpses into the social life of ancient Greece. As the tribe is constituted out of an aggregation of families, so the state is constituted out of an aggregation of tribes. The second book consists in a criticism of political theories (Plato's among others), as well as of existing constitutions. The seventh and eighth books are the most important, as treating of the conditions of the greatest possible happiness in a state, where personal and civic virtue have become identical.* First, Aristotle places the natural conformation

* The idea of "personal" virtue belonged to the new ethics of inwardness, of which Sokrates was the most prominent exponent, and was foreign to the older ethics of the ancient world. In the Politics Aristotle endeavours to find common ground for them.

of the country, proximity to the sea; neither too dense, nor too sparse a population.* For the further conditions the constitution of the state is responsible. Aristotle, while diverging widely from the Platonic-aristocratic state, is nevertheless not favourable to the Greek democracies. While he would concede a large share of power to the middle class, in other words the poorer freemen, which was as far as the Greek conception of democracy extended, he would at the same time have this power checked by the existence of a sovereign.

The Art-philosophy or Æsthetic of Aristotle is chiefly contained in the *Poetics*, a work of which only fragments remain; but expressions on the subject are to be found in the Metaphysics, the Rhetoric, and elsewhere. Art is distinguished from virtue as creation from action. It is further distinguished from the creative activity of nature, which it most nearly resembles, by the fact that the artist realises his end in another body; thus the sculptor fashions brass into a statue, while the plant forms itself, and even the man creates himself, viz., his own character. In spite of this, the analogy is great between natural and artistic action. Art is of two kinds; it may either be designed to complete what nature has begun, as to make man healthy, to protect him from weather, to prepare food for his sustenance, to enable him to live in community, &c., such as, the arts of medicine, of architecture, of cookery, of government, or, in other words, have utility for its end. Or art may have for its end, like nature, to create a world of its own, which since it cannot be a real world must be a world of appearance. Art in this sense, *i.e.* art whose end is its own creation, is termed by Aristotle imitative art, which clearly proves that the distinction between imitation and originality in the fine arts so familiar to us, was not present to the mind of the Stagirite. The sense in which the word imitation (μιμητική) is used, is not quite clear, since Aristotle expressly cites music, the one we should regard as the least so, as the most imitative of the arts. The content of art (imitative) is the beautiful. Art exhibiting the highest

* It must be remembered that Aristotle's references to population only include the minority of actual inhabitants, *i.e.* the free population.

end as accomplished before us, occupies a midway position between theory and practice, between science and life; inasmuch as the object of art is the particular in the universal. In art individual things are idealised, not presented either *in concreto* merely, as in ordinary reality, nor *in abstracto* merely, as in science.

It remains for us, before leaving Aristotle, to give a brief sketch of his *Organon*, or theory of formal logic, which we need scarcely remind the reader contains in all essentials the completed science of the laws of formal thinking. Logic, or Analytics and Dialectics, was to Aristotle merely the propœdeutic to philosophy, and not, as with Plato, the essence of philosophy itself. The classes of concepts, and of propositions, answer to the formal side of reality. The most universal of existence-forms are substance, quantity, quality, relation, place, time, situation, possession, activity, passivity.* The various general propositions respecting the real which are furnished by these concept-forms, Aristotle terms categories. The concept is part of the essence of the real object. The conclusion, *i.e.* the deduction of one judgment from another, is divided into the syllogism which deduces the particular and singular from the universal, and induction, which consists in the assimilation of singulars and particulars, and the construction out of them of universals. In the latter of course we leave the region of the purely formal; the factors of observation and experiment coming into play. The foremost logical principles to Aristotle are "the laws of thought," viz., identity, contradiction and excluded middle; which are immediately cognised through Reason. But more easily (and hence earlier) attainable by the human mind are the simple notions and facts directly conveyed through perceptions—the co-ordination and assimilation of which constitute induction—although in themselves the principles of thought which this process presupposes are prior.

The above brief and necessarily imperfect sketch will suffice to show the enormous range as well as depth of

* We need scarcely observe that, as has been often pointed out, this list is at once defective and redundant.

Aristotle's writings. We can scarcely wonder at the mediæval schoolmen conferring upon him the title of *the* philosopher, so far does his work at once in character and amount surpass that of his predecessors. For even Plato, owing partly to the strong influence of the Socratic method, and partly to his natural temperament, left no works which could have served for ages as standard treatises on the various departments of philosophy, as did Aristotle's Logical treatises, his Ethics and his Psychology.

The bibliography of Plato and Aristotle would fill volumes. The names of some of the best works on Plato have already been given (see above, p. 55). For Aristotle's Metaphysic, Schwegler's *Commentary* is the best book. For the Logical Treatises, Prantl's *Geschichte der Logik* is useful. On the system generally, may be consulted Franz Biese's *Die Philosophie des Aristoteles* (Vol. II. Berlin, 1835–1842); also Zeller's *Aristoteles und die alte Peripatetiker*.

The *De Anima* has been excellently translated, with scholarly introduction and notes, by Professor Edwin Wallace (Clarendon Press.)

FOURTH EPOCH.

ACADEMICS AND PERIPATETICS, STOICS, EPICUREANS AND SCEPTICS.

The Academics and Peripatetics.

This fourth epoch of Greek thought is characterised by the elaboration and combination in various directions of the ideas contained in previous systems. Among the Academics, or Platonists, three periods or "academies" are commonly distinguished, the Old Academy, the Middle Academy, and the New Academy. To the first or orthodox academy belongs Speusippus, the nephew and immediate successor of Plato (347–339), who accentuated the pantheistic tendencies of his uncle; Xenocrates of Chalcedon, who next filled the chair, and who developed the Pythagorean side of the Platonic philosophy; Heraklides of Pontus, the astronomer Philippus, Hermodorus, &c., &c. The middle academy was founded by Arkesilaus (341–315), who took his stand on the sceptical side of Plato, as exhibited in the Parmenides. This soon drifted into the third school or New Academy, the nominal founder of which is Karneades, and where the sceptical direction was still further followed out with the assistance of the theories of Pyrrho. In Philo of Larissa, and his pupil Antiochus of Askalon, and their successors, who, returning to a dogmatic standpoint, endeavoured to read a Stoical tendency into the writings of Plato, some historians have distinguished a fourth and even a fifth Academy.

The Peripatetics, as the successors and disciples of Aristotle were called (Theophrastus, Gadanus, Aristoxenus, Dikearchus, &c., &c.,) directed their attention chiefly to physical research, and to popularising the ethical doctrines of their master, though attempts to modify the main Aristotelian positions in a naturalistic sense were not wanting. With the later leaders of the school, however, all such modifications were abandoned, the text of

Aristotle being regarded as the final arbiter, and the elucidation of its meaning the most important, if not the sole end of the teacher's function. Hence the later Peripatetics are chiefly noteworthy as textual critics and grammarians. Probably the most remarkable of the successors of Aristotle was Strato of Lampsacus (*circa* B.C. 288), whose teaching seems to have made for a materialistic monism, in opposition alike to the spiritualistic elements in Aristotle's speculation, and to the mechanical and pluralistic materialism of the Atomist schools.

The Stoics.

The Stoics, notwithstanding the widely spread influence their school exercised in later times, cannot be regarded as having contributed any essentially new factor to the history of philosophy. Their ethical doctrine has its prototype in Cynicism, their physics in Herakleitanism, and their logic in Aristotelianism. The founder of the Stoic school was the Cypriot Zeno, who was born at Kitium, B.C. 340. After a lengthened study of the post-Sokratic literature he came to Athens, where he was instructed successively by the Cynic Krates, the Megaric Stilpo, and the Academic Polemon.

In opposition to Plato, Aristotle, and even to Sokrates, but in full accordance with the spirit of the Cynical teaching, Zeno so far subordinated the theoretical to the practical, that, not content with defining philosophy as the art of virtue, he sought the ground of its division into Logic, Physics, and Ethics (which he was the first to definitely formulate), in the fact of there being logical, physical, and ethical virtues! The Logic of the Stoics falls into *Rhetoric* or the art of oratory, and *Dialectic* or the art of disputation. It is the auxiliary of Ethics, inasmuch as it serves to enable us to guard against errors. The soul, which is primarily a *tabula rasa*, receives impressions either from external objects or from changes in its own state, through the repetition and remembrance of which an experience is produced. Hence the Stoics maintained, in opposition to Plato, that universals existed merely in the mind, and that only singulars were real. The test of truth was the *conviction* accompanying an experience, whose declaration, when unshakable, must be regarded as final. A conviction or belief of which it is absolutely impossible for us to free ourselves, is true. This criterion was called by the Stoics, the ὀρθὸς λόγος, and is identical with the modern "necessity of thought." As a natural consequence of this doctrine, follow the appeals to the universal consent of mankind, which pervade the Stoic writers. Science is merely the reduction to form and precision of the truths guaranteed by unshakable conviction. Into the logic proper of the Stoics it is unnecessary to enter, since it differs only in a few points of detail from that of Aristotle.

The Stoic Physics, based as they are on the Herakleitan theory, have as their cardinal principle the doctrine of a universal animating fiery ether, called variously Zeus, Soul (πνεῦμα), Reason (λόγος), and Intelligence (νοῦς). The contention that the ultimate form of all reality was spacial and material, was extended to the mind and its states. The distinction was made, however, between the finer and more subtle, the active and formative, matter, which was identified with the divine ether or the world-soul, and with the souls of men and gods, and the coarser merely passive matter of which bodies consist. As with Herakleitos, from the central creative fire arose all things, and into it they must return. The process seems to have been conceived as one of condensation and rarefaction. The opposition of heat and cold also plays a part in the Stoic Physics, the former as active, the latter as passive. The human soul as a fragment of the universal world-soul is of course of the nature of fire. The Aristotelian doctrine of the evolution of form and matter, seems to have been interwoven with the physical theory of the Stoics. Their Pantheism led up to their characteristic fatalism, and to a theory of magical practices, deduced from the kinship, through the all-pervasive world-soul of every portion of the universe.

The celebrated ethical formula of the Stoics, that man is to live in conformity with nature, is attributed to Zeno. By Chrysippus it was limited to living in conformity with one's own nature, and finally assumed the form of living in conformity with the divine Reason. In their interpretation of this doctrine at times they approached the asceticism of the Cynics, though its crudity was mitigated by the high place they gave to culture and meditation. He is the "wise man," for whom all outward things are superfluous, "who has that within" which renders him independent of all that in its nature lies outside his control; who has no desires, and knows no envy.

Kleanthes followed Zeno as leader of the school, but does not appear to have contributed anything new to its doctrines. Chrysippus, his successor, on the contrary, was a voluminous writer, and welded the system into a coherent whole, besides introducing sundry important modifications. Diogenes, a disciple of the last-named, carried Stoicism to Rome, where it spread rapidly. The names of Posidonius, the preceptor of Cicero, of the emperor Marcus Aurelius, and of the slave Epictetus, will at once occur to the reader as instances of Stoics of the Roman period.

That such a thing of "shreds and patches" as Stoicism should ever have attained the importance it subsequently did, would be inexplicable were we to regard it as a philosophical system alone, and forget that it was primarily an ethical movement, and that its ethics partook of that individualist and introspective character, which was yearly growing upon the world, and which culminated in Christianity. Stoicism was no mere system of physics, or logic, or ontology, like Platonism or Aristotelianism, with no very special, or at least, a remote practical bearing, but a doctrine which held out to men a speculative yet practical resting-place from the turmoil of a public life in which the true public spirit was dying out.

THE EPICUREANS.

The founder of the rival system to Stoicism—Epicureanism—was born in Samos B.C. 342, and was thus the contemporary of Zeno. He came to Athens in his eighteenth year, but not till he was thirty-one years of age did he commence lecturing at Athens. Notwithstanding his protestations of originality, there can be no doubt that for the entire framework of his system, Epicurus was indebted to the Atomists and the Cyrenaics. As with the Stoics, philosophy was to Epicurus simply the introduction to the art of living. In the attainment of a happy life, the first requisite was the absence of superstitious fears, and to this end philosophy led up. The Kanonik of the Epicureans, as they preferred to term their logic, included, as with the Stoics, a theory of perception. From the senses all knowledge originally proceeds. Knowledge derived from the senses, without the admixture of any judgment, is free from error. It is in the employment of the understanding that error arises. Repeated sense impressions leave in us the expectancy of their future recurrence. (It is noteworthy how Epicurus anticipated some of the conclusions of modern Empiricism.) That which coincides with "feelings," and with these anticipations, is certain and true. On questions of logic proper, Epicurus seems to have had little to say.

In Physics, he accepted the Atomism of Domokritos with some slight modifications. The supernatural, as embodied in the popular religion, he relegated to the realm of superstition. His well-known assertion to the effect that the gods, in their state of perfect happiness, abstained from all interference with the affairs of this world, was only a veiled way of putting the agnostic position. The Epicureans naturally ridiculed the "Providence" and fatalistic Pantheism of the Stoics. The popular myths they seem to have explained in an Euhemeristic fashion. Man, like every other being, is an aggregate of atoms, the soul consisting of finer, the body of coarser atoms. In either case dissolution is equivalent to destruction. "When *death is*, we are not," said Epicurus; "when death is not, *we are*;" whence the conclusion that death in no way concerns us.

Epicurus reduces all affections to those of pleasure and pain. The thesis that pleasure is the sole "good," is the basis of the Epicurean Ethics. Virtue only possesses value in so far as it leads to pleasure, but by this is not to be understood (as with the Cyrenaics) immediate pleasure, but the greatest sum of pleasure in the long run, or which is the same thing negatively stated, the least sum of pain in the long run. This consideration may sometimes lead us to a course of conduct entailing an amount of immediate pain, when this is the alternative to a greater amount of future pain; and in the same way a present pleasure may be foregone, for the sake of greater pleasure in the future. It is in the determination of the question as to what *is* the greater and what the lesser pleasure or pain, that the philosopher shows his superiority to the common man. Epicurus himself seems to have regarded "moderation," coupled with as much as possible of "apathy" (ἀπαθεία), as the key to the solution of this question.

Among the immediate followers of Epicurus may be cited Metrodorus, his favourite pupil, whom he outlived, Hermarchus of Mitylene, who succeeded him as teacher, Polystratus, Apollodorus (the reputed author of four hundred works), &c., &c. Like the Stoic, the Epicurean sect attained considerable proportions in Rome, where it was introduced by Zeno of Sidon, a pupil of Apollodorus. The celebrated poem of Titus Lucretius Carus, "De Natura Rerum," contains the most complete summary that has come down to us of the Epicurean doctrine, at least, in its Romanised form. As regards this last point it must be remembered, firstly, that the great successes of both Stoicism and Epicureanism were attained after the power and influence of Rome and Roman thought were already established to all intents and purposes throughout the civilised world; and, secondly, that all our information respecting them, with the exception of a few fragments, comes directly or indirectly through a Roman medium.

In Epicureanism we have a more coherent and self-contained doctrine than in Stoicism. It is a doctrine, moreover, embracing some important truths. But it is in no sense original. It established no new truth in philosophy, nor even gave rise to suggestions, by putting old problems in new lights. While Zeno "adapted" in a slipshod fashion the physical side of the philosophy of Herakleitos; Epicurus "adapted," in a manner perhaps not quite so slipshod, but still rather for the worse than the better, the physical doctrine of Demokritos. For their Ethics the one went back to the Cynics, the other to the Cyrenaics. The only original point Epicurus seems to have made was the modification of the Hedonistic doctrine of Aristippus, from the advocacy of the mere immediate sense gratification to that of a calculation of the greatest possible sum of happiness attainable on the whole.

It has been justly remarked that both Stoicism and Epicureanism are rather ethical sects than philosophical schools proper. The doctrines taught were put forward as dogmas to be received and inculcated, rather than sought to be demonstrated as propositions to be heard at the bar of reason. In this respect they show a distinct tendency to revert to a pre-Sokratic standpoint, and as such may be regarded as the first symptoms of the decline of Greek thought in the direction of a reactionary dogmatism. This tendency was encountered by another contemporary school or sect, that of the Pyrrhonists, or Sceptics.

The Sceptics.

The Sceptical school proper has as its founder Pyrrho, of Elis (born about B.C. 360). He was originally a painter, and is said to have followed the expedition of Alexander the Great to India, where he conversed with the Gymnosophists. It is also stated that he studied under a disciple of Stilpo the Magaric, and also of a follower of Demokritos. Pyrrho left nothing in writing, confining himself to oral exposition. As a natural consequence, our knowledge of his teaching is at once scanty and uncertain, all that is really reliable being confined to two or three propositions.

"He who would attain happiness, which is the object of human life," said Pyrrho, "must consider the three following points: What is the nature of things? What should be our attitude towards them? and What will be the consequence of this attitude?" On the first point there is nothing certain, inasmuch as to every proposition its negative can be opposed with equal justice, since neither feeling nor reason can either separately or in combination furnish any safe criterion of truth. From this it follows, as regards the second point, that the course of wisdom is to maintain an attitude of suspense, and to make no assertions concerning things. The answer to every question should accordingly be "I assert nothing;" and instead of saying "it is so," one should rather say "it seems so to me." This applies as much to morals as to knowledge; for just as there is no such thing as an absolute standard of truth valid for all, so there is no such thing as an absolute standard of goodness, to which universal appeal can be made. As to the *third* point, namely, the consequence of the following of this advice, Pyrrho maintained that through it, and through it alone, that perfect calm and equanimity (ἀπαθεία) could be acquired which was the ideal of the life of wisdom. Inasmuch as the ordinary man is led by his feelings and the appearances furnished by his senses, it is the business of the philosopher, so to speak, to strip off the "man." In practical life, however, Pyrrho advised an adhesion to prevalent usage. The doctrines of Pyrrho rapidly acquired numerous followers, especially among the votaries of the Asklepian art, but the school became subsequently obscured by the success of Karneades and the "new academy," which latter was, nevertheless, considerably influenced by it. In ancient Greece, as in modern Europe, the advantages of a subsidised chair, and an "established position" could not but make themselves felt. But the fame of Pyrrho was vindicated at a later period after the "academy" had lapsed into a reactionary dogmatism, when his system was revived with considerable success.

In Scepticism philosophy is directed to the same aim as in Stoicism and Epicureanism, and we may add there is the same want of originality. The positions of Pyrrho, as of Arkesilaus and Karneades, had all of them been forestalled by the Sophists. "Scepticism" was but a Neo-Sophism. The apparently unconscious resuscitation of pre-Sokratic doctrines is as characteristic of this period as their conscious and acknowledged rehabilitation is of the succeeding period, in which, notwithstanding, new elements are introduced, in the shape of Roman and oriental influences.

On this period generally, Zeller's *Stoics, Epicureans, and Sceptics*, may be consulted. For Epicureanism especially, see Lange's *History of Materialism*.

FIFTH EPOCH.

THE ROMAN AND ANTIQUARIAN PERIOD.

The stagnation of thought visible in the previous period, that of the partitioning of the empire of Alexander and the formation of dynasties by his generals, gave way to a steady retrograde · current when the victorious Roman legions had finally disposed of the last vestiges of Greek independence. The Greek grammarians and lecturers now occupied themselves with translating Greek thought into the Latin tongue, and attracted large audiences by their exposition of its doctrines. But philosophy was becoming emphatically a trade—a profitable profession—owing to the new markets opened for it. At the same time all that was required of the philosopher was the statement of already existing systems. When the craving for novelty was felt, there were the old pre-Sokratic systems to go back to; and finally there was the ingenious patchwork of Syncretism, the attempted assimilation of doctrines derived from various systems, to be elaborated. New developments of thought seemed out of the question. It was enough to show the authority of Plato, Aristotle, Zeno, Epicurus, and to interpret, annotate and comment on their written utterances. The three characteristics of this emphatically doctrinaire period, were (1) the establishment of the four chief schools as the recognised philosophicial systems; (2) the resuscitation in their original form and as systems, of older doctrines supposed to have been long superseded; and (3) the harmonisation of various schools affected by the Syncretists. Ritter observes ('Geschichte der Philosophie,' vol. iv. p. 35), "Although the leading *rôle* was still played by the four sects, which had, prior to this, attained the greatest importance, namely, the Academics, Peripatetics, Stoics, and Epicureans, the philosophy of Herakleitos, of the Pythagoreans, of the Cynics and of the Sceptics came once more into prominence. Of these the two last are the most noteworthy, inasmuch as the renewal of the Herakleitan doctrine was very isolated, and the Neo-Pythagorean owed its significance to the mystical tendencies of the Greek-Oriental philosophy." In the present period the theatre of the history of philosophy is removed from Athens and Greece generally to Alexandria and Rome. The history of Greek thought proper, closes with the schools of the generation succeeding Alexander.

The interest the Romans took in philosophy was almost exclusively ethical, and hence it was the ethical side of the Greek philosophies to which they mainly turned. Epicureanism, Stoicism, Scepticism, and Cynicism proved severally attractive to the various orders of Roman temperament. The Academics having somewhat reacted from the Sceptical tendencies of the New Academy, it was left for Ænesidemus of Gnossus, who, it appears, taught in Alexandria in the first century after Christ, to revive the Scepticism of Pyrrho, though its arguments he used rather to establish the Herakleitan position than in the sense of their author. Ænesidemus seems to have left a school of some vitality behind him, which tended to revert more and more to the Pyrrhonistic position.

The physician Sextus Empiricus (about A.C. 200), who was its most prominent member, is justly celebrated for his remarkable work entitled 'Pyrrhonistic Hypotyposes,' also that directed "against the mathematicians," in which the Empirical-sceptical position is put with remarkable clearness and force. The style of Sextus Empiricus has a terseness not usual with ancient writers. Among the other members of the Empirical or Sceptical school may be mentioned Agrippa Saturninus (who must not be confounded with the Gnostic of that name), the pupil of Sextus, and Favorinus, the preceptor of Aulus Gellius. These later Sceptics put forward the following five arguments in favour of suspense: (1) The discrepancy of opinions concerning the same objects; (2) The progression or regression *ad infinitum* of the series of proofs required to establish any given proposition; (3) The relativity of all things, since everything appears differently in different connections and to different persons; (4) The arbitrary nature of fundamental propositions, the dogmatist in order to escape the regressus to infinity of demonstrations, seeking refuge in certain ultimate propositions which he assumes without demonstration; and (5) The *diallele*, namely, that that upon which the proof rests, itself requires proof. This is obviously only a restatement in another form of the second of the five arguments. Sextus brings forward a number of propositions to prove that all demonstration is in its nature tainted with fallacy, inasmuch as it must necessarily move in a circle; he also anticipates Hume in his attacks on causality. The then current theological conceptions, as well as the theories of the Stoics on Providence, are also severely handled by him.

Of the earlier Syncretist schools, that of the Sextians, which flourished in the early part of the first century in Rome, and had considerable influence, seems to have been a compound of Pythagoreanism, Cynicism, and Stoicism. But little is known of the tenets of this school, and next to nothing of its founder, Sextius. Seneca asserts it to have collapsed very soon, in spite of its brilliant opening.

The most celebrated, as the most voluminous Latin writer on philosophical subjects (who belongs, however, to a somewhat earlier date) was Marcus Tullius Cicero (B.C. 106 to 43), who may be described as a disciple of the New Academy tinged with eclecticism. His works contain a mine of information concerning the philosophical views current in his time as well as the manners and customs of the last age of the Republic. In the 'De Divinatione,' Cicero, in characterising the various objects of his own works, states that the 'Hortensius' was designed to exhort to the study of philosophy; the 'Academics' to show the most logical and elegant manner of philosophising, namely, that of the New Academy; the 'De Finibus' to investigate the foundation of ethics; and the 'Quæstiones Tusculanæ,' which may be considered a sequel thereto, to treat of the conditions of happiness; the 'De Natura Deorum,' 'De Divinatione,' and 'De Fato,' which deal with the attitude of philosophy towards the popular beliefs, being designed to conclude the series. Among the Roman Epicureans Lucretius towers supreme, both as regards literary merit and philosophical insight. Stoicism, on the other hand, can boast several exponents of the first rank. Seneca, Epictetus, and Marcus Aurelius all professed the Stoic creed, and all left important literary monuments behind them.

It would be useless to enumerate the obscure grammarians who attempted to resuscitate the various older systems. As a transition to our next epoch, in which the intellect of the classical world makes one gigantic effort to acquire new life and vigour by the absorption of Oriental thought, we may briefly allude to the Neo-Pythagorean school, which arose in the first century before Christ, its founder being, according to Cicero, one Nigidius Figulus. Sextus Clodius, the preceptor of Mark Anthony, apparently belonged to this school. Its most celebrated representative was, however, the celebrated Apollonius of Tyana, who imitated the life of Pythagoras, and achieved enormous reputation for miracle-working.

Men's faces were now definitely set towards the past. It was becoming an undisputed axiom with all thinkers that the whole of wisdom, the key to the great secret, was to be found in the literature and oracles of past ages; the task of the philosopher was henceforward to seek it out, to pierce through the language in which it was hidden and the ceremonies which were supposed to shadow it forth. In a word, it was a kind of philosophical alchemy which was practised, the aim of the philosopher being to transmute the baser elements in all systems, creeds, and formulas into the pure ore of esoteric truth.

SIXTH EPOCH.

NEO-PLATONISM.

THIS last epoch of ancient philosophy is characterised by the fusion of Greek and Oriental thought. Its seat was Alexandria, the meeting-place of Europe and Asia. Founded by the great conqueror who had broken down the barriers between the European and Oriental worlds, had thrown open the mysteries of Egypt, Syria, Persia, and India, it had by the Christian era become the second city of the world. Traders of all nations met in its busy streets and markets; scholars of all nations in its library and lecture halls. Alexandria was the emporium for the exchange of goods between East and West, and not less for the interchange of ideas between East. and West. A crowd of grammarians, philosophers, and men of learned leisure thronged the city of the Delta about the Christian era, all of them affected more or less in their habits of thought by the cosmopolitan atmosphere around them; some finding in the older literatures, newly opened up to them, anticipations of Pythagorean tenets, others discovering that the wisdom of the East had been revealed to the Greeks in the person of Plato, others again in Herakleitos.

Amid these thinkers and writers was a Jew named Philo, one of the considerable colony which the tolerance of the Ptolemies had induced to leave their own land and take up their residence in lower Egypt. Philo, of whose life we know little, was the leading representative of a school of thought prevalent among the learned Jews of this colony, which sought to combine Judaistic theology with Platonic philosophy. The writings of Philo have been transmitted intact, and are of considerable interest in throwing light on the thought of the period. The tendency of Oriential speculation is seen to be just as much to absorb the Greek as the tendency of Greek thought was to absorb the Oriental. Thus in the non-canonical, or so-called apocryphal books of the Old Testament, there are unmistakable indications of this tendency; indeed a similar leaning is discoverable even in the later canonical books themselves. There was a growing anxiety, too, among the Jews to show that all Greek wisdom was implicitly contained in their own Hebrew writings. The Therapeutæ absorbed much of the Pythagorean doctrine. The Essenes were also, in all probability, strongly leavened with Hellenism. Perhaps one of the most remarkable phenomena of this time is the appearance of pseudo-works by semi-mythical personages purporting to be of prodigious antiquity. Of this nature are the writings attributed to the ancient prophet, priest, and king, Hermes Trismegistos.

In Philo himself we find the tendency of the epoch concentrated, and in him we have the germ of the system known as Neo-Platonism, which played so momentous a part in the final struggle of the old Pagan civilisation with Christianity. According to Philo the senses and reason are alike untrustworthy; the highest truth ultimately rests on an internal illumination or revelation, in respect of which the human reason is passive. "God" is absolute being, in whom there is neither quality, quantity, nor relation. "God" is not the creator of matter, but is removed from it by the λόγος γενικώτατος which is equivalent to the supreme idea of Plato and the prime mover of Aristotle, and which may be regarded as containing implicitly the sum total of all the forms or ideas of the real world. The relation of the Logos, or supreme idea, to the inconceivable "God," or "One," is that of emanation, just as the material world is in its turn an emanation from the Logos. The world is often spoken of by Philo in similar language to that of Plato as the "only begotten son of God." But in Philo everything is personified and brought into connection with the Judaic theology and angelology of his time. The world he conceived as actually created by inferior beings—angels and demons—which may be taken as answering to personified ideas or class-names. Philo illustrates his doctrine by the metaphor of rays of light spreading from an effulgent centre, and decreasing in brilliancy as they reach the circumference.

The characteristic of the school of which Philo may be considered as the forerunner, and which was the last effort of ancient thought, lay in the fact that in it human reason fell into the background as insufficient to the attainment of the highest truth. The "dialectic," which for Plato was the great and only highway to supreme wisdom, became subordinate with the Neo-Platonists to the passive "contemplation" which to them was alone adapted for the contemplation of the divine. The science of the Greek world had to yield to the mysticism of Asia. This transformation of philosophy into theosophy, is the key-note of the whole Neo-Platonic movement; in some of its representatives it may be more pronounced, in others more veiled, but it is always present. Neo-Platonism claimed to be not only the reconciler of philosophical systems, but of the diverse religious cults of the ancient world. It took all philosophies and all religions under its wing. It remains to trace briefly the career of this remarkable and unique religio-philosophic movement, which not only furnishes the material for the concluding chapter in the history of the ancient world, but by leaving its impress on its great rival and antagonist, Christianity, has indirectly influenced the speculative thought of the ages which have succeeded. As we have already seen, ever since Greek philosophy ceased to be speculatively productive in the generation succeeding Alexander the Great, and began to confine itself to reproducing and piecing together older doctrines, a change came alike over the object of philosophy and the object of life. Knowledge of the great world-secret was no longer sought after for its own sake, but as a guide to life. It was no longer the welfare of the city, or commonwealth, that concerned the philosopher, but his own individual welfare.

It is true Sokrates was, so far as philosophy was concerned, the father of introspection and individualism, but the time of its triumph had not yet come. His great successors, Plato and Aristotle, found no perfect virtue and no perfect life save in the community. The end of all virtue was still with them, the welfare of the "city." The individual by himself was nothing but an element in the whole. Such was the original view of all ancient peoples, and not least of the Greeks. The beliefs and ceremonials of the ancient religions all tended to this conception of life. But as it declined, the antithetic conception of the import of the individual *quâ* individual, grew. The conflict of Sokrates with the Athenians which resulted in his condemnation and death, may be viewed as the first episode in the struggle of the new individualist ethics with the ancient social ethics. In philosophy proper, the success of the Stoic and Epicurean schools may be taken as indicating the beginning of its supremacy. The consolidation of the Roman empire, and the extinction of the free states of Antiquity, deprived men of even the interest they had left in public life, and threw them more than ever back upon themselves. Soon after this, a movement originating in Palestine, where these ethics of "inwardness" had attained their highest development, spread over the empire, attracting men and women of all conditions in life, in a manner and to an extent, none of the philosophical sects could have ever done. The whole history of the struggle of Neo-Platonism with Christianity, is the history of an effort to reconcile the introspective movement with the existent speculative basis; to satisfy the new individualist cravings without the definite break with tradition which Christianity involved. As such, Neo-Platonism naturally borrowed much from the ethical side of Christianity, but not without furnishing Christianity in return with a groundwork for its theology.

Neo-Platonism* practically dates from Philo, but during the first and second centuries its development is obscure. It is not till the beginning of the third century that we are confronted with a definite personality (if we except the Syrian Numenius, who flourished at the time of the Antonines) in Ammonius Saccas, who died in the year 243. Ammonius, though the nominal founder of the system, himself wrote nothing, and it is said, exacted a pledge of secrecy from his disciples, which it is doubtful if any of them kept.

Plotinus (born 205), his most famous pupil and the typical representative of Neo-Platonism, was, on the other

* The term Neo-Platonism, though its connotation may be understood by all students, is too narrow to indicate the great synthetic movement of Philosophical Paganism which occupied the first four centuries of the Christian era.

hand, a voluminous writer. The doctrine of Plotinus may be briefly epitomised thus:—The highest truth, knowledge, or wisdom, is only to be apprehended by intuition, the highest grade of which is identity with the known—wherein the distinction between being and knowing is abolished. The highest principle is absolute and unconditioned. The "One," the "Existent," the "first God," are the various names which Plotinus employs to express this primal fact, in which all things "live and move and have their being," but which is nevertheless, itself out of all direct relation to the real world. But how can the real world be deduced from such a principle as this? Plotinus replies, by a process of emanation. From the first principle, namely, is eternally and necessarily generated a second, the content of which is less than the first; in other words, which is a weakening, a deterioration (so to speak), of its essence. This stage in the degradation of the primal entity, is the *νοῦς* or intelligent principle, which has as its final aim and goal the Absolute, whence it emanates. Whereas, of the first principle none of the categories of reality could be predicated, the *νοῦς*, or second principle, may be said to unite within itself all contradictions, as the one and the many, rest and motion, the act of thinking and the object thought. The *νοῦς* thus becomes the sum-total of all ideas and general terms, from the highest to the lowest. The third principle, or *hypostasis* (the term by which these successive momenta of the emanation are commonly described), is the *ψυχή*, the universal principle of life and motion, or the world-soul, which is in its turn a weakening, an inferior copy of the *νοῦς*, from which it immediately derives the degree of existence it possesses. As the mere reflex and shadow of the rational principle, though it acts and orders the world in accordance with reason, it does so not by virtue of its own inherent intelligence, but by that of the source whence it emanates. Hence it is, that thought is embodied in all the processes of nature, these processes simply indicating the presence of the ideas which are planted by the *νοῦς*, and which the *ψυχή* mechanically translates into sensible reality. Plotinus in some places speaks of the world-soul as dual—*i.e.*, of a soul tending to matter, which he designates φύσις, and of a soul tending to Reason, for which the term ψυχή is specially reserved. These three hypostases; the πρώτος θεός or primal principle, the νοῦς (Reason) or secondary principle, and the ψυχή (World-soul) or tertiary principle, constitute the so-called Alexandrian trinity. It may be viewed as compounded of the "Good" of Plato, the "Reason" of Aristotle, and the Zeus or universal life of Herakleitos and the Stoics. This Neo-Platonic, *ontological*, trinity is distinguished from the Christian, *theological*, trinity, by its being essentially an immanent as opposed to a transcendent conception of the universe, its momenta being, not persons but aspects, and more definitely by the notion of necessary *emanation* as opposed to that of arbitrary *creation*. The "Matter" of Plotinus, which he opposes to "God," was not corporeal substance, for this, in so far as it is real possesses form, and in so far as it is *in*formed, partakes of the nature of the νοῦς, but like the non-existent sense-world of Plato, or the πρώτη ὕλη (first matter) of Aristotle, it was a mere formless negation—the negation of the rational—as darkness is the negation of light. We shall understand the root-idea of the whole Neo-Platonic ethic, when we remember that it is essentially based on the notion of disengaging the world-soul from the non-existent element, the matter, on which it acts, and of which activity the sense-world is the result. The stage of the Reason is then reached, and lastly that of the Primal One itself. This ecstasy, or absorption in absolute unity without difference, motion, or change, was the aim of the philosopher's life.

Plotinus was followed by his pupil Porphyry, who represents the Roman Neo-Platonism, in which the tendency to theosophy and mysticism was less marked than in the Syrian Neo-Platonism represented by Jamblichos. Porphyry wrote several works against Christianity, which were subsequently burnt. The allegorisation of the Pagan myths and ceremonies occupied an ever larger place in the teaching of Neo-Platonism in proportion as the power of Christianity grew. From the end of the third century all trace of the division of sects is lost, every Pagan thinker succumbing to the prevailing eclecticism, and being classed as a Neo-Platonist. Commentating on the works of Plato and Aristotle became now the main occupation of the philosopher.

After the death of Hypatia, which took place in the fifth century, philosophy was driven from Alexandria, and strangely enough its last place of refuge was Athens. It was here that Proklos, the last eminent representative of ancient philosophy, taught. Proklos was born A.C. 412, at Byzantium. He studied under various teachers, and early devoted himself to Plato. In Proklos the religious side of Neo-Platonism culminated. He had himself been initiated into every Pagan mystery within his reach, and was proud of the title of hierophant of all religions. Christianity alone he held in abhorrence. In philosophy, Proklos approached the Syrian Neo-Platonism of Jamblichos rather than that of Plotinus. The primal principle was with Proklos, itself threefold. From this triadic principle the others emanated. The relation is invariably that what the first *is* the second *has* as predicate. Being, as the predicate of all things, stands above and before all; but inasmuch as reason (νοῦς) implies life as well as being, the second hypostasis is not reason (νοῦς) but life (ζωή). From this latter emanates the reason, which thus forms the third hypostasis. Each hypostasis like the first is triply articulated. These three triads contain the complex of all reality. The first is identified with the divine world, the second with the demonic world, the third with the world of human spirits. The physical doctrine of Proklos differs in little from that of Plotinus. The Platonic division of temporal, sempiternal and eternal, is retained and made to correspond with the division of somatic, psychical, and pneumatic. The first is under the dominion of Fate, the last under that of Providence. Of the Ethic of Proklos there is not much that is new to be said. The end of life was to him as to other Neo-Platonists, the comprehension of, or union with, the divine principle. Immediate inspiration or ecstasy was the highest source of knowledge. For this truth, the soul may be prepared, however, by ceremonies and magical practices. But Proklos, although in a sense a follower of Jamblichos, was distinguished from him by his devotion to all the great Greek thinkers, who, he contended, differed only in form from each other, but whose teaching was substantially identical—though Plato was the culminating point. Proklos died towards the end of the fifth century (485) at an advanced age.

He was succeeded in the chair at Athens by his biographer, Marinos of Sichem; he in his turn appears to have been followed by Isidore of Alexandria, both mere grammarians of no original ability. Damascius of Damascus was the last professional philosopher of Greece. In 529 the schools were closed by edict of Justinian, and Damascius with six friends banished the empire. They repaired to the court of Chosroes, the King of Persia, where they hoped to find the opportunity of establishing a Platonic republic, but returned disappointed; Chosroes, in his treaty with Justinian, stipulating that they should live and die in peace.

About this time lived the senator Boëthius, the last surviving representative of philosophy in Rome, who was executed on a false charge by the Gothic king Theodoric. He is notable as occupying a position apart from the dying Neo-Platonism of the age, having helped to lay the foundation of the Aristotelian supremacy of centuries later. For although they produced no effect whatever on the age in which he lived, his works were counted among the chief text books of the mediæval schools, and contributed largely in the formation of the Scholastic philosophy. It is doubtful whether he was Pagan or Christian, though more probably the former, as even in his last work, *De Consolatione Philosophiæ*, there is no allusion to Christianity.

Night was now fast closing around the ancient world. The old classical civilisation, from which the life had long since fled, was falling to pieces limb by limb and shred by shred. In the sixth century its final dissolution may be said to have taken place. Within a space of little more than fifty years occurred the fall of the Western empire, the closing of the schools of philosophy, and the formal abolition of the consuls. The barbarian was established as master throughout the Western world, including Italy itself, and was pressing hard on the confines of Justinian's empire. The last remains of Paganism had almost disappeared. In the cities the temples sacred to the gods of yore were re-echoing to the litanies of priests and acolytes, while in the country they were silent and neglected. The ancient world was dead, the mediæval world as yet unborn. Such was the sixth century.

It is not without a certain sense of sadness that one can look back at this corpse-like world. Neo-Platonism had succumbed before its great rival—the rival whose mental attitude and spirit it had practically adopted. It would be curious could we but transport ourselves to that age, and inhale for a moment its intellectual and moral atmosphere, and understand the yearning looks cast back toward the ancient traditional rites and faith by many even professing Christians; to talk with the grammarian in his library; feeling that the philosophy it was his delight to study, Plato, Aristotle, Pythagoras, Herakleitos, had been but ill exchanged for the martyrologies, legends of saints, and disputes monophysite or monothelite of the church; to witness the midnight *rendez-vous* of the peasant, as the rites of some local cult were celebrated in secrecy and in silence at the sacred fountain, the traditional grove, or the crumbling wayside altar. One thing that may be regarded as certain, is that the Christianity of that age, formulated and organised indeed, but as yet unembodied in any distinct civilisation of its own, and with the fragments of Paganism, imperfectly assimilated, still clinging to it in their cruder form, was something radically distinct from anything that the word recalls to our minds to-day.

TRANSITIONAL THOUGHT.

THE GNOSTICS AND CHRISTIAN FATHERS.

We must now, before taking a final leave of antiquity, retrace our steps in order to glance briefly at the course of that speculation which was either Christian, or at least dominated directly by the Christian idea, and which thus forms the connecting link between the ancient world and the mediæval.

The attitude of Christianity, and that of all contemporary systems having their source in the Christian idea, was one of hostility to "the world." Every world-historic idea necessarily enters the arena of history as the negation of the actual *status quo*. But the anti-worldliness of the Christian idea, though it included this, went far beyond it. In theology it meant the appearance of the conception of the *supernatural* in direct contradiction of the *natural;* while in ethics it meant the erection of individualism in opposition to the ancient communism, the old, "worldly" conception of citizenship. In short, the *anti*-worldliness of Christianity meant *other*-worldliness This change is traceable in germ as far back as the sixth century B.C. or even earlier. The Hebrew prophets, the first Isaiah, Amos, etc., proclaimed the "gospel of inwardness," with the doctrine of a transcendent god, a "searcher of hearts;" the Buddha again, later, preached the doctrine of individual salvation in Nirvana, from the curse of life, the world, and consciousness; Pythagoras, in Europe, seems to have had a glimpse of the same idea; while, as we have already pointed out, the decline of the old civic or communal feeling threw men more and more back upon themselves as individuals. Sokrates' "Know thyself" was the first definite expression in the Greek world of this ethic of individualism. Coincidently with this, and intimately connected with it, arose the tendency to a purification of the divine and supernatural, by its separation from the human and natural. To the cultured Stoic of the later classical ages, the gods were exalted farther above humanity than they were to the cultured Greek of the earlier age, for even to contemporary popular conception they were hardly any longer mere nature-gods. But in Europe the movement of "inwardness" and supernaturalism obtained, at least in any formulated shape, only among the educated classes. In farther Asia, India, China, and Persia, and also in Palestine, it indeed assumed popular and organised forms, but in Buddhism, Confucianism, Zoroastrianism, and the later Judaism, the future existence of the soul, when taught at all, was taught in a half-hearted, and faltering way; only in the two latter creeds, if even in them, assuming at all a prominent position. It is clear that the spiritualist-individualist movement did not reach its highest phase of formulation or of organisation in any of the faiths mentioned. It first appeared in Europe in an organised and popular form as Christianity. In Christianity, for the first time, moreover, the ethics of individualism became definitely fused with a spritual or supernatural theology; the individual became immortal, not in the vague, metaphysical sense of Platonism or of Neo-Platonism, in which the individual was merged in the Idea or the noetic One, still less in the colourless sense of the primitive ghost, to which the goal of existence was the quiescence of respectable interment,—but immortal *as* an individual, pure and simple, the heir to the life of the blest.

Some maintain the primordial idea of Christianity was that of the messianic kingdom *on earth.* If it had been so, or at least if it had remained so, it would have continued what it was at first, a mere Jewish sect. Its world-supremacy was due to its being the complete expression in an organised form of the rising introspective ethics, in combination with a spiritualist theology. These ideas, previously put forward in an abstract form, and isolated from one another, now became the living and real parts of a complete system. The movement of inwardness and mysticism ever progressing in an unorganised form, and among the cultured classes, now took organised expression among the masses.

The Gnostic systems were the grotesque results of an imperfect assimilation of the new principle at a time when its formulation was incomplete. The relation of the natural and supernatural, and their union in a divine-human being was not as yet crystallised into the same rigidity of dogma that it was subsequently. This especially applies to the earlier period of Gnosticism, when though it was, so to speak, "in the air," it had not attained any definite expression.

The earliest traces of Gnosticism are discoverable in the first generation of the Church. To this period belong the Simonians, whose origin was attributed to the mythical Simon Magus; also the heresies of Corinth, Thessalonica, etc., referred to by St. Paul; but the most noteworthy appears to have been the sect founded by one Kerinthus. They are all connected with Christianity by some form of the doctrine of incarnation.

It was towards the end of the first, or the beginning of the second century, that Gnosticism first attained any real importance as an element in ecclesiastical history. The Gnostic sects may be divided into two categories, represented respectively by the Hellenic Gnosis, whose home was Alexandria, and the Syrian Gnosis, whose home was Antioch. At least, this division seems to have the most to be said in its favour, although others have been made. The Alexandrian Gnostics were dominated largely by Platonic, and Neo-Platonic ideas, and the Syrian Gnostics by the Persian dualism. The chief representatives of the Alexandrian or Hellenic Gnosis are Basilides, who taught about 125, Karpokrates, and Valentinus (*circa* 150), who in all probability originally belonged to the Basilidean school, but came to Rome, where he instituted a sect of his own which attained considerable notoriety and numerical proportions. He died in Cyprus. The Valentinian sect boasted many well-known names, and lingered on till far into the sixth century. The only original

Gnostic work that has survived is the *πίστις σοφία* of Valentinus.

Among the Syrian Gnostics, the most eminent names are its reputed founder, Menander (said to have been a disciple of Simon Magus), who taught at Antioch; Saturninus, Tatian and Bardesanes. As in a sense belonging to this section of Gnostic teachers, though by many historians placed in a division by himself, may be mentioned Marcion, the distinctive feature in whose teaching was the opposition to Judaism, and the Petrine Christianity, and its insistance on a gnosticised form of Paulinism. The notion of the utter corruption of matter may be described as the ground principle of all the Gnostic systems. From the Pleroma or inconceivable and unapproachable Prius of all things, "the immeasurable," the "unfathomable abyss," proceed *æons* or emanations, which in an order variously described in different systems terminate in the sense-world. All the Gnostic principles from the highest to the lowest are personified. It is in the passage from the Pleroma to the world that the main distinction of the various systems lies. The Alexandrian Gnosis gives it, in Neo-Platonic fashion, as a continuous progression, *matter* only becoming real in proportion as it is infiltrated by some higher *æon*. Both the Syrian Gnostics, on the other hand, conceived the process in Zoroastrian fashion, as the invasion of the Kingdom of darkness, matter, by the Kingdom of light, the system of ideal emanations or æons. The dual principle is thus present from the first in this latter case. It should be observed that the process of world-emanation or creation was apparently conceived as actually historical, that is, as taking place in time and space. In Gnosticism, Christ becomes one of the higher æons, proceeding from the personified ideal Kingdom of light, to redeem the world. But the rank assigned to him differs in different systems. In some the Christ is merely one of the lower angels allied to the Demiurgos, or immediate creator of the world, while in others it appears as intermediate between the Demiurgos and the Pleroma. But in all cases, the Christ is distinguished from Jesus the son of Mary, into whom it entered. The Demiurgos is commonly identified by the Gnostics with the god of the Jews—the Jahveh of the Old Testament. But here again there is a difference of view. Thus to Basilides, Valentinus, Karpokrates, etc., he was a fallen angel, whose Kingdom it was the mission of the æon Christ to destroy (a view apparently maintained by Marcion), while with Saturninus Bardesanes and others, he was merely not "good" in the highest sense, the Christ having appeared in order to supersede his lower kingdom of mere righteousness by "goodness." *

Gnosticism forms a strange and fantastic episode in the history of thought. Neither theology nor philosophy, yet something of both, neither Christian nor Pagan, yet something of both—bizarre in an age of prophets, soothsayers, founders of new cults, and revisers of old cults—these curious theosophic systems, originated in the first century, rose to importance in the second, and died away practically in the third, though some of the sects dragged on an existence till the age of Justinian. Manichæanism, which arose on their ruins, achieving a success at one time threatening even to Christianity itself, was little but a modified Zoroastrianism. Its reappearance in the thirteenth century in a Christianised form, as Paulicianism or Albigensianism, its rapid spread and as rapid extinction, though one of the most stirring and remarkable stories furnished by the history of the Middle Ages, does not fall within the scope of the historian of philosophy.

The common doctrine of the absolute and inherent evil of matter, and of its separation from the divine, led with the Gnostics to strangely opposite ethical views. With some, probably the majority, it was the basis of an ethic of rigorous asceticism, but with others, notably the Karpokratians, the Ophites, and the Kenites, it assumed the form of an antinomianism, which regarded all actions as indifferent, inasmuch as they all affected matter only, and with this the divine in man was in no way con-

* In some sects (*e.g.* the Ophites, the Kenites) the antipathy to Judaism was carried to the extent of deifying the things and personages supposed to be most obnoxious to the god of the Jews, as the serpent, Cain, &c.

cerned. Epiphanes, the son of Karpokrates, even enjoined excesses on his followers.

The subject next to occupy our attention is the movement contemporaneous with Gnosticism, going on within the Church, in the persons of the ancient Fathers. This movement had for its end, at once to justify Christianity to the cultivated mind of the age, and to refute the Gnostic heresies (so-called), the form of which was semi-philosophical. The link which the early Fathers thought they discovered between Pagan philosophy and Christian theology was—Plato. Philo and the Neo-Platonists had evolved trinitarianism out of Plato. The task of the "Platonising" Fathers, as those were termed who sought to mediate between the speculative opposition of the old world and the new, was to endeavour to show that what Plato had dimly foreshadowed by the light of reason was supernaturally revealed in the new religion. The great historical importance, however, of the early fathers, consists in their having laid the foundation of the cardinal Christian dogmas.

The first of the philosophic Fathers was Justin, surnamed the Martyr (103–167). He had received an education at the hands of Platonic and Stoic teachers, and we may imagine was of "good" family. It was apparently in his later years that he became Christian. The authorship of two apologies for the Christians, addressed to the Emperors Antoninus Pius and Marcus Aurelius, are ascribed to him, as well as a dialogue between himself and a Jew named Gryphon, and other pieces of more doubtful genuineness. In opposition to the prevailing Polytheism, he urged the impossibility of the ingenerate, changeless essence from whom all things proceed, being other than One. At the same time he admits a measure of truth in the writings, and of goodness in the lives of the ancients. In Sokrates especially, he sees the manifestation of the *logos*, a term he was probably the first to employ in a Christian connection. Plato and Herakleitos, no less than Moses and Elijah, he was disposed to regard as forerunners of Christ, and indeed actually applies to them the epithet Christian.

The doctrines of the fall of man, freedom of the will, hereditary sin, regeneration, are severally expounded on Platonic and Stoic principles.

Next in order to Justin Martyr comes Athenagoras, who also addressed an apology for the Christians to Marcus Aurelius, in which he seeks to furnish a philosophical basis for Monotheism, maintaining the Polytheist to be deceived by demons, and led by them into a confusion between the divine and natural. In this Athenagoras undoubtedly touches the key-note of the essential distinction between Pagan naturalism and Christian supernaturalism. With one the divine is immanent in nature, the gods are simply the personified forces of nature, they are the familiar friends or enemies of man, like himself only more powerful; to the other, nature, in itself dead, is created, animated and governed by the will of a transcendent deity, differing in kind and not in degree merely from man as a natural being.

Theophilus, bishop of Antioch, about the middle of the second century, wrote a treatise addressed to a Pagan friend which contains the first distinct enunciation of the Christian doctrine of the trinity, though the conception of the Holy Ghost labours under some ambiguity, being still partially identified with the *logos*. Irenæus, the pupil of Polycarp (executed 202, at Lyons, of which city he was bishop), was specially concerned with refuting the Gnostics, respecting whom he is one of our chief sources of information. Hippolytus also dealt with the same subject in a lengthy treatise. Minucius Felix defends Christianity on the ground of its ethics. Polytheism he seeks to explain away in Euhemeristic fashion.

More important than any of these from the standpoint of the historian of philosophy is Clement of Alexandria, who flourished in the third century. His *Stromata* are not only a mine of interesting gossip respecting the earlier Greek thinkers, but one of the cleverest of the patristic attempts to found Christianity on a Platonic basis. Clement distinguishes between the πίστις, or faith, which is the root, and the γνῶσις, or knowledge, which is the crown; the means to the attainment of the latter being the understanding (ἐπιστήμη) of what had been previously received by faith. The true Gnosis is distinguished from the false, by the morality and true brotherly love it engenders. The theology of Clement issues in a kind of Pantheism in which all life and activity is identified with God. The Clementine theosophy, as may be imagined, shows many points of contact both with Gnosticism and Neo-Platonism.

Clement's disciple, Origenes (said to have been also a pupil of Ammonius Saccas), is by far the most important figure among the early Fathers. He it was who first made any serious attempt to reduce Christianity to the form of a coherent body of doctrine. Carrying out the idea of Clement respecting faith (πίστις) and knowledge (γνῶσις), he made it his task to formulate the latter, at the same time combating the principles of the heretical Gnosis, and acting as Christian apologist against Paganism. According to Origen, in addition to their literal or *psychical* meaning, the Hebrew Scriptures have a *pneumatic* one. The initiated may discover in them an esoteric signification to which the literal is merely the cloak. Origen, with the Pythagoreans, regards the limited as superior to the unlimited, and hence assigns a limit to the divine power. In the doctrine of the trinity, we notice a development on Justin and Theophilus, inasmuch as Origen fixes the position of the second Person, and pronounces his generation eternal. The Holy Ghost, although spoken of as above all created things, occupies a subordinate and intermediate position. With Origen all creation is eternal, that is, creative activity has neither beginning nor end. Though the present world is not eternal, yet an infinity of worlds has preceded this one. This is not intended to imply the eternity of matter, since the doctrine of creation out of nothing is strongly insisted upon. The spirits which were created first in order, having fallen, were assigned, according to the degree of their transgression, various positions in the hierarchy of existence, including human bodies. The species subsequently took the place of the individual in Origen's doctrine of the fall, individual pre-existence being apparently surrendered. Besides the exoteric or personal relation to the divinity, Origen postulated an esoteric or general one, viz., that of the Church or community of saints. Inasmuch as all creation is destined to absorption in this whole, it would imply a failure of the divine purpose if even the greatest of the fiends ultimately perished.

In proportion as the Church grew as an organisation, grew the desire for the formulation of its doctrines. The Christianity of reminiscence and expectation, of sentiment and vague belief, which had sufficed for the first century, failed to satisfy the second; as a natural result aspirations began to crystallise into a definite system, assimilating the while the various Alexandrian and Zoroastrian doctrines which formed a portion of the general intellectual life of the age. By the second half of the third century this process of crystallisation had approached completion. But even yet the line between heresy and orthodoxy was drawn in a comparatively loose manner, as is evident from the doubtful position Origen occupies in Church history. From this time forward, however, when the position of the Church was assured by its numbers, wealth, and importance, against being crushed out by any persecution that might arise, and when the purely defensive attitude became less and less necessary, increased attention was given to the codification of the mass of dogmas which had now grown up, and to giving them severally increased precision. The *apologetic* Fathers now give place to the *dogmatic*, the link between them being supplied by Origen.

The foundation of dogmatic Christianity was obviously to be sought for in the doctrine of the trinity. Hence it was this which formed the main battleground of the various sects and parties in the Church from the beginning of the fourth century onwards. What relation did the historical Jesus bear to the second Person in the Trinity? What was the relation of the second Person to the first? Were the three Persons co-ordinate? Was it unity or triplicity which constituted the essence of the Godhead? All these, and many subordinate questions began now to occupy the doctors of the Church.

That the Christian trinitarian doctrine first took shape in Alexandria—that seething cauldron of speculation—

during the second century there is no reason to doubt. But its earlier history is wrapped in obscurity. Of the nature and extent of the intercourse between the schools of philosophy and the leaders of the Christian Church in the Delta city, we know nothing; yet that there was an intercourse is evident.* Ammonius Saccas, the reputed founder of Neo-Platonism (which was really founded in all essentials by the Platonic Jew, Philo, in the first century B.C.), is by some writers alleged to have been a Christian, at least originally, though it is evident that during the period of his activity as a teacher, he was altogether outside the pale of the Church. The truth was probably that he took considerable interest in the new system, and probably visited the assemblies of the Christians. He might even have had himself initiated, as a means of ascertaining the nature of the Church's esoteric doctrine. In any case, it is interesting and significant that the Christian Origen is said to have been one of his pupils, in company with the Neo-Platonists Plotinus and Herrennius. But whatever may have been the genesis of the doctrine, the beginning of the fourth century found its definition the subject mainly occupying the attention of the Christian communities. The Judaic monotheism of the Sabellians, in which trinitarianism is reduced to a shadow, was opposed by the paganising tendency of Arius, with whom the *logos* or second Person, was a created being, subordinate in nature to the first. As yet the dogma had not attained the consistency requisite for it as a fundamental thesis of Christian theology. The figure with whom its final formulation as the canon of orthodoxy is indissolubly associated, is that of Athanasius, (298–373), bishop of Alexandria. On the thesis of Athanasius it is unnecessary to dwell, since, after a desperate struggle with Arianism, it obtained what proved a decisive victory at Nicæa, in 325, where it was erected by a large majority into the orthodox Christian doctrine, a position it has maintained throughout Christendom ever since. The attempts subsequently

* According to the critics the fourth Gospel was the immediate outcome of this intercourse.

made to mediate between the two parties, the disputes about a word, and the political, social and religious disturbances caused by the question during the whole of the fourth century, lie entirely outside the history of philosophy.

The last of the Church Fathers that need detain us is St. Augustine (353–412), bishop of Hippo, whose speculative career offers many points of interest, as connecting the ancient and the mediæval world. Of Christian parentage, Augustine subsequently became Manichæan, but after a time reverted to the creed of his youth. Augustine found a refuge from scepticism, like Descartes at a later time, in the certainty of self-consciousness. From this he argues the certainty of being, life, and knowledge, which he maintains are involved in the primary fact of self-consciousness. Reflection on the highest stage of Being shows, he maintains, that the reason in its acts of cognition and judgment, pre-supposes certain fundamental principles, culminating in the eternal truth which unites them in that synthesis which is tantamount to the supreme all-embracing idea of Plato or the creative intellect of Aristotle, but which Augustine identifies with the Christian *Logos.* That this identification of knowledge or consciousness itself with the divinity, is indistinguishable from the Pantheism of the Neo-Platonists is obvious. Indeed Augustine himself admits his Platonism, often designating Plato "the true philosopher." For him the distinction between Faith and Knowledge, Revelation and Reason, does not exist. The one is merely a preparatory stage to the other. Everywhere faith is the beginning, and precedes Reason, although intrinsically Reason is higher than faith. Inasmuch as God is wisdom itself, the philosopher, that is, the friend of wisdom, is the friend of God. God, as the essential object of all knowledge, cannot be conceived under the categories which serve to determine mere objects of sense. He is great without quantity, good without quality, everywhere present irrespective of space, eternal apart from time. He cannot even be spoken of as substance, since no accidents can be predicated of him. The best definition that can be given is that of the *essence* of all things, for outside of, and apart from, him, nothing exists. Since his being knows no limitation, he is better defined in a negative than a positive manner. Being, knowledge, will, action, are in him one. In short, God is the unknowable, absolute, and unconditioned fact which the known, the relative, and the conditioned pre-supposes. But the character of Augustine as Christian dogmatist required that he should not stop at an unknowable God. Hence he proceeds to a consideration of the manifestation of God as revealed to us. This is nothing other than the doctrine of the trinity. Here again the agreement with the Neo-Platonists is strong, though the personal terminology of the Christian doctrine is formally maintained. Indeed Augustine, so far as the letter went, actually put the coping-stone on the work of Athanasius, by not only distinguishing the Holy Ghost from the other Persons, but by co-ordinating it with the *logos;* his doctrine being that in each of the three Persons, the divine substance is equally present

Thus to non-metaphysical ecclesiastics, Augustine might well appear the champion of orthodoxy: though looked at a little more closely, it would be difficult to find a single heresy with which he might not be chargeable.* With all his verbal adhesion to the Christian dogma, it is plain that philosophically he is, in spite of himself, a Platonist and a Pantheist. The world is for him "der Gottheit den ewigen Kleid." The creative power withdrawn, and the world would disappear. Into Augustine's theory of the freedom of the human will, which he identified with the divine will, thereby opening a path to his predestinarian theology, and his controversy with Pelagius on this head, space precludes our entering. It is enough to state that Augustine was, in the exoteric and practical side of his theology, as much the type and embodiment of the Christian theologian, as he was in the esoteric and theoretical side of the Neo-Platonic philosopher. With Augustine the constructive period of Christian dogmatics finally closes. The whole Christian scheme was now

* The passages in which Augustine repeatedly insists on the equal participation of the three Persons in every creative act, might have been written by Sabellius.

mapped out in all its essentials, and many of its particulars. All that remained was to apply this system to the details of life. Augustine practically concludes the line of the ancient Christian Fathers, as his contemporary, Proklos, that of the ancient pagan philosophers. In Augustine we take, as it were, a second, and this time a final farewell of the ancient world. The curtain falls once more. It will rise again on a Catholic and feudal Europe, where the races of modern times furnish the chief actors.

Among the best works on the Christian and semi-Christian speculation of the first three centuries, may be mentioned: in English, Smith's 'Dictionary of Christian Sects and Heresies,' Mansel's 'Gnostics of the Second Century,' Article, "Gnosticism," 'Encyclopædia Britannica,' 9th ed., also separate articles, Basilides, Carpocrates, Cerinthus, &c.; in French, Matter's 'Histoire du Gnosticisme'; in German, Baur's 'Drei erste Jahrhunderte des Christenthums,' Neander's 'Kirchengeschichte' (also translated in Bohn's library), and among recent works Hilgenfeld's 'Ketzergeschichte,' &c., &c. The original works of the early Fathers are translated in the Ante-Nicene library.

MEDIÆVAL PHILOSOPHY.

THE EARLIER SCHOOLMEN.

The first representative of mediæval philosophy occupies so far as speculation is concerned, a somewhat anomalous position. He stands like a solitary obelisk between the ancient world and the middle ages.

The rise and rapid decline of the pure Keltic civilisation is an interesting phenomenon in the history of mediæval Europe. Its greatest architectural monument remaining is the cathedral of Iona; its greatest literary monument, the works of Johannes Scotus Erigena. Erigena, the first mediæval philosopher, is the solitary representative of Platonism among the schoolmen, if, indeed, he can be properly classed as a schoolman.

The spirit of scholasticism, or at least of the earlier scholasticism, was one of subordination. The function of the reason was to act as the handmaid of dogma, in defining, applying, justifying it; in Erigena, however, we see a much freer tendency. In him, Reason takes precedence of dogma, since even the dogmas laid down and formulated by the fathers, were arrived at by the help of Reason. Erigena is fond of saying that philosophy and religion are one, that true philosophy is true religion, and *vice versâ*. At the same time, he proceeds to explain the world on Platonic principles, into which the Christian scheme enters only incidentally.

Scotus Erigena was born in Scotland, or Ireland (it is uncertain which, though most probably the latter), about the year 800. He doubtless received his education in one of the monastic schools which then covered Ireland and Keltic Britain, and where Greek was still taught in conjunction with Latin. In 843 he was called to the court of Charles the Bald of France, and entrusted with the Chair of the Schola Platina, a position he retained for many years. The tradition which assigns to him an academical post in the University of Oxford, under Alfred the Great, is generally considered unauthentic. Scotus Erigena, in all probability, died in Paris about the year 877.

The totality of all Being or Nature* falls, according to Erigena, under four classes; the Uncreated-Creating, the Created-Creating, the Created-Uncreating, and the Uncreating-Uncreated. By the first and the last of these classes, God in His pure essence is indicated; the former denoting God as the ground of all Being, the latter as the final end and goal of all things. The second, which stands in direct opposition to the fourth, as does the third to the first, comprise between them the totality of real or related existence. It may be remarked that the first three classes are discoverable in both Plato and Aristotle, not to speak of later thinkers, while the fourth is plainly indicated by the Neo-Platonic writers. Of the five books into which the philosophical treatise of Erigena is divided, the first treats of God as the Uncreated-Creating; as that in and through which everything exists. He is the beginning, the middle, and the end, and hence, says Erigena, justly regarded as the unity of three Persons. This trinitarian conception may also be viewed in another light, as the unity of being, willing, and knowing, or again of essence, potentiality, and actuality. The same trinity is discoverable in the soul of man, the "image of God," it matters not whether we adopt the first of the classifications just given, which was that of Augustine, or the second, which is that of the other Fathers. In agreement with Augustine, Erigena denies any of the categories of thought to the essence of God, who he insists can best be defined as *pure nothing*.

The first passage or progression is to the subject-matter of the second book, which deals with the created, which is also creating. This is nothing other than the system of the Platonic ideas, or ideal prototypes, in other words, the *logos* which embraces all things as the beginning, in

* As will be seen, Erigena employs the word Nature as synonymous with Being, and not in the usual limited sense, of the world as perceivable.

which all things were created, as the wisdom in which they were intuited. Although created, they are nevertheless eternal, inasmuch as the process of creation is not in time, but co-eval with time. As with the Neo-Platonists these principles stand to each other in a graduated order of participation. They comprise within them the principles and forms of all real things, which are only real in so far as they participate in the essence of these forms. It is thus that they may be regarded as the direct causes and principles of the real world, or of that nature which is created, but does not itself create. This complex of individual objects forms the theme of the third book. The latter comprises a cosmology with which, by a process of allegorisation, the Biblical is forced into accordance. Man is the *officina creaturarum*, in whom the consciousness of the whole lower creation is gathered up. He is now out of paradise, inasmuch as he is divided from God by the sense-world. But this is not the end of his being. He is destined to a reconciliation with God, a reabsorption in the divine essence. Respecting this, the fourth and fifth books treat. In these the Pantheism of Erigena is most pronounced.

Evil has no substantial existence, since the ground and essence of all reality is God. Similarly evil has no positive cause. It is *incausale.* Free will, to which many have referred the existence of evil, only determines itself to evil, through want of knowledge, that is, through our mistaking evil for good. (We call the attention of the reader to the fact that this is an echo of the Sokratic doctrine.) Since its object is a mistaken one, since it is evil, and therefore negation, the will remains unsatisfied, its end being unaccomplished. This we term punishment, and therefore that only can be punished which does not exist. The purpose of punishment is hence, not the destruction of the substance of the sinner, but merely the accident of this substance, the misdirected, and therefore essentially negative, will. On this ground Erigena insists with Origen on the ultimate union of all things in God, on the reabsorption of the whole creation into the substance from which it sprang, after all that is evil, *i.e.*, negative in it, has been finally purged away.

This re-absorption should logically exclude individuality; but Erigena does not appear to contemplate this, at least more than to a limited extent. The antitheses of creator and created, heaven and earth, male and female, indeed disappear, but the individuality remains, though in what sense it is difficult to determine. As in the order of creation, so in the order of absorption or *deification*, there are degrees according to purity, or the reverse.

The great work of Erigena, *De Divisione Naturæ*, is written in the form of a dialogue between a master and disciple.

ANSELM.

WE pass over a period of two hundred years, during which no names of special note occur in the schools. This brings us to the eleventh century, a most important one in the history of scholasticism, since it gave birth to two of its most prominent figures, Anselm and Abelard. The former was born in 1035 at Aosta. He was educated first at Avranches and subsequently at the Abbaie de Bec in Normandy, where he followed Lanfranc as prior, and afterwards as abbot. In the archbishopric of Canterbury, which he occupied from 1089 till his death in 1099, he was also a successor of Lanfranc.

With Anselm philosophy becomes avowedly the handmaid of theology. Its object is the justification of dogmatics, although its procedure, Anselm declares, must be independent of dogma. In Erigena we saw that the idea of personality and conscious volition in the Godhead and the world-order (the fundamental feature in all theology—as such, Christian or otherwise—the feature which distinguishes it from metaphysic proper), was left very much in abeyance. In Anselm, on the contrary, as might be expected, it assumes a much more prominent place, since Anselm was no searcher after truth, but a philosophical advocate on behalf of the doctrines of the Church. His chief work is the *Proslogium*, which contains the first serious attempt to base theology on the so-called ontological argument. Anselm argues the existence of God from the mere conception of a supreme being which obtains in the mind. All things, inasmuch as they can be expressed by predicates, point to this ultimate concept, just as the predicate great points to the concept greatness, the predicate good to goodness, &c. Anselm agrees with Augustine in defining God as the *Essence of all things*. In three dialogues *de veritate, de libero arbitrio*, and *de causâ diaboli*, Anselm developes the thesis that the being of the real world is essentially negative, and in this way explains creation out of nothing; the meaning of which is that the being of the world is the negation of the being of the Deity. Its purpose is the glory of the Deity, to which even the fall of man has contributed, by enabling man to become conscious of that glory. The freedom of the will is also dealt with, in a libertarian sense.

Anselm occupies the position of a link between the Platonism of Erigena and his successors, and the pure Aristotelianism of the schoolmen proper. The great scholastic controversy—Nominalism *versus* Realism—was yet to come, although near at hand. Its immediate starting-point may be considered the, in the first instance, purely theological polemic of Anselm against Roscellinus, canon of Champiegne, whose doctrine on the subject of the trinity tended in the direction of Tritheism. Anselm in this dispute takes the realist position against Roscellinus, who is the representative of the most extreme nominalism. The former, like all his predecessors, and in spite of the Aristotelian tendency of much of his own thought, had never doubted that universals were to be regarded with Plato as having a substantive existence apart from the particulars and singulars in which they were realised. The latter maintained the then paradoxical (and in truth equally one-sided) position that universals had no significance except as words, that they were *flatus vocis*. It is noticeable how the great metaphysical problem which had occupied the ancients—the relation of matter and form—was now becoming whittled down to a mere logical or even psychological issue, in which its kernel was entirely lost and its bearings totally changed. It is remarkable also how this mere question of the schools was made the arena for the strife of Church parties and the battleground of twelfth-century orthodoxy and heresy. At first the

I 2

weight of the Church's authority was thrown into the realist scale. This was to be expected, not only owing to the heterodox theological attitude of the first representative of nominalism, but also because it gave to sense-perception the foremost place, besides cutting at the root of the ontological and all similar arguments. The pantheistic tendencies of Realism, when logically carried out, were apparently not discerned at this time.

Abelard.

The leading representative of the great scholastic controversy was Abelard (born 1079), a native of Pallet, or Palais, near Nantes. He studied first under Roscellinus, and afterwards in Paris under the Realist William of Champeaux. The result was a dissatisfaction with the teaching of either, but especially with that of the latter, which led Abelard to challenge his master to a public disputation. This ended triumphantly for Abelard, inasmuch as William was compelled to a formal recantation of his extreme Realism. Abelard's reputation as the greatest dialectician of the age now grew rapidly, and scholars flocked from all sides to hear the *Philosophus Peripateticus*, as he somewhat arrogantly styled himself. Rising higher and higher in public estimation, in spite of a lengthened remission of labour owing to ill-health, as well as of the not unnatural animosity of his former master and now humiliated rival, William of Champeaux, whom he had literally driven from Paris, Abelard attained the chair of the great Cathedral school of Notre-Dame, being at the same time nominated canon.

It was now that the romantic episode occurred which was destined to overshadow the whole of Abelard's subsequent career, and which has given to the dialectician and schoolman the undying place he occupies in popular imagination. It would be out of place in a manual like the present, to enter into a detailed account of the well-known story of the seduction of the canon Fulbert's niece by Abelard, of Abelard's passion, and Heloïse's life-long devotion. A subsequent secret marriage, though for a time it appeased the indignation of Fulbert, did not prevent the perpetration of the crime which, to a large extent, shattered Abelard's subsequent life. He was not born for the cloisters, and his attempt to retire from active work to the abbey of St. Denis was a failure. He reappeared as teacher, seemed to be regaining his old popularity, was condemned on a charge of heresy, again fled from the world, this time into the wilderness, was sought out by the students, again induced to teach, was once more driven by new dangers to the desolate abbey, Gildas de Rhuys, in Brittany, whence was penned his share of the well-known correspondence with Heloïse. The final blow to Abelard's reputation was the *fiasco* of his attempt to answer St. Bernard, to whom his dialectics were an abomination. Condemned once more for heresy, Abelard was on his way to plead his cause in person at Rome when his health broke down, and he died shortly after, on the 21st of April, 1142, at the priory of St. Marcel. He was buried at the convent of the Paraclete (erected by his own scholars), of which Heloïse, who subsequently shared his tomb, was Superior. Their bones, after many vicissitudes, now lie in Père la Chaise.

Abelard was in a sense the founder of Scholasticism, that is, the method of philosophising (for a system Scholasticism was not), which has for its end the rational formulation of the Church's doctrines. In Abelard we first find that exclusive ascendency of Aristotle, which is its main characteristic. Plato, before the chief storehouse for the philosopher and theologian, henceforth remained a sealed book until the Renaissance. It was Abelard, too, who fixed the question of universals as the central one. In antagonism alike to the extreme Realism of William of Champeaux, and the extreme Nominalism of Roscellinus, he maintained, formally at least, the Aristotelian position, *universalia in rebus.* We say formally, as it is doubtful how far Abelard saw the metaphysical bearings of the question. But at least he joined with the Nominalists in ascribing full reality only to sensible concretes, while he repudiated the *flatus vocis* doctrine, proclaiming the existence of the universal in the concrete, and declaring it to emerge in the act of predication.

The doctrine of Abelard has been termed conceptualism ;

but the applicability of this designation rests upon the assumption that Abelard concerned himself with the mere psychological question of the mental subsistence of the universal. It is most probable that he never clearly grasped the distinction between the metaphysical and the psychological problems. He was pre-eminently a logician who took delight in dialectical combats for their own sake, as his contemporaries of the sword took delight in combats with the lance for their own sake. With ethics, however, Abelard occupied himself to some extent, and some of his observations in this department are acute, and in certain points even anticipate the remarks of modern thinkers, although awe of the Church's authority prevented him from treating the subject in any thorough manner.

THE ARABIANS AND JEWS.

We must turn aside now from the Schools of Catholic Europe, with the controversy raging between Nominalism and Realism, where Aristotle was being exploited in the interest of the Church, to a series also of Aristotelian thinkers, trained, not in the fathers, but in the Koran, and who appear first of all in the East, and afterwards in Spain. For their acquaintance with the writings of the Stagirite, the Arabians were largely indebted to the Nestorian Christians of Syria. The physician of the Prophet himself was a Nestorian. But it was not until the reign of the Abbassides, in the eighth century, that the medical and philosophical Greek literature came generally into vogue with the learned Saracen. The first Arabian translation of Aristotle dates from the beginning of the ninth century.

About the same time, or rather later, flourished Alkendi, to whom the English Roger Bacon was much indebted. He was the first to attempt to place the Islamite theology on a rational basis. As Professor Wallace observes (*Encyclopædia Britannica*, 9th ed., art. "Arabian Philosophy"), "there were schoolmen amongst the believers in the Koran, no less than amongst the Latin Christians. At the very moment when Mohammedanism came into contact with the older civilisations of Persia, Babylonia, and Syria, the intellectual habits of the new converts created difficulties with regard to its very basis, and proved themselves a prolific source of diversity in the details of interpretation."

Looking at the philosophical problem from the point of view of Mohammedan monotheism, the difficulty was to reconcile the ascription of manifold attributes to a being whose essence was unity. The next in interest was the relation of the Divine omnipotence to the freedom of the human will. But the philosophical genius of the Semitic mind was not sufficiently great to deal with these questions satisfactorily to itself without the assistance of European thought. It is a noteworthy circumstance that the philosophy of Aristotle appears in its purest form in the Middle Ages, in the works of the Arabian writers. Next to Alkendi comes the so-called Alfarabi, who died A.D. 950. His philosophy was buried in the darkness of a secret order, such was the suspicion with which his rationalising tendencies were regarded.

One of the most important of the philosophers of the East, was Avicenna (born 980). In him the question of Nominalism and Realism resolved itself, not after the manner of Abelard in the West, by a destructive criticism of the rival theories, but by a recognition of their equal justification. According to Avicenna, all universals exist *ante res* in the Divine understanding, *in rebus*, as the real predicates of things, and *post res*, as the abstract concepts formed by the human mind. At the head of Avicenna's metaphysic stands the absolutely simple, necessary, and perfect essence. This is the Good towards which everything tends, and from its participation in which its relative perfection is derived. Notwithstanding its unity, this principle embraces as determinations of its thought, the necessary (as distinguished from the merely contingent) in all real objects. Opposed to this abstract principle of *form*, is the *hyle* or *matter*. The matter of Avicenna is, like that of Aristotle, Plato, and their successors, merely the principle of limitation, of non-being, of contingency, in which the whole sense-world partakes; in other words, the principle of plurality and potentiality, as against that of unity and actuality. Nature is the synthesis of these fundamental principles. The passage from the higher to the lower is to be conceived as eternal. The cause which gives reality to things is equally necessary to preserve their reality. It is an error to suppose that once brought into being, objects would remain so of themselves. Avicenna, as a natural consequence of this doctrine, teaches the eternity of the world.

It is unnecessary to enter upon the manner in which Avicenna brings this dualistic system into conformity with his theological creed. Suffice it to say, that any contradiction between the doctrine of reason and the revelation of the Prophet, is to him an impossibility. In practice he advocates asceticism as a means of freeing the soul from the bondage of *matter*, and raising it to the intelligible world, which is its proper destination.

Al Ghazzali (born 1059) represents the sceptical side of Arabian philosophy, as Avicenna does the mystical. His work may be described, like that of the late Dean Mansel's 'Limits of Religious Thought,' and Mr. Balfour's 'Defence of Philosophic Doubt,' as an effort to resuscitate a popular theology by a demonstration that philosophic conceptions are as unreliable, and as susceptible to negative criticism, as those of common experience, which philosophy pretends to undermine. The consequence of the scepticism of Al Ghazzali was the triumph throughout the East of unphilosophical Mohammedan orthodoxy. Spain became henceforth the chief theatre of Saracen learning.

Tho first figure that strikes us in the Moorish Empire is Abu Beker, who was born at Saragossa, towards the end of the eleventh century. He wrote only small treatises, most of which are lost. The most famous of these, 'The Guide of the Lonely,' treats of the stages through which the soul rises from the instinct that it possesses in common with the lower animals, to the active intellect, which is an emanation of the Deity Himself. This is, as with Avicenna, by a progressive freeing of itself from the potentiality and multiplicity of sense. Abu Beker is chiefly interesting as leading up to the greatest of all the Mohammedan thinkers, Averroës.

Averroës was born at Cordova in the year 1120, and died in Morocco, as physician, in the last year of the century. His veneration for Aristotle amounted almost to adoration. his works chiefly consisting of commentaries on the master,

Averroës is strong in his polemic against the doctrine of creation out of nothing, and in his rehabilitation of the Aristotelian principle of evolution. What is called creation is nothing but the transition from potentiality to actuality. Matter contains within it all forms, according to their possibility; they do not require to be superinduced upon it from without, as in the Platonic doctrine of Avicenna, but to be merely evolved, the distinction betweeen *potentiality* or *possibility*, *i.e.*, *matter*, and *actuality*, *i.e.*, *form*, existing only in our limited thought, The philosopher should recognise this. He should see that the oft-repeated question as to whether *chaos* or *matter* has preceded or followed *order* or *form*, from his point of view, has no meaning, since the merely temporal distinction of possibility and actuality is for him merged in the higher category of necessity. Averroës found in his religion what he was expounding in a rational form, shadowed forth in images and symbols. Only a few could attain the highest goal, viz. philososophical truth; for the rest, the popular creed was necessary. With Averroës the series of the Saracen thinkers closes. Their influence is readily discoverable in the writings of Albertus Magnus, Thomas Aquinas, and indeed, all the later schoolmen.

Before proceeding to again take up the thread of Western speculation proper, we must cast a glance at the contemporary Jewish philosophy, a type of which we may find in Maimonides. This, although possessing no especial bearing on what immediately follows, will have its importance when we come to treat of Spinoza.

The Jewish philosophy of the middle ages consists partly in the Kabbala, which was a secret doctrine, claiming great antiquity, but in all probability not dating from earlier than the middle of the ninth century; and partly in a Judaistic Aristotelianism, traceable immediately to the Arabian thinkers, especially Averroës. The doctrine of the Kabbala is comprised in two books, called respectively *Jezirah*, or Creation, and *Sohar*, or Illumination. It is the former book which contains the original Kabbalistic doctrine, the latter being avowedly the production of a Spanish Jew of the thirteenth century. It will suffice to state that the doctrines contained in these books are simply a mixture of Neo-Platonic, Neo-Pythagorean, Parsic, and other theosophies.

The Moorish Empire was the happy hunting-ground of all searchers after knowledge and speculative freedom in the middle ages. In spite of not unfrequent bursts of intolerance, thought was probably freer in Spain than in any other European country. It was not alone Mussulman thinkers and scholars that found a home there; Christians and Jews taught and studied side by side with them. The civilisation which produced the Alhambra and the Escorial can boast not only Averroës, but Avicebron and Maimonides.

The first Jewish philosopher of any note is Avicebron, author of the work *Fons Vitæ*, much quoted by the schoolmen. He was born at the beginning of the eleventh century, at Malaga, and died about 1070. His main thesis is the universality of the opposition of Matter and Form (or, which is the same thing, of Genus and Differentia), throughout the sensible, no less than the intelligible and moral worlds; and at the same time, their indissoluble conjunction. Will alone transcends this opposition, and hence cannot be defined, but only seized by intuition. Avicebron was a pronounced Pantheist, and his work was in consequence shunned by the orthodox, no less among the Jews than the Christians.

Moses Ben Maimon, or Maimonides, who was a native of Cordova, was born 1135, and died, 1204, at Cairo. He was alike among his co-religionists and the outer world the most highly esteemed of all the mediæval Hebrew thinkers. Although much influenced by his Mohammedan contemporaries and predecessors in the field of philosophical research, having studied under the famous Averroës, he none the less cultivated with assiduity the writings of Aristotle himself. He was a voluminous writer, not only on philosophy but also on law and medicine. His main doctrines were the impossibility of predicating any positive attributes of the Deity; with this was connected his division of all existence into the Makrokosmos and Mikrokosmos, terms which play such a large part among the alchemists and the pseudo-physicists of a later age. Maimonides, in spite of his devotion to Aristotle, refused to admit the eternity of the world *a parte ante*. The divine intelligence is, according to his doctrine, connected with the singular or individual through the human intelligence. In itself it only contains the universal forms of things.

The writings of Maimonides soon became widely circulated, and were much commented upon. It was chiefly through his contemporary, Gersonides, that they were made known to the Gentile world.

THE LATER SCHOOLMEN.

Albertus Magnus.

This eminent schoolman and reputed magician was born in Swabia, about the year 1193, receiving his education at the university of Padua. In his thirty-sixth year Albertus repaired to Cologne, as professor in the Dominican College there. He is also said to have taught in several other places, amongst them Strasbourg and Paris, but subsequently returned to Cologne at a time when Thomas Aquinas was beginning to achieve distinction. After much wandering in France and Germany, he died in the year 1280, having outlived his famous pupil "the angelic doctor."

Albertus Magnus was the first of the schoolmen to expound the Aristotelian philosophy in systematic order, at the same time taking account of its various Arabian commentators, and to seek to bring the whole mass—original form and later developments—into possible harmony with ecclesiastical dogma. He expounds his modified version of "the philosopher" in a series of writings which form a running commentary on the Aristotelian text. His theory of the Universal is nearly identical with that of Avicenna. It is *universale ante rem* in the divine mind; *universale in re* in the synthesis of reality; and *universale post rem* as the mental concept. Albertus is careful to separate the Trinitarian doctrine of the Church and the dogmas connected therewith from his rational or philosophic theology. He none the less rejects the Aristotelian doctrine of the eternity of the world, holding fast in this case to the Church dogma of a creation in time. Albertus, with Aristotle and Plato, contends for the materiality of the soul and its independence of the body so far as its existence is concerned, although not in respect of it as an active agent in the real world. The ethics of Albertus rest entirely on the principle of the freedom of the will. His attempt to combine the Aristotelian morality with the Christian is more ingenious than successful.

THOMAS AQUINAS.

Thomas of Aquino, born 1225, at the castle of his father, a Neapolitan count, is the central figure among the later schoolmen. His abilities being early recognised, he was sent to the Dominican School in Cologne, where Albertus Magnus was then lecturing. He followed Albertus to Paris, and back again to Cologne, there assuming the position of Magister Studentium. He subsequently gave courses of lectures in most of the chief universities of Europe, while at the same time engaged in affairs of State, both in France and Italy, and active in all the public business of the Church. He died in 1274.

Thomas Aquinas may be described as the spirit of Scholasticism incarnate. His *Summa Theologia* is an attempt to realise the scholastic ideal of an all-embracing system of knowledge comprehending philosophy proper, theology, and such physical speculations of an alchemistic character, which then did duty for science.

The grand principle on which Aquinas based his system was that there were two sources of knowledge,—revelation and reason. The chief characteristic of revelation is the mysterious and incomprehensible guise in which its truths are conveyed, but which are to be believed in spite of this. The channels of revelation are the Hebrew Scriptures and Church tradition.

The Reason of Aquinas is not to be confounded with the individual reason. It is the other main source of knowledge, its artery being the writings of the Greeks, especially of Plato and Aristotle. In both these two channels of knowledge there is a higher and a lower sphere, the latter of which, alone, man can hope to attain. Though distinct for us, in the last resort, Reason and revelation alike draw from the same ultimate source, namely, God, or the Absolute One. Thomas Aquinas did for the Christian theology what Averroës did for the

Moslem, and Maimonides for the Jewish. He supplied it with a fairly coherent, philosophical dress. In his theory of the universal, Aquinas follows his master, Albertus Magnus, who, as we have seen, in his turn follows Avicenna. Realism (whether Platonic or Aristotelian), and Nominalism, alike have their relative justification. In the agreement of things with the eternal ideas consists *their* truth; in the agreement of our thoughts with the things, consists the truth *for us*. The connection between the metaphysic and theology of Aquinas is seen when he comes to treat of *Form* as independent Substance, in which way the existence of spiritual being is explained. The angels of Aquinas, like those of Philo, are simply personified universals.

In treating the Scholastic period generally, but more especially a writer like Aquinas, it is hard to say where philosophy ends and theology begins, for in spite of St. Thomas's primary distinction, we find the theological method named pervading the whole current of his thought, as of that of the Schoolmen generally.

The influence of the "Angelic Doctor," as he was termed, on the thought, and more than all, on the terminology of subsequent ages, must not be measured by the comparatively limited space we can afford, or, indeed, that it is necessary, to devote to him, in a work like the present. "Were the importance of a school determined by the number of its adherents and its long continuance," says Erdmann, "none could compare with that of the Albertists, as they were originally, or the Thomists, as they were afterwards called. There are even many who see in Thomas at the present day the incarnation of the philosophical reason." The present pope Leo XIII., in 1879, constituted Thomas Aquinas the, so to speak, official exponent of the philosophical side of Catholicism. Not long after his death, however, he had already obtained the same position among the Dominican order to which he had belonged. There can be no doubt or question, whatever may be our opinion of the value of the scholastic philosophy in general, or of that of St. Thomas in particular, that he was one of the subtlest and acutest intellects that have ever lived. The services he has rendered in giving precision to philosophical terminology must alone, apart from all question of the particular tenets associated with his name, render him deserving of the gratitude of all subsequent thinkers.

Duns Scotus.

John Duns Scotus, the precise year and place of whose birth are somewhat uncertain, though the probabilities seem in favour of a Scottish origin, flourished during the latter half of the thirteenth century. He is reported to have studied at Merton College, Oxford, where he became remarkably proficient in all branches of learning, especially mathematics. In 1301 he was appointed Professor of Philosophy at Oxford, and attracted great attention, a fact expressed in the legend that no less than thirty thousand students attended his classes. He acquired his title of "Doctor Subtilis," on account of the dialectical ingenuity he displayed in his defence of the doctrine of the immaculate conception, a dogma which was maintained by the Franciscans, to whom Scotus belonged, against the Dominicans. He died, it is said, in the thirty-fifth year of his age at Cologne, in November, 1308.

Though the Scotists, or followers of Scotus, continued, till the close of the Scholastic period, the rivals of the Thomists in the learned world, it must not be supposed that he was any the less a realist in philosophy than Aquinas himself; indeed, Scotus may be regarded as representing the harder and more uncompromising form of the realist doctrine. He also indicates a reaction against the eclecticism of Aquinas in another respect. Aquinas, as we know, gave to reason an amount of authority independent of dogma; Scotus, on the other hand, will not admit of any other channel of knowledge than the ecclesiastical one. In accordance with this position, he rejects the ontological arguments offered by Aquinas in favour of the existence of the Deity, whose being and attributes he proclaims altogether outside the sphere of reason. The most important of the writings of Scotus consisted of commentaries on Aristotle and Lombardus. His strength consists rather in negative criticism than in constructive thought. This is connected, according as we view it, either as cause or consequence of his fundamental position, which amounted to denying for the reason any sphere of use other than that of undermining its own pretensions. To him who proclaimed the unconditional acceptance of the Church's doctrines in their very letter as the primary duty, it was not likely that any attempt at constructing a rational theology would find much favour. Scotus is what Occam was still more, a Christian Al Ghazzali.

All things, according to Scotus, are constituted of Form and Matter combined. The principle of individuation he finds in Form. The special individual determination or the Thisness (*hæcceitas*) imposes itself as Form on the Matter which is constituted of generic and specific character. The essence of individuation is distinguishable in the things as well as in the intellect, although it has no existence separable from them, *i.e.* the Universal is not merely potentially present in the object, but actually so. Scotus is particularly strong in his assertion of the freedom of the will, which he declares capable of self-determination without motive. It will be sufficiently clear from this brief sketch that by his doctrine of the Thisness (*hæcceitas*), or principle of individuation, not implying any limitation or deterioration of the Whatness, or quiddity, but rather the completion and perfecting of it, Scotus has discarded the last remnant of the older Platonic realism, according to which the sense element, or in other words, this same principle of individuation was the purely negative *matter*, limiting the perfection of the universal *form*, which inhered in it.

William of Occam.

William, born at Occam (now Ockham), in Surrey, a Franciscan and pupil of Duns Scotus, was for some time professor in Paris. Opposed to the temporal power of the Hierarchy, in accordance with the principles of his order, he threw himself with ardour into the conflict between the French Monarchy and the Papacy on the side of the former. Persecuted by the papal party, he fled to Padua, and subsequently to Munich, where he placed himself under the protection of Ludwig of Bavaria. He died in Munich about the year 1347.

In William of Occam, the swan of scholasticism sang its death-song. For from Occam's new arguments and re-statement of the position of Nominalism, which he championed, resulted the bankruptcy of the school-ardently philosophy. Occam was as much opposed to Scotism, the dominant philosophy of his order, as he was to the Thomism of the Dominicans. His definition of a Universal is interesting. "A Universal is," he says, "a particular intention of the mind, itself capable of being predicated of many things, not for what it properly is itself, but for what those things are; so that in so far as it has this capacity it is called Universal, but in so far as it is one form really existing in the mind, it is called singular."

With Occam the great controversy respecting Universals became consciously narrowed to a purely psychological issue. The coincidence between much in his writings with the doctrines of the later English Empiricist school is, allowing for scholastic terminology striking. According to Occam, the Species (*intelligibiles*) of the Scotists are superfluous entities. It is rather the *actus intelligendi* itself which is the sign of the thing. By sign, William understands that by which one thing is distinguished from another thing. He draws a line between natural signs, or signs of objects over which our will has no control, and those general terms formep in the mind which can be called up and dismissed at pleasure. The former constitute our perceptions or thoughts of *things*, the latter are merely states or modifications of the soul caused by these perceptions. But it would be just as irrational to suppose that even the first of these, *i.e.* our necessary thoughts, or our perceptions through sense, resemble the things perceived, as to suppose that the sigh resembles the pain which causes it, or the smoke the fire. Here we have a plain statement, albeit couched in scholastic phraseology, of the ordinary empirical doctrine of a world of "things-in-themselves," which are the *cause* of our perceptions but concerning which we know nothing more. The second order of *signs*, our ideas or general concepts, have, according to Occam, no connection whatever with things, but are merely built up of our perceptions of things and serve to indicate these. They are mere words or names, having no more resemblance to the perceptions which gave rise to them than the latter in their turn have to the *things* by which *they* are caused.

The principle of Occam's philosophical method is well expressed in his favourite maxim : *entia non sunt multiplicanda præter necessitatem. Sufficiunt singularia, et ita tales res universales omnino frustra ponuntur.* He makes short work of distinctions which, until then, had passed as the common property of the learned. The same tendency to simplification is observable in his theology. Like his master Duns, he denies the possibility of basing theology on reason.

With William of Occam, the philosophy of the Church virtually closes. After him there is no original figure. The various schools continued to furnish writings and disputations up to the period of the Renaissance, and even later, but there is little to record concerning them.

Among the best works giving a general view of the philosophy of the Middle Ages may be mentioned *Haureau, de la philosophie scolastique* (2 Voll. Par. 1850); *Kaulich, Geschichte der scholastischen Philosophie* (Prague, 1863); *Stöckl, Geschichte der Philosophie des Mittelalters* (Mainz, 1862–66); *Prantl, Gesch. der Logic im Abendlande.* Maurice, Mediæval Philosophy, in Vol. I. of his Moral and Metaphysical Philosophy, which contains perhaps the best and fullest English monograph on the subject. For the Arabians and Jews may be consulted *Munk, Mélanges de philosophie juive et arabe* (Paris, 1859); *Ernest Renan, Averroes et l'averroïsme* (Paris, 1852; 2nd Ed. 1865); *Geiger, Moses ben Maimon* (Breslau, 1850); also *Beer, Philosophie und philosophische Schriftsteller der Juden* (Leipsic, 1852).

About the time that Scholasticism was declining, a curious movement sprang up in Germany. This was the so-called "German Mysticism" of the fourteenth and fifteenth centuries. It is in the main concomitant with the rise of that German national literature which was brought to an untimely end by the Thirty Years' War. This mystical movement may be said to have originated with the Master

Eckhart, who, tired of the teachings of the schools, broke away from them in a direction which led directly to Jacob Böhme, and indirectly to the Lutheran Reformation. Johannes Tauler, of Strasbourg, may be also mentioned as one of the leaders of this movement. Though he did not add much in substance to the speculations of Eckhart, he was possessed of a literary style which his predecessors lacked, and thus contributed to popularise them.

The most important work of this school in its influence on German thought was one by an unknown author, subsequently published by Luther as "A German Theology" (*Eyn deutsch Theologia*). The burden of the whole school is the evil and unreality of the phenomenal world; true reality only being recognised in a world outside the limits of time and space to which man must attain ere he rises to his higher life. We have in them an apt illustration of history repeating itself. To Eckhart and his followers, as to Plotinus, the goal of the reason is found in the absolute all-embracing Unity wherein all difference is abolished, Indeed this German Mysticism of the later Middle Ages is little but a reproduction of Neo-Platonic theories, considerable as was its practical influence and results.

On the German Mystics the best work is *Praeger's Geschichte der deutschen Mystik im Mittelalter* (1st Part, Leipsic, 1875); *Rosenkrantz, Der Deutsche Mystik*, Königsberg, 1836). In French, Albert Barran, *Études sur quelques tendences du mysticisme avant la réformation* (Strasbourg, 1868).

TRANSITION TO MODERN PHILOSOPHY.

THE PHILOSOPHY OF THE RENAISSANCE.

FEUDALISM was in ruins. Industry and Commerce were rising into power. Catholicism was rapidly disintegrating as a system even in spiritual matters, while as a controlling factor in the affairs of the world it was merely one, by no means the greatest, among several contending forces. The philosophy of the schools was everywhere in disrepute among earnest and independent thinkers. The art of printing had just been invented, and was of itself revolutionising older habits of thought. The New World was being opened up by enterprising Spanish and Portuguese mariners. And last, but not least, Constantinople had but recently fallen before the crescents and horsetails of Mahomet II., and its treasures, literary and artistic, been, in consequence, dispersed throughout the Western World. Such was Europe as the fifteenth century closed, and the sixteenth opened. Among a crowd of diverse, yet connected factors, each contributing its quota to the formation of the mental character of an epoch, it is difficult to assign the relative importance of any one in particular. Yet it is sufficiently obvious that it was the last event mentioned which gave its immediate colouring to the philosophy of the period.

Little as the so-called Renaissance has in common with the Middle Ages pure and simple, it yet possesses a distinct mediæval character of its own, just as the period of the Christian Roman Empire has the stamp of the civilization of antiquity upon it, notwithstanding the gulf which divides it from the ancient world properly so called. The industrial middle class of the fifteenth century were so far nearer allied to the yeomen and free tenants of feudalism than to the commercial classes of modern times. In the same way the hatred of scholasticism and the desire to start afresh on the lines of ancient thought in its purity did not prevent the philosophical literature of the period from having a distinct mediæval and scholastic flavour.

Early in the fifteenth century, there was a society established in Florence by a Greek named Plethon, the commentator of Plato, under the special protection of Cosmo de Medici, for the study of the works of Plato untrammelled by theological scruples. Marsilius Ficinus (1433–1499), who taught in the school, was the author, in addition to a work entitled *Theologica Platonica*, of a well-known Latin translation of Plato. Another prominent reviver of Platonism was John Picus of Mirandola. Turning from Platonism to Cabbalistic mysticism and charlatanry, Picus of Mirandola repaired to Rome to propound nine hundred theses on every conceivable subject, logical, ethical, mathematical, metaphysical, theological, magical, which he offered to defend against all comers. By these he succeeded in achieving great notoriety at the time, though not without falling under the suspicion of heresy. Picus died at the early age of thirty-one, in the year 1494.

Ficinus and Picus may be taken more or less as types of the average philosophical product of the Renaissance in Italy. Scholars like them crowded the court of the Medicis. The great speculative result of the classical revival of the fifteenth and sixteenth centuries may be seen in the Paganism which became fashionable among the upper classes, extending even to the Papal chair itself. A state of things prevailed similar in many respects to that presented by the French pre-revolutionary salons of the eighteenth century, of which it was indeed the precursor. The dominant classes, while amid their own circle avowedly anti-Christian, were publicly, and before the common people, devout members of the Church.

The cultured indifferentism of Italy was in striking contrast with the earnestness felt and displayed in religious matters the other side of the Alps. To Leo X. the sale of indulgences seemed a short and easy method of raising money, as little objectionable as any. This opinion was doubtless shared by the higher clergy, and all those who, whether Italian or not, had come directly under the influence of the Renaissance. *Populus vult decipi et decipiatur* was their motto; and it was surely only fair that the *populus* should pay for its deception. To Luther and his *confrères* of the German Reformation, whose contact with the Renaissance was only indirect and second-hand, and who possessed in addition, the fierce earnestness of the northern temperament, the whole body of Christian dogma was of serious and vital moment. To the man who believed himself to be continually wrestling with the devil, it is obvious the sale of free leave of sinning was horrible in the extreme. The great religious conflict of the period known as the Reformation, was not so much the struggle of a new religious idea with the old Catholic one, as with the class-culture of the Renaissance. It may be roughly characterised as a conflict between the two great natural groups of western Europe—the Latin and the Teutonic. The former would have had two creeds, that of a Paganised culture for the upper classes existing concurrently with abject superstition in those below them in the social scale; the latter contended for the right of the growing middle classes to independent judgment within certain limits; *i.e.* what they deemed the fundamental articles of Christian belief. To them the free-thought and ecclesiastical superstition of the Latins were alike abominable.

But it was an indispensable condition, even in Italy itself, great as was the latitude allowed in speculation, that none should endanger the authority of the Church. GIORDANO BRUNO, born 1548, near Naples, originally a Dominican, found this to his cost. In consequence of his having come to disbelieve the ecclesiastical dogma, he left his order, a fact which in itself must have constituted him a fool, and a somewhat dangerous one to boot, in the eyes of his brother Italian churchmen of the period. To this noble-minded man the lip-service and speculative chicanery of other clerical scholars was abhorrent. He, at least, could not continue professing a creed, or serving a church, in whose pretensions he disbelieved. He was hence compelled to leave Italy. At first he repaired to Geneva, then the capital of the Reformation; but the "reformed" doctrines, so-called, were to his logical mind even less satisfactory than the Catholic orthodoxy he had forsaken.

From thence he went to Lyons, Toulouse, Paris, and ultimately to Oxford and London. He found a temporary resting-place at the Court of Queen Elizabeth, and held disputations at Oxford. It has even been conjectured, though on perhaps insufficient grounds, that while in London, Bruno made the acquaintance of Shakespeare, and that certain philosophical allusions occurring in "Hamlet" may be traced to the influence of his conversation on the poet. But the spirit of wandering again seized Bruno; he travelled to Wittenberg, thence to Prague, subsequently visiting Frankfort-on-the-Maine, where he remained some little time, and from which place an evil fate seems to have drawn him once more across the Alps into his native country. He fell into the hands of the Inquisition soon after his arrival, and was conveyed to Rome in 1593. There he suffered an imprisonment of some years' duration, during which time every attempt, whether by force or cajolery, to induce him to recant his views was nobly and successfully resisted. When, at the beginning of 1600, he was sentenced to death, Bruno is reported to have said in the presence of the Court, "It behoves you to have greater fear in pronouncing this sentence than I have in receiving it." He was burnt at Rome on the 17th of February, 1600. A statue has been erected to his memory at Naples, before which the students, on one occasion, burnt an encyclical letter of Pope Pius IX.

Bruno is certainly by far the most important and original philosophic figure to which the Renaissance gave birth. An ardent disciple of the new physical doctrines of Copernicus, he was not satisfied with philosophising on the old Platonic or Aristotelian lines, but sought a theory of the universe which should embrace the new science. Bruno's admiration for the older Greek philosophers was great; he placed them before either Plato or Aristotle, for the latter of whom he seems to have had a genuine hatred. Anaxagoras, Herakleitos, Pythagoras, he held in high esteem; but the thinker who most immediately influenced him was perhaps Nicolas of Chusa, the celebrated German ecclesiastic and mystic of the fifteenth century.

To Bruno God was simply the immanent principle of the universe, or world-soul. Bruno attacks what he conceives the dualism of Matter and Form; the Form is immanent in all Matter of which it is only an aspect. Like his enemies, the Scholastics and the Arabian Aristotelians, he held to the three-fold existence of ideas, or universals, *ante res*, *in rebus*, and *post res*—metaphysically in the ultimate unity or world-soul, physically in the real world, and logically in the sign, symbol or notion. God, or the universal substance of all things, is related to the real world as the universal to the particular. In the laws of nature, which are the expression of his being, Bruno discovers true freedom. But the determining and infinitely *actual* principle presupposes a *possible* principle, which *becomes* determined. The other pole of the philosophic equation is therefore the old principle of Matter, or the infinitely *possible*. Thus, as might be expected from the nature of things, Bruno was bound, when once he attacked the ultimate philosophical problem, to express himself in that same Aristotelian fashion which he elsewhere condemns as dualistic. The position held by Bruno in reference to the problem of Monism or Pluralism is not quite clear. His work *De Monade Numero et Figura*, seems to incline to the latter; the *De Immenso et Innumerabilibus* to the former; but possibly he had never clearly propounded the question to himself. God, or the universal principle, inasmuch as it embraces the sum of things, is the *maximum possibile;* inasmuch as it is equally present in every atom, the *minimum possibile.* It comprehends in itself every other contradiction; thus, that which is everywhere centre, is at once everywhere and nowhere periphery, &c. The one principle is the same, not only in kind, but in degree, whether in the plant, the animal, or the stone. The infinite possibilities of the one substance are realised successively in the order of time, which is also infinite. As Erdmann remarks, if on the one side Bruno may be regarded as a forerunner of Spinoza, on the other he is none the less a forerunner of Leibnitz. The monad is the principle of the working of the soul. Every order of beings is perfect according to its kind; there is no absolute, but only a relative evil. These principles are developed on Pythagorean lines.

Bruno is remarkable for having been the first to attempt

the incorporation of the new scientific conceptions into a philosophical system. He is moreover interesting from his having been the first thinker in the modern world who openly and definitely broke with Christianity. A true son of the Renaissance, in spite of his originality, his philosophy, like his character, was essentially formed on a Pagan mould, and he knew it. But unlike the rank and file of the scholars and grammarians of the age, he boldly attacked the dogmas which he disbelieved, and which were abhorrent to him, and attacked them too in no compromising or half-hearted manner.

In this he was not followed by his countryman and contemporary Thomas Campanella, also a man of considerable original power, though inferior to Bruno. Campanella is chiefly noteworthy as the immediate predecessor of Descartes, in making the certainty of the actual moment of consciousness the starting-point of his philosophy; and also in having employed the ontological argument to prove the existence of the Deity. In many respects he approached Bruno, even in the latter's Pantheism, but he nevertheless always contrived to keep on good terms with the Church, being in his later years a strong advocate of Papal domination.

THE SIXTEENTH-CENTURY ALCHEMISTS AND COSMIC SPECULATORS.

THE sixteenth century was eminently an age of travelling scholars. The whole of civilized Europe was at this period of universally awakening intellectual activity, literally overrun with students who contrived to support themselves chiefly by obtaining hospitality in return for some slight service, educational, medical, or divinatory; among these were brilliant disputationists and scholars like Giordano Bruno and Johannes Reuchlin, &c., but the vast number obtained a meagre subsistence by soothsaying, fortune-casting and healing (or the reverse). It was an age of restless intellectual cravings and of ceaseless wandering. The

Faust legend—the last instance in history of the complete envelopment of a personality in myth—is a perfect embodiment of the spirit of the sixteenth century. It was emphatically the epoch of the *occult sciences*, so-called. The strange lore which had lain buried in monasteries, shunned by all but a few doctors during the Middle Ages, was now the common property of every man possessed of a little learning. Add to this, that the new culture of Greek and Hebrew had opened up sources hitherto sealed. As Italy may be taken as the typical country for the more purely literary and artistic side of the Renaissance, so Germany (understanding by the term the German-speaking countries of Central Europe) may be regarded as the typical country of this magical-theosophic aspect of it, though, of course, in neither case is any exclusiveness implied. The intermingling of theosophic lore with the rising physical science was most systematically carried out in Germany. Most of the theosophic and alchemistic notions which now became popular, the elixir vitæ, the philosopher's stone, the elemental spirits, are immediately traceable to the Kabbala (see above, p. 121), the authors of which probably drew from Coptic, Persian and other Oriental sources, in addition to the Talmud and other Rabbinical writings.*

The first to introduce the study of Hebrew, and especially of the Kabbala, into Germany was Johannes Reuchlin, who studied under Picus of Mirandola and Ficinus in Italy, and subsequently settled at Tübingen. The story of his successful conflict on behalf of Hebrew literature with the monks of Cologne, in which he was supported by the reformers Melancthon and Ulrich von Hutten, is well known. He wrote a treatise *De arte cabbalistica.* After Reuchlin may be mentioned Cornelius Agrippa von Nettesheim (1486-1530), who wrote a treatise *De occulta philosophia.* Agrippa was a true son of his century, spending his life in courts, universities, on the battle-field, and anon in studious retirement, seldom remaining more than two or three years

* The Rosicrucians, the Freemasons, the Illuminati of the eighteenth century, all date indirectly from this Alchemistic or rather physico-theosophic movement of the sixteenth century. The attempt to connect Freemasonry with the mediæval craft-guild of masons can only pass muster with those who have not studied the period in question.

at the utmost in the same place. Like Giordano Bruno, these writers, especially Agrippa, drew much from the writings of the mystic Nicolas of Chusa, whose mathematical speculations furnished material for many of the magical formulæ of the time.

But the man in whom the whole intellectual and moral temper of the century was most perfectly embodied is in the erratic person who rejoiced in the name of *Philippus Aureolus Theophrastus Bombastes von Hohenheim*, though better known by his surname of PARACELSUS (1493-1541). He is a true prototype of the Goethean Faust. The contempt for traditional and academic teaching and teachers, the universal scepticism culminating in the attempt to wring from nature her secrets by magic;

"Ob mich durch Geistes Kraft und Mund
Nicht manch Geheimniss würde kund;"

the ceaseless wandering, the alternations of drunkenness and debauchery with real attempts to pluck out the heart of the mystery of nature, make the parallel complete. Some apology may be deemed necessary for introducing the physical speculators, of whom we take Paracelsus as the type, into a manual of the history of philosophy. From a narrow interpretation of the word philosophy it might perhaps be out of place, but the interest attaching to the first dawnings of physical science, and the quaint blending of theosophy and physics, which coloured more or less the whole thought of this epoch will, we fancy, render any formal apology unnecessary to those who take a broad view of the evolution of speculative thought.

Paracelsus spent most of his youth in the manner we have described as common at the time, that is, wandering from city to city and country to country, practising astrology, palmistry and magic and alchemy generally. He is said to have been initiated in these pseudo-sciences by sundry ecclesiastics. In the course of his travels he visited nearly all the most prominent universities of Europe. Owing to the reputation gained by some cures effected on important personages, he obtained, in 1526, the professorship of medicine in the University of Basel. His first act on assuming the chair was to publicly burn the treatises of Aristotle and Galen, for whom he had a special antipathy. His discourses appear to have been delivered in a manner which, whether Paracelsus originated it or not, has ever since been associated with his name, the word *bombastic* dating from the medical lectures of Bombastus Paracelsus at Basel. Drunkenness compelled him to resign his chair, and again take to the life of wandering medicus, divinator and astrologer. He died, like his friend Cornelius Agrippa, in great poverty, at Salzburg, in 1541.

Paracelsus was believed by his contemporaries to have unveiled the secret arcana of nature, to have become possessed not only of the power of transmuting metals, but of the philosopher's stone, the elixir of life, and many other things. He is usually decried as a mere charlatan by historians, but probably with insufficient cause. There is little reason for doubting that Paracelsus believed in the main in the principles he was propounding, and at least in the general possibility of obtaining the powers he claimed for himself. Living in a magical age, the whole of Nature presented itself naturally enough to his mind as a system of "occult" properties, affinities and agents. Those who stigmatise Paracelsus as a conscious impostor must surely forget the state of science at the time, and the universality among the learned of the belief in astrology and alchemy. These beliefs were reduced to systematic form by Paracelsus. The idea traceable throughout the period is that theosophy supplies a key not only to the theoretical interpretation of Nature, but to the practical application of its laws in medicine, &c. Still, on the confines of the Middle Ages, when everything, from the highest relations of Church and State to those of the trade or handicraft, had a mystic religious significance, it was but natural the new physical science should be conceived in this spirit. A scientific method did not exist, and men had not as yet become accustomed to the habit of specialisation, which characterises our thought in this transitional age of mental and material anarchy.

The cosmological system of Paracelsus, for with metaphysic he did not occupy himself, was based on the conception of the tripartite division of nature and man. Nature was the macrocosm, man the microcosm. Man, as the pinnacle of nature, embraced in his body the elements of all other things. Without astronomical, physical and theological knowledge, it is impossible for the physician to understand the true nature of the human body or its diseases. The trinitarian principle was all-pervading, the *prima materia*, understanding by this a physical substance, contains within it the potencies of all things; but even in this may be traced a triple nature, generally designated by Paracelsus as salt, sulphur, and mercury, though sometimes as *Balsamum*, *Resina*, and *Liquor*. Paracelsus is careful to insist he does not mean these substances in the gross bodily form presented to us, but their spiritual essences. All material things contain these principles; thus in wood that which forms smoke is the mercurial principle, that which burns is the sulphurous, while what remains as ash is the saline. In man, the body represents salt, the animal soul sulphur, and the intellectual principle mercury. In the combination and separation of these, the variety of things appears. The so-called four elements as we know them are the offspring of the *spirit* or *vulcanus* inhering in them. What in the elements is *vulcanus*, appears in composite individual things as their *archeus*, or individual force. Man, who is the quintessence of all things, is dependent upon all: his intellect is divine, his animal soul astral, his body terrestrial. Hence his state in sickness can only be understood by referring it to the particular element which is its cause. A knowledge of water and earth only gives the clue to the body of man. The macrocosm embraces heaven as well as earth, and to man's spiritual nature, which corresponds to the former, a knowledge of the heavenly bodies is requisite, for with these it has its affinity. To investigate this is the function of astrology. The visible stars are to Paracelsus only the body (corpus) of the invisible essences which animate them. But it is needless to enter further into the details of Paracelsus' system (if it can be termed such), with its sylphs, gnomes, kobbolds and salamanders; its far-fetched and fanciful analogies; its strange medley of Cabbalistic, Platonic and Christian doctrines. Its key-note is the correspondence between macrocosm and microcosm. As the macrocosm is divided into its upper and lower parts (the heavens and the earth), so is the microcosm into body and animal soul. Outside these spheres which constitute the subject-matter of human science is the divine order, the subject-matter of theology, the divine science. To this belongs the rational and moral nature of man, and the creative activity by which the universe is sustained and governed. On this ground human reason is inadequate, and revelation (esoterically interpreted) is the only guide. A point that strikes one in reading Paracelsus is that with all his hatred of Aristotle and Scholasticism, he is unable to dispense with the well-known Scholastic distinctions and terminology. The school-philosophy, even in its decay, asserted its influence on friends and foes alike.

It is an apt illustration of the truth of what we before said as to the tendency of the age, that much the same views as those of Paracelsus were enunciated by an Italian contemporary, also a physician, who, so far as we are aware, had no knowledge of him or his works. HIERONYMUS CARDANUS (or Cardano, as it is in Italian), well-known for his interesting and curious autobiography entitled *De vitâ propriâ*, was born in 1500, at Milan. His fame as a mathematician and scientific investigator, which in his own day was great, has not proved enduring, owing to the fact, as observed by a recent writer, that he was compelled to labour, "partly in fields of research where no important discovery was then attainable, partly in those where his discoveries could only serve as the stepping-stones to others by which they were inevitably eclipsed." Like Paracelsus, Cardanus was an ardent believer in astrology, which he sought to establish on inductive principles, as well as in the "occult sciences" generally. His two philosophical treatises are entitled respectively *De subtilitate rerum*, and *De varietate rerum*. In these, as we have said, we find much the same order of speculation as in the works of Paracelsus; the same fanciful analogies; the same subtle affinities; the same haphazard guesses. The "elements" from which, like his elder contemporary, Cardanus excludes that of fire, though for different reasons, naturally play an important part in his system. Even the elemental spirits and other extra human intelligencies assumed by Paracelsus, are to be found in Cardanus. At the same time there are remarkable glimpses of later thought which open out now and again in the works of the Italian. Even the doctrine of evolution appears in a crude form, while the truth that the end of man's being is social rather than personal, is clearly indicated in more than one place. Cardanus is probably the first writer who hinted at the idea of a philosophy of history. In fact, the whole of his thought, even where most fanciful, tends to the recognition of an orderly sequence in events, in short, of the prevalence if not the universality of law, in every sphere of existence. Cardanus, who was also a great traveller, died at Rome in 1576.

Among works dealing with the physical speculations of the sixteenth century may be mentioned Rixner und Siber's *Leben und Meinungen berühmten Physiker im 16ten und 17ten Jahrhundert*, forming a part of the *Geschichte der Physiologie*. Sprengel's *Geschichte der Arzeneikunde*, Thiel III.; Erdmann deals fully with this subject in Vol. II. of his History.

MODERN PHILOSOPHY.

FIRST EPOCH, A.

THE ABSTRACT-DOGMATIC SYSTEMS.

WE have now traced briefly the development of speculative thought from its rise in the sixth century B.C. to the close of the ancient world; we have seen the transition of philosophy in the hands of the Church from its ancient forms into Scholasticism, in which it became the slave of dogma; we have witnessed the decline and fall of Scholasticism at the Renaissance, and its replacement by the resuscitation of classical systems, through the scholars of Italy, and the crude physical speculations of men such as Agrippa, Paracelsus, and Cardanus. Henceforth we have done with the Middle Ages, and enter a period with which current thought is directly affiliated; in short, the period of *Modern Philosophy*.

We noticed that, notwithstanding their declamations against Aristotle and the schoolmen, the writers of the Sixteenth century still employed scholastic expressions and followed a more or less scholastic order of thought. The great negative characteristic of the earlier stages of the modern period (we say earlier stages, though it is a characteristic which it has retained in some of its most recent developments) is the entire absence of all Aristotelean terminology and method. The reaction against scholasticism had at last done its work. With the quibbling and word-jugglery of the schoolmen were swept away the all-important distinctions of the Stagirite himself. But philosophy was now for the first time since the earlier Roman Empire more or less independent, not only of positive dogma, but of any special and determinate intellectual tendency. In the Seventeenth century the foundations of modern civilization in all its aspects were laid; the era of "free contract" (so called) had fairly dawned; the hierarchy of the Middle Ages was spasmodically gasping in its death-throes; authority and status were undermined in all directions; the middle class was asserting its power against all forms of feudal domination; the battle between Catholicism and Protestantism, which had raged in the preceding century in the various countries of Europe, was now practically decided one way or the other; in those lands where the middle class was powerful, Protestantism having become the dominant creed. Philosophy, although now free from the physical persecution of ecclesiasticism, still indirectly felt the influence of dogma, an influence, however, which affected it less and less as time went on, while the oppression it exercised was more of a moral and social than a legal character.

There are two main contemporary streams of philosophic development constituting the speculative history of the Seventeenth and Eighteenth centuries, which may be termed respectively the Abstract-Dogmatic and the Empirical-Sceptical. The reputed founder of the first of these lines was the French Descartes, that of the second the English Bacon. The Abstract-Dogmatic schools consist (I.) of the Cartesians proper, (II.) of Spinoza and his followers, and (III.) of Leibnitz and those who drew their inspiration from him, such as the Germans, Wolff, Baumgarten, &c. The Empirical-Sceptical schools embrace the names of Bacon, Hobbes, Locke, Berkeley, Hume, Reid, and the Scotch psychologists. The French sensationists and materialists of the Eighteenth century are also an offshoot of this line of thought.

The Abstract-Dogmatic schools postulate the *reality* outside of experience of the *forms of thinking* which alone possess meaning in the system of knowledge or experience. They assume concreteness in what is really only a detached element of the concrete; they assume, that is, the conditions of the whole synthesis as present, while *ex hypothesi* they are making abstraction from them.

The Empirical-Sceptical schools profoundly ignore Metaphysic, and confine themselves to psychology; yet they in the long run usually fall into the metaphysical assumption of an independent external world as the *cause* of the individual mind's impressions. The next step is Scepticism, in which the mere individual impression or idea *per se* is hypostasised; that is, made the ultimate reality. In Scepticism the bankruptcy of Empiricism becomes manifest. Philosophy degenerates into a mere negative criticism. There is, however, one way of escape. and that is Materialism, in which the concrete corporeal substance of the universe is made absolute. In this doctrine a truth is presented, though inadequately, because torn from its connection. It is nevertheless the truth of Empiricism, its logical and, in a sense, valid result.

DESCARTES.

RENÉ DESCARTES was born on March 31st, 1596, at La Haye, in Touraine, and educated in the Jesuit College of La Flèche. The early training of Descartes in mathematics and philosophy had the effect for many years to disgust him of all such pursuits. For some time he occupied himself with play and the chase. Subsequently he entered the army of the Netherlands as a volunteer. During this portion of his career he began again to interest himself in intellectual pursuits. He soon exchanged his commission in the army of the Netherlands for one at first in the Bavarian, and afterwards in the Imperial army then engaged in the "Thirty Years' War." It was now that Descartes began to occupy himself in earnest with mathematical investigations chiefly connected with algebra and geometry. He shortly after resigned his commission and devoted himself to travel, as a private individual, visiting in succession Holland, France, Switzerland, and Italy. He afterwards settled in Holland, occupying himself with his studies, until an invitation from Queen Christina of Sweden induced him to remove to Stockholm. The severity of the climate proving too much for his health, never very robust, he died on the 11th of February, 1650, in the last-named city. The principal philosophical works of Descartes are his *Principia Philosophi*. his *Meditationes de prima Philosophia*, his earlier *Essais Philosophiques*, and his short treatise, the *Discours sur la Méthode*.

Descartes' Doctrines.

The system of Descartes starts from the celebrated 'Methodic Doubt,' as it is termed by his followers. Descartes' earlier alienation from philosophy had been largely due to the loose literary spirit of scepticism then prevalent in France among the educated classes, and which is embodied in the writings of Montaigne. It was clear, therefore, that before Descartes could enter with any zeal upon a new course of philosophic investigation, he must make up his account with the scepticism that, with him no less than with others, had discredited the traditional methods of the schools, methods which he had satirically characterised as affording the student the means of "talking glibly on all subjects in a manner to excite the wonder of the less instructed." With the object, therefore, of forestalling the destructive effects of sceptical arguments on the system he hopes to rear, he, so to speak, inoculates it with scepticism at birth.

The 'Methodic Doubt,' above alluded to, forbade anything to be taken for granted that could possibly be questioned. But could not everything be questioned? "No," answers Descartes, the evidences of the senses may; the most apparently indestructible declarations of the intellect may; but there is one thing which all doubt itself presupposes, and that is the doubter. I exist doubting, but doubting is only a form of thinking; therefore this is as much as to say I exist thinking. Descartes' formula for this fundamental position of his philosophy is the celebrated *Cogito ergo sum.* The logical form of this proposition was obviously vulnerable, and Gassendi's criticism of it, from his point of view, undoubtedly justified. But the form of statement does not really affect the point at issue. Descartes wished to insist upon the intuitive character of the proposition, "I am conscious." In this he regards as indistinguishable the fact of existence and the fact of consciousness, of the matter, *I*, and the form, *thought*, a circumstance which, as we shall see later on, has had a bearing on the Kantian and post-Kantian philosophy of Germany. Furnished with this primal deliverance of consciousness, Descartes thought he had discovered the one true foundation on which philosophy can stand. The *Cogito* was the philosophic bantling whose system had been purified of debatable matter, such as might subsequently prove soil for scepticism, by the lymph of the "Methodic Doubt." Here, therefore, was the criterion of truth, all that stood or fell with this axiom partook of its certainty, and partook of it in proportion to its inseparability from the act of consciousness. From the above criterion of truth Descartes deduces the theorem that the clearness of a conception is the test of its truth. This, however, is limited by the possibility that a being superior to myself might deceive me. Hence the necessity before proceeding farther of determining the question of the existence and attributes of such a being.

Now, no idea which obtains in the mind can represent more than the object from which it is formed or which causes it. Of some ideas, as for instance that of a doubting or thinking being, it is quite clear that I might have them, even if I alone existed; for I myself should be their prototype. "But there is one idea," proceeds Descartes, "which it would be impossible could arise within me in the latter case; to wit, the idea of an infinite Being. This I can neither draw from myself, since I am finite, nor can it come through an abstraction from anything finite without me." I can very well arrive by abstraction at the conception of a *negative infinite*, in other words, of an *indefinite*, but not at the positive conception of an infinite excluding all limitation whatever. I can think, for instance, of an endless space by abstracting from the limits of the known space. But this is infinite only in a particular sense, it is not absolutely infinite. Every conception of the merely negative infinite, the infinite of one kind only (*i.e.* the *indefinite*) presupposes that of the positive infinite. The latter idea it is not in my power to diminish by the abstraction or to increase by the addition of anything, and consequently, says Descartes, "nothing remains but to admit this idea as coeval with my creation, in other words, as co-extensive with the idea of myself."

The presence of the idea of the infinite within us demonstrates, according to Descartes, the existence of an infinite Being without us who is its original, and who has Himself implanted it in us. Even viewing the matter *à posteriori*, I should require a cause, though I existed from eternity, for without it I could not continue in existence. To be maintained in existence is to be continuously re-created. But the argument for the existence of God upon which Descartes most plumes himself is his celebrated "ontological" argument. The existence of God, according to this argument, must be drawn from his very conception itself; for inasmuch as the idea of a triangle contains that of three sides, so does the idea of the Infinite contain that of necessary existence, since contingent existence would imply dependence or limitation and therefore contradict the notion of infinity. Descartes distinguishes his ontological argument from the somewhat similar one of Anselm by the remark that it does not rest simply upon the mere significance of a word, upon the fact that we conceive God as existent—since all we think of, in so far as we think of it, is thought of as existing—but upon the *necessity* which attaches to the thought of existence in this particular case, and upon the fact that this thought is not a mere figment of the mind, but a necessary, because innate, idea.

The existence of God is the second position in the Cartesian construction. "Self" and "God" satisfactorily accounted for, the next proceeding is to establish the existence of the "World." Descartes having found as the ultimate postulate of his philosophy the clear and determinate conception of himself as a thinking being, and having proclaimed clearness of perception the test of truth, barring the possibility of deception from a superior being, next proceeded to determine the existence and the nature of this being. In the course of the investigation, the notion of an infinite being was shown to exclude all limitation and all imperfection of any kind whatever, in other words, to involve the notion of absolute perfection. But the deception is irreconcilable with *moral* perfection, and hence must be excluded from our conception of divinity. Yet were it the case that our perceptions which appear to represent an existent world did not really do so, we should be compelled to assume deception, *i.e.* moral imperfection, in our Infinite Author. The canon is therefore now established without reserve, that that of which we have a clear perception exists. To the objection that the above argument proves too much, since it precludes the possibility of human error, Descartes replies, that error does not consist merely in the imperfect apprehension of things *per se*, but in the individual's act of will by which that imperfect apprehension is accepted as true. In this connection he draws a distinction between the unsophisticated thought which instinctively accepts the dictates of common-sense without hesitation (*e.g.* the belief in external objects), and the thought which comes of reflection and which is voluntary.

Now that the validity of his canon of investigation has been settled, Descartes naturally proceeds more quickly in the construction of his system. He distinguishes between those conceptions which pre-suppose, *i.e.* are limitations of, other conceptions or ideas, and those which are independent, or which are conceived *per se*. The only ideas which are capable of being conceived *per se*, Descartes finds to be those of *extension* and *thought*. Each of these can be thought of without the assistance of the other or of any foreign idea whatsoever except that of infinity. These independent self-existent ideas, Descartes terms *attributa*, which he derives from the etymology *à natura tributa sunt*. The former class of ideas—those which are derivative, that is, are merely limitations of other ideas—he terms *modi*. Although *extension* and *thought* are the only *attributa* of things known to us, Descartes declares that in God, in whom of course there are necessarily no *modi*, inasmuch as these would imply limitation, "the attributes are many." This portion of Descartes' system is especially important in its bearing on Spinoza. In this respect also Descartes' definition of the independent subjects of the attributes, which he terms substances, is particularly noteworthy. A substance, says Descartes, is "that which requires nothing else to its being or conception;" in other words, it is an absolutely independent existence; for, as he expressly asserts, an incomplete substance is a contradiction. Still further remarkable is it that (in his *Principia*) he actually touches Spinozism in conceding that, according to the literal terms of his definition, there could only be one substance, namely, God. He gets over this somewhat inconsequently by extending the definition as regards the supposed created substances in which the attributes of extension and thought are assumed to inhere, namely *mind* and *matter*, by declaring that though not absolutely independent, inasmuch as they have their ground in the Supreme Being, yet they are relatively so, that is, as regards all other created things. The existence of *body* (*matter*) and *mind*, as substances, Descartes finds guaranteed by his conception of them as such, and *à fortiori*, by the trustworthiness of the Deity. Inasmuch as they are substances they mutually exclude each other. *Thought* is pure inwardness, having no analogy whatever with *extension*, which is pure outwardness. There can be no question of any community between them. This extreme dualism was the rock upon which Cartesianism split. It is true Descartes thereby separates himself from Spinoza, but he also logically separates himself from Leibnitz, although there are not wanting indications in his works of a tendency, at times, to Leibnitzianism.

The practical consequence of the dualistic character of Descartes' metaphysics is, that the two departments of physics and psychology are entirely severed from one another. Descartes always regarded his physics as the most important part of his work. Its problem was to formulate all that can be discovered in nature by reflection thereupon. In this, it is clear, abstraction must be made from the sensuous qualities of objects, for these sensuous qualities are no more than states or feelings of the perceiving mind, which have as much resemblance to that which causes the feeling as mere words have with the ideas of which they are the signs: "All the sensuous qualities of things lie in us, *i.e.* in the soul," Descartes repeatedly insists. Hence physical investigation demands that we abstract from all that does not pertain to the objects themselves, or to the modes by which they are related to us, as for instance time, number, &c. The only quality which, according to Descartes, inheres in bodies themselves is *extension* in its three dimensions of length, breadth, and thickness. Space and matter are coextensive, an empty space involving a contradiction. Descartes maintains *extension* as the sole quality of matter *per se*, not even excluding gravity. The result of this is that he was enabled to identify physics with mathematics, and to claim for his physical doctrine the certitude of geometry. In accordance with this view, he excludes all idea of purpose in nature from his investigations. He, of course, did not deny divine purpose in the world, but declared speculation with regard to it impious. All which follows from the conception of *extension*, and nothing but this, is to be affirmed respecting this corporeal world. Hence there are neither atoms nor limits in the world. The capacity of division, of figure, and of motion, is comprised in the conception of *extension*. To their realisation these capacities require a cause outside themselves, which cause is God. The first principle of realisation is motion; the variety of bodies consists in nothing but the different motions of themselves or their parts. A curious anticipation of modern thought is seen in Descartes' principle of the constancy of the sum of matter and motion in the universe.

In his *Monde*, a work containing his theories on physical science proper, he starts with the hypothesis of a new world to be created on mechanical and mathematical principles alone. In this he furnishes many interesting anticipations of modern science, in addition, as might be expected, to many untenable hypotheses, such, for instance, as the celebrated "theory of vortices," and some of his theories respecting physiology, though in this department he also achieved some valuable results. Animal bodies, including the human, he regarded, in accordance with his fundamental physical principles, as purely automatic. It is the psychical principle, or soul, in man, which alone distinguishes him from the lower animals.

This leads us to the Cartesian Psychology, or doctrine of the soul. As the attribute of body is *extension*, so the attribute of soul is *thought*; just as the material substance, inasmuch as extension is its attribute, can neither exist nor be conceived without extension; so the mental substance whose attribute is thought, can neither be conceived nor exist apart from thought. The soul is always conscious—always thinks—just as light always illumines, as heat always warms, &c. Even the babe in the womb is conscious. There is no such thing as dreamless sleep; it is merely memory failing us, which leads us to think this possible, and memory, Descartes is careful to remind the reader, is a purely bodily state.

Descartes divides ideas as concerns their clearness into adequate and inadequate, or complete and incomplete; as concerns their origin, into self-made ideas (*fictæ*), into borrowed ideas (*adventitiæ*), and inborn ideas (*innatæ*). The will is always dependent on consciousness, that is, on an act of perception; but there may be acts of perception apart from any act of will. Error consists in the affirmation by the will as true of an inadequate perception or idea. Hence, in God, in whom is no inadequate idea, error is impossible. In the latter case truth consists in his affirmation of it, in the fact that he wills such and such to be true. In the same way goodness is purely determined by the Divine will. Truth and goodness are, therefore, with Descartes, dependent in the last resort solely on the arbitrary fiat of a supreme being. Descartes, of course, maintains the freedom of the human will, but at the same time regards indeterminateness as the lowest stage of willing. He who possessed clear and distinct ideas of the good and the true, would never hesitate in choosing it, and hence would not be indifferent. The highest freedom and the highest perfection obtains, when error has become impossible through knowledge. The Sokratic doctrine thus once more appears in the history of ethical speculation.

When Descartes comes to speak of Anthropology, that is, of man, as a personality in which *thought* and *extension* appear in union, his dualism naturally gives him some trouble. The union he declares to constitute only a *composition*, which is purely empirical, resting upon a supernatural fact, that is a special act of the Divine will. Although the soul is in union with the whole body, this union is effected immediately by means of a specific organ, to wit, the *pineal gland*, which according to Descartes, is the source of the 'animal spirits,' and for this and sundry other fanciful reasons the most suitable seat for it. On the above theory, Descartes proceeds to explain the effects of the emotions and passions. The contest of the mind with the appetites is not one between a higher and a lower soul, but between the soul and the so-called 'nervous fluids' or 'animal spirits.' The practical side of Descartes' ethics falls to be dealt with in this connection. The most important point, however, in his anthropological doctrine, for the subsequent history of the Cartesian school, is the virtual assumption of a perpetual miracle in the union of body and soul.

In the foregoing pages we have endeavoured to give a clear general view of the Cartesian system as it left the hands of its founder. Its strength and its weakness will appear in the course of the succeeding historic development. Criticism is unnecessary of a doctrine which the average educated reader will now-a-days readily see is fatally vulnerable in many of its cardinal principles. The sceptical attitude assumed at starting gives way, after the first stage in the construction has been reached, to so much obvious sophistry even in essentials, that whether they be right or wrong in fact, we can hardly wonder at the attitude of those critics who have regarded it as a "blind," consciously put forward to guard certain vulnerable points in the coming construction which had been in reality assumed from the first. *Facilis ascensus cœli*, to the aspiring philosopher. But be this as it may, Descartes' position, as the founder of modern philosophy, is not to be gainsaid. Of a rather feeble moral nature, he lived in a continual dread of unpleasant notice being taken of him by the Church; his obsequiousness in this respect being remarked even in an age of theological subservience. This makes it difficult in estimating Descartes and his work, to determine in some cases whether a particular doctrine is to be attributed to mental servility or real conviction. But the historian of philosophy must console himself with the maxim *chacun a les défauts de ses qualités.*

Cartesianism, though in the end successful all along the

line, did not pass without encountering a brisk fire of adverse criticism. Descartes himself formally replied to the more important objections raised against his system in a separate work. Amongst the critics with whom he deals were Hobbes and Locke; for in addition to objections from the side of Scholasticism, and the resuscitated Greek philosophy of the Renaissance, Descartes had to encounter the contemporary British movement. The new system made its way notwithstanding. The university of Utrecht, in Holland, was the first official home of Cartesianism. But in Leyden we find the most brilliant series of teachers, foremost among whom is Geulincx. The other Dutch universities soon caught the infection, and Holland, which had long been the home of Descartes himself, became the principal seed-ground of his philosophy. Clerical opposition, more or less successful, there was, of course, but this in the long run rather helped than hindered its germination. In theology, in medicine, in physical science, Cartesianiam became the order of the day throughout Western Europe, Great Britain excepted. The philosophy of Descartes was not without its influence on the decadence in the belief in magic, witchcraft, and the "occult sciences," which took place so rapidly among the educated towards the close of the century. Belthasar Bekker published in 1691 his celebrated work 'The Enchanted World,' in which he attacked these superstitions on Cartesian grounds. This treatise, originally written in Dutch, had not been published long before it was translated into all the more important European languages.

The celebrated Port-Royal Logic (*L'art de penser*) was perhaps the principal product of Cartesianism in the land of its founder's birth, upon the culture of which it made a deep impression.

MALEBRANCHE.

The first successor of Descartes who can be regarded as having at all developed the master's doctrines was the French ecclesiastic, Nicholas Malebranche, born at Paris in 1638. His *Recherche de la vérité*, first published in 1674, passing through six editions during the lifetime of its author. It was followed by a large number of treatises, metaphysical, theological, and ethical, up to the time of the death of Malebranche, in 1715.

The main problem for Malebranche was to bridge over the gulf between the two opposed substances of Descartes' *Thought* and *Extension;* to define their relation alike to the finite individual and their infinite ground. Malebranche was not satisfied with the hesitating and superficial manner in which Descartes had attempted to explain away the difficulties which arose on this head. The arbitrary act of the Divine will by which perception was produced was too clumsy an hypothesis for him. The celebrated saying of Malebranche, that he saw "all things in God," of itself indicates the link between the dualism of Descartes and the Pantheism of Spinoza. To the former the relation of the two subordinate substances alike to each other and to the one infinite substance was indefinite and arbitrary. Malebranche sought to give that relation a systematic basis. Starting from the conception of the Infinite Being, which Descartes had formulated, he brought *Thought* and *Extension*, and through them *Individuation*, nearer this being, deduced them more directly from this being than Descartes had dared to do. Unlike Descartes, he does not separate the idea or notion, from the existence, of the infinite. "We conceive of the infinite being," says Malebranche, "by the very fact of our conceiving of being without thinking whether it be finite or not; but that we may think of a finite being we are compelled to sever or deduct something from the general idea of being, which we must therefore possess beforehand; thus, the mind apprehends nothing whatever except in and through the idea it possesses of the infinite; so far is it from the truth that this idea is formed by the confused mass of our notions of particular things, as the philosophers maintain, that on the other hand, all these particular notions participate in the general idea of the infinite, in the same way that all creatures imperfectly participate in the Divine being, whose existence itself cannot be derived from them." (*Recherche III., Part II., Chap.* 6). The external world is unintelligible in itself, and only becomes intelligible by our perceiving it in and through the being who contains it in an intelligible manner. "Hence," says Malebranche, "unless in some sense we saw God, we should see nothing else." In short, our consciousness, whether of ourselves or of external objects, is nothing more nor less than a limited portion of the divine consciousness. From this doctrine of Malebranche of all "things in God" to the *unica substantia* of Spinoza was scarcely a step. The only *modus vivendi* between *Thought* and *Extension*, mind and body, was found in the divine essence or substance; but Malebranche not merely shrank from the obvious conclusion to which all his reasoning points, that of identifying them with the substance, but, strange to say (that is, strange were it not so common a phenomenon in history), denounces in scurrilous language the man who was at once honest and logical enough to draw this conclusion.

SPINOZA.

BARUCH DE SPINOZA, born Nov. 24, 1632, at Amsterdam, belonged to a well-to-do Jewish family of Portuguese origin settled in Holland. He received a thorough education in the hands of the Rabbis of his native town in all that pertained to Jewish learning as then understood, besides studying Latin and natural science, under other teachers. Previous reading of the semi-rationalising Jewish philosophers of the Middle Ages, notably Maimonides, had already given Spinoza a speculative groundwork when he took up the study of the works of Descartes. Spinoza occupies a unique position at this time. His heterodoxy had already caused his expulsion from the synagogue, and he thus found himself unpledged to any set of traditional dogmas. To this fact we may attribute the perfect freedom and honesty displayed in his writings. The fawning of Descartes to Christian doctrines naturally disgusted the man who had severed himself from family connections, social intercourse, and even risked life itself for his convictions. But, nevertheless, the system of Spinoza is the direct and logical outcome of the principles enunciated by Descartes. After a generally quiet and uneventful life, occupied either in the pursuance of his livelihood as a glass-lens polisher, or in study and writing, Spinoza died at the comparatively early age of forty-five, in the year 1677. The respect with which he was regarded by all who knew him is illustrated in the well-known story of his landlady, who, aware that he belonged to no recognised religious persuasion, asked his opinion as to whether she was justified in going to Church and otherwise practising the rites of the orthodox Calvinistic faith. He had comparatively but few friends, but among these several correspondents, notably Oldenburg, one of the founders of the English Royal Society.

SPINOZA'S DOCTRINES.

With Spinoza the method of philosophy is identical with that of mathematics. In his Ethics he places Definitions, Axioms, and Postulates, at the head of every book. The Geometrical method appeared to him as the most adequate for the expression of "clear and distinct" ideas, and as the one which most effectually excluded the possibility of the entrance into philosophy of personal or other bias—it was the only purely disinterested method.

Hegel observes, that Spinoza, the Jew, first introduced into European thought the conception of the absolute unity in which finite and infinite are merged. It would be perhaps more correct to say that he was the first to give distinct expression to this monistic point of view, which is implicitly present in many previous thinkers.

Spinoza distinguishes two kinds of errors to which the mind is subject, those of *abstraction* and those of *imagination*. These two errors he finds invariably united in *opinion*. An abstraction means any imperfect conception in which the elements of a whole are separately treated as wholes. Clear and distinct thought must discern the necessary relation of any finite thing or notion to the whole system of things or notions. This is expressed in Spinozistic language by what is termed the distinction between mere modes of substance and substance itself. The progress of knowledge necessarily limits this abstracting tendency. Imagination comes to the aid of abstraction in enabling the mind to picture the thing without its surroundings, or in other words, apart from the conditions necessary to its real existence. Such conceptions as that of a talking animal, a horse with a man's head, an extended figure without weight or resistance, are common and obvious instances of this combined power of abstraction and imagination. Teleological explanations of the world have their root entirely in the foregoing tendency of the mind. "All such opinions," says Spinoza, "spring from the notion, commonly entertained, that all things in nature act for the same reason as men themselves act, with an end in view." Human will and action are abstracted from the only whole of which they can form a part, namely the human being, and transferred by the imagination to external nature, and even the Absolute itself. The consequence of this is exhibited in religion, in the anthropomorphic conception of God as having "made all things for man, and man that he might worship Him." In the Appendix to the first book of the *Ethics*, Spinoza demolishes this view with his usual clearness and vigour.

In philosophy Spinoza demands the elimination of all time-relations, in other words, that the philosopher should be understood as viewing the world *sub specie æternitatis*. By this, of course, he meant that the province of metaphysic is to expound the world in its logical, rather than its temporal sequence. Hence, the starting-point of his system is not any first cause of all things in the ordinary sense of the word, but that which all things logically presuppose; that by means of which all other things are conceived, but which is in itself independent and ultimate. In this great advance is made on Descartes, whose God was little more than the first cause of the world. This unconditioned ground, the *one substance* of Spinoza, contains within it the sum-total of all reality. Although he did homage to current prejudices by employing the word *God* for his conception, it is only fair to remember that he distinctly disclaims using the word in any current sense.

Erdmann well observes that those who connect the usual religious significance with the word *God*, had better, in reading Spinoza, substitute for it the word *Nature*. It is constantly insisted upon that all things proceed from the One Substance by the same necessity as that by which it exists, since they form an essential part of its existence. Of the infinite attributes of the infinite, eternal, and all-comprehending substance, two only concern us, *i.e.* Thought and Extension. As with Descartes, they are mutually opposed in every respect, in all save the one fact of their common ground. At last the Cartesian problem is solved in the only way possible on Cartesian principles. Thought and Extension, Mind and Body, assume for the first time a position of mutual equality; while they at the same time lose the last shred of their independence of the Infinite. The real world is simply made up of *modes* of these two *attributes*. By *mode*, Spinoza understands that which exists through something else, or which is the determination of something else. There are eternal *modes*, by which is probably meant the necessary determinations of things termed by us laws of nature, and individual or finite things. As, however, the place of individuals in Spinoza's system is not unobscure, we give some of his utterances on this head in his own words. In Proposition XXIII. of Part I. of the *Ethics*, we read, "*Every mode, which exists both necessarily and as infinite must necessarily follow either from the absolute nature of some attribute of God or from an attribute modified by a modification which exists necessarily and as infinite.* Proof. A mode exists in something else through which it must be conceived (Def. v.), that is (Prop. XV.), it exists solely in God, and solely through God can be conceived. If, therefore, a mode is conceived as necessarily existing, and infinite, it must necessarily be inferred or perceived through some attribute of God, in so far as such attribute is conceived as expressing the infinity and necessity of existence, in other words (Def. viii.), eternally; that is, in so far as it is considered absolutely." "A mode therefore which necessarily exists as infinite must follow from the absolute nature of some attribute of God, either immediately (Prop. XXI.), or through the means of some modification which follows from the absolute nature of the said attribute; that is (by Prop. XXII.) which exists necessarily and as infinite (Prop. XXIV.). *The essence of things produced by God does not involve existence.* Proof. This proposition is evident from Def. i. For that of which the nature considered in itself involves existence is self-caused, and exists by the sole necessity of its own nature. *Corollary.* Hence, it follows that God is not only the cause of things coming into existence, but also of their continuing in existence, that is, in scholastic phraseology, God is cause of the being of things (*Essendi rerum*). For whether things exist or do not exist, whenever we contemplate their essence, we see that it involves neither existence nor duration; consequently it cannot be the cause of either the one or the other. God must be the sole cause, in as much as to Him alone does existence appertain. (Prop. XIV. Corollary 1.) Q.E.D. (Prop. XXV.) *God is the efficient cause not only of the existence of things but also of their essence.* Proof. If this be denied, then God is not the cause of the essence of things; and therefore, the essence of things can (by Ax. IV.) be conceived without God. This by Prop. XV. is absurd. Therefore God is the cause of the essence of things. Q.E.D. *Note.* This proposition follows more clearly from Prop. XVI. for it is evident thereby, that given the Divine nature, the essence of things must be inferred from it no less than their existence—in a word, God must be called the cause of all things in the same sense as he is called the cause of Himself. This will be made still clearer by the following corollary. *Corollary.* Individual things are nothing but modifications of the attributes of God, or modes by which the attributes of God are expressed in a fixed and definite manner."*

It will be sufficiently evident to the reader that Spinoza has only carried to its consistent issue the Cartesian principle which Malebranche had indeed enunciated, but without admitting its full bearing, namely, that unless we knew the Infinite, or God, we could know nothing else, inasmuch as the human mind is simply a modification of the Divine Substance. The idea of this absolute unity is involved in the idea of every particular thing, and the only reason ordinary men are unable to discover it is because their ideas are confused, in short, because, owing to the illusions of sense and imagination, they are unable to arrive at a clear and distinct idea of anything.

* Now and always I quote from the excellent translation of Spinoza's works by Mr. Elwes, published in 'Bohn's Philosophical Library.'

Spinoza insists on the parallellism between the world-order in *Thought* and the world-order in *Extension.* "*The order and connection of ideas,*" he says (Ethics, Prop. VII.), "*is the same as the order and connection of things.*" This is as much as to say the One Substance may be viewed either as thinking or as extended. "Whatsoever follows from the infinite nature of God in the world of extension (*formaliter*), follows without exception in the same order and connection from the idea of God in the world of thought (*objective*)." And again: "Substance thinking and substance extended are one and the same substance, comprehended now through one attribute and now through the other." "In the same way the mode of extension and the idea of that mode are one and the same thing, though expressed in two ways. For instance, a circle existing in nature and the idea of a circle existing, which is also in God, are one and the same thing displayed through different attributes. Thus whether we consider nature under the attribute of extension, or under the attribute of thought, or under any other attribute, we shall find the same order, and one and the same chain of causes—that is, the same things following in either case." "I said that God is the cause of an idea—for instance, of the idea of circle—in so far as He is a thinking thing, and of a circle in so far as He is an extended thing, simply because the actual being of the idea of a circle can only be perceived as a proximate cause through another mode of thinking, and that again, through another, and so on to infinity; so that so long as we consider things as modes of thinking, we must explain the order of the whole of nature, or the whole chain of causes, through the attribute of thought only. And in so far as we consider things as modes of extension, we must explain the order of the whole of nature through the attribute of extension only; and so on in the case of other attributes. Wherefore of things as they are in themselves, God is really the cause, inasmuch as He consists of infinite attributes. I cannot for the present explain my meaning more clearly."

The impressions of the senses and the mind, namely, that which in the world of thought corresponds to the particular or finite modifications of extension, are termed *affectiones*. There has been much discussion among students of Spinoza as to the relation of the attributes to the individual mind. In his definition of attributes, Spinoza says (I. Def. iv.): "By *attribute* I mean that which the intellect perceives as constituting the essence of substance." This has been by some interpreted in the sense of Psychological Idealism, as implying that the attributes are simply the marks by which the One Substance is individualised in the finite mind, or by which it becomes aware of itself. According to this view, the attributes are not essential distinctions in the substance itself, but only indicate its nature to the reflecting intellect, that is, they are the form under which the latter apprehends it. On the other hand, there are Spinozists who strenuously deny this phenomenal acceptation of the doctrine, and maintain that the attributes represent a noumenal fact. For the first of these views, it may be alleged that Spinoza in his definition (Def. iv.) when he refers to the perceiving intellect, seems to make an intentional deviation from Descartes, who speaks of the attribute simply as constituting the essence of the substance. The second view, on the other hand, is supported by the assertion of the infinity of attributes. We suspect that the point was one upon which Spinoza was not very clear himself; also that here, as elsewhere in the Cartesian school, the effects of the reaction against scholasticism which was manifested in the neglect of Aristotelian distinctions, is responsible for much ambiguity, and possibly some confusion of thought.

Extension is spoken of by Spinoza as infinite, no less than Thought; but the relation of the unconditioned to the conditioned form of these attributes is imperfectly indicated. All limitation must be abstracted from the attributes conceived as *natura naturans*, and this applies as much to thought as to extension; hence, God is no more to be conceived as will, which is only a particular limitation of thought, than He is to be conceived as body, which is only a particular limitation of extension. Spinoza distinctly repudiates (Ethics, Part II. Prop. XLIII.) any such thing as an unconscious idea; he carefully warns us against understanding by idea a mere prototype which can never enter into consciousness, and demands that we should regard it as a conscious act of thought. Inasmuch as the One Substance is the foundation of all being, it is the foundation of corporeal no less than of mental processes. Every such process is conditioned by another such, and that by another, and so on to infinity. (See quotation, p. 162, *supra.*) Of course this occurs only in the same attribute, for we have already seen that there is no passing over from the one to the other; no more from the mental to the corporeal, than from the corporeal to the mental. By Spinoza's rigid division it is needless to say all idealist explanations in physics, no less than all materialist explanations in psychology, are excluded.

Turning now to *natura naturata*, we find the principles of the corporeal world were, to Spinoza, rest and motion. All modifications of body he attributes to the velocity and direction of motion in its parts. The so-called union of body and soul only means that the same thing is viewed now under one attribute, now under another. The mind is nothing more than the idea of the body, but inasmuch as an idea is only a product of thought-activity, the *idea corporis* is a conscious act of the mind with which is bound up the reflected knowledge of this act, that is, the idea of this idea, which is nothing other than the *idea mentis.* Just as the modification of extension, or body, of which the real or empirical world consists, is brought about by differences of rest and motion—in short, as an individual body is a determinate system of the modifications of body or extension—so an individual mind is a determinate system of the modifications of thought, *i.e.* of ideas. The world of eternal modes, or *natura naturata*, roughly corresponds to the world of Ideas in Platonic systems. The *natura naturata* is, of course, also to be conceived under the dual attribute. It consists of *motion and rest*, and what Spinoza terms the *intellectus infinitus.*. Just as *motion and rest* contains the possibility of the actual corporeal world in its entirety, so the *intellectus infinitus* is the complex of all ideas and minds, *i.e.* the possibility of the actual ideal world in its entirety. Just as every individual body is conditioned by *motion and rest*, so is every individual mind conditioned by the *intellectus infinitus*.*

Inasmuch as Spinoza regards man merely as a portion of nature, his Anthropology and Ethics are one. Man's bodily state is conditioned by the bodies which surround him, his *milieu*, as it might now be expressed. He is at once active and passive. His activity is continually obstructed and affected by his surroundings, and his whole career is a continuous striving to realise himself, or, which is the same thing, to *assert* his own being, against this obstruction. The consciousness of striving is primarily appetite or desire, which leads, according as the struggle fails or succeeds in any particular instance, to joy and sorrow; hope and fear being further modifications of these fundamental emotions (*passiones*). With the passions are directly connected the conceptions of good and evil, which can have no meaning in any other than a human relation. The proposition, "this is good for me," is perfectly justified, but not so the proposition, "this is good" (absolutely). The presence, with the *emotion* of joy or sorrow, of the *idea* of the object causing it, produces love or hatred.

The result of Spinoza's Ethics proper (contained in the third part of the treatise under that name, the first two parts being purely metaphysical), which, as we before said, is identical with his Anthropology, is in many points similar to that of his contemporary, Helvetius. He is a rigid necessarian, and pure disinterestedness he regards as an illusion, since man acts according to the dictates of his nature, the stimulus to action in men being only possible to be mortified or destroyed by a stronger stimulus. This of course forms the foundation for Spinoza's political theory. Spinoza was the first consistent advocate of universal toleration, although he does not recognise formally the "rights of man" as such. Like most political theorists of the seventeenth century, all his hypotheses were based on the as-

* Between the individual mind, with its manifold of reality, and the pure undetermined attribute of *thought*, stands the determination of this attribute as Infinite Intellect, *i.e.* as comprehending under its eternal modes the infinite complexity of the real world.

sumption of the incurable stupidity of the many; but he at the same time regards that state as most secure in which there is the greatest amount of personal liberty. The great truth which the present century has brought to light of the dependence of the political and other forms of society upon its economical conditions had not then dawned, any more than the truth that the social organism obeys certain definite laws of development just as does the animal organism.

Apart from this, however, perhaps what strikes one most in reading Spinoza is the modernness of his style and standpoint as compared with other seventeenth-century thinkers. There are passages in the "Tractatus Theologico-politicus," as well as in the "Ethics," which might have been written by a modern scientist. As an instance of Spinoza's capacity for scientific exposition, we quote a passage from a remarkable letter of his to Oldenburg. He is endeavouring to explain to Oldenburg the principle that every part of nature agrees with the whole, and is associated with all other parts: "Let us imagine, with your permission, a little worm, living in the blood, able to distinguish by sight the particles of blood, lymph, &c., and to reflect on the manner in which each particle, on meeting with another particle, either is repulsed or communicates a portion of its own motion. This little worm would live in the blood, in the same way as we live in a part of the universe, and would consider each drop of blood, not as a part, but as a whole. He would be unable to determine how all the parts are modified by the general nature of blood, and are compelled by it to adapt themselves, so as to stand in a fixed relation to one another. For, if we imagine that there are no causes external to the blood, which could communicate fresh movements to it, nor any space beyond the blood, nor any bodies whereto the particles of blood could communicate their motion, it is certain that the blood would always remain in the same state, and its particles would undergo no modifications, save those which may be conceived as arising from the relations of motion existing between the lymph, the chyle, &c. The blood would then always have to be considered as a whole, not a part. But, as there exist, as a matter of fact, very many causes, which modify, in a given manner, the nature of the blood, and are, in turn, modified thereby, it follows that other motions and other relations arise in the blood, springing not from the mutual relations of its parts only, but from the mutual relations between the blood as a whole and external causes. Thus the blood comes to be regarded as a part, not as a whole. So much for the whole and the part."

In many points Spinoza anticipates Kant, but his fundamental conception is still abstract. The *Unica Substantia* is, after all, at bottom, the Being-in-general of the Cartesians and of Malebranche. His system is an ontology, and an ontology, too, in which all traces of "theory of knowledge," as such, are absent.

Spinozism found an immediate success in Holland. Numerous works appeared, some containing views obviously drawn from the Ethics, others attacking those views. About the close of the seventeenth century, it appears to have gained some ground in France.

Spinoza's is the only pre-Kantian system which has been revived in modern times. In fact, the interest in Spinoza dates mostly from Goethe and Schleiermacher. The works which have been published during the last half-century, dealing with the Dutch thinker, would fill a library. There are not wanting, at the present day, men of eminence who declare that in him is contained the fulness of modern science manifested. With Spinoza closes the main line of Cartesian development. We now proceed to consider a subsidiary branch springing from the same stem.

Among recent English works treating of Spinoza and his philosophy may be mentioned, Willis's 'Spinoza, his Life, Letters and Ethics,' Frederick Pollock's 'Life and Works of Spinoza,' Martineau's 'Spinoza,' &c., &c. The German works on the subject are numerous and well-known.

LEIBNITZ.

Gottfried Wilhelm Leibnitz was born, 1646, at Leipsic, and was educated in the university of that town. An omnivorous reader, he early attained considerable acquaintance with the history of philosophy. In Jena, where he subsequently studied, he read Hobbes and Locke, in addition to Kepler, Galilei, and other scientific writers. His journey to Paris, though it failed in its immediate purpose of inducing Louis XIV. to undertake an Egyptian expedition, had as its result the mathematical education of Leibnitz. It was in Paris, in 1676, that he discovered the differential calculus. Here, also, he first began seriously to study Descartes and Spinoza. In 1684, Leibnitz removed to Berlin, and shortly after undertook a lengthened archæological expedition to Italy. On his return to Berlin, he became president of the newly constituted Prussian Academy, as well as the occupant of a diplomatic post. With the death of the Queen of Prussia in 1711, his connection with Berlin ceased. He died in Vienna, in 1716, loaded with honours. The latter part of his life is said to have been embittered by his quarrels with the Newtonians.

LEIBNITZ'S DOCTRINES.

In philosophy Leibnitz stands in one sense at the opposite pole to Spinoza. He is chief representative of what is commonly known as Pluralism in metaphysic, *i.e.* he regards individuation as an ultimate and irreducible fact. The result of Leibnitz's scientific studies had led him early to accept the atomistic theory of the ultimate constitution of matter. This atomism he carried into the sphere of metaphysic. To Leibnitz, substance was infinitely many. The infinitely numerous eternal, and simple substances, unities, or forces, as they may perhaps with equal right be termed, Leibnitz designates *monads*, a word originally employed by Bruno. The *monads* being simple, could only come into being by creation, or cease from being by annihilation, and besides them nothing exists. Although destitute of parts, extension, figure, or divisibility, they must, nevertheless, have qualities, "otherwise," says Leibnitz, "they would not even be entities; and if simple substances did not differ in their qualities, there would be no means by which we could become aware of the changes of things, since all that is in compound bodies is derived from simple ingredients; and *monads*, being without qualities, would be indistinguishable one from another, seeing also that they did not differ in quantity." Every *monad* must differ from every other, for Leibnitz postulates the axiom that "there are never two beings in nature perfectly alike, and in which it is impossible to find an internal difference, or one founded on intrinsic determination."

But the metaphysical monads of Leibnitz differ from the physical atoms of Demokritos, in that they are determined by an internal principle of change, and are uninfluenced by anything external to themselves. "But besides the principle of change," proceeds Leibnitz, "there must also be a detail of changes, embracing, so to speak, the specification and the variety of simple substances. This detail must involve multitude in unity or in simplicity, for as all natural changes proceed by degrees, something changes and something remains, and consequently, there must be in the simple substance a plurality of affections or relations, although there are no parts." (*Monadologie*, 12, 13.) The section which follows is interesting as characteristic of Leibnitz's mode of thought, and as showing the first distinct enunciation of a doctrine which has played a not unimportant part in subsequent speculation—that of the unconscious perception or idea. "This shifting state, which involves and represents multitude in unity, or in the simple substance, is nothing else than what we call perception, which must be carefully distinguished from *apperception*, or consciousness, as will appear in the sequel. Here it is that the Cartesians have specially failed, making no account of those perceptions of which we are not conscious. It is this that has led them to suppose that spirits are the only monads, and that there are no souls of brutes or other Entelechies. It is owing to this that they have vulgarly confounded protracted torpor with actual death, and have fallen in with the scholastic prejudice, which postulates souls entirely separate. Hence, also, ill-affected minds have been confirmed in the opinion that the soul is mortal."

Leibnitz, of course, strenuously opposes all mechanical explanations of perception. "If we imagine a machine so constructed," he says, "as to produce thought, sensation, perception, we may conceive it magnified —the same proportions being preserved—to such an extent that one might enter it like a mill. This being supposed, we should find in it, on each inspection, only pieces which impel each other, but nothing which can explain perception. It is in the simple substance, therefore—not in the compound, or in machinery—that we must look for that phenomenon; and in the simple substance we find nothing else—nothing, that is, but perceptions and their changes. Therein also, and therein only, consist all the internal acts of simple substances." Leibnitz recognises a progression or hierarchy among the monads, from the simple monad which is purely unconscious or confused, to the monad which has attained to self-consciousness or clearness. The term *soul* he would reserve for the latter. When we are in a profound and dreamless sleep, or in a swoon, "the soul does not differ sensibly from the simple monad; but since this state is not permanent, and since the soul delivers herself from it, she is something more." In much of this we see Leibnitz as a true successor of Descartes; the Cartesian distinction between confused and clear perception being made noumenal. The impossibility of the entire absence of perception in the thinking subject here receives a new application, in so far as perception is formally distinguished from consciousness. If there were no distinction in our perceptions, we should continue for ever in a state of stupor: "and this," adds Leibnitz, "is the condition of the naked monad." "Where there is a great number of minute perceptions, but where nothing is distinct, one is stunned, as when we turn round and round in continual succession in the same direction, whence arises a vertigo which may cause us to faint, and which prevents us from distinguishing anything."

Memory, according to Leibnitz, gives to the soul a consecutive action, but must be distinguished from reason. Leibnitz is prepared to recognise a large measure of truth in the English Empiricist school. Memory, or the consecutiveness of perceptions, is shared in common by men and animals. It is the scientific reason which especially distinguishes man. The distinction between empirical knowledge derived from the former source, and that derived from the latter, is illustrated by the following familiar instance: when we expect the sun to rise to-morrow, we judge so empirically, because it has always done so hitherto; but the astronomer makes the same judgment by an act of reason. In the same way the difference between a quack and a physician consists in the fact that the one has only practice, or knowledge picked up in a casual way to rely upon, while the other derives his knowledge from scientific theory. The celebrated proposition directed by Leibnitz against Locke, "nihil est in intellectu quod non prius in sensu fuerit, *nisi ipse intellectus*," expresses in a sentence this cardinal distinction between *empirical* and *necessary* truth.

The God of Leibnitz is the supreme monad or primitive unity, the simple original substance of which all the created or derived monads are the products, and which are generated, "so to speak, by continual fulgurations of the divinity from moment to moment, bounded by the receptations of the creature of whose existence limitation is an essential condition." Like the God of the schoolman, he is *actus purus*, to which the created monads approach in varying degrees, "according to the measure of their perfection." The created monads can only act upon one another through the medium of the divine monad. It is only through it that one can be dependent upon the other. Leibnitz bases his optimism on the principle of *sufficient reason*. The principle of *sufficient reason* declares that no fact can be "real, or existent, no statement true, unless there be a sufficient reason why it is thus, and not otherwise, although these reasons very often cannot be known to us." This principle leads us to infer that since out of the infinite number of possible worlds, this one has been created by the Divine mind, it must contain within it the greatest possible measure of perfection. "And this connection, or this accommodation of all created things to each, and of each to all, implies in each simple substance relations which express all the rest. Each, accordingly, is a living and perpetual mirror of the universe. And as the same city viewed from different sides appears quite different, and is perspectively multiplied, so, in the infinite multitude of simple substances, there are given, as it were, so many different worlds which yet are only perspectives of a single one, according to the different points of view of each monad. And this is the way to obtain the greatest possible variety with the greatest possible order: that is to say, the way to obtain the greatest possible perfection." Every monad contains the infinity of being in itself. It would lose nothing if all other monads were destroyed, nor gain anything if they could act upon it. The monad is a self-sufficient microcosm, and an omniscient eye might see in its present state the whole past and future of the universe. "But each soul can read in itself only that which is distinctly represented in it. It cannot unfold its laws at once, for they reach into the infinite." Every organic body is a species of "divine machine," surpassing all human mechanisms by the infinite complexity of its relations. Each portion of matter expresses the universe; that is, each portion of matter has its special formation energy or soul. "Every particle of matter," say Leibnitz, "may be conceived as a garden full of plants, or as a pond full of fishes. But each branch of each plant, each member of each animal, each drop of their humours, is in its turn another such garden or pond.' Death, chaos, and barrenness, exist only in appearance, owing to the imperfection of our point of view. It must not be supposed, however, that each entelechy, force, or soul, has a special portion of matter for ever united with it; for all bodies are in a perpetual flux, like rivers, their particles for ever coming and going. "That which we call generation is development and accretion, and that which we call death is envelopment and diminution." There is no destruction either of the soul or the body, strictly speaking. They each follow their proper laws, and coincide by virtue of the "pre-established harmony," which exists between all substances as representations of one and the same universe. Leibnitz maintains that had Descartes known the laws of motion, he would have been led to discover this principle of the "pre-established harmony," by which, to quote his words, "bodies act as if there were no souls, and souls act as if there were no bodies; and yet both act as if the one influenced the other."

The foregoing exposition we have taken almost verbatim from the summary of his system, written by Leibnitz in 1714, for Prince Eugene of Savoy, and published after his death as the "Monadology." The inconsistency and mutual incompatibility of several of the main positions taken up are apparent at a glance. Leibnitz is emphatic in declaring that the monads have "no windows," while at the same time postulating a direct relation between them and the supreme monad, and an indirect relation with one another. It is difficult to see, on Leibnitzian principles, how psychological idealism is to be avoided. The self-centred microcosm *ex hypothesi* knows only its own universe. In this it is absolutely shut up. How then has it any right to pronounce on the absolute nature of things outside this universe? It may be quite true that other self-centred monads may exist as the centres of different worlds, but of them it cannot possibly know anything. Those who postulate a plurality of ultimate world-principles can never logically answer the questions raised by "theory of knowledge." Leibnitz is involved in additional difficulties by his theism, and above all, by his attempts to render his system compatible with theological orthodoxy. A hierarchy of *self-centered* and *essentially independent* beings, extending from the lowest sentiency to the highest consciousness, may be a pretty and symmetrical conception, but will certainly not bear the test of criticism, as an explanation of the universe.

But Leibnitz, who after all was more of a litterateur than a philosopher, gives us, nevertheless, many acute suggestions and able pieces of analysis in his writings. His individualist Pluralism he was fond of placing in opposition to Spinoza's Monism, when charged with the latter by thinkers too logical to conceive the possibility of a serious thinker treating individuation as an ultimate metaphysical fact.

Leibnitz, of course, admits freedom of the will, but his freedom is neither absolute indifference, nor is it determination without motive. It is a free choice of one line of conduct rather than another from among two or more that are, physically speaking, equally possible. God alone is absolutely free. Human freedom merely means that the determination of the will is contingent upon the character. In this sense, "the understanding may determine the will according to the prevalence of perceptions and reasons of one kind which, since it is certain and infallible, may incline without necessitating it" (*Nouveaux Essais*, XXI.). In a certain sense, a ball might be said to be free after it has been struck by a racquet, in so far as its movement is not hindered. In another sense, the motion of the ball is contingent, in other words, not free.

Leibnitz warns the student against the misuse of the Cartesian principle of "clearness and distinctness" in idea, as a test of truth. Very often that appears to us clear and distinct, which is really dark and confused. The test of clearness and distinctness is only applicable when it is the result of exact observation and faultless deduction. As we have seen, in one sense nothing is clear and distinct; for example, our perception of matter is in its nature confused: matter which is composed of an infinity of unextended substances, to our perception appears as a continuously extended whole.

Leibnitzianism is in every sense the logical antithesis of Spinozism. To Spinoza there existed naught but the one substance and its modes; to Leibnitz existence comprised an infinity of monads and their perceptions. To Spinoza, extension is an ultimate fact, co-relative with thought; to Leibnitz it is an illusion due to confused apprehension. To Spinoza, all teleological explanations are to be rigidly excluded in philosophy; to Leibnitz, they form an integral part of its method. To Spinoza, philosophy had no part nor lot with theology; to Leibnitz, the justification of theology is its end and aim. Leibnitz was essentially an eclectic; an eclectic in religion (he had sought, as one of the great objects of his life, to find a *modus vivendi* between the Catholic and Protestant churches); an eclectic in philosophy, an eclectic in science, and last of all, an eclectic in his attempts to reconcile philosophy and theology.

The somewhat flashy system of Leibnitz, as was natural, made an immediate and widely extended impression on the culture of Europe. It almost entirely superseded Cartesianism in the university and in the *salon*, and indeed was the dominant academical philosophy of the Continent until the time of Kant, if not in its original form, in one but slightly modified.

We pass over intermediate writers, and come to CHRISTIAN WOLFF, the first follower of Leibnitz who erected an independent system on the principles of the master. Wolff was born in 1679 at Breslau, and became, in 1706, professor of mathematics in Halle. He subsequently entered upon a professorship at Marburg, but owing to alleged heretical tendencies in his doctrines he was recalled, and retired again to Halle, devoting himself mainly to literary work till his death, on the 9th April, 1754. Wolff is noteworthy as being the first academical thinker who wrote in German. He was the author of a large number of works dealing with every department of philosophy. He attempted to combine Leibnitzianism with the older Aristotelian doctrines of the schools. The pre-established harmony he regards simply as an admissible hypothesis. He also denies the unconscious perception of Leibnitz, that is, he refuses to admit perception in any monads below the rank of the Leibnitzian soul. On the other hand, he adheres to the optimism of his master no less than to his doctrine of the will. His division of philosophy into Ontology, or the doctrine of being in general; Rational Psychology, or the doctrine of the soul as unextended and simple substance; Cosmology, or the doctrine of the physical universe; and Rational Theology, or the doctrine of the existence and attributes of God, is interesting and noteworthy in its relation to the "critique" of Kant, as we shall presently see. Practical philosophy (an expression since much used in Germany, of which apparently he was the originator) he divides into Ethics, Economics, and Politics (the old Aristotelian division). Wolff bases his "practical philosophy" on the idea of perception, which is the law of our rational nature.

Wolff left an extensive school behind him, the most noteworthy name of which is that of ALEXANDER GOTTLIEB BAUMGARTEN (born, 1714, in Berlin, died, 1762, in Frankfort). Baumgarten is chiefly remarkable for two things;

firstly for having attempted to construct a philosophy of æsthetics, and secondly for having been the thinker who probably had most share in the earlier philosophical education of Immanuel Kant. Baumgarten was Kant's type of the dogmatic metaphysician, as often appears in his works. The only other member of the school worthy of notice, and for the same reason, is CHRISTIAN AUGUST CRUSIUS (born, 1712, died, 1776, professor of philosophy at Leipsic). He also had an influence on the philosophical education of Kant, and is often referred to by him.

MODERN PHILOSOPHY.

FIRST EPOCH, B.

THE EMPIRICAL SCEPTICAL SCHOOLS.

BACON.

We have now traced the course of the dogmatic schools of the Continent from the rehabilitation of philosophy, after the fall of scholasticism had been succeeded by the brilliant literary revivals of ancient systems, followed by the fantastic physical speculations of the sixteenth century; and after these in their turn had collapsed—in other words, from the period of Descartes. We have followed this development to the middle of the eighteenth century, that is, to the time of Immanuel Kant. Here we must retrace our steps to the period at which we started in the survey just concluded, *i.e.* to the beginning of the seventeenth century, for the purpose of following the contemporaneous, though essentially distinct Empiricist movement in the British Islands.

The first name we meet with in this Empiricist movement is that of Francis Bacon, Lord Verulam. "By eliminating the theosophic character which Natural Philosophy had acquired during the transitional period," says Ueberweg (vol. iii. p. 35), "by the limitation of its method to experiences and induction, and by raising the fundamental characteristics of this method to a philosophical dignity free from the narrowness attaching to any special circle of physical research, Bacon of Verulam (1561–1626) is the founder, not indeed of the empirical method in natural science, but of the empiricist line of development in modern philosophy." The notion of reorganising human knowledge on a new basis was, it is said, a favourite dream of Bacon, even in his boyhood. Like his younger contemporary, Descartes, he had been early disgusted with the metaphysic of the schools. The growing enthusiasm for physical science had seized him also; but, unlike the Frenchman, he did not dream of bringing knowledge back to the primitive *cogito* by any drastic scepticism.

In his 'Instauration of the Sciences,' Bacon makes a survey of knowledge, as it then existed, as a preliminary to the work of reform. It falls under three heads, Memory, Imagination, and Reason. In this portion of his great work, Bacon points out what he conceived as the fundamental sources of error in the human mind, to which he gives the name of Idols in the Greek sense of the word (εἴδωλον). This, perhaps the most interesting and important part of the work in question, is succeeded by a dissertation on the three branches of human science which fall respectively under the above heads, viz., History, Poetry, and Philosophy. Philosophy, according to Bacon, concerns itself with God, Man, and Nature. The first department, that of natural theology, consists of the attempt to show that the series of physical causes implies a first cause and a Providence. On the positive nature and attributes of God, natural or philosophical theology has nothing to say. Similarly, in the second department, that which has Man for its object, it is not the immaterial soul of man which is immediately breathed into him by the Deity that philosophy deals with, but the animal soul, which is of a thinner, finer, corporeal nature than the body, but not immaterial.*

Natural philosophy, the third department, is divided into two sections, speculative and operative. Speculative natural philosophy is again divided into physics and metaphysics; the first in so far as it is concerned with proximate causes, the second in so far as it deals with ends. Operative natural philosophy is divided into two corresponding sections, as applied physic it is termed mechanic,—as applied metaphysic, natural magic. The fundamental conceptions and axioms which lie at the root of all philosophy, such as those of being and non-being, similarity and diversity, &c., or such an axiom as that two things that are equal to the same thing are equal to one another, form the subject-matter of

* The coincidence of this with the doctrine of Paracelsus is curious.

what Bacon terms *philosophia prima* or *scientia universalis*. Mathematics is merely the auxiliary science of physics. Anthropology, or the science of Man, refers partly to the human body and partly to the soul, in the sense above indicated. Bacon ascribes all the elements of bodies to perception, which he explains mechanically as the result of attraction and repulsion. Like Leibnitz at a later date, he distinguishes between mere perceptions, and feelings accompanied by consciousness, although perhaps not so clearly. Logic and ethics, no less than politics, fall to be dealt with in this department. It is in the portion of the "*Novum Organum*" dealing with method, in which the idols of the mind are treated of, that the doctrines are to be found to which the subsequent philosophic development may be most directly traced. Bacon discovers in the natural constitution of the human mind a tendency towards a deceptive anthropomorphism, as for instance, to the substitution of final causes for proximate or efficient causes in physic, fallacies occasioned by which are termed by him *Idola Tribus*. He finds also many fallacies attributable to some special bias of the individual, which he terms *Idola Specus*; or again, others occasioned by the mis-use of language; yet others, which spring from traditional prejudice; the latter being styled respectively *Idola Fori* and *Idola Theatri*. The mind has to free itself as far as may be from these infirmities before it is in a position to arrive at truth. "We must," says Bacon, "neither draw everything from ourselves, as the spider its threads, nor merely gather together like the ants, but gather together and work up as the bees their honey." Induction, as taught by Aristotle and the schoolmen, the so-called *inductio per enumerationem simplicem*, he condemns, since it fails in this latter point, namely, the subjective working-up, by which Bacon means the methodical and systematic reduction of the individual instance under the general rule. Negative instances are to be taken account of as much as positive, as well as differences of degree. The reduction is to be undertaken with the greatest care, not by springing at once from the singular to the universal, but by proceeding step by step through all the intermediate stages.

HOBBES.

The next English thinker we have to notice is Thomas Hobbes, the contemporary and friend of Bacon. Hobbes was born at Malmesbury in 1588, and as a young man became tutor in the house of the Duke of Devonshire. Subsequently, after a journey through France and Italy, he studied Mathematics and Natural Science in Paris, and became as enthusiastic as his nature allowed in the rising physical science, as represented by Kepler, Copernicus, Galilei, and Harvey. He produced a number of works, the most famous being his treatise "On Human Nature," and the celebrated "Leviathan; or the Matter, Form, and Authority, of Government." Hobbes died in 1679.

Hobbes defines philosophy as the cognition of effects or phenomena from their causes, and of the causes from the observed effects, by means of correct deduction. Its object is practical, namely, that we may foresee effects, and thereby make use of them in life. Hobbes shares Bacon's mechanical mode of regarding things, which he in many respects exaggerates. He may justly be regarded as the father of British psychology. Without him there could have been no Locke. A distinct stand is taken on experience and observation as the sole source of knowledge. There is no metaphysical problem any more than one as to the constitution of our knowledge. "Concerning the thoughts of Man," says he (Leviathan, Chap. I.), "I will consider them first singly, and afterwards in a train of dependence upon one another. Singly, they are every-one a *representation or appearance* of some quality or other accident of a body without us, which is commonly called an object, which object worketh on the eyes, ears, and other parts of a man's body; and, by a diversity of working, produces diversity of appearances. The original of them all is that which we call *sense.* There is no conception in a man's mind which hath not at first, totally or by part, been begotten upon the organs of sense. The rest are derived from that original."

In Hobbes we have the first distinct expression of the English empiricist doctrine—the doctrine which has maintained its ground in this country up to the present time. Philosophy in the English school, of which Hobbes is the earliest direct representative, is reduced in its main issue to a mere question of psychology. Is the mind a *tabula rasa* receiving its knowledge ready-made from an external source? or does it possess innate ideas by which it is enabled to form judgments of a higher validity than those which can be referred to a succession of particular experiences? In other words, is there any essential distinction between *contingent or empirical truth* and *necessary truth*, or is the distinction that exists between them merely one of degree? The problem as to what constitutes *reality*, which is of course involved in these questions, is here altogether lost sight of. The completed categories of consciousness which the *real* world implies, the entire synthesis of experience, is assumed from the outset.

The confusion between metaphysic, psychology, and physics, so characteristic of the English school, is present from the first. Hobbes sees that sensible qualities can exist only in the percipient, but he nevertheless, as appears in the above passage, assumes the existence of the mysterious entity, a "body without us," which, in an equally mysterious manner "worketh upon the eyes, ears, and other parts of a man's body, and by diversity of working, produces diversity of appearances." Hobbes, of course, postulates an atomism which he bases upon the assumption that that which moves others must also in itself be moved at least in its smaller parts, since motion apart from matter or at a distance is an impossibility. The senses of men and animals are affected by motions which propagate themselves from the senses to the brain, and from the brain to the heart, whence the reverse process takes place, which reverse process constitutes feeling. We see an anticipation of Leibnitz in the assertion that all matter possesses potentiality of feeling. From feeling all knowledge is ultimately derived. General notions, so called, are nothing more than words serving as signs for an aggregate of similar objects. All thought is merely the addition and subtraction, the combination and separation of perceptions.

The original state of man in society, Hobbes declares was that of war; this was substituted at a later stage for a formal contract by which unconditioned obedience to an absolute ruler was pledged on condition that he, holding the balance of power, should protect individual members of the society to which this contract was to give birth, against one another. This theory of society was accepted in substantially the same form to that laid down by Hobbes as axiomatic, by almost all political thinkers till the end of the eighteenth century, and forms the basis of that great text book of the French Revolution, the "Social Contract" of Jean-Jacques Rousseau. Morality Hobbes regards as the direct result of the Political State. That is good which is sanctioned by the absolute power in the state; the reverse, evil. Religion and superstition have this in common, that they both imply the fear of imaginary powers; the difference between them consists in that the fear or worship of those imaginary powers which are recognised by the state is religion, while the fear or worship of those not recognised is superstition.

LOCKE.

John Locke was born in 1632 at Wrington, near Bristol. He studied at Westminster, and afterwards at Oxford. In 1664 he went on a diplomatic mission to Berlin, which lasted some twelve months. A few years afterwards, having in the meantime resided at Oxford, he undertook a journey through France and Italy. For a long time he remained as tutor in the house of the Earl of Shaftesbury. The 'Essay on the Human Understanding,' though commenced in 1670, was not published until some years later. Shaftesbury's resistance to the absolute tendencies of James II. brought him to the Tower; but being acquitted by the jury, he repaired to Holland, where he was followed by Locke in the year 1683. In consequence of the revolution of 1688, which placed the Prince of Orange on the English throne, Locke returned to his native country; he soon received an official appointment, first as "Commissioner of Appeals," and afterwards as "Commissioner of Trade and Plantages." Locke died in the seventy-third year of his age, in 1704. In addition to the famous 'Essay,' Locke was the author of numerous treatises on ethical, political, and economical subjects.

The great principle of Locke's philosophy is, that the origin of all knowledge is in experience, and that the derivation of all concepts is from experience. The first book of his essay is occupied almost entirely with a polemic against the doctrine of "innate ideas," that is, of ideas existing in the mind independently of experience. Did the individual really possess such ideas, they would be discoverable in children and savages. The fact that the abstract notions supposed to be innate do not exist in these cases, proves that they are not universal, while a little consideration of their nature shows them to presuppose a relatively high degree of culture. The case of savages proves conclusively that there is no single ethical proposition which is regarded as binding by all men alike. The same reasoning applies to the elements of our complex ideas as to the ideas themselves; there are none which are innate. The understanding is originally a *tabula rasa*. The second book deals with how this blank tablet is engraved with the writing of experience. There are two "receivers," so to speak, of different orders of experience, the external senses, *sensation* proper, and the internal sense, or the capacity of *reflection*. But whether what we perceive be an outward or an inward fact, our understanding is in either case nothing more than the mirror in which it is reflected—the smooth surface of the *camera obscura* which is the passive vehicle of the influence of the light of experience. There are thus ideas derived from sensation, and ideas derived from reflection. The capacity of an object to produce an idea in our understanding is called its *quality*. Where the idea is similar to the state of the object producing it, it is termed a *primary quality*. There are two primary qualities in external objects—*extension* and *impenetrability*. Our idea of an extended thing implies a real externality of the particles to one another; our idea of resistance a real configuration of the body producing it. But with most qualities the case is otherwise. These *secondary qualities*, as they are termed, such as colour, odour, taste, roughness, smoothness, beauty, ugliness, pleasantness, and unpleasantness, &c., only indicate a certain relation between our organs and the object, but nothing existent in the object itself. Indeed, the object has as little analogy with those ideas it produces in our minds, as the heat of the sun has with the softness of the wax which it melts. It is the cause of these effects in us, but no more. This distinction of *primary* and *secondary* qualities is with Locke a cardinal one. The ideas of sensation, then, are the effect of the qualities of outward things upon our understanding; those of reflection, the effects of our own inward states upon our understanding. Out of these two kinds of ideas is made up the whole sum of our knowledge.

As the immense variety of words is constituted of the twenty-six letters of the alphabet, so the number of primitive ideas out of which all our concepts are constructed is relatively small, and may be readily enumerated. In forming an inventory of them, it is advisable to begin with those derived from a single sense, such as colour, sound, odour, &c., and then to proceed to those which are produced by a combination of several senses, such as that of dimension, which involves the idea of a measured or determined extension or space. We may then proceed to ideas having their origin in reflection, such as thought, will, duration, or measured time; and finally to ideas derived from both sources, namely, sensation and reflection, such as those of unity, force, &c. The complex ideas which are produced by the combination of these simple ideas, Locke divides into three classes—ideas of modes, of substances, and of relations.

By "modes," Locke understands "such complex ideas which, however compounded, contain not in them the supposition of subsisting by themselves, but are considered as dependencies or affections of substances; such are the ideas signified by the words 'triangle, gratitude, murder,' &c."—Book II., Chap. III., 4. Modes are subdivided into simple or mixed, the first kind being such as are produced by the combination of the same simple idea, "as a dozen, or a score; which are nothing but the ideas of so many distinct units added together," and the second being compounded of various kinds of simple ideas, such as "beauty," "theft," &c. Ideas of substances are "such combinations of simple ideas as are taken to represent distinct particular things subsisting by themselves, in which the supposed or confused idea of substance, such as it is, is always the first and chief."—(II. VI.) "Relation" consists in the "consideration and comparing one idea with another."—(*ib.* VII.)

The simple ideas which come to us directly through experience, are ektypal, *i.e.* they always have something real corresponding to them. The complex ideas, on the contrary, since they are the figments of our own minds, are archetypal, and have no reality corresponding to them. All words, except proper names, are concerned with the latter order of ideas, i.e. general or abstract concepts, and must therefore not be regarded as representing anything real, for there is nothing real but what is individual. Here, we may remind the reader, we have Locke taking up the parable, though possibly unconsciously, of Occam, and the later nominalistic schoolmen. The third book of the 'Essay' is devoted entirely to a discussion on the question of language, to the misapprehension of the true nature of which Locke attributes most of the fallacies of the metaphysicians.

One only of the complex ideas does Locke admit to denote any reality; this exception is the idea of substance. We are compelled, says Locke, whatever be the reason, to postulate a substratum as that in which the qualities of things inhere, and which, although we have no evidence of it in experience, and can even form no definite idea of it, we cannot help regarding as real. The idea of substance, although a complex idea, corresponds therefore to a reality, albeit an unknown reality.* Substances we know only by their qualities, and hence we can only classify them according to their qualities. In this way we may divide substances into two classes—those capable of thought or cogitative substances (mind), and those not

* We may observe that Locke's use of the word "substance" is not that of Aristotle's *οὐσία*, or of most of the schoolmen, but answers rather to the Aristotelian *πρώτη ὕλη*, and to the Kantian *thing-in-itself*, or *noumenon*.

so capable (matter). We are by no means justified, however, in dogmatically asserting the former class to be immaterial, like Descartes; indeed, their susceptibility to decay rather gives colour to the hypothesis that they are material in nature. Thought may very well be conceived as quality of matter. It is just as incorrect to regard the thinking substance as necessarily always conscious (another error of Descartes); for this is plainly contradicted by experience.

The further combination of ideas gives us cognition or knowledge, expressed in language in the form of the proposition, which may be either instructive or demonstrative, according as to whether it is immediately perceived or arrived at through the interposition of middle terms. To these two modes of cognition, may be added a third, namely: the immediate sensuous perception of external objects. Our conception of God is attained by a process of reasoning, in other words, is demonstrative. It is composed of ideas derived from our experience of finite minds, with the idea of infinity, that is, the negation of limits superadded. When the constituent elements of a cognition are universal notions, it is a universal axiom.

The utility of universal propositions should neither be over nor under-estimated. We should always bear in mind, while employing them, that they are ultimately mere abstractions from our experience of individual facts. It is also important to make a distinction between those general propositions in which the predicate adds something to our knowledge of the subject, and those which are merely verbal and identical. The statement that a triangle is a triangle, or that the triangle has three sides, is a mere play of words, since the word triangle implies a figure comprising three sides and three angles. On the other hand, the assertion that the outer angle is greater than either of the internal and opposite angles is a statement carrying with it a distinct increase to our knowledge of the triangle; the predicate, in short, contains something more than what is already contained in the subject. This distinction appears later in Kant as that between analytic and synthetic judgments.

Locke divides the whole of knowledge into *natural philosophy* which deals with things, *moral philosophy*, which deals with the means by which the good and useful is attained, and *logic* which deals with symbols and words. Locke's treatise entitled the 'Elements of Natural Philosophy,' is concerned with the first of these departments. The second is treated of in a fragmentary way in his 'Thoughts on Education,' in his two 'Treatises on Government,' and in his 'Letters on Toleration,' &c. Nowhere, however, does he go into the fundamental questions of ethics in any thorough manner. The third or logical department, is discussed in the 'Essay on the Human Understanding,' as well as in that 'On the Conduct of the Understanding.'

Locke's views on Education had a very wide influence, and form the basis of Rousseau's 'Emile.' His political treatises breathe the spirit of the typical English Whig, their ideas and reasoning having been since dressed up in many a Whig speech and pamphlet. The resemblance of certain of Locke's political doctrines to those of Hobbes as expressed in the *Leviathan* would seem too strong to be accounted for by mere coincidence or contemporaneity, although Locke himself disclaimed all knowledge of the *Leviathan*.

The influence of the writings of John Locke, especially the 'Essay on the Human Understanding,' on the subsequent course of philosophic thought has been immense. That it has been so, is in many respects surprising, considering how little there is in his works that is not to be found in those of his elder contemporary Hobbes. His main position indeed is traceable much further back, and amounts to little more than the nominalism of Occam and his followers as expressed in the famous formula *Nihil est in intellectu quod non prius in sensu fuerit*. The popularity of his style, and the forcible manner in which he returns again and again to the charge in his efforts to refute his adversaries, real or imagined (for it is extremely doubtful whether any thinker ever seriously believed in the innate psychological concepts which are Locke's particular *bête noire*), and to establish his own position, will, however, account to a large extent for the hold he not only obtained but kept on men's minds. He gathered, so to speak, into one focus the arguments against the older metaphysic, and gave to the empirical doctrine of Bacon and Hobbes a definite psychological standing-ground. Locke was an Englishman of Englishmen, alike in his character and writings. There is in the latter all the common-sense force of the English character, with all its lack of subtility, and we may add, all its honest contempt for the qualities it does not itself possess.

We have now to trace the development of the principles laid down by Locke, first in the hands of Berkeley, Hume, Reid, and the so-called Scotch Psychological School, and afterwards in those of the French Sensationist and Materialist School.

BERKELEY.

LOCKE'S ideas were developed in various directions by his pupil Shaftesbury, by Clarke, Hutcheson, and others. But the most important among his immediate successors from the point of view of the historian of philosophy is George Berkeley, born at Thomastown in Ireland, in 1685, of an old Royalist family. Berkeley studied with avidity contemporary philosophical literature, especially Locke and Malebranche. He took advantage of a visit to Paris to pay his respects to the latter, but the interview proved fatal to the aged ecclesiastic, then suffering from inflammation of the lungs, who died a few days afterwards. After spending some years in travel, he returned to Ireland, having been meanwhile presented to the deanery of Derry. This post he subsequently threw up, to engage in an abortive missionary enterprise in the Bermudas. It was on his return thence, that he was made Bishop of Cloyne. He died at Oxford in 1753.

Berkeley's standing-ground is Lockeian; Empiricism pushed to its logical conclusion in the shape of a thorough going nominalism, which denied abstraction altogether. "Knowledge and demonstration," it is true, are about universal notions, but it does not follow they are formed by abstraction. The universality consists rather in the "relation it bears to the particulars signified or represented by it, by virtue of which it is that things being in their own nature particular are rendered universal"— ('Principles of Human Knowledge' Introduction, xv.) There is no such thing as a universal idea. When I speak of a triangle, says Berkeley, I do not mean a triangle that is neither "equilateral nor scalenor, nor equicrural, but only that the particular triangle I consider, whether of this or of that sort, it matters not, doth equally stand for and represent all rectilinear triangles whatsoever, and is in that sense universal." That which is inseparable in existence is also inseparable in thought. It follows that general names so-called, must be the names, not of general ideas (which can have no existence), but must be expressions by which we represent classes of individual objects, characterised by common features with special reference not to the individual peculiarities of the objects, but to their common characteristics. It is in the doctrine of abstract ideas that this belief in an independent external world ultimately rests: "for can there be a nicer strain of abstraction than to distinguish the existence of sensible objects from their being perceived, so as to conceive them existing unperceived?" (Principles v.)

"If we enquire into what the most accurate philosophers declare themselves to mean by *material substance*, we shall find them acknowledge they have no other meaning attached to these sounds than the idea of being in general, together with the relative notion of its supporting accidents." (XVII.) Now all ideas, whether (in the language of Locke) they be ideas of "sensation" or of "reflection," are nothing but states of our mind or spirit. Even the upholders of the current doctrine admit with Locke, that the ideas of colour, odour, &c., do not represent any independent quality in things outside us, but they notwithstanding, inconsequently, assume them to express a relation to such things. The distinction between primary and secondary qualities is a purely arbitrary one, of no validity whatever in proof of the existence of an external world, since the former can, by the same reasoning as is used with regard to the latter, be shown to have no existence apart from the mind perceiving them.

The *material substance* or *substratum*, which to Locke was a necessary assumption, falls away therefore, together with the inherence in it of the so-called primary qualities. It is surely simpler and more rational, instead of imagining an unknown something behind the qualities perceived in the sense-world, to acknowledge that matter is nothing but the constant sum of these perceived qualities—that the thing is what is perceived and nothing else—or once more, that the *being* of things consists in their *perception*, that their *esse* is *percipi*. But the assumption of a world independent of perception is not merely gratuitous, it involves a self-contradiction. The notion of hardness, extension, figure, that is, of certain affections of our minds, existing apart from our minds, is plainly absurd. All would recognise the absurdity if any one were to assert the independent existence of the feeling of pain caused by burning, apart from its being felt. Strange to say, they do not recognise that the independent existence of the fire itself, that is, of the assemblage of sense affections or ideas (as Berkeley, following Locke's terminology, calls them) connoted by that word, is equally absurd on the very same grounds. The substratum of Locke and the philosophers is just as untenable. For did such independent existence obtain, it is evident that we, neither philosophers nor anyone else, could know anything about it. In so far as the philosophers predicate its existence, they profess to know something about it, in which case it is not independent of perception, since they must have arrived at it sooner or later through perception, and therefore the same reasoning will apply.

Under no hypothesis can one escape the dilemma: if the term matter expresses something known, it is only an idea; if not, it is for us an altogether meaningless phrase. To the objection that the idea may be the copy of a reality, Berkeley replies that an idea can only resemble another idea: "If we look never so little into our thoughts, we shall find it impossible for us to conceive a likeness, except only between our ideas. Again I ask whether these supposed originals or external things of which our ideas are the pictures or representations be themselves perceivable or not. If they are, then they are ideas, and we have gained our point; but if you say they are not, I appeal to anyone whether it be sense to assert a colour is like something which is invisible; hard or soft, like something which is intangible, and so of the rest." (VIII.)

The conclusion Berkeley draws from his analysis is that "there is not any other substance than spirit or that which perceives." For, that an idea should subsist in an unthinking substance is a manifest contradiction, to have an idea being the same as to think or to perceive, and hence the only possible substratum for external objects is a mind or minds in which they are perceived. The distinction between ideas of sense and their reproduction in reflection is that the former are implanted in us immediately from their source, the divine mind, while the latter are derived immediately from our perception of the former. "Some truths there are," says Berkeley, "so near and obvious to the mind, that a man need only open his eyes to see them. Such I take this important one to be, to wit, that all the choir of heaven and furniture of the earth, in a word, all those bodies which compose the mighty frame of the world, have not any subsistence without a mind; that their being is to be perceived or known; that consequently so long as they are not actually perceived by me, or do not exist in my mind or that of any other created spirit, they must either have no existence at all, or else subsist in the mind of some eternal spirit,—it being perfectly unintelligible, and involving all the absurdity of abstraction, to attribute to any single part of them an existence independent of spirit. To be convinced of which the reader need only reflect, and try and separate in his own thoughts the being of a sensible thing from its being perceived." (VI.) The existence of external things consists in their being eternally present in the mind of God, by whom they are revealed to us. Hence, in a sense, it is true that they exist independently of our mind, but only so far as they are present in the divine mind. There exists, in short, only active entities (spirits) whose nature consists in thinking and willing, and ideas or modifications of these entities. The resemblance of Berkeley's doctrine to that of Malebranche in this point is not to be denied, but the two men approached the question from opposite points of view. Malebranche never relinquished the Cartesian Dualism, while Berkeley's whole system is a polemic against Dualism.

Our knowledge of an object is made up of distinct kinds of sensations, *e.g.* sensations of sight and sensations of touch. These are absolutely independent and distinct; yet their constant association, by means of which each becomes for us the "sign" which suggests the possibility of expressing the other, is independent of any control of the precipient mind. It follows for Berkeley that this arbitrary yet orderly and invariable connection must have its source in the work of a creative intelligence outside our own.

Berkeley, it must be remembered, had a distinct aim in view in his philosophical writings other than the mere search for truth, to wit, to cut the ground, as he believed, from under "scepticism, atheism, and irreligion." This object he thought he attained through the refutation of the doctrine of an independent external world of matter. Berkeley's system may be described as a thorough-going phenomenalism or empiricism. How this system, which was to annihilate all scepticism and atheism, was itself the groundwork of a systematic philosophy of doubt, we shall see.

The complete works of Bishop Berkeley have been more than once republished, the best edition being that of Professor Frazer, in four volumes, 8vo., London, 1873. In addition to his main philosophical essay, entitled 'A Treatise Concerning the Principles of Human Knowledge,' in which his leading positions are expounded at length, he wrote 'Three Dialogues between Hylas and Philonous,' containing the main arguments for immaterialism in a more popular form. His celebrated 'Essay Toward a New Theory of Vision,' contains an exposition of the psychological side of optics which has formed the foundation for every subsequent scientific exposition of the subject. Berkeley there endeavoured to show that judgments of distance rest entirely on an empirical basis. 'Alciphron, or the Minute Philosopher,' at the time his most popular work, is a dialogue designed to refute the fashionable bon-vivant "freethinker" of the day, a figure which belongs to that era,—the era of chap-books, "wit," coffee-houses, highwaymen—in short, which is peculiar to eighteenth-century social life, and heard of no more after the French Revolution. In addition to some mathematical treatises, the only other work of importance is the 'Siris,' written towards the close of Berkeley's career, in which he starts from a dissertation on the virtues of tar-water, and proceeds to descant on the physical nature of things in general, winding up with a learned disquisition on theosophy, Egyptian, Platonic, and Christian. All Berkeley's writings are interesting from their quaintness of style.

Berkeley's position may be summed up by saying that he put a "new question" as to the meaning of the general name "matter." Hume, as we shall see, in effect took up the application of his method at the point at which Berkeley dropped it, and proceeded to inquire into the meaning of the general name "mind."

HUME.

David Hume was born on the 26th of April, 1711, in Edinburgh, at the university of which city he was educated. He subsequently entered a merchant's office in Bristol, but finding the occupation little to his taste, availed himself of a small independence to migrate to France, where he remained four years. Hume's first philosophical work, the 'Treatise of Human Nature,' was published in 1728, but fell almost stillborn from the press. This was followed in 1741 by a volume of general essays, entitled 'Essays and Treatises on Various Subjects,' which attracted considerable attention. Encouraged by this success, Hume ventured upon a condensed restatement of his philosophical position, which saw the light between the years 1748 and 1752. It consisted of three portions, the 'Enquiry concerning Human Understanding,' the 'Dissertation on the Passions,' and the 'Enquiry concerning the Principles of Morals,' besides appendices.

The 'History of England' which subsequently made his fame in another direction, does not interest us here. His final work was his autobiography. He died on the 26th of August, 1776. The 'Dialogues concerning Natural Religion' and the 'Essays on Suicide,' were published after his death.

Hume closes for practical purposes the great line of British thinkers initiated by Bacon and Hobbes. We say closes this line, inasmuch as there is little or nothing to be found in the Scotch psychological school of Reid, Beattie, &c., which is not a repetition, or at most, amplification of what we find in the writings of these thinkers. Hume's place in the history of philosophy is that of the immediate successor of Berkeley. His main advance on Berkeley was this: the Anglican bishop, while rejecting the Lockeian substance—that is, the substratum of qualities—in so far as the external or material world was concerned, never once thought of rejecting the same conception with regard to the internal or mental world. To Berkeley "the only possible substratum for external objects was the mind or minds by which they are perceived." To Hume, on the contrary, the immaterial substance "mind," "spirit," or "soul," had as little justification in reason, as the material substance against which Berkeley's polemic was directed. An achievement in its consequences even more momentous for the subsequent evolution of thought, was the attention Hume called to the problem of causation, for this it was which Kant tells us first directed his thought towards the deeper issues of which this was only one, involved in Theory of Knowledge.

Locke and Berkeley had both of them employed the word "idea" for the objects alike of sense and reflection. Hume makes a distinction between impressions and ideas. "We may divide," he says (Inquiry, Sect. 2), "all the perceptions of the mind into two species, which are distinguished by their different degrees of force and vivacity.* The less forcible and lively are commonly denominated Thoughts

* It is singular how persistently the thinkers of the empirical school missed the point of the distinction between the real and the psychological order in resting satisfied with this pitiable makeshift of a definition.

or Ideas. The other species want a name in our language and in most others; I suppose because it was not requisite, for any but philosophical purposes, to rank them under a general term or appellation. Let us therefore use a little freedom, and call them *impression*, employing that word in a sense somewhat different from the usual. By the term *impression*, then, I mean all our more lively perceptions when we hear, or see, or feel, or love, or hate, or desire, or will. And impressions are distinguished from ideas, which are the less lively perceptions of which we are conscious, when we reflect on any of these sensations or movements above mentioned." Every idea has its origin in an impression or combination of impressions. The having of impressions is feeling, the having of thoughts is thinking. Among ideas may be distinguished those of memory, and those of imagination; the former, as being nearer their sense original, being the more, and the latter the less, lively. The fundamental principles of connection or association among ideas, Hume finds to be three, namely, *Resemblance*, *Contiguity*, and *Cause and Effect*. "A picture naturally leads our thoughts to the original (Resemblance); the mention of one apartment in a building naturally introduces an inquiry or discourse concerning the others (Contiguity); and if we think of a wound, we can scarcely forbear reflecting on the pain which follows it (Cause and Effect). But that this enumeration is complete, and that there are no other principles of association except these, may be difficult to prove to the satisfaction of the reader, or even to a man's own satisfaction. All we can do in such cases is to run over several instances and examine carefully the principle which binds the different thoughts to each other, never stopping till we render the principle as general as possible. The more instances we examine, and the more care we employ, the more assurance shall we acquire, that the enumeration which we form of the whole is complete and entire." (Inquiry, Sect. 3.) We quote the above passage, as it contains a concise statement of the empirical method in psychology.

The objects of human reason or inquiry may be divided into "relations of ideas," and "matters of fact." The former alone are susceptible of demonstration. All reasonings concerning matters of fact are founded on the relation of cause and effect. And here comes in Hume's celebrated doctrine that "causes and effects are discoverable, not by reason, but by experience." With this is connected the categorical denial of any causal nexus, of any principle, that is, uniting the cause with the effect. The belief in this nexus is attributable, according to Hume, to the fact that custom or habit leads us unhesitatingly to expect a certain effect to follow a given cause; in other words, it is by experience alone that the belief in the necessary connection of cause and effect is obtained. "The nature of experience is this: we remember to have had frequent instances of the existence of one species of objects, and also remember that the individuals of another species of objects have always attended them, and have existed in a regular contiguity and succession with regard to them. Thus we remember to have seen that species of object we call flame, and to have felt that species of sensation we call heat. We likewise call to mind their constant conjunction in all past instances." (Treatise, Part III., Sect. 6.) The effect is totally different from the cause, and can never be discovered therein. There is nothing by which we could tell *à priori* that the impact of one billiard ball with another should result in the motion of the second. Constant conjunction is all we can predicate of this or any other instance of causation. It is CUSTOM OR HABIT alone which leads us to believe that the future will resemble the past. Hume in a similar manner disposes of the ideas of power, force and energy.

Hume's treatment of the subject of the freedom of the will is based on his theory of causation. Because, he says, we are accustomed to believe in the necessary connection between a cause and its effect in the external world, and do not feel any such connection between our volitions and the acts which follow them, we regard our will as free, in contradistinction to the necessity we imagine to exist in other instances of causation. This distinction Hume, of course, regards as altogether spurious, and therefore as having no place whatever in philosophy. "All mankind," he says, "have ever been agreed in the doctrine of liberty as well as in that of necessity," the whole discussion concerning which "has been hitherto merely verbal." "For what is meant by liberty when applied to voluntary actions? We cannot surely mean that actions have so little connection with motives, inclinations and circumstances, that one does not follow with a certain degree of uniformity from the other, and that one affords no inference by which we can conclude the existence of the other. For these are plain and acknowledged matters of fact. By liberty, then, we can only mean a *power of acting or not acting according to the determination of the will;* that is, if we choose to remain at rest, we may; if we choose to move, we also may. Now this hypothetical liberty is universally allowed to every one who is not a prisoner and in chains. Here then is no subject of dispute." (Inquiry, Part I. Sect. 8.) Being once convinced that we know nothing of causation of any kind beyond "the *constant conjunction* of objects and the consequent inference of the mind from one to another, and finding that these two circumstances are universally allowed to have place in voluntary actions, we may be more easily led to own the same necessity common to all causes." If man had but begun by investigating the true nature of the belief in the connection of cause and effect in the external world, the free-will controversy would never have arisen.

The attack upon the doctrine of the Soul-Substance occurs in the 'Treatise on Human Nature.' Hume contends that this is no less an absurdity than an independent substance or substratum of matter. "This question," says Hume (Treatise, Part IV. Sect. 5), we have found impossible to be answered with regard to matter and body. But besides that in the case of the mind it labours under all the same difficulties, it is burthened with some additional ones which are peculiar to that subject. As every idea is derived from a precedent impression, had we any idea of the substance of our minds, we must also have an impression of it; which is very difficult, if not impossible, to be conceived. For how can an impression represent a substance otherwise than by resembling it? And how can an impression represent a substance, since according to this philosophy it is not a substance, and has none of the peculiar qualities or characteristics of a substance?"

All we know respecting the mind is a succession of certain states, seeing, hearing, feeling, willing, &c. The assumption of a substratum in which they inhere has no warrant in experience and is a purely gratuitous fiction of the philosophers. Hence the question whether our thought inheres in a material or immaterial substance is altogether unmeaning. We have presented to us a series of impressions and ideas. This is all we know of matter or mind; the assumption of anything further is an illusion. Hume's speculative doctrine thus resolves itself into a systematic Scepticism or Phenomenalism. The transition of these impressions and ideas is purely arbitrary. The Berkeleian conception of the Divine "mind" having been shown to be as meaningless as the Lockeian conception of "matter," it is clear we have no ground for belief—except what is entirely based on association—in any uniformity of nature, whatever. The only utility of metaphysics is to exhibit the limits of human inquiry.

The proper objects of abstract thought are quantity and number; in Mathematics alone can we have demonstration. "All other inquiries of men," observes Hume (Inquiry, Rule XII. Part 3), "regard only matter and existence; and these are evidently incapable of demonstration. Whatever *is* may not be; no negation of a fact can involve a contradiction; the non-existence of any being is as clear and distinct an idea as its existence. The proposition which affirms it not to be, however, false, is no less conceivable and intelligible than that which affirms it to be. The case is different with the sciences, properly so-called. Every proposition which is not true is there confused and unintelligible. That the cube root of 64 is equal to the half of 10 is a false proposition, and can never be distinctly conceived; but that Cæsar or the angel Gabriel, or any being never existed, may be a false proposition, but still is perfectly conceivable and implies no contradiction." Questions of existence can only be proved by arguments from cause and effect, and hence are merely contingent. Hume characteristically closes his

'Inquiry concerning Human Understanding' with the following words: "When we run over libraries, persuaded of these principles, what havoc must we make? If we take in our hand any volume—of divinity or school metaphysics for instance—let us ask: *Does it contain any abstract reasoning concerning quantity or number?* No. *Does it contain any experimental reasoning concerning matter of fact and existence?* No. Commit it then to the flames; for it can contain nothing but sophistry and illusion."

Hume regards as much more important than any mere theoretical research that into the basis of morals. Will and action exhibit a perfectly regular mechanism, the laws of which can be as clearly presented as those of motion and of light. He is thus a thorough-going determinist, as this doctrine is generally understood. The very admission of motives involves this principle, according to Hume, while the punishment of the criminal is a practical application of it; for if his action were not the necessary consequence of his character, no end would be served by his punishment. This, however, does not exclude moral judgment, any more than the fact of the beauty or ugliness of an object, not being under its control, hinders an artistic judgment on that object.

Hume's main division of the emotions and passions, is into "calm," and "violent." "Of the first kind is the sense of beauty and deformity in action, composition, and external objects. Of the second are the passions of love and hatred, grief and joy, pride and humility." (Treatise, Book II. Part I., sect. 1). A further division of the "violent" passions is into "direct" and "indirect." "By direct passions," says Hume, "I understand such as arise immediately from good or evil, from pain or pleasure. By indirect, such as proceed from the same principles, but by the conjunction of other qualities." Under the indirect passions are included pride, humility, ambition, vanity, love, hatred, envy, pity, malice, generosity, with their dependents; and under the direct passions, desire, aversion, grief, joy, hope, fear, despair, and security. From the primitive impressions of "pleasure and pain" proceed the "propense and averse motions of the mind." The reference of these to the cause of the impressions, according as it is present or absent, produces joy or sorrow, hope or fear, &c. These direct passions lie at the foundation of the more complex, indirect ones. Hume endeavours to show the results of association of ideas and impressions, in the modification of the primitive passions.

The philosopher cannot properly accord praise or blame to moral action; ethical judgments being on the same footing as critical (æsthetic). Hume is thus in agreement with Shaftesbury and Hutchison in placing virtue in the same category with beauty, and in the hypothesis of a moral sense, as the foundation of ethical judgments, which he asserts express nothing more than the pleasure or the reverse which an action occasions in the spectator. The possibility of this is deducible from the feeling of *sympathy* or reciprocal communicability and receptivity, which unites us with all sentient creatures, but especially our fellow men. The condition of a moral judgment is, that the action should not be regarded as an independent event, but as the sign of a disposition of character. Hume divides all virtues into natural and artificial, the first including such as spring directly from sympathy, and which in themselves are good and useful. The second arise through the exigencies of society, and are hence conventional, although not arbitrary: such as probity, truthfulness, &c. Hence the idea of an original social contract is groundless, or rather, the reverse of the facts. The *societas* becomes a *civitas*, when a definite government arises. A dictatorship becomes necessary when the society is threatened from without, from which it follows that the first form of government is absolute monarchy. Since the state mainly exists for the sake of protection, there are circumstances under which its justification might cease.

Such is the course of the evolution of thought that, as we have seen, what Berkeley had intended to put an end to "Scepticism" and "Atheism," became the most powerful solvent of the foundation of traditional belief that the eighteenth century produced in this country.

REID.

In Thomas Reid we have the progenitor of the large and long-lived school of the Scotch psychologists. His philosophy, which started with a polemic against Hume, has been the fountain at which psychological Scotsmen have drunk from that time to this. His writings have been read, re-read, annotated and amended by four generations of Scottish thinkers. Born in 1710 at Strachan, in Kincardineshire, Reid lived an uneventful life. He graduated in due course at Aberdeen, where he afterwards was appointed Professor of Moral Philosophy. On the resignation of Adam Smith, he succeeded to the same post in the more important University of Glasgow. In 1780 Reid resigned, passing the remainder of his life in study and retirement. He died in 1796. Reid's complete works first appeared in 1785, but have been several times reprinted, the best edition being that issued with annotations by Sir William Hamilton.

The secret of the success of Reid among his countrymen may be supposed to lie in his professed appeal to common-sense, alike against the scepticism of Hume, and the psychological idealism of Berkeley. To Reid the well-known aphorism will aptly apply, that he said many things that were true, and some things that were new; but unfortunately, that the things which were true were not new, and the things which were new were not true. His appeal to common-sense, in-so-far as it meant anything, is certainly not new; his assumption that his contemporaries, Berkeley and Hume, denied the fact of common-sense, or that its dictates were practically irresistible, is as certainly not true, notwithstanding some rhetorical passages in Hume which might give colour to such a conclusion.

Reid starts by taking for granted as axioms an astounding number of propositions, the first and foremost being the immediate dicta of consciousness. "If a man should take it into his head to think or to say that his consciousness may deceive him, and to require proof that it cannot, I know of no proof that can be given him; he must be left to himself, as a man that denies first principles, without which there can be no reasoning. Every man finds himself under a necessity of believing what consciousness testifies, and everything that has this necessity is to be taken as a first principle." ('Essays on the Intellectual Powers,' I. 2). In this solemnly-expressed platitude is summed up the whole of the Common Sense Philosophy. This thesis, expanded into three volumes, may be apt to suggest to the irreverent mind the hackneyed saying, by no means always true, so far as our experience goes, about the Scotchman and the joke. Reid proceeds to "take for granted," as he expresses it, personal identity based on a "thinking principle" or mind. He sagely remarks that "every man of a sound mind finds himself under a necessity of believing his own identity and continued existence. The conviction of this is immediate and irresistible; and if he should lose this conviction, it would be a certain proof of insanity which is not to be remedied by reasoning" (*ibid.*).

Reid further assumes as a first principle the very point in dispute with Berkeley and Hume, namely, the existence of external objects. Though he intends to take up the argument against them, they would justly have insisted that his whole attack was simply an *ignoratio elenchi*, and that that of which he ostentatiously paraded the assumption they had never questioned.

But after all that may be justly said in derogation of Reid's claims as a thinker, it is not to be denied that there are some acute observations scattered here and there throughout his works, and also that he makes some scores against his more brilliant adversaries, as for instance (Essays I. 1), where he touches the vulnerable point in Hume's doctrine (which he received, by the way, as a legacy from Locke), viz. the formulation of the distinction between the outer and the inner orders of conscious states as one merely of "force and vivacity." Reid truly observes, "To differ in species is one thing; to differ in degree is another. Things which differ in degree only must be of the same species. It is a maxim of common-sense, admitted by all men, that *greater* and *less* do not make a change of species. . . . To say, therefore, that two different classes or species of perceptions are distinguished by the different degrees of their force and vivacity is to confound the difference of *degree* with the difference of *species*, which every man of understanding knows how to distinguish." And again: "Common-sense convinces every man that a lively dream is no nearer to reality than a faint one, and that if a man should dream that he had all the wealth of Crœsus, it would not put one farthing in his pocket." All this is very apposite criticism on Hume, so far as it goes, but it certainly does not help the Reidian philosophy.

The fact is, that Reid saw a flaw in Berkeley and Hume, and his whole system is a bungling attempt to discover its real nature. But it was not by wholesale assumptions and pragmatical assertions that this could be done. Poor Reid's struggles to extricate himself and human reason from the meshes of Scepticism, only resulted in worse entanglement. There was at this time a young *Privat-docent* at the Prussian University of Königsberg, who was also trying his hand on the same theme, but of him we shall hear more anon. Reid's philosophy continued to be taught in the Scotch universities by James Beattie (1735–1803), Dugald Stewart (1753–1820), Thomas Brown (1778–1820), &c.

THE FRENCH MATERIALIST SCHOOL.

WE now pass from Scotland to France, where we shall see the influence of the same movement of thought, namely, that originating with Hobbes and Locke, exhibited in the writings of the Abbé de Condillac, Bonnet, Helvetius, &c., leading up to the great French materialist school of the eighteenth century.

ÉTIENNE BONNOT DE CONDILLAC was born in 1715 at Grenoble. He published his *Essai sur l'origine des Connaissances Humaines*, in which he introduced Locke to his countrymen, in 1746. His most important work is, however, his *Traité des Sensations* (1754), in which his special line of differentiation from Locke is shown. His *Logique* appeared shortly before his death in 1780. His completed works (Paris, 1798) comprise twenty-three volumes.

After carefully sheltering himself from the Church's censure, Condillac proceeds to develop the thesis known as Sensationism, namely, that sensation is the one source and vehicle of knowledge,—the "thought" or "reflection" admitted by Locke being nothing more than transformed sensation. This he illustrates by the fiction of a statue endowed successively with the five senses. He first admits the sense of smell, and seeks to show the extent of knowledge this sense alone would suffice to procure. He then proceeds to discuss how the world would appear to a being thus limited, on the addition of taste, hearing, &c. In this he assumes that the simultaneity of an impression with the remembrance of a previous one, in itself constitutes a judgment. The sense of feeling is singled out by Condillac from among the rest, as being that through which alone is obtained the idea of objectivity proper; the remainder only furnishing us with the impression of our own affections or states. It is only the solid which leads us to the knowledge of a world outside our own organs. The superiority of our sense of feeling primarily distinguishes us from the lower animals.

The ideas of good and evil, like everything else, are ultimately traceable to sensation. Condillac criticises Locke's doctrine of the association of ideas, while adopting it in the main. Repeated coincidence of ideas leads to their being necessarily combined. This is the origin of complex ideas, which may thus be said to make themselves. Nothing facilitates so much the fixation of these complex or combined ideas as the use of signs representing them. Hence the power of language. The want of the capacity for language in animals is as great a drawback to their intelligence as regards the combination of ideas as their imperfect sense of feeling is as regards the elements of such a combination. But though ideas may be combined and recombined, it matters not in how complex a manner, yet they are all ultimately reducible to sensations. *Penser c'est sentir*, is the motto of Condillac's system.

Condillac's contemporary, Charles Bonnet (1720–1790),

was independently working out the same line of thought. Curiously enough, Bonnet even hit upon the illustration of the statue, when he became aware of the fact that Condillac had worked out the same idea five years previously. Bonnet was in many respects more widely read at the time than Condillac, though his philosophical writings did not exercise so great an influence on the French eighteenth-century movement. Bonnet was in a sense the founder of what is known as physiological psychology. In both his scientific and theological positions he approached Priestley. He endeavoured to show the complete conditioning of thought and sensation by cerebral and nervous action; but, like Priestley, he sought to elude the theological consequences of this doctrine by a resort to the hypothesis of miracle.

CLAUDE ADRIEN HELVETIUS, another contemporary writer, (1715–1771), further carried out the ideas of Condillac. Helvetius declines to regard the "soul" as anything else than the sum of its ideas. Since all ideas are ultimately traceable to sensations or impressions of external objects, all mental differences which we find among men are the result merely of chance and outward circumstance, the most potent influence in the formation of character being education. The end of life is happiness, by happiness being understood the greatest possible amount of animal pleasure. There is no such thing as disinterested conduct. Since society is merely the sum of individuals, individual satisfaction, as such, contributes to the general well-being. Self-love is the only motive of conduct; its import in the moral world being analogous to that of gravitation in the physical. It is the lever of psychological no less than of practical action. All knowledge is dependent upon the attention and study which arises from the desire to escape *ennui*. Still more obvious is it that all practical action in life is traceable to self-interested motives. From this it follows that no moral teaching, whose aim is not to show that virtuous conduct is that most conducive to individual happiness, is of any value. The state, by acting on this principle in its system of jurisprudence, that is, by making punishment attend criminal conduct, shows the true philosophic instinct. Helvetius is distinguished by considerable literary facility, and his works have been more than once republished in a complete form.

Another influential writer of this period was JULIEN OFFROY DE LA METTRIE (1709-1751) who was originally led through observation of the delirium produced in fever, to a conviction of the absolute dependence of the psychical on the physical. Like Condillac, Bonnet, and Helvetius, whom he preceded by a few years, he proclaimed the ultimate reduction of thought and will to feeling. Intelligence would be impossible in a man brought up outside human intercourse. In ethics La Mettrie was the determined opponent of asceticism, his conception of life being ably set forth in his "L'art de jouir." His polemic against the convention and hypocrisy of human life generally is especially effective. La Mettrie was a great friend of Frederick the Great, who offered him an asylum at his court from the persecutions on account of his materialism which drove him successively from France and Holland, and at his death composed an elegy on him, which was read before the Berlin Academy of Sciences. Voltaire facetiously styles him the "Court atheist."

A survey of any department of French eighteenth-century literature would seem incomplete without some notice of the great names of Voltaire and Rousseau. Their significance for the history of philosophy is, however, of the smallest. Voltaire, whenever he touches on a philosophical subject, does so from the standpoint of mechanical eighteenth-century Deism. Rousseau is satisfied with a sentimental Deism, and is extremely bitter against the materialists. In his Social Contract, as already mentioned, he develops in a remarkable manner hints which were thrown out by Hobbes, Locke, &c. But original reflections on philosophy proper are entirely absent.

DIDEROT.

THE most important original figure produced by the French eighteenth-century movement in its more strictly philosophical aspect is undoubtedly DENIS DIDEROT, born 5th Oct. 1713. Diderot was originally destined for the priesthood, but this career he soon abandoned for law, and this again for literature. Diderot had a truly encyclopedic mind—a mind eminently adapted to be the organising power of the great literary work with which his name is most intimately associated. He possessed, moreover, what in Voltaire and Rousseau was undoubtedly lacking—a considerable speculative faculty. Diderot may be said to have focussed the materialist movement. The reading and translation of Shaftesbury's works first shook his faith in his early creed, and resulted in the *Promenade d'un Sceptique*, which, being impounded by government before publication, did not see the light till after his death. He soon developed into a deist in the ordinary sense of the eighteenth-century man of letters, but was too acute to rest long at this standpoint, and in the course of a few years passed over to a logically carried-out materialism. Diderot, after a life of many vicissitudes, alternately persecuted and patronised in France, finding a refuge at the court of the Empress Catherine of Russia, &c., died 13th July, 1784.

The pieces in which the mature Diderot is most clearly exhibited on his philosophical side are the *Interprétation de la nature*, the *Entretien entre D'Alembert et Diderot*, and the *Rêve de D'Alembert*, in the two latter of which, as may be judged by the titles, his friend and coadjutor on the *Encyclopédie*, D'Alembert, plays a prominent part. Several of the articles in the *Encyclopédie* itself are rendered almost valueless owing to the fact that worldly prudence induced the printer to modify them in an orthodox sense before their publication.

Diderot may most accurately be described as a materialistic monist. To him all nature was one; the difference between organic, inorganic, animal and human, were only differences of degree. There was no such thing as dead matter; the molecule was no less an active agent than the man. To employ an illustration of his: "the great musical instrument we call the universe plays itself." It does not require a demiurge or *deus ex machinâ* to evoke its harmonies and discords. Matter is itself active by its very nature, itself sentient, itself conscious, potentially when not actually. In other words matter, i.e. physical substance, is the ultimate ground of all existence; nature is the sum of its combinations. One set of combinations manifests itself as so-called inert, inorganic matter; another set as organised sentient matter; yet another as the thinking, feeling, willing, animal or human body. Diderot admits, however, an original diversity in the primal constituents of the various orders of material existences: "I term elements the various and heterogeneous *material substances* necessary to the general production of the phenomena of Nature, and I term *Nature*, the actual general result, or the successive general results, of the combinations of these elements" (*De l'interprétation*, lviii.). Diderot proceeds to suggest that animality had from all eternity its specific elements," "confounded in the mass of matter," that they gradually became united, and that thence vegetable, animal and human life resulted.

The materialism of Diderot is rather akin to the doctrine of Anaxagoras, than to that of Demokritos (it was Dynamism rather than Atomism). It is for this reason that we class him as a monistic materialist, in spite of certain passages which seem to make for a contrary assumption; more particularly since these are mainly to be found in the earlier work just quoted. For instance, in the *Entretien* we read: "There is but one substance in the universe; in man or in animal. The bird-organ is of wood; the man is of flesh. The canary is of flesh, the musician is of a flesh differently organised; but both have the same origin, the same formation, the same functions, and the same destiny." There is a remarkable passage in the *Rêve*, where Diderot, speaking through the mouth of the sleeping D'Alembert, gives an almost exact reproduction of the doctrine of the *Homoiomerai*. "Everything is more or less some one thing, more or less earth, more or less water, more or less air, more or less fire, more or less of one kingdom or of another; for nothing is of the essence of a particular being. No, assuredly, since there is no quality of which some being is not participant, and it is the greater or less amount of this quality which makes us attribute it to one being rather than to another. You speak of individuals, indeed, poor philosophers! Let your individuals be; answer me! Is there an atom in nature strictly like another atom? No. Do you not admit that everything in nature hangs together, and that it is impossible there can be a break in the chain? How then about your individuals? There are none; there is but one great individual, and that is the All. In this All, as in a machine or an animal, there is a part which you call this or that; and when you give the name individual to this part of the whole, it is by virtue of as false a conception as if in a bird you were to give the name individual to a wing or to a feather of the wing. And you talk of essences, poor philosophers! Let your essences be! Behold the general mass, or, if your imagination is too narrow to embrace that, behold your first origin and your last destiny. Oh Architas! you who have measured the globe, what are you? A little ashes. What is a being? The sum of a certain number of tendencies. Can I be anything else than a tendency? No, I am advancing towards an end (*Je vais à un terme*). And species? Species are only tendencies towards a common end which is their own. And life? Life is a succession of actions and reactions. Living, I act and react in mass; dead, I act and react in molecules. I do not die then? No, assuredly I do not die in this sense; neither I nor anything else. To be born, to live and to pass away, is but change of form. And what matters, one form or another? Each form has its own good and ill fortune. From the elephant to the grub, from the grub to the sensible and living molecule, the origin of all, there is no point in all nature which does not suffer or enjoy."

And again, in the short essay *Sur la Matière et le Mouvement:* "I cast my eyes over the general aggregation of bodies; I see everything in action and reaction; everything destroying itself under one form, everything recomposing itself under another; sublimations, dissolutions, combinations, of all kinds; phenomena incompatible with the homogeneity of matter; whence I conclude that it is heterogeneous; that there exists an infinity of diverse elements in nature; that each of these elements, by its diversity, has its particular force, innate, immovable, eternal, indestructible; and that these forces within the body have their action without the body; whence springs the movement, or rather the general fermentation of the universe." The force inherent in matter is at once the varying and uniting principle of the whole. It will be readily seen that the materialism of Diderot differs in some not unessential points from the scientific materialism of the present day, and also that his several statements of the doctrine are not always consistent with one another. The first is but natural and to be expected. Our admiration for the luminous suggestions of the eighteeenth-century writer will not be lessened by the few crudities from the point of view of modern science which cling to them; while as to the second point, it must be borne in mind that Diderot was primarily a man of letters rather than an exact thinker.

In method, Diderot is of course a thorough-going empiricist. Materialism is the logical development of empiricism, the truth which it implicitly contains. In the *Entretien*, D'Alembert is made to observe that according to the system propounded by Diderot it is impossible to conceive "how we form syllogisms, or how deduce their consequences." To this Diderot replies that we do not deduce them, that they are deduced for us by nature. "We do but proclaim conjoint phenomena of which the connection is either necessary or contingent, phenomena which are known to us through experience; necessary in mathematics, rigorous in physics and other sciences; contingent in morals, politics and the rest of the speculative sciences." To the question whether the connection between phenomena is less necessary in one case than in another, Diderot replies, "No, but the cause is subject to too many particular vicissitudes which elude us, for us to be able to reckon infallibly on the effect which will ensue. The certainty we have that a violent man will be irritated by an insult is not the same as the certainty that a body which strikes a smaller one will set the latter in motion."

We have quoted from Diderot at comparative length, inasmuch as he represents the most finished literary expression of the materialist movement. But the classical text-book of this movement is not to be found in the elegant and chatty dialogues and essays of the French littérateur, but in the more systematic though drier pages of the *Système de la Nature*, originally published under the name of the elder Mirabeau, but now known to be the work of the Baron d'Holbach and the habitués of his salon.

D'HOLBACH.

D'HOLBACH, or to give him his full title, Paul Heinrich Dietrich, Baron von Holbach, was born 1721, at Heidesheim, in Germany, and educated in Paris, where he spent the greater part of his life, amid the wits, men of letters, and "philosophers" of the pre-revolutionary era. He died 21st February, 1789.

The *Système de la Nature* is a systematic embodiment and exposition of the principles of the dominant materialism. In it we find the Empiricism of the British school, the Sensationism of Condillac, its pendant, the self-interest ethics of Helvetius, the physiology and epicureanism of Lamettrie; the whole forming the bible of materialism as understood in France during the eighteenth century. The only existence is matter, i.e. physical substance and the motion that is inherent in it. The complex of all things is termed nature, which constitutes the whole, inasmuch as all things stand in a causal relation to one another. Hence everything in nature is necessary. The three conditions of motion in the physical world are inertia, attraction, and repulsion. Motion is brought about through the inequalities in the degrees of attraction and repulsion in bodies. The same forces appear in the moral world as self-interest, love and hate. The only difference between the physical and the moral consists in the difference between the visible motion of masses, *i.e.* of complex systems of molecules, and the invisible motion of the molecules themselves. Thought, will, and feeling consist in the molecular motion of brain and nerve substance. Owing to this not having been recognised, dualism, or the doctrine of two substances, a mental and a material, with all its train of fallacies, has arisen. Perception is nothing but the setting in motion of the molecular system of the brain and nerves by impact from without. It cannot be decided whether sensibility is, as Diderot suggested, present in every portion of matter, or whether organisation is its essential condition. Moral action is a necessary consequence of temperament, which simply denotes the relative proportions of the solid and the fluid matters in the system. There is nothing more *spiritual* in love and hate, or in the numberless passions of which these two are the foundation, than there is in the phenomena of gravitation or of impact. The only difference is, as before said, that in the one case we can see the material motion which produces the phenomenon, in the other it is hidden from us.

It was only natural, after men had constituted themselves into a double existence, that they should extend this theory to the universe at large. Hence arose the conception of a God over against the world, a conception which explains nothing, does no one any good, frightens the foolish, and the folly of which is manifest in the fact that it can be expressed only by negations. The contradiction of ascribing to the deity human passions and morality, after removing him altogether from the sphere of the conceivable, is dwelt on. To the rational man there is no god beyond the force which moves the universe, appearing now as mechanical motion, now as sensibility, now as thought; to him there is no providence but the invariable laws of nature. D'Holbach and his friends are uncompromising in their attacks on the eighteenth-century theory, which justified superstition, on the ground of edification. To teach error for the sake of curbing the passions of men, is like instilling poison lest strength and health should be misused.

The doctrine of free-will is stigmatised as a cunning device for maintaining the credit of the deity in the face of the evils of the world. The adherents of the doctrine forget that an uncaused event would suppose quite a different world from this, and that a really free agent could be nothing less than a creator. The immorality of the belief in a future life is also insisted upon as tending to the neglect of the real world and of its pleasures and duties. A thorough-going materialism is alone consistent with common-sense and human dignity, inasmuch as it frees men from the degrading fear of imaginary evils and from useless regrets. The materialist has neither concern for the future, nor remorse for the past; all that happens, moral no less than mechanical actions, being the necessary outcome of the nature of things. Vice and crime are to the materialist mere disease. The latter would supplant the preacher and the judge by the teacher and the physician. He would be content to make men healthy in body, and to train them to see that their own interest lies in virtue, knowing that crime would thus become ever more rare, until it altogether ceased.

The *Système de la Nature* marks an epoch. Though, for obvious reasons, it has been persistently depreciated, its power, honesty and logicality, produced an immediate and widespread effect on contemporary thought. It succeeded in sweeping away the cobwebs of traditional belief from many a mind, and in utterly discrediting the sentimental Deism then popular. As against the inconsequent doctrines, philosophical and other, which were opposed to it, it was unanswerable, while its noble and humane moral teachings were the inspiring and sustaining power of numbers a few years later, whether in civil conflict or in the tumbril carrying them to the guillotine.

The ideas contained in the *Système de la Nature* were developed on their scientific side by various *savants*, notably *Cabanis*, *Claude*, and *Testutt de Tracy*. *Cabanis* (1758–1808) made a distinct advance on D'Holbach by identifying psychological processes rather with chemical and organic than with mechanical action. *Cabanis* is, however, chiefly famed for his crude and singularly unhappy analogy between the cerebral and visceral systems.

Of analogous nature to the error of D'Holbach in failing to distinguish between organic or vital processes and mechanical, is that which he exhibits in failing to see the difference between physiological and social processes. He would trace the existence of vice and crime to certain pathological states of the individual's body or mind, rather than to the economic and social conditions into which the individual is born.

MODERN PHILOSOPHY.

SECOND EPOCH.

KANT AND THE POST-KANTIANS.

INTRODUCTION.

Retrospective and Prospective.

We have now passed in review since the beginning of the modern period, two distinct lines of philosophic thought, the one springing from Descartes and his school, and the other from Bacon and Hobbes. In the first the abstract concept arrived at by reflection is made the unconditional test of truth, its validity that is, is apart from and even outside all experience. Descartes began his new departure in philosophy by the illogically constructed proposition, *I think, therefore I am.* This was the fundamental axiom of all knowledge, the certainty of certainties. But what was this *I* of which Descartes talked? Upon this question much hinges.

In the view of the present writer, eminent authorities to the contrary notwithstanding, the result clearly showed it to have been the "internal" object arrived at by reflection—the individual mind. At least if Descartes meant anything other than this at starting, he certainly very soon lost sight of it; for the whole of his philosophy proceeds on the foregoing assumption, and proceeds on it simply enough. The thinking individual once postulated as the *prius*, "the clearness and distinctness" of its ideas or abstract mental concepts, becomes naturally the basis of truth and its only ultimate criterion, in other words, the reflective reason is the key to the problems of philosophy, unalloyed by the baser matter of sense. The idea of God is attained in this way, similarly that of an independent though created external world, &c., &c. The possession of certain fundamental ideas justified the construction out of them of a dogmatic system irrespective of experience. Malebranche, accepting the main Cartesian positions, and taking his stand on the idea of substance, asked how two distinct substances, mind and body, could come into a position of reciprocal relation. This question he answered by constituting the Divine substance which was the origin of both, the *modus vivendi* between them. The abstract conception substance as defined by Descartes became the fulcrum upon which his philosophy turned. This principle was further and independently carried out by Spinoza, who, taking the same concept, denied, by its very definition, the possibility of a plurality of substances. He accordingly affirmed God to be the one substance, of which mind and body or Thought and Extension were the attributes, the reality and correspondence of which were given only in their relation to this substance. Out of the two psychologically "clear and distinct" ideas of substance and attribute, the system of Spinoza was formed.

Leibnitz, starting essentially from the same principle, though endeavouring to give it precision by sundry limitations and corrections, the principle, namely, that the "clearness and distinctness" of the mental concept is the ultimate criterion of all truth, evolved a pluralistic ontology, the antithesis on this historical plane of the Spinozistic Monism. Wolff, Baumgarten, Crusius, &c., all adhered to the same principle of method, though introducing various modifications into the results of the Leibnitzian speculations.

These schools, springing from Descartes, are what are termed the DOGMATIC or ABSTRACT metaphysical schools. They are systems to be received from the hands of a teacher—what the ordinary man has confusedly in his mind when he rails at all things metaphysical. Side by side with this development on the Continent, there was, as we have seen, another going on in this country. Bacon had laid down the inductive principle, had pronounced the method of all investigation to be the observation, collegation and comparison of individual facts. This Hobbes had adopted in his philosophical investigations, which consisted in the study of what passed in his own mind, in other words, of the manner in which the individual mind opens up (so to speak) to the perception of a fully-fledged objective world—of the world as known. Locke, following on this line, attacked the theory of "innate ideas," as he termed them, by which he probably meant the Cartesian mental concept, this polemic constituting the framework of his essay. For Locke, the main question of philosophy was, is the individual born into the world with any ready-made, concrete ideas in his mind, or does he derive all his knowledge through experience?

The question as thus put, it was, of course, not difficult to answer, and to answer in the sense in which Locke did answer it. He said in effect, all knowledge is derived from experience, or to put it popularly, through the senses. Berkeley pursued this idea to its logical conclusion on the one side, when he denied that an external world of "matter" had any existence except in a perceiving mind, for, said he, we only know it through experience *as perceived*, any other kind of existence we can only infer, and as he demonstrated, illegitimately infer. Hume, accepting the conclusions of Locke and Berkeley, carried them to an equally logical conclusion, on another side, when he showed "mind" or "soul" itself, regarded as an entity, to be an illegitimate inference from the succession of thoughts and feelings which is all that experience gives us. Empiricism, the necessary outcome of inductive psychology, issued as necessarily when fully carried out in pure phenomenalism or scepticism. The French sensationists and materialists, starting from Locke's incomplete Empiricism, are the counterpart of Berkeley's Idealism, their analysis being equally correct as far as it went, but equally incomplete and inadequate. While Berkeley rejected the entity "matter" but retained the entity "mind," they got rid of the entity "mind" but retained the entity "matter." On the basis of his sole existence, "mind," Berkeley sought to establish a dogmatic Theism or Spiritualism. On the basis of their sole existence, "matter," they sought to rear a dogmatic Materialism or Mechanicism. Though we are far from placing the positive results of the two procedures on a level; we must point out that, philosophically viewed, they are on precisely the same plane. The practical difference between their results is, that Berkeley's work, important as it was, was mainly negative, while that of the materialists laid the foundation, to a large extent, of modern science.

Both the foregoing lines of investigation, as will be seen, started from the individual mind as object. It was the "clearness and distinctness" of the concept that the individual mind forms, which was the test of truth for the Cartesian. It was the reproduction of a world already assumed as existent in the mind of the individual, that was the problem to be investigated for Hobbes and Locke. Even for Berkeley, the "finite spirits" and the "infinite spirit" respectively, in and for which alone matter existed, were concrete individual minds of men, and the similarly concrete and individual, though magnified mind of the creator, which was, so to speak, over against and distinct from them, as they were from each other. Similarly for the Sensationists the problem was the action of the assumed material world upon the sensory system of the individual. Hence it is that Spinoza's Monism was such a riddle to his contemporaries and successors till the present century, dogmatic metaphysicians and empirical psychologists alike.

The main speculative result of this evolution, both dogmatic and empirical, was the distinction of subject and object, that is, of perceiver and perceived, thinker and thought, knowing mind and known world. This was the main issue of a whole series of problems and distinctions which had never troubled the schoolmen or the ancients, but which rose up before the seventeenth and eighteenth century thinker, once he had decisively turned his back on the classical and mediæval speculative landscape. Not until Kant, however, did the distinction receive definite expression and become cardinal. The definite fixation of this distinction, which belongs essentially to the empirical or psychological plane of thought, discloses the inherent contradiction in Empiricism. Hence Kant represents at the same time the culmination and the bankruptcy of this line of thought. In the *Critique* he endeavours to treat the deeper issues involved in 'Theory of Knowledge,' of which he was the first to catch a glimpse, on the lines of this mere psychological distinction. His success and his failure were alike written in the history of the subsequent philosophic evolution.

The above, then, was the state of philosophy in the second half of the eighteenth century. On the one side were the dogmatic metaphysicians, assuming the clearness and distinctness of the thinkers' concepts, to be a test of their objective truth or reality; on the other, the empirical psychologists, who maintained all concepts to be originally derived from concrete experience, which was hence at once the source and ultimate criterion of truth.

Kant, following a hint dropped by Hume, namely, his distinction between the necessity attaching to mathematics, and the contingency of "matters of fact and experience," was led to put the crucial question, What is experience? *i.e.* what is this concreteness we call reality? With the Lockeian school, Kant admitted that every concrete concept can come only through experience—indeed, this was of the nature of a platitude to him—but his great merit lies in having seen, if imperfectly, the issue which lay beyond this mere psychological question, the question, namely, as to the conditions of experience itself? In investigating this, Kant found that experience or perception was not wholly sensuous, that the phenomenon was more than a ready-made impression passively received from without, that it involved a thought or active element—in short, that the mere sense-impression had first of all to be determined by a category or pure concept before it could become experience. Further investigation proved this to lie deeper than the object of reflection, the individual self, with which alone philosophers had been hitherto concerned. The pure concept, which entered so intimately into the essence of the concrete, was universal and necessary, while all that existed for the individual as such was merely empirical and contingent. Kant proceeded to trace the categories or pure concepts, determining the real (which he had hit upon in a somewhat haphazard manner) back to their source, and original first principle. This proved to be, not the self or mental synthesis determined in time by memory, but the *I* for which time is, and which Kant designates the original synthetic unity of consciousness or apperception. The old antagonism of Materialism and Idealism is clearly absorbed in this more thoroughgoing analysis. "Mind" and "body" cease to be separate entities, mutually exclusive of one another, and are disclosed as the same fact differently categorised. A short sketch of the successive changes of attitude implied in the passage from the common-sense view of the non-philosophical man, through Empiricism to that of Kant and the post-Kantian thinkers, may facilitate an understanding of much that follows, which, without some kind of key, would be scarcely intelligible to the reader unversed in the matter.

The ordinary man believes the phenomena of the world to be things existing in themselves and apart from their cognition. The Berkeleian or Humean philosopher dispels this belief of his by a *reductio ad absurdum*, to wit, by pointing out to him that the thing, object, or matter, all, namely, that is perceived externally to ourselves, is nothing but a congeries of affections or determinations of consciousness, as much so as the thoughts, feelings, and volitions which are unmistakably peculiar to himself as an individual. He is therefore immediately seized with a sense as of living in a dream-world, a world of phantasms, since the outer world is shown to have no more independence of the fact of being known, felt, and perceived, than the inner. Both alike consist of impressions and ideas, and he fails to discover—his old land-mark, independent existence, being removed—any ground of distinction between them. The real table and his recollection of the table are alike determinations of his consciousness. But this state of mind cannot permanently endure. The absurdity of confounding empirical reality and empirical ideality in one category, the instability of an attitude which logically carried out makes the individual absolute, at once centre and periphery of the universe, carries its own *reductio ad absurdum* with it. The world refuses to be philosophised away, and forces to a reconsideration of the problem.

The first departure from a state of innocence established one fact, namely, that a world outside consciousness is nonsense and a contradiction in terms. A return to crude realism therefore is out of the question. The head and front of the offending difficulty is not to be found in the first position of philosophy arrived at in the departure from common-sense, which reduced the world to a system of determinations of a feeling and thinking subject. May it not lie in a loose employment of the words knowledge, feeling, consciousness? Our philosophical neophyte proceeds to examine them. This examination proves that these words have been used in a different sense in the premises of the argument to that in which they have been used in the conclusion, in short, that it involves the fallacy *à dicto simpliciter ad dictum secundum quid.* The first position of philosophy merely reduced reality to determinations of knowledge, or feeling and thinking, *i.e.* of a conscious subject. The conclusion implicitly or explicitly drawn as to the illusoriness of reality is based on the assumption that the subject referred to is the subject which is at the same time object, the synthesis determined by memory, that is, reproduced in time, the *individual mind.* All within the sphere of this latter, or psychological synthesis, is of course of merely individual significance, is purely empirical. The conclusion arbitrarily imports into the terms used a psychological meaning, as implying the completed actuality immediately present in the individual mind, while in the premises no such limitation is contained.

But, says our empiricist, I only know of thought or feeling as appertaining to myself as an individual. No, interposes the speculative thinker, who at this stage steps in to the rescue. In this assumption consists the *cul-de-sac* in which you find yourself caught. You assume knowledge or consciousness to be identical with the reproductive synthesis constituting the individual mind, but analysis—nay, ordinary experience itself—gives the lie to this assumption. The objective world, which you have already seen to be nothing more than related feelings (or states of consciousness, if you will), refuses to be reduced to a mere series of your personal feelings or states of consciousness. You and I alike perceive the table, the same table, not two different impressions of an occult table in itself, as the imperfectly developed empiricist supposes, nor two different tables, as the psychological idealist must needs suppose; else thought and language have no meaning. This *objective point*, at which our consciousness ceases to be distinguishable as mine and yours, but which to me and to you, so far as we are individuals, *is given as for all possible consciousness*, is not a mere determination of me, *i.e.* of my mind, like my personal thoughts, feelings, and desires, but is a determination of that *ego* or subject for which my mind itself is object, of the *I* which is never *in* consciousness, inasmuch as it is the subject of consciousness. The objective, then, is that element or factor in knowledge which though *per se* extra-individual, the individual makes his own by reproducing in his concepts. Psychology is the science which traces the process of reproduction. For the individual it is *mediate*, unlike his thoughts and feelings which are immediate. This necessary and universal or *object*-element in knowledge or consciousness, it is, which constitutes its reality. The term *real* distinguishes it from the merely psychological element which is popularly expressed by the word *ideal*.

In accordance with the foregoing, there are three points of view from which the world may be regarded. There is the standpoint of physical or natural science, which concerns itself exclusively with the objectively real. Here abstraction is made from the self-determining subject, and the processes of the production of the real, as well as those of its reproduction in the individual mind, in other words, of the problems of metaphysic and psychology respectively. The abstract real, the fully-fledged object in space and time, but abstracted from the principle of its generic possibility, and treated as an existent, is viewed in the same way as by the unreflective commonsense of the ordinary man and the crude empiricist. The ultimate expression of the objective real is, physical substance, static and dynamic, the "matter and motion" of the materialists. To physical substance and to its categories of determination, and to this alone, the whole sum of things is legitimately reducible from this point of view.

Again, there is the standpoint of psychology, which views the world simply as reproduced in the "mind.'

This is the standpoint of Berkeleian idealism proper, As in science, "matter" is treated as an abstract entity, so here, "mind" is treated as an abstract entity, as the receptacle of "impressions and ideas," also regarded as independent existences. The universe of psychology is "mind" and "ideas."

Lastly, there is the synthetic point of view of the speculative method, which treats the world under its most comprehensive and concrete aspect, as a system of determinations of knowledge or consciousness—or rather of the Subject, the *I*, or *I-ness*, which is the ultimate condition of the possibility of consciousness-in-general, and which, as such, can never, *per se*, be object of consciousness, like the self or mind of psychology. On this principle the *concrete-real* is seen in the last resort to consist in the syntheses of relations, or *I*-determinations. How from this is deducible the method by which all evolution is determinable we shall see later on.

We may observe respecting the three ways of approaching the world-problem, that the *materia prima* of natural science is corporeality, extending-resistance; its *universal form* is *motion*. This is the lowest term to which the universe is reducible on the lines of "common-sense" and "abstract" reality, *i.e.* the universe in space-and-time. Outside this there is no rational principle of explanation—in other words, there is no phenomenon in space-and-time which cannot be expressed in terms of matter-motion. Again, the *materia prima* of psychology is *mind*, its *universal form* being *ideation*. The psychological universe which is in time merely, is reducible to terms of mind (impressions and ideas). Finally, the raw material, the *matter* of "Theory of Knowledge" is *I-ness*, i.e. *the potentiality of consciousness*, its universal form being *experience*, *knowledge*, or *consciousness - in - general*. "Theory of Knowledge," it will thus be seen, embraces, while it transcends the two former standpoints.

It must not be supposed that the foregoing is to be found, in so many words, in Kant. Like all intellectual pioneers, Kant clung to many of the crudities of his predecessors even till the end. He never completely disengaged himself from crude realism, or at least from its survival in the Lockean doctrine; for the "things-in-themselves" of Kant are essentially a hybrid between the "substance" of Locke and the Leibnitzian monads with which Kant's earlier philosophical training had familiarised him. The whole *Critique of pure Reason* (Kant's greatest work) is, moreover, cast in a psychological form, although the true nature of the problem it is concerned with continually forces its way through.

But though the above exposition is not expressed in so many words by Kant, it is indicated in every page of his writings, and was substantially the result evolved from his main position in the course of the post-Kantian Movement.

KANT.

IMMANUEL KANT was born April 22nd, 1724, at Königsberg, in which city he resided with but few intermissions throughout a long life. He was of Scotch descent on his father's side, the name having been properly spelt Cant.* Kant entered the university of his native city as a theological student, a faculty which he subsequently forsook in favour of philosophy. His first work was an academical essay entitled "Thoughts on the true estimation of the Vital Powers." Shortly after the publication of this treatise he left the city, and for several years occupied the post of private tutor in various aristocratic families. In 1755 he returned to Königsberg, where he obtained the position of *Privat-docent* in the university. He now began to devote himself in earnest to literary work. The Latin essay which preceded his installation in his academical functions, sought to mediate between Wolff and Crucius. His next important work, the 'General Natural History and Theory of the Heavens,' is similarly designed to effect a *modus vivendi* between Newton and Leibnitz. Various logical, metaphysical, and scientific essays followed in rapid succession. The Latin dissertation "On the form and principle of the sensible and intelligible world," constitutes the turning-point in Kant's philosophical career. Therein we find the awakened Kant endeavouring to formulate the problem of which the 'Critique' was to be the attempted solution. This work was his test-essay for the professorship of philosophy, which he entered upon in 1770. For eleven years subsequently, Kant was ceaselessly occupied with the problems indicated in this dissertation, the result of his cogitations being the appearance in 1781 of 'The Critique of

* The reason for change of orthography assigned by Kant himself, is the rather enigmatical one that it was in consequence of the tendency of his countrymen to pronounce the name as though it began with Z (Zant).

the Pure Reason,' a work which, in spite of its long inception, in actual writing out only occupied its author five months. This was followed in 1783 by the 'Prolegomena to every future Metaphysic,' an abstract of the last-mentioned treatise; by a second and somewhat mollified edition of 'The Critique' in 1784; by 'The Foundation for the Metaphysic of Ethic' in 1786; by the 'Metaphysical Foundations of Natural Science' in 1787; and the 'Critique of Practical Reason' in 1788. In 1790 appeared the 'Critique of Judgment,' a work exhibiting a visible falling-off in power, which may also be said of 'Religion within the boundary of Mere Reason' (1793). The last important work from Kant's own pen was the 'Anthropology,' which saw the light in 1798. Subsequently to this, however, Kant's lectures on "Logic," on "Physical Geography," and on "Pedagogic," were all published by his pupils during his lifetime. Kant died the 11th of February, 1804, aged eighty.

Three complete editions of Kant's works have been issued, that of Hartenstein (Leipsic, 1838–39, second edition 1866) in ten volumes; that of Rosenkranz and Schubert, comprising a biography and a history of the Kantian Philosophy (Leipsic, 1840–42) in twelve volumes; and the latest, that of Kirchmann (Berlin, 1868) in eight volumes, with a supplementary volume of annotations by the editor.

"The Critical Doctrine."

The guise in which the great problems comprised under what is termed "Theory of Knowledge," problems which touch the foundations of consciousness and reality, presented themselves to Kant, fresh from the reading of Hume and the Empirical school, was the at first sight unpretentious psychological question, "How are synthetic propositions *à priori* possible?" The classification of propositions into *analytic*, or those in which the predicate is already contained in the subject, and which are therefore virtually identical; and *synthetic*, or those in which the predicate adds something to the subject which is not already contained in its definition, we have already found in Locke, although in other words. The distinction is practically the same as that between *verbal* and *real* predication. Now there is no doubt that all analytic propositions are *à priori*, that is, independent of any particular experience; also that they carry with them a logical necessity and universality. There is equally little doubt, that most synthetic propositions (the Empiricists would say all) have their origin in particular experience, in other words, are *à posteriori*. Kant, however, found certain propositions, such, to wit, as the fundamental axioms of mathematics, and some others of equal, or even greater importance, whose nature we shall see directly, which by the "universality and necessity" that characterised them, proclaimed their origin, as independent of any number of particular or individual experiences whatsoever, in short, as *à priori*. Experience itself presupposed them; they formed part of the constitution of every particular experience; without them, experience would be impossible or meaningless; it would no longer *be* experience. This universality and necessity was not merely logical, like that of analytic judgments, but entered into the constitution of reality. The apparently simple and unpretentious psychological query thus assumed a far more formidable aspect. The question was now nothing less than: "How is experience itself possible?" what is this "necessary and universal" element that goes to the making of, or that underlies that real experience, which the Empiricists take as a matter of course, and about which they talk so glibly? What is the principle or principles from which it is deducible, and what is the method and order of deduction? Such is the problem to which Kant addressed himself in the 'Critique of the Pure Reason,' and we may add also, to which the series of German thinkers with whom Kant was the starting-point, and which culminated in Hegel, addressed themselves.

The disadvantage, as we have already observed in our section on the transition to Kant, which Kant laboured under, in attacking this problem from a psychological base (so to speak), from which he was unable or unwilling to cut himself off, is manifest in every page of his philosophical writings. A terminology derived now from the old dogmatic systems, and now from empirical psychology, hampers his thought at every turn, making him in some cases inconsistent with himself, and in others scarcely intelligible. Kant sometimes speaks as though he viewed "Theory of knowledge," merely as the vestibule of a possible metaphysic, at least he puts it forward as the preliminary question, which all metaphysicians must answer, before they can properly proceed to construct a system, professing to deal with the time-honoured problems of philosophy. He hesitated to formally insist, as he might have done, and as indeed he frequently hints, that the answer to this question exhausts the whole problem of metaphysics, and of itself constitutes philosophy. He felt that some place must still be left for the old speculative inquiries. With Kant, the chief end of philosophy still remained the answer to questions, as to God, the Soul, and Freewill. It is true they were not to be answered in the spirit of traditional dogmatism. They had no longer any theoretical *locus standi* in philosophy, but their determination, direction, and formulation, in the interests of practice, was still its chief function. In this, as in other respects, the separate influences of the two sides of Kant's philosophical education display themselves. Empiricism proclaimed the limitation of all knowledge to experience. The dogmatists of the Leibnitz-Wolfian school, whose works formed Kant's earliest philosophical pabulum, constituted the discussion of the nature of God, of the human Soul as an independent entity, and of the absolute constitution of the World-order, as the sole end and object of philosophy. Although Kant saw that "Theory of knowledge" was concerned with nothing but experience; although he saw that no speculative science, as such, could be concerned with anything higher than this; he nevertheless felt himself bound to make up his account, in some way or other, with the old questions. The ingenuity with which he endeavoured to effect this without invalidating his main speculative position we shall presently see.

Just as little as the Empiricists considered what was implied in that experience to which they were so fond of insisting (and with justice) that our knowledge is limited, did the dogmatists consider the significance and application of the conceptions which *they* so freely assumed to transcend all experience. The former assumed experience as a thing given, the latter assumed the absolute validity of certain of the concepts which experience presupposes as part of its own constitution beyond that constitution. The Empiricist never stopped to ask himself what are the conditions which render experience possible. The Dogmatist never stopped to enquire whether his abstract concepts had any validity outside experience; or how he came by concepts which appear to transcend experience.

The thinker who wakened Kant from his dogmatic slumber, as he expresses it, was Hume. Hume had shown that the notion of causality does not spring from experience, but is somehow or other imposed by us on the events which are given us in experience. The sceptical attitude assumed by Hume, as regards metaphysics, was merely the result of his imperfect analysis. Had he not limited his researches to the conception of causality alone, he would have discovered that the whole of pure mathematics consists of similar—as Hume would have deemed them—arbitrarily constructed syntheses. This would have sufficed to "give him pause," inasmuch as he must either have straightway abandoned mathematical certainty, or have reconsidered his position with reference to metaphysics. To profit by Hume's genius as displayed in his researches into the causation problem, and to repair the errors arising from his shortsightedness, we must institute the enquiry into how we come to form such combinations or syntheses, which carry with them "necessity and universality," in other words, as to the nature and conditions of knowledge or experience-in-general—an enquiry distinct from the merely psychological one, as to what falls within individual experience. Kant, nevertheless, in spite of his insisting on the distinction, is apt only too frequently, to mix up the respective points of view of "Theory of knowledge" and psychology.

Transcendental Æsthetic.

Kant understands by "Transcendental" all that belongs to the conditions or possibility of experience as opposed to "Transcendent" by which he understands that which professes to transcend, or pass beyond experience. Transcendental enquiries are simply enquiries into the conditions which experience presupposes, without reference to the *content* given in any particular or individual experience. The sum of such enquiries constitute what is called *Transcendental philosophy*. Transcendental Æsthetic denotes therefore, with Kant, the enquiry into the *à priori* or transcendental conditions of Sensibility. These Kant finds to be space and time, together with all that is directly deducible from them. In these two forms of Sensibility are contained the possibility of the axioms of mathematics. They are not given to us through the senses, like our individual impressions; these latter constitute the matter, or the purely empirical element in our Sensibility. On the other hand, space and time constitute the *formal* element, which helps to give reality to these impressions. The *formal* element of space-time combines the manifold *matter* of sensibility into intuition or perception. Upon the *matter*, the sense-impression which is received from without, Sensibility imposes its own unifying forms. In space the manifold impressions of sense are united in *co-existence*, in time in *succession*. The *à priori* nature of space and time is proved by the fact that we cannot make abstraction from them even in thought, as we can from all that is merely empirical. That they are different from conceptions abstracted by the understanding is evident, since space or time do not presuppose individual spaces or times, but on the contrary, individual spaces or times can only be thought of as parts of the one universal space or time. Further, that they only reside in our Sensibility, and not in the object itself, is evidenced by the fact that purely spacial distinctions cannot be described objectively, but only with reference to the cognising subject. "What can more resemble my hand or my ear, and be in all points more like, than its image in the looking-glass? And yet I cannot put such a hand as I see in the glass in the place of its original; for when the latter is a right hand, the one in the glass is a left hand, and the image of a right ear is a left one, which can never take the place of the former. Now there are no internal differences that could be imagined by any understanding. And yet the differences are internal, so far as the senses teach us, for the left hand cannot, despite all equality and similarity, be enclosed within the same bounds as the right (they are not congruent); the glove of one hand cannot be used for the other. What then is the solution? These objects are not presentations of things as they are in themselves, and as the pure understanding would cognise them, but they are sensuous intuitions, *i.e.* phenomena, the possibility of which rests on the relations of certain unknown *things in themselves* to something else, namely, to our Sensibility." (Kant's 'Prolegomena,' § 13, Bohn's edition.) By means, then, of the forms of space and time, we combine the various impressions of sense together into a whole. Intuitions, presentations, or phenomena (*i.e.* appearances) consist therefore of formed, or in other words, timed and spaced, feelings or impressions.

It is, however, only time that can be predicated of all phenomena whatever, for although space and time are alike mere subjective conditions of our Sensibility, yet space only belongs to the impressions of external Sensibility, and does not apply to our internal states; on the contrary, time is immediately only the form of a connection of inward states or affections, in short, of internal Sensibility; but since there is no external impression that is not accompanied by the internal intuition of self, time is indirectly the form of external intuitions also. The *matter* of Sensibility, that is, the manifold impressions of sense therein, being the empirical and casual element, it follows that this formal and necessary element of space-time must be pure and *à priori*. But if space and time are the *à priori* forms of all phenomena, intuitions, or perceptions, it is obvious that all the temporal and spacial determinations of phenomena admit of prediction in a universal and necessary manner. Now these determinations constitute the subject-matter of mathematical science. Arithmetic (and those departments of mathematics based upon it) is concerned with the repetition or *succession* of the unit, in other words, is founded on *time*. Geometry again deals with the configuration of space. The axioms and postulates of these sciences, inasmuch, therefore, as they are already implicitly present in our Sensibility itself, are universally and necessarily predicable of all that falls within it. But this also proves that mathematical propositions are strictly limited in their application to the phenomena given through sense, and in no way apply to things-in-themselves.

In brief, according to Kant, Sensibility, with its primordial forms of space and time, is the receptive vehicle of impressions received by it from without, though of this "without" we can know nothing whatever.*

TRANSCENDENTAL ANALYTIC.

Transcendental Æsthetic, while exhibiting the principles of the passive or receptive side of knowledge or experience, has also answered the question, How are synthetic propositions *à priori* possible, in so far as mathematics is concerned? But as yet we have only one of the elements constituting the completed synthesis of real knowledge. We have next to treat of the active element which all complete synthesis or unification implies. It has been justly remarked that space and time, in "the critical philosophy," are the warp of knowledge, across which the shuttle of thought has to throw its woof before reality, objectivity or experience can obtain. A world of three-dimensioned space, and of one-dimensioned time, forms the warp. This material is supplemented by the spontaneity of the Understanding or pure form of thought. The

* This doctrine Kant designates as at once *transcendental idealism* and *empirical realism*. He claims that it differs from what he terms the *empirical idealism* of Berkeley; inasmuch as, while Berkeley denied the existence of objects while admitting the existence of space, he would deny the existence of space while admitting the existence of objects.

function of the understanding may be compared to the action of the electric spark, passing along and illuminating the whole series of sensations. Sensations, even though unified in space or time, are, to use Kant's expression, "blind," until they are reacted upon by the Understanding. The Understanding synthesises them, and thereupon a fully-fledged real or experienced world arises. This system of experienced objects—the real world—is the *nature* with which science is concerned. Science, no less than common experience, is based upon the pure thought-forms or categories, as Kant, following Aristotle, terms them.

As in the case of Sensibility and its product, intuition or perception, the pure form or necessary element disclosed itself after the matter or empirical (*i.e.* contingent) element had been abstracted from, so here the pure concept or category is arrived at, by abstracting from the matter of the logical judgment; we then see the necessary conditions which every judgment presupposes. The clue to the discovery of these universal categories of consciousness Kant thus found in the ordinary logical table of judgments.

The following is the list as given by Kant:—

LOGICAL TABLE OF THE JUDGMENTS.

1. *According to Quantity.*	2. *According to Quality.*
Universal.	Affirmative.
Particular.	Negative.
Singular.	Infinitive.

3. *According to Relation.*	4. *According to Modality.*
Categorical.	Problematical.
Hypothetical.	Assertorical.
Disjunctive.	Apodictic.

Parallel to this table runs the Transcendental table of the categories which Kant derived from it, but of which the logical judgments are, or should be if Kant's derivation is correct, the applied form.

TRANSCENDENTAL TABLE OF THE CONCEPTIONS OF THE UNDERSTANDING.

1. *According to Quantity.*	2. *According to Quality.*
Unity.	Reality
Plurality.	Negation.
Totality.	Limitation.

3. *According to Relation.*	4. *According to Modality.*
Substance and accident.	Possibility.
Cause and effect.	Actuality.
Community (action and reaction).	Necessity.

As a matter of fact, Kant's derivation of the categories from the judgments is in many cases forced and arbitrary.* The distinctions contained in the original table are themselves often of doubtful value, and sometimes altogether untenable. This, however, does not affect the philosophical importance of Kant's analysis. The accuracy or inaccuracy of the list of categories furnished, does not touch the point that experience is determined by thought in a manner at least generally corresponding to the Kantian categories.

But to proceed with our analysis. Having gathered together these categories in the somewhat hap-hazard manner we have seen, it remained for Kant to justify their place in a doctrine professing to be systematic by deducing them from some primary datum or principle of consciousness. This he seeks to effect in his sections on the deduction of the categories, one of the most important portions of the 'Critique.' It is necessary to remember that the deduction is no demonstration, in the ordinary sense of the word, but like every other "transcendental" exposition, is designed to show that reality or experience itself presupposes the successive stages of the argument as its necessary conditions; that on ultimate analysis, all knowledge is resolvable into these, as its constituent

* The student may observe that in the categories of *Quantity* and *Quality* (the mathematical categories, as Kant termed them), the order of the corresponding table of judgments is reversed.

elements. The sections on the deduction of the categories are very different in the two editions of the 'Critique.' It is here that the crucial point, separating Theory of Knowledge from Psychology, is to be found.

We have seen that the phenomena furnished by the Sensibility to the Understanding are simply presentments or presentations, in other words, determinations or limitations of Sensibility. Looking at the question from the standpoint of Psychology, with its hard and fast distinction of subject and object, inner and outer, mind and matter, it seems utterly enigmatical that I should have a right to affirm universal or objective validity of the categories; for instance, to say that the conception of cause and effect can never be contradicted by any experience. "There are only two possible ways," says Kant, "in which synthetical representation and its objects can coincide with and relate necessarily to each other, and, as it were, meet together. Either the object alone makes the representation possible, or the representation alone makes the object possible. In the former case, the relation between them is only empirical, and an *à priori* representation is impossible. And this is the case with phenomena, as regards that in them which is referable to mere sensation. In the latter case—although representation alone (for of its causality, by means of the will, we do not here speak) does not produce the object as to its existence, it must nevertheless be *à priori* determinative in regard to the object, if it is only by means of the representation that we can cognise any thing as an object." (Kant's 'Critique,' p. 77: Bohn's edition.)

We have, it must be remembered, to distinguish between two distinct processes; two presentations may combine themselves in an individual consciousness, in a certain time-order, *i.e.* in the empirical ego, which itself consists simply in a synthesised series of impressions on the internal sense determined in time. In this case the judgment, together with its contained conception, its root, is merely a *judgment of perception.* These have merely a subjective and individual validity; in other words, they are purely empirical and contingent. Or, on the other hand, they may be combined in a manner valid not alone for the individual consciousness, but for all possible consciousness; that is, they may be combined in a consciousness-in-general. "The business of the senses," says Kant, "is to intuite, that of the understanding to think. But to think is to unite presentations in a consciousness. This union is either merely relative to the subject, and is contingent and subjective, or is given unconditionally, and is necessary or objective. The union of presentations in a consciousness is judgment. Thinking, then, is the same as judging, or referring presentations to judgments in general. Hence, judgments are either entirely subjective, when presentations are solely referred to a consciousness in one subject, and are therein united, or they are objective when they are united in a consciousness in general, that is, are necessarily united therein. The logical momenta of all judgments are so many possible modes of uniting presentations in a consciousness. But if they serve as conceptions of the *necessary* union of the same in a consciousness, they are therefore principles of objectively valid judgments. This union in a consciousness is either analytic by identity, or synthetic by the combination and addition of different presentations to one another. Experience consists in the synthetic connection of phenomena (perceptions) in a consciousness, in so far as this is necessary. Hence, pure conceptions of the understanding are those under which all perceptions must be previously subsumed, before they can serve as judgments of experience, in which the synthetic unity of perceptions is presented as necessary and universal." (Kant's 'Prolegomena,' § 22: Bohn's edition.)

But these pure conceptions of the understanding, to which perceptions are immediately referred, before they can become real or objective, themselves presuppose synthetic processes lying (so to speak) still deeper in the nature of consciousness. These are *the synthesis of apprehension in intuition*, of *reproduction in the imagination*, and of *recognition in the conception* itself. The material originally supplied by sense requires a unification other than that furnished by the passive forms of sense. This unity is afforded in the primary act of intuiting, or perceiving the sense-manifold furnished in time and space. Each impression given in an instant of time would be lost, were it not gathered up in the act of intuition, and connected with those which precede and follow it. This is what Kant terms the *synthesis of apprehension.* More than this is necessary, if a unity is to be formed out of these several points of perception. To this end they must be reproduced in the imagination and retained for combination with fresh impressions. This *synthesis of reproduction* in imagination is therefore inseparably bound up with the foregoing *synthesis of apprehension.* Lastly, before the completed categories can come into operation a further step has to be traversed. "Without the consciousness," says Kant (the passage, I may mention, occurs in the first edition of the 'Critique' only), "that what we think is the same as what we thought a moment before, all reproduction in the series of presentations would be in vain. For there would be a new presentation in the actual state, not in any way belonging to the act whereby it must have been gradually created, and the manifold therein would still not constitute a whole, inasmuch as it would lack the unity which this consciousness alone can give it. If I forget in counting that the unities which are at present before my senses have been successively added together by me, I should not understand the creation of multitude through this successive addition of one to one, and hence I should not understand number, a conception consisting simply in the consciousness of this unity in synthesis." The last-named consciousness is what Kant terms the *recognition in the conception,* which is necessary before the categories can obtain. Now we need scarcely say that all these acts or processes are *à priori,* that is, precede all particular experience; that they are further removed from the latter, even than the categories themselves, notwithstanding that each of them can be distinguished empirically, that is, in its application to given experience. The two first unite empirically in perception, and the third gives us the empirical consciousness of the identity of these reproduced perceptions, with the phenomena whereby they were originally given.

But deeper than any of these syntheses, deeper even

than the *unity of apprehension in sense*, lies the original *synthesis of the consciousness*, the *unity of apperception* as Kant terms it. All the unifying acts we have been considering find their ground in time; this one, on the contrary, is not *in time*, but time is *in it*. The necessary and universal identity of the knowing subject in respect of all presentations, or determinations of consciousness whatsoever, is the necessary condition of the possibility of consciousness. This primary *synthesis* is identified by Kant with the productive or pure *ego*, the ultimate datum of "theory of knowledge," as opposed to the empirical *ego* or subject-object with which psychology is concerned. The transcendental synthesis of apperception includes the secondary or psychological synthesis (the empirical self) as it does the whole world of experience. From the *synthesis of apperception*, the primordial "I think," every other synthesis is deducible. In so far as it refers to the categories and their conditions which we have just been considering, it is the "pure Understanding" which creates them.

Having now arrived at the fundamental and general grounds of the distinction between propositions which are necessary and universal, and such as are contingent and singular, it remains to deal with their application to phenomena. We have now clearly distinguished between the world of sense as such and its ordered connection, which we term Nature. Furthermore, we have seen that the distinction does not lie in that the one resides more, the other less in our consciousness, but that both elements constituting real experience, the world of mere sense-impressions, no less than the same world as modified by Understanding, is in the one case a series, and in the other a system, of determinations of a *conscious subject possible or actual*. Kant, after repeatedly assuring us that this alone is *our* world, proceeds somewhat inconsequently to postulate a world of things in themselves outside this system or world of experience. With this, however, we are not at present concerned.

Just as the laws determining intuition of phenomena as sense-presentations, reside in the Sensibility itself and constitute *pure mathematics*, so the laws which regulate the co-ordination of phenomena must be sought for in the Understanding and constitute *Pure natural science.*

The transcendental Analytic falls into two parts; *analytic of conceptions*, which is the statement of the ultimate forms to which unification may be reduced, and *analytic of principles*, which exhibits these elements of unification, as syntheses in the concrete world itself. In this way the question, "How are synthetic propositions *à priori* possible?" is answered generally so far as natural science is concerned.

But although it has been shown how the universal axioms of experience and of science are possible in general, it remains yet to consider more nearly the manner in which the sense-material is subsumed under the pure conceptions of the Understanding. This is the problem of those sections of the 'Critique' which are occupied with the schematism of the pure conceptions of the understanding. The mediator between the radically disparate elements of sense and intellect is the pure form of *time.* This, in the words of Kant, "is the third thing, which on the one side is homogeneous with the category, and with the phenomenon on the other, and so makes the application of the former to the latter possible." "This mediating representation," he continues, "must be pure (without any empirical content), and yet must, on the one side, be intellectual, on the other sensuous." But time is at once sensuous and pure, and, therefore, answers this condition. The immediate form of the category as applied to the sense-world must, therefore, be one in which it is united with time, or reduced to a time-determination. This form is what Kant calls the schema, which gives us the category as susceptible of direct application to the phenomenon.

As the Sensibility is the faculty which furnishes the sensuous-material of knowledge, the Understanding that which creates the categories, so it is *the productive imagination* which produces the *schema*, whose function it is to determine time and space by means of the categories. There is naturally a parallelism between the categories and the schemata. For the categories of Quantity the schema is *number*, which we have already seen to be a time-determination; for those of Relation the schema is the time-determinations—*change and continuance, succession, simultaneity;* for those of modality the time-determinations—*sometime, now, always.* All this is plain-sailing enough, but the category of Quality offers a little difficulty. The empirical element of feeling has here to be introduced, and the category of Quality can only be schematised as that of *filled, filling, and empty* time. "Between reality (presentation of feeling) and zero, *i.e.* the complete emptiness of intuition in time, there is a difference which has a quantity. For between each given degree of light and darkness, between each degree of heat and complete coldness, each degree of weight and of absolute lightness, each degree of the containing of space and of totally empty space, progressively smaller degrees can be thought of, and similarly between consciousness and complete unconsciousness (psychological darkness) continually smaller [degrees] exist. Hence no perception is possible that would prove an absolute void; for instance, no psychological darkness that could be viewed otherwise than as a consciousness, which is but surpassed by another stronger consciousness, and the same in all cases of feeling." (Kant's 'Prolegomena,' § 24, Bohn's edition.) This Kant calls the second application of mathematics to natural science (*mathesis intensorum*); the first, of course, being the original schema of number (*mathesis extensorum*). The schemata of Relation and Modality, which, like the corresponding categories, are of course dynamic, are always subordinate to those of Quality and Quantity, which are mathematic. To the schemata naturally, as to every other stage in the construction of experience, the synthetic unity of apperception, the ever-present "I think," is the ultimate motive power.

These *à priori* categorised time-determinations may be summarised as representing the time-series, the time-content, the time-order, and the time-complex. They severally furnish us with the metaphysical principles of science. The schema of number or of the time-*series* gives us the *axioms of intuition or perception*, which express in a general principle the fact that an object of perception is always an aggregate of parts, an extensive magnitude; the *anticipations of perception* supply the rule for the fact that every sensation, feeling or conscious state, though it have no *ex*tensive magnitude, has nevertheless *in*tensive magnitude or degree (*quantitas qualitatis est gradus*); in other words, both these principles are based on number; in the one case it is a number of parts outside one another, or time-*series*, in the other, a number of successive, and therefore anticipatory, gradations of feeling or time-content. The principles corresponding to the schemata of Relation, viz. change and continuance, succession, and simultaneity, and which fix the time-*order* of the phenomenon, Kant calls *analogies of experience.* They are, that the quantity of material substance in the universe is unchangeable; that every change has an external cause, and that in the communication of motion, action and reaction must always be reciprocal. Finally, the three postulates of *empirical thought in general*, based on the categories of Modality, give us the rules for the physically possible, aotual, and necessary, or in other words, of the time-*complex.*

These principles Kant insists are all that a metaphysic of nature can furnish us with *à priori;* the rest must be left to observation and experiment, according to the method of induction.* There follows on this a long section on the division of all things into "phenomena and nomena," in which Kant develops at length his distinction between the "thing-in-itself" and the appearance or phenomenon in consciousness—between sensible and intelligible being. The appendix to this section on the "Amphiboly of the conceptions of reflection," deals with the subject of the confusion of the empirical use of the Understanding with the transcendental. To this confusion Kant traces much of dogmatic metaphysics, notably the doctrines of Leibnitz. At the close of the Transcendental Analytic, Kant, in the second edition of the 'Critique,' appends a dissertation on the relation of criticism to the empirical and dogmatic idealistic theories of Berkeley and Leibnitz which need not detain us.

* For a full development of these fundamental principles in their relation to matter and motion, the reader is referred to my translation of Kant's 'Metaphysical Foundations of Natural Science,' in Bohn's Philosophical Library.

We have now reached the conclusion of the constructive or constitutive portion of Kant's Philosophy, that is, the portion in which he seeks to lay before us what goes to the making of experience, the data or principles which completed or real experience presupposes. The question, How is experience possible? is now for Kant fully solved. But how about the problems with which dogmatic metaphysics had hitherto been concerned, which had exercised the genius of a Leibnitz and the talent of a Wolff; which were so essential to morality and political stability; questions as to the first cause, the immortality of the soul, freewill, &c. Up to this point the tendency of "Criticism" had been unmistakably to show the utter absurdity of all such inquiries. In the next portion of the 'Critique' the "Transcendental Dialectic," which Kant distinguishes from the first part, by affirming it to deal with *regulative* rather than *constitutive* conceptions, he proceeds to treat of these problems in his own fashion, first "critically," and afterwards "practically."

Transcendental Dialectic.

This third division of the 'Critique' discusses the question: How metaphysics in the dogmatic sense is possible? just as the two previous divisions had discussed the question: How is experience possible? We are here concerned with the Pure Reason, properly so called, as we have before been dealing with the Pure Understanding and Pure Sensibility. The two latter were the faculties of Perceptions and of Conceptions respectively; the Reason is the faculty of Ideas. By "Ideas" Kant understands those conceptions which, though they do not enter into the constitution of experience like the categories, are nevertheless, according to Kant, universally present in human consciousness as "practical" or "regulative" principles, in the shape of problems, postulates and requirements. Just as the material upon which the understanding exercises itself is Sensibility, so the material upon which the Reason operates is the reality or experience, constituted by the combination of the two former elements.

For this reason the Ideas transcend alike sense-forms and categories, while, at the same time, they have a determination entirely different from either of them. The former are constitutive of experience itself; the latter, on the other hand, are merely speculative, being concerned with problems which experience indeed suggests but which do not affect its constitution, and which its nature precludes it from solving.

The distinction formulated by Kant himself between the Understanding, the logical function of which is judging, and the Reason, whose logical function is syllogising (if I may coin a word), is so obviously artificial, and dictated by Kant's love of symmetry, that it need not detain us, more especially as it plays no important part in the subsequent exposition of the "Ideas." Sense and Understanding are concerned with what *is*, the Reason on the other hand with what *should be*. Were we only sense and understanding, we should have no impulse to travel beyond the region of phenomena. This faculty of Ideas, the Reason, forces us, however, beyond the conditions of the given world of experience. As the phenomenon only exists in its relation to ourselves and to that which produces it, the sphere of experience is essentially the sphere of the relative, the finite, and the conditioned. Now, all the demands of the Reason turn upon the search for the absolute, the infinite, and the *un*conditioned. The great error we are liable to in the employment of the Ideas of the reason, is to forget or to ignore their true character, and to treat them as constitutive. The temptation to this is sometimes great, and when yielded to the reason becomes sophistical or dialectical. Whenever the reason dogmatises, that is, ventures assertions on matters outside all possible experience, it falls into this error. There are cases, however, in which such a proceeding seems inevitable. And in these cases the sophistications, or dialectic of reason, form part of its essential nature, and we can no more help our subjection to them than we can help ourselves being subject to the illusion that the sun moves, or that the moon is larger when near the horizon than at other times. But just as in the latter cases, although the sense-illusion itself does not disappear when we know that it is the earth and not the sun that moves, and that the moon does not vary in its dimensions, yet it is nevertheless rendered harmless, inasmuch as we cease to treat it as reality. The same with the illusions of the reason. As soon as criticism has unmasked their true character, philosophy must cease to rely upon them.

The Ideas of the Pure Reason embrace the Paralogisms, the Antinomies and the Ideal of Pure Reason. The first concern the absolute nature of the soul, the second the absolute constitution of the world-order, and the third the absolute existence of God. The paralogisms are so called because in them it is sought to show that the soul is simple and therefore immortal; that it is substance; that it is distinct from the body; all which propositions are based on so many paralogisms. In his treatment of this subject Kant first deals with the arguments of Mendelssohn and of Reimarus, and, it may be added, that of his teacher Knutzen, all of whom emphasised the unity of the self-consciousness as the ground of proof of the soul's immateriality and immortality. The paralogism here rests on the fact that by means of the Idea of the unconditioned, the reason demands that the ego shall always occupy the place of subject and never that of predicate; that all its presentations shall be referred to its own unity; and finally, that all which it perceives shall be regarded as other than, and external to, itself. It is sought to change these valid requirements, which are all fulfilled in experience, into dogmatic assertions respecting the nature of the soul apart from experience.

The confusion at the basis of this, as of the other paralogisms, consists in the failure to distinguish between the ego of the primordial apperception which, inasmuch as it is that which renders experience itself possible, can never become an object of experience, with the soul, that is, the object of the internal sense (as Kant terms it), or in other words, the individual mind or personality. This latter is as Hume had shown, given us as a series of "impressions and ideas," but, as Kant added, knit together and realised under the category of "substance" and the schema of "permanence." This confusion is the parent of other fallacies;

thus out of the logical unity of the subject is constituted a real simplicity; from the fact that I am for myself identical in every moment of consciousness, it is concluded that the soul is objectively an identical personality; lastly, from the distinction between the internal and external sense and its object, the subsistence of the soul independently of the body is inferred. "From all this it is evident," says Kant, "that rational psychology has its origin in mere misunderstanding. The unity of consciousness, which lies at the basis of the categories, is considered to be an intuition of the subject as an object; and the category of substance is applied to the intuition. But this unity is nothing more than the unity in *thought*, by which no object is given; to which, therefore, the category of substance (which always presupposes a given intuition) cannot be applied." Consequently, the subject cannot be cognized. "The subject of the categories cannot, therefore, for the very reason that it cogitates these, frame any conception of itself as an object of the categories; for, to cogitate these, it must lay at the foundation its own pure self-consciousness (the very thing that it wishes to explain and describe). In like manner, the subject, in which the representation of time has its basis, cannot determine, for this very reason, its own existence in time. Now, if the latter is impossible, the former, as an attempt to determine itself by means of the categories as a thinking being in general, is no less so." ('Critique,' Bohn's edition, p. 249.)

The sum of Kant's investigations into the paralogisms of the Pure Reason is that every "rational psychology" which claims to be dogmatic, that is, to establish doctrines concerning the real nature of the soul, rather than to be critical or determinative of our attitude towards the question, is, and must be, a delusion and a snare.

The criticism of Cosmology consists in the discussion of *the antinomies of the pure reason.* The Idea of the unconditioned requires us to expect a completed system of all phenomena, or in other words, a *world.* This world-Idea is determined according to the four classes of categories, and may thus be split up into eight propositions, consisting on the one side of the assertions of the Wolffian cosmology, and on the other, of their sceptical antitheses. They are as follows :—

Thesis.	*Antithesis.*
The world has a *beginning* (boundary) in time and space.	The world is *infinite* in time and space.
Thesis.	*Antithesis.*
Everything in the world consists of *simple* (parts).	There is nothing simple, but everything is *composite.*
Thesis.	*Antithesis.*
There are in the world causes, through *Freedom.*	There is no freedom, but all is *Nature.*
Thesis.	*Antithesis.*
In the series of world causes, there exists a *necessary* being.	There is nothing necessary, but in this series *all is contingent*

According to Kant, the natural dialectic of the Pure Reason is exhibited in these propositions; for, while the theses are grounded on universally admitted axioms, the antitheses, which are equally well accredited, directly contradict them. Each of the eight propositions is thus a correct consequence from self-evident premises. The inherent contradiction is thereby shown to lie in the nature of the reason itself. For of two mutually contradictory propositions both cannot be false unless the conception at their basis be itself contradictory. Kant's Transcendental or Critical Idealism, which distinguishes between phenomena and things-in-themselves, and rescues the word "phenomenon" from its sceptical implication of "illusion," is the sword which is to cut this Gordian knot. The two first antinomies (the mathematical) are disposed of by a demonstration of the fallacy alike of thesis and antithesis, inasmuch as *phenomena* are here treated as *things-in-themselves.* It is just as impossible to say the world is infinite as it is finite, for neither of these conceptions can be contained in experience, "because experience is neither possible respecting an *infinite* space, or an infinite time, or the boundary of the world by an empty space or a previous empty time; these things are only Ideas." On the other hand, since both conceptions pertain to the forms of sense, it would be manifestly absurd to predicate either of them of the world as thing-in-itself. The same reasoning applies to the second antinomy which concerns the division of phenomena. For here again the parts only exist as given, that is, *in* the act of division, in other words, in experience, and hence only extend as far as experience reaches. But it is no less impossible for experience to dogmatically fix a limit to the division of phenomena than it is for it to follow out that division to infinity.

The two second antinomial pairs are not like the first, mathematical, that is, concerned with the *quantum* of the world, but like their corresponding classes of categories, dynamical, that is, concerned with a determination of the world-order in a special manner. "In the first class of antinomy (the mathematical), the fallacy of the assumption consisted in that what is self-contradictory (namely, phenomenon and thing-in-itself), was represented as capable of union in one idea. But as regards the second, or dynamical class of antinomy, the fallacy of the assumption consists in that what is capable of union is represented as contradictory, and consequently, as in the first case, both contradictory assertions were false; so here, where they are opposed to one another merely through misunderstanding, both may be true." (Kant's 'Prolegomena,' Bohn's edition, § 53.)

In this no less than in the previous instance, it is the distinction between phenomena and things-in-themselves which solves the difficulty, though in another way. Both propositions may here be true, if the thesis be referred to things-in-themselves, and the antithesis to phenomena. It is quite conceivable that, while in the phenomenal world all the actions of man are the necessary consequences of his empirical character, outside this phenomenal world in his capacity of thing-in-itself, existing out of time, man may be the self-determining cause of his actions. It is thus that Kant reconciles liberty with necessity. Similarly with the fourth antinomy, it may be quite correct according to the assumption of the antithesis, that, as in the world of phenomena, every event has a cause—the *regressus* no less than the *progressus* of causes being infinite—the idea of a first or uncaused cause is absurd, inasmuch as this could only be discoverable could we arrive at the completion of the series of subordinate causes, which is obviously impossible; and nevertheless, the thesis may still obtain outside phenomena, *i.e.* outside the world of experience, in that of things-in-themselves. There is nothing contradictory here in the assumption of a self-existent, necessary being, for although the existence of such a being can never be proved, yet it can be just as little disproved, time and causality only applying to the phenomena of sense, and not to things-in-themselves.

The criticism of rational Theology is contained in the section of the 'Critique' on the Ideal of the Pure Reason. Kant has already led up to it in his discussion on the fourth antinomy. In the *Ideal of the Pure Reason* the Idea of the Unconditioned claims to be presented *in individuo* but not *in concreto*, being determined by itself alone. "The idea of humanity in its complete perfection supposes not only the advancement of all the powers and faculties, which constitute our conception of human nature, to a complete attainment of their final aims, but also everything which is requisite for the complete determination of the idea; for of all contradictory predicates, only one can conform with the idea of the perfect man. What I have termed an ideal, was in Plato's philosophy, an *idea of the divine mind*—an individual object present to its pure intuition, the most perfect of every kind of beings, and the archetype of all phenomenal existences." ('Critique,' Bohn's edition, pp. 350–1.)

This idea of the sum-total of all perfection, and of all reality, conceived as concentrated in an individual being, constitutes the idea of God, or the Ideal of the Pure Reason. Kant describes the progress of the reason in proceeding first to the hypostasisation, and finally, to the personification of this conception of a sum-total of all reality; but that the reason itself has a lurking suspicion that in the course of this procedure it has broken altogether with experience, is shown by the desperate attempt to justify itself exhibited in the three arguments (the ontological, the cosmological and the teleological), which it puts forward in proof of the objective existence of its ideal. Kant proceeds to show the illusoriness of all these arguments.

But if all the pretended proofs of the existence of the Deity are based on illusions of the Pure Reason, the atheistic demonstrations of the opposite are equally baseless, on the other hand. The non-existence of God can just as little be demonstrated as his existence.*

"The reason does not here," observes Kant, (with reference to this third or Theological Idea) "as with the pyschological and cosmological ideas, start from experience, and is not by a [progressive] raising (Steigerung) of the grounds, misled into an endeavour to contemplate the series in absolute completeness, but wholly breaks therewith, and from mere conceptions of what would constitute the absolute completeness of a thing-in-general, consequently by means of the idea of a most perfect original being, descends to the determination of the possibility, and thereby also to the reality, of all other things." (Kant's 'Prolegomena,' Bohn's edition, § 55.) Thus much as to the form in which the Ideal is conceived. As regards its content, its real purport and meaning, it is an indispensable regulative conception for our study of nature, no less than for our conduct; that is, the reason requires that we regard nature *as though* created and governed by God, and that we act *as though* we were accountable to God. The regulative, or disciplinary function of the Pure Reason as regards scientific method, and the systematisation of knowledge, is developed in the closing sections of the 'Critique,' which treat of the "Transcendental doctrine of method."

Kant's practical or moral philosophy is contained most fully in 'The Metaphysic of Ethics,' and in the 'Critique of Practical Reason.' The basis of Kant's Ethic is the "categorical imperative" by which the Practical Reason affirms its domination over the natural impulses. The moral man is, according to Kant, not he who is by nature benevolent, but he who acts well against his natural inclinations. The great distinction of Transcendental

* From Kant's "practical" standpoint, this fact has an important bearing, and therefore the stress he lays upon it is justified. Not so with our modern Positivists, Agnostics, and others with whom it is no more than a verbal quibble, and whose repudiation of Atheism can but denote mere social servility.

Idealism between *noumenon* or *thing-in-itself* and *phenomenon* or *appearance* in consciousness, of course plays an even more important *rôle* here than in the theoretical side of the critical philosophy. Man's will, as *noumenon*, proclaims the moral law which man's will, as *phenomenon*, receives. The categorical imperative, the "*ought* of that which has never happened," as Kant expresses it, can only have a meaning for me in so far as I feel within me the possibility of my accomplishing the demand made upon me. The fact that it does appeal to me affords all the proof requisite for me that the will is free. Inasmuch as without freedom no *ought* or moral law is conceivable, the latter is itself as much a demonstration of the former as the former is the foundation of the latter. The conviction of this moral freedom must, however, in no way be conceived as extending our theoretical knowledge. It simply affords a subjective demonstration of what the Transcendental Dialectic had already declared possible, though incapable of any positive theoretical proof. We have at the same time a subjective confirmation of another fact, which the Transcendental Dialectic had proclaimed conceivable, though not demonstrable, namely, that of our dual nature. While we are sensuous beings in time, we are intelligible beings apart from time. It is in my noumenal, intelligible, or which is the same thing, my moral nature, that I am really free, this freedom consisting in the power of the unconditioned commencement of a series of events in time. Thus practical necessity compels us to make assumptions which would be unwarranted were we to confine ourselves to the theoretical aspect of the case. In this we see the superiority of the Practical over the Pure Reason. These assumptions are the postulates of the Practical Reason by which we are to understand its necessary presuppositions for practical purposes, but which have no theoretical or speculative bearing whatever. In this connection, Kant steadily adheres to his original contention that a man is no more able to increase his knowledge by mere conceptions, than a merchant is to increase his riches by adding noughts to the balance of his account.

It will be seen from the foregoing that Kant's basis of Ethics is absolute intuition. The dictates of conscience are ultimate, and not traceable to any higher external source. Kant polemicises against the moral philosophy which places the principle of the action in the object desired, such as happiness, perfection, &c. It is quite evident that that is desired which affords pleasure, but this is obviously only an empirical principle. Even the principle of perfection is open to the criticism that it only puts forward conditional demands, and consequently affords no adequate distinction between expediency and morality. This objection is obviated, once we place the criterion of morality in the commands of the Practical Reason, and recognise them as ultimate, and *per se* of universal validity. The formula of this universal principle may be thus stated: so act that the maxims of your conduct may serve as a rule valid for all.

The conformity of the action with the above formula constitutes the conduct legal, the conformity of the motive makes it moral. The metaphysic of Ethics may be divided accordingly into the doctrine of right (jurisprudence) and the doctrine of virtue (Ethics proper). The first comprises the external and legally binding; the second, the duties with which conscience is concerned. The one is treated of in Kant's "Theory of Jurisprudence" the other in his "Theory of Virtue."

Kant's views on the philosophy of history, the conception of which was at that time recent, are contained in a remarkable little essay entitled, "Ideas for a Universal History from a Mundane Point of View." Kant here enunciates the now familiar but then novel conception that "individuals and even entire peoples, little imagine that in following their own interest, and often in struggling with one another, they pursue each in their own way, as a conducting filament, the design of nature, to them unknown, and co-operate in an evolution which, even if they had an idea of it, would signify little for them." And again, "there remains but one issue for the philosopher, and that is, it being impossible for him to suppose in the play of the actions of men a reasonable design of their own, he must endeavour to discover in the apparently absurd concatenations of human affairs, a natural design which renders it possible to trace among creatures, who themselves proceed without plan, a history conformable to a plan determined by nature." The following are the principal points in the little *brochure* from the introduction to which the above passages are taken. Kant admits a continuous development, subject to constant laws, in human history. The aspirations, the struggles, and the work, of one generation, bear fruit and are realised in the next, only to become in their turn the material for further development. This conception gives to the present a real bond of union with the past and the future. The primitive savage condition, to a large extent abolished in the relations between individual men, still exists in the relations of states to one another. This can only be terminated by the institution of an international federation of states. The solidarity of all the members of the human family, their union in a world-republic in which the distinction between Ethics and Politics would cease, and the conscious end of which would be the well-being and progress of humanity as a whole, such was for Kant the goal of history.

That Kant was stirred to these thoughts by the spirit and events of the time (the essay was written in 1789) there is no doubt; but how different the scientific value of Kant's contribution to the great question, trifling though it is in dimensions; how vastly deeper and more comprehensive his conception of the true bearing of history, than is to be found in any other of the writings of the "age of reason!" These, one and all, saw in the past little, if anything, more than a seething mass of conscious knavery and folly, which it was the function of mature human reason to unmask and denounce. Kant saw in it the parent of the present. He saw that history is no more the fortuitous concatenation of knaveries and follies the men of the *Aufklärung* declared it, than it is the arbitrary dispensation of the supernatural being the theologians declared it. Of course we find the inevitable shortcomings of an eighteenth-century view of the subject. That political forms are merely the outcome and seal, so to speak, of the several stages in the social, and, more particularly, the economical development of society, was a truth not even the most far-seeing eighteenth-century thinker could be expected to grasp. And Kant, of course, did not grasp it. With him, as with his contemporaries generally, the political and juridical aspect of human affairs was the fundamental one: so far as progress was concerned, their reconciliation with individual morality and liberty the final statement of the problem to be resolved.

On the 'Critique of the Faculty of Judgment,' the third of the great critical treatises of Kant, in which he formulates a theory of the sublime and beautiful, space precludes our entering. The work, as before remarked, is visibly inferior—look at it from what point of view we may—to its predecessors. It is needless to say it is not without happy and valuable suggestions, but, taken all in all, it must be pronounced arid, confused and unappreciative. Kant's character was especially deficient on the artistic side, and it is not surprising that his efforts to deal with art, and the emotions of which art is the expression, should have resulted in something like a failure.

Upon the wide influence of Kant on general culture, it would carry us beyond the province of the present volume to dilate. Well-nigh every department of learning, received an impulse from the founder of 'The Critical Philosophy.' The reception which 'Criticism' met with was unparalleled. "Many regarded Kant," says Vaihinger (*Commentar*, pp. 9–10), "as a prophet of a new religion, and Reinhold declared that in an hundred years Kant would have the reputation of Jesus Christ. The Jena *Allgemeine Literatur Zeitung* proclaimed a *novus ordo rerum.* In the course of some ten years three hundred attacks and defences of Kant's philosophy appeared. The enthusiasm aroused the hatred of opponents. Herder characterised the whole movement as a St. Vitus dance, while fanatical priests sought to degrade the name of the sage of Königsberg to a dog's name. We must not only be acquainted with the books written from a more or less impartial standpoint, but also with the subjectively coloured pamphlets and letters belonging to the period, if we are to form an adequate idea of the, at present, almost inconceivable commotion. The powerful impression of the Kantian philosophy on all classes in the nation, implied a corresponding influence on every sphere of intellectual activity. Theology, jurisprudence, philology, even natural science and medicine, were soon drawn into the movement, quite apart, of course, from the special philosophical disciplines which were subjected to its mighty influence."

The effect produced, however, was not quite immediate. Little notice was taken of the original "dissertation," which contained all the ideas of the 'Critique' in germ, while, as regards the only important review of the 'Critique' itself, it cannot be denied that it justified Kant's stricture, that the criticism had preceded the study of the work criticised. Among the earliest and best known of the popular writers on Kantianism was K. L. Reinhold, who, in his "Letters on the Kantian Philosophy," endeavoured to show that all the oppositions which had hitherto divided philosophy were disposed of by the new system. The foundation in 1785 of the Jena *Allgemeine Literatur Zeitung* contributed much to its spread. By the last decade of the century there was scarcely a German university in which the new philosophy was not taught; while its name at least, and in some cases more than the name, had spread far and wide throughout western Europe. Among the men of letters most powerfully influenced by Kant, were, Frederick Schiller, and Jean-Paul Friedrich Richter.

Among the most prominent opponents of the 'Critical Philosophy' may be mentioned Johann Gottlieb Herder. Herder was at one time a pupil of the Königsberg sage, but was more especially influenced by Hamann, a friend of Kant, but at the same time an opponent of the Kantian philosophy. The subtle distinctions of the 'Critique' repelled Hamann, who from a Humian-sceptical attitude in philosophy, sought refuge in a mystical religious illuminism. Herder's position was similar; like Hamann, Herder lays great stress on language as that which crucially differentiates man from the higher animals. But Herder none the less insists on the natural or human, as opposed to the supernatural origin of language. In the "Ideas for a philosophy of history" he seeks to show that in order to understand the microcosm, man, it is necessary to understand the universe; since man's place in or above nature is determined by the planet in which he lives, by the geographical, topographical, climatic, environment into which he is born, and finally by his original organisation. The whole of Herder's thought is permeated by a poetical pantheism and nature worship akin to the spirit of the eighteenth century, but totally alien to that of Kant, against whom Herder polemicises with bitterness in his '*Metakritik.*'

The special representative in philosophy of the above religio-mystical opposition to Kant, however, was Friedrich Heinrich Jacobi (1743–1819). Jacobi, while accepting Kant's limitation of knowledge to experience, and acknowledging the invalidity of all reasoning respecting the unconditioned, joins issue with him on the matter of the "faith" which is to rehabilitate the dogmas that are excluded from the province of reason. Kant's "practical necessity" will not suffice for Jacobi. For him certainty of the existence of God, the soul, &c., is afforded by an immediate intuition which is itself ultimate. The powerlessness of reason with regard to the question, is of the same nature as its powerlessness to prove or disprove an immediate intuition of sense, which is also ultimate. Of the nature of such an intuition is the "faith" of Jacobi. Jacobi's position, it may be observed, was but a revival of the stoical test of truth as consisting in "strength of individual conviction," and in a modified form, of the Neoplatonic "ecstasy." At such a point of view philosophy necessarily ceases to be philosophy, and becomes mere theosophy and mysticism.

In the flood of philosophical literature which the Kantian movement produced, the most prominent names beside that of Reinhold above mentioned, are those of Schulze, Fries, Beck, Maimon, and Bardili, all of whom occupied a more or less critical position with regard to the master, while acknowledging the fundamental positions of the new philosophy.

In attempting to discover a *modus vivendi* between the Dogmatism which professed to transcend experience and the Empiricism which accepted experience as an ultimate fact, without further inquiry into its nature or significance,

Kant struck upon the crucial distinction between *elemental* or *transcendental* and *real* or *empirical* condition. For the first, the self-consistency of thought, necessity in the order of coherence in the given whole, is the ultimate criterion; for the second, the necessary relation of events in *time* as determined by *causality*. Kant was unable to keep the distinction steadily in view, a circumstance not to be wondered at, considering the difficulties which he, as a pioneer, had to contend with, in striking out his new "footpath" as he termed it. Many a time does he wander back into the old beaten road of Empiricism or Dogmatism unintentionally, and even without knowing it, when in the midst of following out a transcendental argument. This is facilitated by his employing on the one side the arrangement and terminology of the empirical psychologists, and on the other that of the Leibnitz-Wolffian dogmatists. The distinctions of subject-object, mind-world, *phenomenon-noumenon*, &c., frequently mislead him as to the real bearing of his own thought, and make him forget that his point of view properly transcends all these distinctions. The pedantic working-out of the system, the forced symmetry striven for at every turn, which has been so often animadverted upon, on the other hand, is largely to be accounted for by the influence of the dogmatic system, which he made his model as far as the order and arrangement of his exposition was concerned. The symmetry is sometimes attained by the most obvious verbal quibble, as for example, where in order to make a perfect parallel between the ideas and the categories, a laboured piece of augmentation is introduced to derive them from the form of the syllogism, the categories having been derived from the form of the judgment. Many other instances will occur to the reader versed in the 'Critique.'

"Criticism" viewed as a system occupies a position of unstable equilibrium. Its professed solutions, in almost every case, have the effect of opening up deeper issues. There are many things in it that are so plainly "survivals" from the dogmatic and empirical schools which criticism professed, and, in the main with justice, to have superseded, that no student of logical mind, who had once grasped the central thought of the new system, could rest satisfied with it as it stood. For instance, he could hardly fail to see that the Leibnitz-Lockeian "things-in-themselves," the occult cause of the sense-impression, which were nevertheless wholly outside that "experience" for which alone, as Kant had been careful to demonstrate, the conception of cause and effect had any meaning or significance—were a "survival" certainly not of the fittest. But, after making all due detractions, Kant remains the most encyclopædic thinker the world had seen since Aristotle, a veritable sun in the intellectual firmament. There is no subject which Kant's philosophy did not cover, and to which he did not himself apply it. But the great heritage he left was not the "critical" *system*, but the "critical," elemental, or transcendental *method*, the method which was discovered in principle by Kant, himself by no means fully aware of its wide-reaching importance, and perfected as regards form by Hegel. This method, we must once more repeat, consisted in the *reduction by analysis of a given synthesis to its elementary constituents in order to reconstruct it in the forms of abstract thought from its primary datum.* This method is the method of philosophy *par excellence.* The thought of Plato and of Aristotle is based upon it, but from their time to that of Kant it had been more or less lost sight of. In our next thinker, Fichte we shall see this "re-reading," as it has been called, of experience, this reconstruction of the concrete or real world according to its elemental conditions, more successfully carried out than by Kant. Fichte found the track already cut, and it only remained for him to widen the path, and to clear away as far as possible the dogmatic and empirical débris which still encumbered it.

FICHTE.

Life.

Johann Gottlieb Fichte was born, May 19, 1762, at Rammenau in Ober-Lausitz. He received his higher education at the universities of Jena and Leipzig, where he entered in the faculty of Theology. For some years subsequently he resided in Switzerland in the capacity of private tutor. Shortly after he left Switzerland, having meanwhile abandoned his intention of entering the church, he became acquainted with the new philosophy of which the 'Critique' was the organon. His enthusiasm knew no bounds, and resulted in the production of a work on Kantian principles, entitled a 'Critique of all Revelation,' for which Kant procured him a publisher, and which was mistaken by many persons at first for an anonymous work of the master, so thoroughly had he assimilated the style, as well as the thought of the Titan of Königsberg. In Switzerland, whither Fichte again repaired in order to get married, in 1793, he published anonymously a lecture 'On the Claims of Free Thought,' together with a work, 'Contributions towards Rectifying the Public Judgment on the French Revolution,' in which he ardently championed the cause of the people against the then governing classes, royal, noble, and ecclesiastical. These were followed by some magazine articles on Schulze's 'Ænesidemus' in 1794. In the same year, Fichte was called to Jena, to succeed Reinhold in the Chair of Philosophy. The small *brochure* on the 'Conception of Theory of Knowledge,' which appeared soon after, contains the programme of his lectures. This was followed almost immediately by his first great work, 'The Foundation of the Complete Theory of Knowledge,' '*Grundlage der gesammten Wissenschaftslehre*.' Next came 'The Foundation of Natural Right on the Principles of Theory of Knowledge,' in 1796, and the 'Theory of Ethics,' in 1798. A cry of atheism that was raised against him, led to the publication of his appeal to the public in 1799, but he lost his professorship at Jena, notwithstanding. Fichte then repaired to Berlin, and in a short time obtained the Chair of Philosophy at Erlangen. Finally, in 1809, he became professor at the Berlin University, and retained the post till his death on January the 27th, 1814.

He published his 'Destiny of Man' and his 'Close Commercial State' in 1800; his 'Sun-clear Statement' in 1801; his 'Characteristics of the Present Age,' and 'Nature of the Scholar,' in 1806; and his 'Addresses to the German Nation,' in 1808. Fichte's complete works have been issued by his son; first the posthumous writings (vols. iii., Bonn, 1834), and subsequently a collected edition of the works published during the elder Fichte's lifetime (vol. viii., Berlin, 1845).

THE WISSENSCHAFTSLEHRE, OR "THEORY OF KNOWLEDGE."

Though Fichte's system, to which he gave the above name, is primarily based on Kant, it was modified directly by a study of the exponents and critics of 'Criticism,' Reinhold, Schulze and Maimon. The influence upon it of Fichte's early study of Spinoza is also not to be overlooked. Spinoza's Monism had early attracted Fichte, and contributed powerfully to mould his subsequent thought. Fichte rightly signalises as the epoch-making work of Kant, his having directed philosophy toward transcendental inquiries. While other sciences investigate the nature of known objects, it is the function of philosophy to discover the nature and conditions of knowledge itself. Philosophy is hence entitled to be called the "science of knowledge," and its doctrine "theory of science," *par excellence*.

Inasmuch as philosophy is occupied with knowledge alone, as its subject-matter, the philosopher cannot recognise any substantive existence or thing-in-itself outside knowledge. Furthermore, philosophy which is concerned not with the content, but with the conditions of knowledge, has no more concern with the object of psychology than it has with any empirical object of external intuition. The task of philosophy is rather to give a transcendental deduction of the process of knowing. Scientific method demands that this deduction should proceed from a single fundamental principle or axiom, this fundamental principle being one which precedes the distinction between speculative and practical that Kant had formulated. The test of the correctness, nay of the very existence, of a "theory of knowledge" consists in its ability, from a fundamental axiom, to deduce the subordinate momenta or syntheses of consciousness. Of course since consciousness is the fact to be explained, this principle cannot fall within consciousness as any *part* of its content. It must not be supposed, however, for this reason that "Theory of Knowledge" is a mere fiction of the imagination: it is rather the disclosing of the mechanism by which empirical consciousness comes to pass—a mechanism which cannot *per se* be object of that consciousness, inasmuch as it is the *conditio sine qua non*, which that consciousness presupposes.

"Theory of Knowledge," as science, must constitute a system which must contain implicitly the principles of all other sciences. The fundamental axiom on which "Theory of Knowledge" rests, must be one by which the matter and form of knowledge are alike conditioned. "We have," says Fichte (*Werke*, vol. i., p. 91), "to search for the absolutely primal ultimate and unconditioned principle of all human knowledge. As an absolutely primal principle it does not admit of *demonstration* or *definition*. It must express that deed-action (*Thathandlung*) which does not and cannot appear among the empirical determinations of our consciousness, but which rather underlies all consciousness, and alone makes it possible." The primal act in and through which the unity of the subjective and objective and all other syntheses is given, Fichte finds in the assertion by the ego of its own being. The form in which he expounds this ground-principle of his philosophy is rather calculated to give rise to the very misconception against which he guards his readers in the passage above quoted, namely, that it can be proved. He connects it at starting, that is to say, with the logical law of identity of which the formula is A = A. Fichte's only purpose in this, however, is to convince the formal logician with whom the above principle is ultimate, that this very "law of thought," ultimate as it seems, is only valid provided that A be originally posited; in other words, that the law of identity is only the abstract formula of the original act of "self-positing." The true formula for the latter is the proposition *I am I.*

This first position of Fichte, as will be seen, is identical with the "original synthetic unity of apperception" of Kant. "*That whose being (essence) consists merely in that it posits itself as existent*, says Fichte, "*is the ego as absolute subject.*" Fichte wards off the common confusion between the *I* of apperception, the ego as absolute, universal subject, and the Me of empirical thought, the ego as relative, individual object. "One often hears the question propounded: *what* was I before I came to self-consciousness? . . . The possibility of the above question rests on a confusion between the ego as *subject*, and the ego as *object* of the reflection of the absolute subject, and is in itself utterly inadmissible. The ego forms the presentment of itself, articulates itself in the form of presentation and becomes *something*, an object; consciousness acquires in this way a substratum which *is* . . . such a state is postulated, and it is asked what was I then, *i.e.* what is the substratum of consciousness. But at the very time this question is asked *the absolute subject* is assumed as the above substratum of intuition; in other words, that is surreptitiously replaced in thought of which abstraction was professed to have been made; and the question thus contradicts itself. We cannot think at all without presupposing in thought the Ego as conscious of itself; we can never abstract from self-consciousness, hence all questions of the above kind are unanswerable, for they are, when properly understood, impossible (*Werke*, vol. i. p. 97).

From the Ego as absolute subject or activity all reality is deducible. There is no reality but what is translated, so to speak, by and from the absolute subject. It will be now sufficiently clear to the reader that by the *I*, or (to put it in its latinised form to which the English reader is more accustomed) the *Ego*, Fichte understands what Kant had confusedly in his mind when he spoke of the *pure* as opposed to the *empirical* Ego, the pure self-consciousness which is the basis of all empirical thought, and which the Königsberg thinker subsequently identifies with the Practical Reason. Fichte clearly enunciates what Kant does but indistinctly suggest, namely, that the individual Ego is in the order of transcendental deduction at the opposite pole to the pure Ego. What was with Kant merely a notion arrived at more or less incidentally in the course of the working out of his system, becomes with Fichte the cornerstone of the whole. The attitude of the philosopher towards pure Egoition (*Ichheit*) is not that of mere introspection, but it may be rather termed intellectual intuition in which individual existence passes out of view, and the object of intuition is not so much existence as activity. That this primary act of egoition suffices to explain all the facts of consciousness it remains for the development of the system to show. Inasmuch as the categories are only so many momenta or determinations of the Ego, and inasmuch as it is they which determine the possibility of the object, it is obvious that the latter is only possible in so far as it is given by the Ego.

The second axiom of Fichte affirms the necessary *op*-position of the *non*-ego as the correlate of the original position. The corresponding logical form to this act of *op*-position (*Anstoss*) is *A is not B*. The primary act of position is incomplete without this secondary act of op-position. With the fulfilment of these two postulates the third is already given, for, as they mutually negative one another and nevertheless are both of them absolute—the one, absolute affirmation, the other, absolute negation, their synthesis must be *determination*, that is, the abolition of the absolute character of either of them *per se*, and the assertion, so to speak, of absolute relativity. The first axiom was unconditioned, alike as regards matter and form; the second is conditioned as regards its matter but unconditioned as to its form; the third is unconditioned as regards its matter but not as regards its form. In these three axioms, *thesis*, *antithesis*, and *synthesis*, we have the framework of the *Wissenschaftslehre*.

The reader will observe in them a further progress towards the completion of the Dialectical method. According to Fichte, we have here the categories of quality and quantity in their pure form, and derive them from their only source. In this primitive synthesis furnished by (I.) the original self-positing I-ness or Egoition, (II.) the non-ego posited by the first as op-position (*Anstoss*), (III.) the resultant limitation of the former by the latter, thereby abolishing its absolute character, all other syntheses are contained. We have now a clear road before us along which to arrive at the solution of Kant's problem: How are synthetic propositions *à priori* possible? or, which is the same thing, How is experience possible? a road unencumbered by extraneous and useless hypotheses such as "things-in-themselves," &c.

As yet, however, we are far from the complex, concrete synthesis—experience—of which we are in search. We must first see whether the original synthesis itself does not contain implicitly its own antithesis, which, in its turn, may pave the way for a second synthesis. In this analysis or search for antitheses, and their combination into syntheses consists the method of philosophy, a method, as before observed, already shadowed forth by Kant in his table of the categories. This, of course, might be carried on to infinity, were it not that the thesis embracing all antitheses and syntheses, the self-identical Ego or absolute principle of I-ness, forms at once the starting-point and limit of our investigations. The goal of "Theory of Science" namely, is to reach this principle which is its absolute commencement at the completion of the circle of its journey. It then appears as Kant's "law giving" or "practical" reason, as a striving for that which can never be fully realised, in short, it re-appears at the limit of the theoretic and practical, as *idea*. Midway, so to speak, between the absolute commencement and the absolute goal, falls the finite, limited, divisible Ego of individuation. The third axiom or synthesis, which embraces the whole of "Theory of Knowledge," may be briefly formulated thus: the Ego posits itself and the non-ego as reciprocal and determining. It is plain that this proposition involves two. First, the Ego posits itself as determined by the non-ego; and second, the Ego posits itself as determining the non-ego. In this distinction is indicated the fundamental division of "Theory of Knowledge" itself into theoretical or speculative, and practical. The first has to solve the problem of Kant's Æsthetic and Analytic, namely, how the Ego, or (which is the same thing with Fichte) the pure and absolute Reason can arrive at a knowledge of the object? The second deals with the problems of Kant's "Dialectic" and "Practical Reason," and contains the answer to the question: How does the Ego or Reason come to ascribe causality to itself?

"Philosophy," says Fichte (*Werke*, vol. i. p. 425), "has to assign a foundation for all experience; its object therefore necessarily lies outside all experience . . . . finite reason has nothing outside experience; experience contains the whole matter of its thinking. The philosopher necessarily stands under the same condition, hence it seems incomprehensible how he can lift himself above experience. But he can abstract, that is, he can separate by the free action of his thought what is combined in experience. In experience the thing, namely, that which is determined independently of our freedom, and to which our knowledge has to direct itself, is indissolubly bound up with the *intelligence* which cognises it. The philosopher can make abstraction from either of them, and he has then abstracted from experience and raised himself above it. If he abstracts from the former, he retains intelligence *per se*, that is, abstracted from its relation to experience; if he abstracts from the latter, he retains the thing *per se*, that is, he abstracts from the fact that it enters into experience; he retains it as the only ground of explanation of experience. The first proceeding is called *Idealism*, the second *dogmatism*." So much as to the standpoint of the older philosophy; but what as to that of "Theory of Science," which cannot rest satisfied any more with the mind-in-itself of the subjective Idealists than the thing-in-itself of the dogmatists?

Kant, who saw that the empirical idealist and the dogmatic materialist were each right as against the other, endeavoured to unite them mechanically. Hence his repudiation alike of idealism and materialism as such, and hence, also, his characterisation of his system as at one and the same time *empirical realism* and *transcendental idealism*. This mere mechanical combination will not suffice for Fichte. "Theory of knowledge" requires a deduction from one central principle. The "productive imagination" of Kant, by which Fichte understands the activity of the Ego as self-determining, which we have arrived at as the original synthesis of the absolute Ego and its negation, is the basis of the distinction of subject and object on which the old abstractions turn. We now see wherein the shortcoming of the old idealism and realism, respectively, lay. Inasmuch as the presentation is for the Ego a limitation of its activity, it is regarded as foreign to it.

Let us hear Fichte on this point. "Taking our stand firmly at the point at which we are arrived (namely, that of the primary synthesis), an opposition (*Anstoss*) takes place in the infinite activity of the Ego which, because it is infinite, contains no ground of distinction; and the activity thereby in no way destroyed is reflected, forced back, and thus acquires a diametrically opposite direction. We may represent the infinite activity under the figure of a straight line passing from A through B into C, &c. It might be arrested within C or beyond C. Let us assume then that it is arrested at C. The ground thereof will then, according to the above, lie not in the Ego but in the Non-Ego. Under the given condition the direction of the activity of the Ego going from A to C is reflected from C to A, but nothing can act upon the Ego, in so far as it is Ego without an equivalent reaction. In the Ego nothing can be destroyed, not even the direction of its activity. Therefore the activity reflected towards A must, in so far as it is *reflected, at the same time* react to C. And so between A and C we have a double conflicting direction in the activity of the Ego, in which that from C to A may be regarded as passive, and that from A to C as mere activity; both together constituting one and the same state of the Ego. This state, in which diametrically opposite directions are united, is the activity of the 'imagination'*; and we have now definitely obtained the object of our search, an activity which is only possible through a passivity, and a passivity which is only possible through an activity." (*Werke*, vol. i. p. 46.)

From this it will be seen why, on Fichtean principles, an Idealism which would make the activity of the Ego the immediate source of objects, is as incorrect and onesided as the Realism according to which the object-world is entirely independent of the activity of the Ego. The category of

* Of course the word is always employed in a transcendental, never in an empirical sense.

Ideal-realism, as Fichte sometimes calls his system, is not that of cause-and-effect, or substance-and-accident, but rather that of action-and-reaction. The formula for the theoretical or speculative side of the doctrine is indeed that "the Ego posits itself as limited or determined by the Non-Ego;" this is supplemented, however, on the practical side by the formula, "the Ego posits the Non-Ego as determined by itself (viz. the Ego)." Objects then are given us through the "productive imagination." Needless to say, we are still dealing with momenta prior in nature to empirical consciousness. The object appears here merely as limitation. It yet remains for Fichte to deduce the remaining stages in the production of concrete experience. In this exposition (which is given most fully in some of the shorter pieces written subsequently to the *Grundlage* itself) the main feature is, always keeping in view the fundamental axiom that there is nothing in the Ego but what is posited by itself, that the object as object is a reduplication, so to speak, of the original act of opposition, in other words, that it must become *for itself* what in the first place it was *for us*.* The Ego, in order to reflect on any moment of it determination, and thereby to constitute it object, must be already beyond that moment—must have left it behind.

The first stage or moment is that of in-itselfness, *mere feeling*, in which, as yet, there is no distinction between outer and inner, feeling and felt. In the next stage the Ego distinguishes itself from its *feeling*, and views the latter as in a sense outside itself. In this moment of *outlooking*, feeling becomes differentiated, pluralised—it becomes mutual independence (space) and onesided independence (time). At this point, says Fichte, the student may take up Kant's Transcendental Æsthetic. Just as the indefinite possibility of feeling becomes by limitation or differentiation, Intuition (*Anschauung*), so the indefinite possibility of Intuition becomes fixed, reduced to actuality by the limitation imposed upon it by the Understanding (*Verstand*).

In the syntheses of the understanding the *real* is

* This is important in view of the Hegelian Dialectic.

properly contained. The intuitions ordered and fixed by its categories became henceforward real objects. The feeling which the "productive imagination" distinguishes into inner and outer in the previous moment is the chaotic sense-world of Kant. The categories must not, however, as with Kant, be regarded as so many ready-made forms or moulds, but rather like the schemata, as modes in which the "productive imagination" operates in its creation of objects. The necessity for any formal deduction of the categories is, of course, done away with, inasmuch as they fall into the natural course of the exposition itself.

The intelligence, when it passes beyond the limits fixed for it by the Understanding, becomes abstract or reflective; in the consciousness of the possibility of this consists the "Pure Reason" of Kant, in which self-consciousness proper is first explicitly given. The intelligence has thus come to a consciousness of itself as such; the circle is complete. "Theory of Science" on its speculative side is now perfect as a system. We close this section with a quotation from Fichte on the method employed in the deduction of the system:—"In realising this deduction, he (the philosopher) proceeds as follows: *He shows that the first fundamental law which was discovered in immediate consciousness, is not possible, unless a second action is combined with it, which again is not possible without a third action; and so on until the conditions of the first are completely exhausted, and it is itself now made perfectly comprehensible as to its possibility.* The teacher's method is a continual progression from the conditioned to the condition. The condition becomes again conditioned, and its condition is next to be discovered. If the pre-supposition of Idealism be correct, and if no errors have been made in the deduction, the last result, as containing all the conditions of the first act, must comprise the system of all necessary representations, or the totality of experience;—a comparison, however, which is not instituted in philosophy itself, but only after that science has finished its work." (Fichte, *Werke*, vol. i. p. 446.)

Practical "Theory of Knowledge."

Speculative "Theory of Science" while explaining the process by which consciousness comes to pass, the conditions of its possibility, although it indicated the fact of the opposition or limiting by the Ego of its own activity, failed to demonstrate the ground of this limitation, a task reserved for the practical side of the Fichtean philosophy, which has to answer the question, How the Ego becomes conscious of itself as an active principle in the events of the world?—in short, as a moral agent. The answer lies in the proposition above given as constituting the formula of the practical side of Fichte's doctrine, to wit, the Ego posits itself as determining the Non-Ego. This, which is its starting point, is also its goal. Hence the supremacy Kant had already averred the Practical Reason to possess over the Theoretical. The fundamental axiom of "Theory of Knowledge" was the affirmation by the Ego of its own being as absolute. The question now arises, How is the finite objective activity which has been deduced reconcilable with this basal thesis? only in one way, answers Fichte, and that is, If the finite activity be conceived as means, and the infinite, end. This occurs when the Ego is conceived as a striving towards infinity, or, practically expressed, as conscious of its own activity as cause, which can only happen in so far as it overcomes a resistance; all striving implying resistance to be overcome.

"By as much as the Ego opposes to itself a Non-Ego, it creates *limits* and places itself in these limits. It distributes the totality of the existence posited generally, between the Ego and the Non-Ego; and so far posits itself as necessarily finite." (*Werke*, vol. i. p. 255.) This is as much as to say, since the activity of the Ego is now no longer occupied with itself, but with the Non-Ego, it has become objective (Fichte clinches his argument by a reference to the German word for object *Gegenstand*). "The object is only posited in so far as an activity of the Ego is resisted; no such activity of the Ego, no object. The relation is, that of the determining to the determined. Only *in so far* as the above activity is resisted can an object be posited; and in so far as it is not resisted there is no object." (Ibid. 259.) The object, therefore, is necessary to the realisation of the Ego's activity; it creates the object-world not for the sake of that world, but for the sake of *realising* itself in the *negation* of that world. The Ego thus affirms itself in a higher form, attains reality, in other words, consciousness of its freedom, in the negation of its own negation—in the overcoming of that resistance which it has set up over against itself.

The Ego now affirms itself as Will. The correspondence of Fichte's doctrine at this stage with that of Schopenhauer, it may be observed in passing, is noteworthy. Here then we have the ground of the original antithesis or opposition. This could not be deduced from a merely theoretical or speculative point of view. The first division of Theory of Science was obliged simply to postulate the antithesis as a necessary compliment to the thesis, without being able to give any further account of the matter. "It is now," says Fichte, "obvious how this question is to be answered. With the positing of the Ego all reality is posited; in the Ego all is posited; the Ego must be absolutely independent, but all must be dependent upon it. The agreement of the object with the Ego is therefore required, and the absolute Ego it is which for the very reason that its being is absolute requires it." (Ibid. 260.) Since Theory of Knowledge finds its highest ground not on its theoretical but on its practical side, it may be fitly called "Practical Idealism." "The result of our investigations," says Fichte, "is accordingly as follows: The pure activity of the Ego, which returns in upon itself, *in respect of a possible object* is a *striving*, and indeed, as above shown, an *infinite striving*. This infinite striving is to all infinity the *condition of the possibility of all object;* no striving, no object." The same method obtains in the practical as in the speculative side of the doctrine—here as there progression is spiral, so to speak. The *in-itselfness* of every moment of determination must become a *for-itselfness* in the next moment. The "productive imagination," the striving after the creation and articulation of the object, becomes, when pursued into the region of the practical, the striving for moral satisfaction—

the ethical impulse or tendency. The basis of the Ego as "Productive Imagination" was the Ego as Pure Apperception." The goal of the Ego as Freedom, Tendency, Will, is the Ego as *Idea* or *Ideal*. The Ego as Absolute Subject is unconditioned *Possibility;* the Ego as Ideal is unconditioned *Actuality*. Neither the one nor the other can be realised in the plain of empirical consciousness which is the sphere of the limited or conditioned, although its knowledge presupposes the first and its ethical impulses the second. In this the essential unity of the system is shown. What with Kant had two distinct roots, namely the theoretical and practical, and which it was impossible to bring into connection otherwise than in a purely mechanical manner, is by Fichte identified in one fundamental fact. The categorical imperative "the *ought* of that which has never happened" of Kant, becomes, with Fichte, the universal striving, the impulse, manifested on the one side in the production of the real world as the presentment of the Ego, and yet as independent of the Ego, and on the other by the ethical tendency, the aim of which is to abolish this independence and bring it back into subjection to the Ego.

It has been remarked that there has never been a system so antipathetic to "nature" as Fichte's. Since with Fichte nature is identified with the non-ego, which it is the ethical function of the Ego to abolish; his position with regard to it is identical with that of the Buddhist ascetic, for whom it is the *maya*, "that which is not and ought not to be," or with the less logical Christian ascetic. This side of Fichte we shall find developed in Schopenhauer. Just as Kant only admits theology in so far as it serves as a prop to Ethics, so does Fichte. He stands, moreover, by the distinction of Kant between *the legal* and *the moral*, between which Fichte maintains that there is no sort of connection, the object of law being to supply the means by which its mandates are to be maintained, even though justice and good faith should have vanished from among men. Hence law justly ignores morality, for morality deprives law of its *raison d'être*; the just man being a law to himself. It is in dealing with these questions, more especially in the *Grundlage des Naturrechts* (*Werke*, vol. iii.), that Fichte gives his deduction of a plurality of individuals or rational beings. This deduction is on the same lines as that of the original opposition (*Anstoss*). At first sight it is not easy to comprehend the possibility of deducing from the one indivisible Subject, or impersonal Reason, the plurality of individual subjects, but, says Fichte, the Ego must be conscious of itself as active, that is, must "ascribe to itself a free activity in the sense-world." It cannot do this "without ascribing it to others, and therefore assuming other finite rational beings outside itself."

The absolute Ego had already posited objects as the material for its activity to work upon. But they can only serve their purpose in so far as their necessity is given. The seal is affixed on this necessity when the testimony of others is added to my own. The universal Ego or I-ness, which is the condition of all consciousness, must therefore posit itself as individual Ego in a world of individual Egos, united under the category of reciprocity. The conception of individuality "is obviously a reciprocal conception, that is, one which can only be thought, in and through the thought of another, and it is indeed conditioned by the same thought as to its form. It is only possible in any rational being in proportion as it is given as completed by another; it is therefore never *mine*, but on my confession *mine and his, his and mine*; a conception common to both, and in which two minds are united in one. . . . The complete union of conceptions described, is only possible in and through actions. The consequence therefore is that it consists only in actions, and can only be required for actions. Actions occupy here the place of conceptions, and conceptions in themselves apart from actions do not and cannot concern us." (*Werke*, vol. iii. pp. 47–48.)

To each individual Ego a portion of the world-whole is preserved as the sphere of its own exclusive freedom, and the limits of these spheres constitute the rights of the individual. Within its own sphere the individual Ego justly ascribes to itself causality. That portion of my sphere of freedom which is the starting-point of all the changes to be wrought by me in the world of sense, is my body. This therefore is the immediate object of right or law. There can be no question of any obligation on the part of the individual to enter the state of law, but once entered therein, it follows as a natural consequence that he respect this state. We see evidences here of the inevitable social contract theory. Like Kant, Fichte sees in the state the instrument for giving sanction to rights by force, or, as he might define it, the condition of the realisation of right. Fichte's view of the state is that of the protector of the personality, in other words, of individual freedom. Property he considers as necessary to the maintenance of the personality. But the state exists for Fichte merely as a convenience, whose highest aim should be to abolish itself by rendering itself unnecessary. We must not leave this subject without noticing the remarkable anticipations of Socialism to be found in Fichte. In his early essay on the French Revolution he proclaims labour the sole basis of wealth, and hence the sole justification for its possession. In speaking of the collective organisation and subdivision of labour, and the possession by each citizen of the full product of his labour and this alone, he says, "Property will thus be universalised; none would have superfluities while there were any wanting necessaries, for the right of property in articles of luxury has no foundation while any citizen lacks his necessary portion of property. *Agriculturists and workmen will associate themselves for the production of the greatest possible amount of wealth with the least possible amount of labour.*" Other socialistic passages are to be found in the *Geschlossene Handelstaat.* "Each desires to live as pleasantly as possible; and since every man demands this, and no one is either more or less than man, all have an equal right to make the demand. The division must be made accordingly on the basis of this equality, so that each and all may live as pleasantly as possible." Fichte boldly proclaims it the function of his "state" to secure an equal enjoyment of the products of labour among its members.

Fichte's Ethics (*Sittenlehre*) are, like the "Jurisprudence" (*Rechtslehre*), divided into three sections, the first containing the deduction of the principles of morality, the second deducing its reality and applicability, and the third dealing with the system of duties. Fichte maintains in the first the necessity, even in the absence of any end, of regulating action in accordance with a pre-determined standard, to be the fundamental axiom of man's moral nature. He here expresses, in a dry hard formula, the basis of a whole school of Ethic—a school which embraces all the so-called Ethical or universal religions of the world. Wrapped up in imagery, in rhetoric, and concealed by theological theories, the corner-stone of the morality of these religions, all turn upon this arbitrary premiss, if we do but pursue it far enough. As will be already apparent to the reader, it is a legitimate consequence from what Fichte terms the practical side of his "Theory of Knowledge." He there showed us the Ego erecting a world over against itself for no other purpose than to realise its power in the subjugation of that world. That the individual should determine his actions for the mere sake of determining them, is the necessary corollary from this. Fichte has the merit of being the only thinker who has grasped the ground axiom of the morality which has been current among men for ages, and has logically carried it out. He proceeds to develop his doctrine respecting the moral tendency as causal factor in the events of the world, distinguishing between the sensuous impulse, or impulse to happiness, and the moral impulse. The moral impulse leads to a satisfaction, a happiness, which could never be obtained were it the object immediately sought after. Ethical theory frees men from the worship of this idol, happiness, and proclaims the end of all action to be the realisation of the Ego as Idea, viz. the "moral order of the world," to which Fichte applies the term "God." This is the basis of religion as understood by Fichte, which is identified with the moral impulse in its highest form. Its object, as idea, can of course never be realised in empirical consciousness; the relation of human life to this Idea must ever remain like that of the asymptote to the hyperbole, a continuous approximation, a becoming which never becomes, which is never finished. Fichte polemicises against the conception of God as existing object. Those who conceive the Absolute as *being* have really emptied the conception of its content. It is obvious from the main principle of Fichte's philosophy that the Absolute must not be considered as an existence over against ourselves. We must rather, in our own personality, be it and live it. The conception of the Deity as substance or personality, in however vague or refined a form, Fichte stigmatizes as the last remnant of Paganism from which it is the function of "Theory of Knowledge" to deliver men; any question as to an author of the "moral order of the world," is to Fichte just as inadmissible as the question as to the cause of the Deity would be to the ordinary Theist. Existence is a sensuous conception which has no *locus standi* in these matters. With the Ego as Idea, as "the moral order of the world," the system of Fichte reaches its final conclusion. It is not uncommon to divide the Fichtean doctrine into two periods; the later developments of the system, however, show no essential points of difference. The terminology employed is sometimes more carefully chosen with a view of accommodation to the Theological faculty which had procured his expulsion from the university of Jena, but that is practically all.

With Fichte, as with Kant, Ethics is conceived abstractly. In this respect the systems of both thinkers may be alike regarded in the light of attempts to reconstitute the Christian and introspective Ethics, threatened by the collapse of the dogmatic system of which they form part, on a more secure basis. In many post-Kantian thinkers, but notably in Fichte, we find this deification of morality as such, this assumption of morality as an end in itself, nay, as the *telos* of all. A great deal of the enthusiasm called forth by Kant may be referred to the belief that he had rehabilitated the old theological morality against the mere negations of the revolutionary writers and effectually rendered it independent of any theological basis. This hope, as might be imagined, proved but short-lived. The impossibility of a Christian Ethic apart from a Christian Theology has been conspicuously illustrated in the collapse of the Kantian and post-Kantian schools, a collapse almost wholly traceable to their staking their existence upon the achievement of this impossible feat. The fallacy running throughout them may be found in the hypostasis of the mere abstract form of the moral consciousness, viz. freedom. The effect of this galvanised introspective ethics was in the long run decidedly chilling. Well might Maria von Herbert complain to Kant that when put seriously to the test, his "categorical imperative" availed her nothing. It was no abstract "imperative" or "freedom," with a personified "sum-total of all reality," or an impersonified "moral order of the world" as its goal that inspired a St. Bernard, a St. Francis, or a Thomas-à-Kempis. The ethics of inwardness was in them a living reality, because it grew out of a speculative belief which to them was a living reality also.

The distinction between the introspective ethics of the old Christian theology and that of Kant and the post-Kantians, is as the distinction between life and electricity, between nature and art. The sooner it is recognised that the "ethics of inwardness" is a part of a whole, that it cannot live separately from a particular conception of the world, and of man's relation to the world, in other words, from a religion of the *supernatural* or *spiritual* as such, the better for consistent thought. The non-recognition of this is only an instance, albeit a serious one, of the common fallacy of regarding as fundamental in human nature what is merely the characteristic of a special epoch of historic evolution.

In the earlier periods of history,—not to speak of the vast pre-historic era—the individual, as such, did not exist, morally speaking, so completely was he absorbed in the social whole—in the *gens*, the tribe, the "city." Morality was then purely outward; men sacrificed themselves for the community as a matter of course; in active devotion to the community consisted all religion and all duty. The decay of the old social and race ideals was synchronous with the rise of another religion and morality, that of the individual as such. This was the religion and morality taught by the so-called "ethical religions" of the world, and which reached its ultimate expression in Christianity. It formed part of a new conception of the universe, in which the old standing-ground was radically changed, by the introduction of the notion of the *spiritual* over against the *natural*. Religion and morality, from being social and natural, became individual and supernatural; the test of the value of the individual was no longer to be found in his relation to the community existing without him, but in his relation to the divinity revealed within him. The spiritual or the supernatural abhors the natural as much as the "nature" of our grandfathers abhorred a vacuum, and hence the essence of the ethics of "inwardness" has always consisted in the negation of the "natural man," in other words, in self-renunciation for its own sake—in asceticism. It is this ethics of "inwardness" which Kant and the post-Kantians thought to rehabilitate apart from the supernatural theology, with which it is both logically and historically connected. The most pronounced representative of this ill-fated attempt was Fichte.

The author of the *Wissenschaftslehre* proclaimed in all its baldness the doctrine that the negation of the phenomenal individual is the final end of all morality. His desire to assert the ethics of inwardness blinded Fichte to the crudely abstract nature of the doctrine he propounded. As the outcome of supernatural religion, with its mystical relation of the individual to the divinity, it is real enough. The necessity of connecting it with something corresponding to the old "spiritual" ground was vaguely felt by Fichte, as it had been felt by Kant, and is expressed in his conception of the "moral order of the world" as idea; but the support was too weak to hold it.

All morality of course involves a possible sacrifice of the individual in the interest of something "not himself" *as* individual. The fallacy of the introspective ethics when proposed as a rational basis for conduct consists in treating this purely abstract element—this negative moment—of the moral consciousness as though it comprised the whole concrete synthesis of that consciousness. Ethics, concretely viewed, does not, as the doctrine of "inwardness" assumes, either begin or end with the individual *per se*, be it as regards *affirmation* or *negation*. Its reference to the individual as such is purely secondary and incidental.

The Fichtean negation of the natural impulses of the

individual is therefore utterly barren and objectless, since such negation only acquires meaning when directed to a definite social end.* The bare form of the moral consciousness, freedom, the glories of which Kant and his successors trumpet so loudly, is a mere abracadabra apart from a positive content? and such a positive content, if not furnished it by the arbitrary mandates of a supernatural being, revealing himself directly to the individual, must be supplied by the needs of the social whole into which the individual enters. The determination given to this "freedom," or which is the same thing otherwise expressed, to this possibility of subordinating directly personal interests to those which may be termed impersonal (*i.e.* as to what natural impulses shall be suppressed, and what not suppressed) is conditioned entirely by the forms of the social environment.

Any ethic which leaves this out of account, whether it be based on the "categorical imperative," the idea of the "moral world-order," or what not, remains abstract and dogmatic, which is as much as to say, it belongs to the past and not to the future. As a matter of fact neither Kant, Fichte, nor their successors really rested satisfied with the abstractions they professed to glorify; they read into their categories, and necessarily so, the current morality. The result was to close up their avenue of vision to a true view of the subject, by making them postulate the morality of the age as absolute.

It will probably have been evident to the reader, apart from all this, that there is a distinct line of cleavage

* In Ethics, if anywhere, we have presented the category of "reciprocity," or mutual determination, rather than that of "causality," or one-sided determination. In the *individual* resides the "moral tendency," the potentiality to the pursuance of impersonal aims. This is only actualised, only receives a determination when the individual is regarded as entering into the constitution of Society. Here the negation of individual interest is realised as affirmation of social interest. For Fichte and his school (*vide supra*) society exists only as food (so to speak) for individual "freedom" (*i.e.* for the moral impulses of the individual), which is its only *raison d'être.* This monstrous hypostasis is, we are well aware, the basis of the current morality, but it is as fallacious a "subreption" as any which Kant gibbets in his "paralogisms." An act of self-restraint apart from a definite social end is as barren ethically as a proposition respecting "pure being' is speculatively

between the speculative and practical sides of "theory of knowledge" as conceived by Fichte, which he vainly endeavours to conceal. The fundamental opposition between the moral and the natural, by which it is the function of the Ego, as practical activity, to abolish that which the Ego, as theoretical activity, had called into being, can hardly fail, we think, to strike the average student as a result somewhat arbitrarily imposed upon a doctrine which begins by annulling the absoluteness of the distinction between the Ego and the non-Ego, upon which the old dualism rested, and affirming their ultimate unity. One would have imagined such a doctrine should rather have led, as its practical issue, to a "rehabilitation of the body" to a declaration of the unity of man and nature, which it has shown to be, after all, a part of the ultimate essence—a crucial moment in the realisation of consciousness—rather than to an Ethic of asceticism and self-negation. The negation of nature would then mean merely the negation of its antagonism to man, not the absolute negation for which Fichte contended.*

The *Wissenschaftslehre*, as might be expected, found opposition not only from the representatives of pre-Kantian views, whose influence and numbers by this time had considerably diminished, but also from the Kantians and semi-Kantians, who were by no means disposed to recognise Fichte for what he himself claimed to be, the representative of the logical development and perfecting of the critical system. Not to mention the disciples of Kant, who all took up the quarrel, the master himself disclaimed all connection or sympathy with Fichte in the most emphatic manner. Jacobi and his school also joined in the onslaught. The *Wissenschaftslehre* thus found itself simultaneously attacked by Kantians, pre-Kantians, and religious illuminists. In addition to these, there were of course the popular writers, who, in spite of protestations and expla-

* For an interesting account of the life and philosophy of Fichte, the student is referred to Professor Adamson's 'Fichte,' in Blackwood's series. This little volume also contains one of the clearest condensed statements in popular English of the "speculative" principle and method, that we have seen.

nations, persisted in treating the absolute Ego of Fichte as though it referred to the individual Ego, and who amused themselves and their readers by affirming that "Professor Fichte regarded himself as the Creator of the world." But notwithstanding the opposition raised against him, Fichte succeeded in gathering together a small but enthusiastic circle of disciples. Foremost among these was the thinker with whom we shall next have to deal.

SCHELLING.

FREDERICK WILHELM JOSEPH SCHELLING was born January 27, 1775, at Leonburg in Würtemburg. In his sixteenth year he entered the Theological Seminary at Tübingen, where, in addition to theology, he occupied himself with philosophical and philological studies. Some years later he went to Leipzig, where he devoted himself chiefly to Mathematics and Natural Science.

In 1798, he taught, together with Fichte, at Jena; in 1803 he was called to the chair of philosophy at Würzburg. He became subsequently secretary to the Academy of Sciences at Munich, after which he lectured at Erlangen for some years. The last official position he held was in the university of Berlin, but this he gave up some years before his death, which took place in Switzerland, August 20, 1854. Schelling's works, which occupy 14 volumes, were published in a complete edition, between 1856 and 1860.

SYSTEM OF IDENTITY.

Schelling's Philosophy, or "The System of Identity," as he termed it, exhibits some not inconsiderable variations in its earlier and later form. As already intimated, Schelling was originally a follower of Fichte. His fundamental divergence from the *Wissenschaftslehre* consisted in an accentuation of the indifference of the basal principle of knowledge as regards the distinctions of subjective and objective, real and ideal, mind and nature. These and all minor distinctions are implicitly contained, and yet resolved, in the original identity, the Absolute.

The Idealism of Fichte, Schelling found to be too subjective. We have already seen that Fichte started with the Ego as the primordial activity, which all knowledge presupposed, to end with the Ego as Idea, which all morality presupposed. The Fichtean system is thus to some extent open to the criticism Fichte had himself made as regards the "Critical Philosophy," namely, that it did not form, so to speak, a complete circle. The fault is, according to Schelling, that it was one-sided; that although it might lay claim to the title of "Ideal-Realism," it could not be called at the same time "Real-Idealism."

Knowledge consisting of an agreement of an objective with a subjective, the problem of Philosophy or "Theory of Knowledge," is, according to Schelling, to determine how the object, the sum-total of which we call nature, can enter into consciousness, and also how the subjective, or rather the sum-total of its determinations, mind, or intelligence, can become object as part of nature. "The sum of all that is purely objective in our knowledge we may call *Nature*, while the sum of all that is subjective may be designated the *Ego*, or Intelligence. These two concepts are mutually opposed. Intelligence is originally conceived as that which solely represents Nature, as that which is merely capable of representation; the former as the conscious; the latter as the unconscious. There is, moreover, necessary to all knowledge, a mutual agreement of the two—the conscious, and the unconscious *per se*. The problem is to explain this agreement." Philosophy thus necessarily falls into two main divisions, "Nature-Philosophy," which deals with the problem, so to speak, of the subjectivisation of the object and "Transcendental Philosophy," which treats of the objectivisation of the subject. "Transcendental Philosophy," in Schelling's sense, regards Nature as the visible organism of the Understanding, while "Nature-Philosophy" has to explain the Understanding, as a product of Nature. In order to account for the progress of Nature from the inorganic to the organic and psychic, Schelling has recourse to the time-honoured theory of a world-fashioning principle or world-soul. "The necessary tendency of all natural science," says Schelling, "is to proceed from Nature to Intelligence, this and nothing else lies at the basis of the endeavour to reduce natural phenomena to theory. The completed theory of nature would be one which resolved the whole of nature into intelligence. The dead and unconscious products of nature are only the unsuccessful attempts of nature to become conscious of itself. Dead nature is only unripe intelligence, hence its phenomena, notwithstanding that they are unconscious, reveal a character of intelligence. The final goal of becoming completely object to itself is attained by nature in its highest and final reflection, which is nothing other than man, or, expressed more generally, than what we term Reason. It is here that nature first returns completely in upon itself, whereby it is evident that nature is originally identical with that which is in us recognised as conscious and intelligent."

Transcendental Philosophy has for its problem to deduce the necessity of our assumption that things exist outside of us. It is not within everyone's power to do this, but it requires a special faculty, that of "internal intuition." The philosopher seizes the act of self-consciousness in the moment of its becoming. In this of course Schelling is in agreement with Fichte. Inasmuch as in the free act of the Ego, no other being is posited but itself, it has to make an arbitrary act its object. The task of Transcendental Philosophy on its theoretical side is from this act to deduce the necessity present in objective experience. "The one fundamental prejudice to which all others are reducible, is this: that there are things outside of us; an opinion which, while it rests neither on proofs nor on conclusions (for there is not a single irrefragable proof of it), and yet cannot be uprooted by any opposite proof (*naturam furcâ expellas, tamen usque redibit*), lays claim to immediate certainty; whereas, inasmuch as it refers to something quite different from us—yea, opposed to us—and of which there is no evidence how it can come into immediate consciousness, it must be regarded as nothing more than a prejudice—a natural and original one, to be sure, but nevertheless a prejudice. The contradiction lying in the fact that a conclusion which in its nature cannot be immediately certain, is, nevertheless, blindly and without grounds, accepted as such, cannot be solved by transcendental philosophy, except on the assumption that this conclusion is implicitly, and in a manner hitherto not manifest, not founded upon, but identical, and one and the same with an affirmation which is immediately certain; and to demonstrate this identity will really be the task of transcendental philosophy."

Schelling divides the process of the production of the Real into three stages; the first extending from original blind feeling to productive intuition. Feeling, as given limitation, has its ground in a previous activity which cannot fall within consciousness, inasmuch as its result, passive limitation of feeling, is the primordial stage of consciousness. The progress from this stage to the following one consists, according to Schelling, in the outgoing of the infinite activity beyond its previous point of determination; what it then was *for us* it now is *for itself*. At this point Schelling seeks to show why the perceived or intuited feeling must appear spacially in three dimensions, in other words, as matter. Then begins the second period, from *productive intuition* to *reflection*. Here again, the course of the deduction consists in showing how the intuition comes to be *for itself* what it was previously for the act of contemplation. This period contains the whole multiplicity of the objective world as the consciousless production of the Ego, besides the deduction of time and space and the categories, which latter, however, are much reduced by Schelling, the categories of relation being indicated as the ground of all the rest.

The category of Reciprocity phenomenalised in time and space is expressed in Organisation. The interconnection of the parts of an organism is not a case of cause and effect, but of action and reaction. The universe viewed under the category of reciprocity may thus be regarded as an organic whole. In this also is given the ground of individuation in the subject, the explanation why the Ego hitherto limited merely by the object in general, passes into a second limitation by which it is compelled to intuite the universe from certain limited points of view, each one of which stands in the relation of accident to the sum of things. The third epoch embraces a third limitation, which is the foundation of Will. It is clear that the question why I regard a portion of the universe as specially belonging to myself, as my organism, is intimately connected with the question, how I come to regard the remainder of the universe as altogether independent of myself? Schelling's answer to this is that it takes place through an act of will. The transition from the theoretical to the practical sides of Schelling's philosophy are thus effected in a manner precisely analogous to that of Fichte. There is little indeed in Schelling's transcendental deduction which shows any essential variation on the corresponding division of the *Wissenschaftslehre.* The gist of the deduction is well given by Schelling himself when he says, "As natural science produces idealism out of realism, by mentalising the laws of Nature into the laws of intelligence, or superinducing the formal upon the material, so transcendental philosophy produces realism out of idealism, by materialising the laws of nature, or introducing the material into the formal."

In his practical philosophy Schelling is still mainly at one with Fichte. What Fichte calls the deduction of the opposition (*Anstoss*) constitutes the starting-point. The act of will has to be explained, the inherent contradiction between freedom and necessity which must be conceived as united in it has to be resolved. The category of reciprocity effects this, inasmuch as it is shown that this is brought about by the action of intelligences outside the individual Ego. The co-operation of many intelligences produces a world common to all. Through the interaction of individual intelligences arises the limitation of individuality. The world common to all is the arena of our conscious action, the sphere within which we know ourselves as causal agents. This turns upon the fact (and here Schelling's substantial agreement with Schopenhauer comes into view) that what we call action is only a modified form of perception, since perception itself is ultimately nothing but unconscious action. For this reason, *i.e.* because they are ultimately identical, Nature and Freedom can never really conflict. How at once the objective world conforms itself to ideas in us, and ideas in us conform themselves to the objective world, it is impossible to conceive, unless there exists between the two worlds (the ideal and the real) a pre-established harmony. But this pre-established harmony itself is not conceivable, unless the activity, whereby the objective world is produced, be originally identical with that which displays itself in volition, and *vice versâ*.

"Now it is undoubtedly a (productive) activity that displays itself in volition; all free action is productive and productive only with consciousness. If, then, we suppose, since the two activities are one only in their principle, that the same activity which is productive *with* consciousness in free action, is productive *without* consciousness in the production of the world, this pre-established harmony is a reality, and the contradiction is solved." Freedom can never transcend the laws of Nature, and the fact that impulse falls within the sphere of Nature, does not affect its intrinsic character. (This, be it observed, is nothing but Kant's phenomenal necessity united with noumenal freedom otherwise put.) Schelling proceeds to build up on the basis of the above a social, political, and historical theory, which, in spite of occasional suggestiveness, shows no real advance upon Fichte.

The main difference between Schelling and the author of the *Wissenschaftslehre* appears conspicuously in the "Philosophy of Art," and here again we find a striking correspondence with Schopenhauer. The fundamental distinction between nature and art is that between conscious and unconscious production. Nature has the appearance of design without being consciously formed according to design. The Ego is *for itself* and *in itself*, at one and the same time conscious and unconscious, in the art-perception. In art, which is the product, so to speak, of an inspiration which is itself unconscious, consciously exercised, is realised that Ideal which practice or morality is ever striving to attain but never reaches. Art is the resolution of an infinite contradiction; beauty is the incomprehensible miracle by which the ideal is materialised and the material is idealised, by which Nature is presented as the infinite possibility of freedom, and freedom as the definite reality of Nature.

The æsthetic faculty occupies the same pre-eminent position with Schelling that the moral impulse or conscience does with Fichte. Artistic perception is the objectivised transcendental. Art and philosophy have it in common that their subject-matter is a reality, but an idealised reality. The production of the artist and of the philosopher is alike a reproduction of the world which is in himself. The æsthetic or artistic consciousness forms therefore the conclusion of the system. Its commencement is intellectual intuition, its close is artistic intuition. Intellectual intuition, inasmuch as it does not fall directly within empirical consciousness, can only be appreciated by the philosopher who can distinguish it, and hence philosophy, as philosophy, will never be available for everybody. The æsthetic intuition, on the contrary, is merely the highest and most complete phase of empirical consciousness, and therefore art is available for all, potentially, if not actually. As Philosophy and Poetry were in the infancy of mankind united in Mythology, so its maturity will produce a new mythology, which will present in idealised form, not the history of any individual hero, but of the whole human race.

The departure of Schelling from Fichte is crucially shown in his constituting "Philosophy of Nature," coordinate with "Transcendental Philosophy." In this, obviously, "Transcendental Philosophy" is conceived as a science purely of the subjective, to which a corresponding science of the objective is a necessary complement. The opposition between them is resolved by Schelling's notion of the Absolute as pure "indifference" or "identity." In philosophy of Nature, Nature is regarded as productive (*natura naturans*), not as product (*natura naturata*). Nature is here viewed as self-limiting productivity; on the one hand maintaining its own infinity, while at the same time crystallising itself in limited products or phenomena. As the stream flows endlessly on, notwithstanding the continuous passage into nothingness of its individual drops, so it is with Nature; it is ceaselessly creating and annihilating itself in its products. Nature may thus be viewed as a struggle between the principles of universalisation and individuation, a struggle manifested in a series of attempts, so to speak, to realise an equilibrium. This is called by Schelling the "dynamic process" of Nature, and is worked out by him in the form of an emanation-theory.

Schelling, as we have already seen, defines the Absolute Reason as the complete indifference between object and subject. This conception is attained by distinguishing between the act of thinking and the thought. This absolute identity is the true in-itself-ness of things, and to know "things in themselves," is to know them as they are in the Absolute Reason.

The "absolute identity" of Schelling is, in spite of Schelling's protestations to the contrary, in no way distinguishable from the absolute Ego of Fichte, all quantitative difference, of course, falling within the region of the finite. The fundamental formula for the Absolute being A = A, that for the Relative is A = B, subject and object being combined in various proportions. *In itself* of course, nothing is relative. Were we able to take in the universe in an "infinite glance," we should discover perfect quantitative equilibrium between subjective and objective; it is only in individual things that proportionate differences between these two elements occur. There is nothing outside the whole; the notion of anything existing apart from the system of things which is the manifestation of the Absolute is due to the error of reflection which separates and individualises the inseparable and the universal. The quantitative differences existing in finite things as to the subjective or objective element they contain are termed by Schelling *potences.* The first potence is matter in which the two elements or momenta are united as gravity. Here we have the preponderance of the object; the second is light, the preponderance of the subject; the third is the synthesis of both—organisation—which, according to Schelling, is common to all matter. The correspondence of Schelling with Leibnitz is apparent when he speaks of inorganic matter as a sleeping plant and animal world. The doctrine of evolution, it cannot be denied, is distinctly present in Schelling's *Naturphilosophie.* Man is simply the result of the entire process of organic metamorphosis. What we term inorganic matter, contains within itself the potentiality of life; it represents, in its present form, the abortive product of the attempt of nature to become organic. In the ideal sphere the potences are, Knowledge, Action, and Reason. The first gives us the "true," the subsuming of matter under form; the second the "good," the subsuming of form under matter; and the third, the synthesis of these—the "beautiful."

The later developments of Schelling show an ever increasing tendency to go off into mere mysticism and theosophy. From 1804 onwards a strong Neo-platonic bias is shown in all his writings. This culminated after a lengthened study of the mediæval mystics of Germany, and of Jacob Boehme, in literary productions which amount to little more than fantastic rhapsodies of a religio-poetical nature. The exposition of these need not detain us, inasmuch as they have no important bearing on the subsequent history of philosophy in Germany, such influence as they exerted being purely on mystical litterateurs, such as Schlegel, Tieck, Novalis, &c., if we except some slight impulse they may have given to mythological studies.

Schelling's system as a whole can hardly be regarded as embodying any solid advance on Fichte, although there are certain departments in which Fichte was especially lacking upon which Schelling is suggestive. This is notably the case as regards Art. Fichte, like Kant, in his apotheosis of that emptiest of all simulacra "moral freedom," entirely ignores the Art-consciousness. In Schelling's Philosophy of Art, though there is much that is artificial and of no speculative value, there are also some luminous thoughts of which Hegel and later writers on Æsthetics have availed themselves. As regards method, Schelling is distinctly retrograde, if indeed he can be said to have any method at all. His system is, moreover, based upon the purely psychological distinction of subject and object, the importance of which Fichte had to some extent gauged at its true value. Schelling assumes the distinction as ultimate, and then endeavours to transcend it by a mere phrase. Well might Hegel complain that Schelling's Absolute appears in his system "as though it had been shot out of a pistol." The later writings of Schelling show him to have been essentially rather what the Germans called a *schöngeist*—the cultured man of letters with a religio-æsthetic cast of mind—than the philosopher pure and simple.

The "System of Identity" succeeded in obtaining a following, not only in the philosophical world, but, as was to be expected, amongst purely literary men. It was eminently congenial to the spirit of the romantic school, then in the height of its renown. That it should have attracted men of science, may seem somewhat surprising, yet so it was. The naturalist, Oken, the botanist, Von Esenbeck, the physiologist, Burdach, among others may be mentioned as disciples of Schelling. Among the philosophical adherents and expanders of the system may be named, G. M. Klein, J. J. Wagner the theosophist, F. Von Baader and K. C. F. Krause. The two latter, although they are sometimes regarded as the founders of independent systems, have in all essentials drawn from Schelling. The celebrated theologian Schleiermacher also belonged to the school of Schelling.

Before entering upon an analysis of Hegel's system, which at least, so far as method is concerned, forms the culmination of the line of thought we have been considering, we propose to turn aside in order to take a survey of two other schools of thought, which also have their origin in the "Critical Philosophy." Kant, as we know, makes an absolute distinction between Sensibility and Understanding. Sense is always with Kant the material principle, Understanding, the formative principle, in the synthesis of Reality. "Æsthetic" and "Analytic" are the two co-ordinate pillars on which the structure of the Critical Philosophy rests. The Sense-element in Knowledge is as incapable of reduction to terms of the Understanding as the Intelligible-element is to terms of Sense. Fichte, in his deduction of experience from the one fundamental principle of Egoition, took his stand on Kant's formal element, the Understanding, the starting-point of his system, being discoverable in the deduction of the categories from the original "unity of apperception." Fichte is, perhaps, not always quite consistent, since he sometimes, especially in his later writings, seems to identify his primordial activity with a mere alogical impulse; but nevertheless his sheet-anchor is, as he repeatedly insists, *self-consciousness*—the formal unity, the "I think"—of Kant. Fichte, in other words, starts with a formal principle; with him *for*-itself-ness is practically ultimate, and includes *in*-itself-ness; concrete reality is thus deducible from the formal activity of thought alone, the "I" is confounded or identified with the "think."

It is not proposed to pursue the subject further now, inasmuch as we shall have to recur to it again in treating of Hegel, in whom we find the principle fully and consistently carried out. We shall then endeavour to show its inevitable effect, as it appears to us, in the working out of the speculative method. Our only object in mentioning it here is to point out the position occupied by the line of thought, of which Schopenhauer and Herbart represent the two opposite poles, and which is based on the Transcendental Æsthetic. With these schools, the *Alogical*, whether as *impulse* (will) or *feeling*, constitutes the *prius* of experience. Schopenhauer analyses experience into the momenta of an impersonal all-determining Will; Herbart into discrete self-centered units of feeling. For the one, Reality is a continuous whole; for the other, a congeries, so to speak, of separate points; the basis of the one is Monistic, that of the other Pluralistic. Both these schools alike reject the speculative method, as is only natural, considering that they found on the "Æsthetic" side of the "critical philosophy." The idea which is confusedly present in Schelling's system is distinctly formulated by Schopenhauer. Schelling sought for a principle other than thought, and imagined he had found it in the phrase "Absolute Identity," or "Indifference." Schopenhauer asserted that the principle other than thought—the matter of which thought was the form—was Will undetermined by any specific content. Schelling seems to have a confused consciousness of what is lacking in Fichte when he charges him with subjectivism, a defect he evidently thinks his principle of "indifference" supplies. Schelling's grasp of the speculative method was, however, so weak, especially in the later writings, that he has little importance in this connection.

SCHOPENHAUER.

ARTHUR SCHOPENHAUER, the founder of Modern Pessimism, was born 22nd February, 1788, at Dantzig. His father, a successful merchant in the old Hanseatic town, was a great traveller for those days, besides being a man of considerable culture. The wandering life of his youth was doubtless not without its influence in the formation of young Schopenhauer's character. He resided for some time both in France and England, the pietism of the latter country proving particularly obnoxious to him. Early in 1805 Schopenhauer entered a merchant's office, where he remained, much against his inclinations, for twelve months; after which, his father having died in the meantime in consequence of an accident, he entered the university of Gotha, with the intention of devoting himself to literature. He subsequently left Gotha for Weimar, then at the zenith of its literary splendour, his own mother, Johanna Schopenhauer, the novelist, being a prominent figure there. In 1807 he repaired to Göttingen, where he matriculated in the medical faculty. After some further travelling, in the course of which he visited Italy, he finally settled down at Frankfort-on-the-Maine, where he remained, with but little intermission, until his death on September 21st, 1860, and where most of his works were written.

Schopenhauer, though not so voluminous a writer as Fichte or Schelling, possesses a literary charm, wanting in all other German philosophers. He was an ardent student of those remarkable products of Oriental thought, the Upanischads, and it is to these, conjoined with Kant, that his conception of a systematic Pessimism must be immediately traced. Schopenhauer's chief work is his 'World as Will and Presentation.' He is also the author of a treatise, 'On the fourfold Root of the principle of adequate cause' (his first work), of two charming volumes of miscellaneous essays to which he gave the name of 'Parerga and Paralipomena,' of a treatise on 'Will in Nature,' and other less important pieces.

Philosophy of Schopenhauer.

In his earliest work, 'The Fourfold Root,' Schopenhauer takes his stand on Kant's reduction of space and time to subjective forms. He, however, blames Kant for having assumed twelve categories where one only, that of Causality, is necessary. He also criticises Kant's separation of perception from thought, since space and time themselves are but one of the four forms of the principle of causation which is as much sensuous as intellectual. The four forms of the principle of causality, in question, are termed by Schopenhauer respectively the *ratio essendi, fiendi, agendi, et cognoscendi.* The two first forms are constructive of the object itself. The *ratio essendi* is nothing other than the space and time form of the inner and outer sense—succession and co-existence. The *ratio fiendi* is the relation of things as cause and effect, properly so called. By this relation, causality constitutes the object in time and space, real. Through causality alone can it become object; hence the notion of an object apart from the relation implied in causality (*e.g.* a first-cause) is a contradiction in terms. The three chief phases of *cause-and-effect* are mechanical impact (inorganic), irritability or reflex action (organic), and motive (psychic). Every change of state pre-supposes a prior state; hence the absurdity of the assumptions of Theism. Matter is the only reality, inasmuch as a timed, spaced, and caused object, must necessarily be material. The *ratio fiendi* of Schopenhauer, unlike Kant's category of cause and effect, is not, as it were, thought *into* the object by the understanding; the causal relations proper, of the latter, are as much intuited as its time and space relations. The third principle, the *ratio cognoscendi*, is not, like the two former, constructive of the object, *i.e.* not creative; it is the faculty of discursive thought, which by Kant, Fichte, Schelling, and their school, has been falsely, under the name of the "Reason," given a pre-eminence over those principles which go to the construction of the real. The *ratio cognoscendi* is, in short, merely the faculty of forming abstract conceptions. The fourth form of the principle of

Cause, the *ratio agendi*, shows us the principle as determined from within, but none the less *necessarily* determined, in other words as *individual will* or *motivation*. To sum up: the principle of Cause in its four forms, interpenetrates the world, but inasmuch as it is only a principle belonging to our faculty of presentation, it follows that the world itself is nothing but our presentation. The Ego itself is but phenomenal, and appears as individual in so far as it is an object in time and space, since they may be called the *principia individuationis.* My body has as much right to the appellation *microcosmos* as the universe has to the appellation *makanthropos.*

The foregoing exposition, which is contained in 'The Fourfold Root,' may be regarded, taken by itself, as little more than a rectified Kantism. This view is modified directly the main position of Schopenhauer is taken into consideration. Schopenhauer's philosophy does not rest satisfied with an analysis of the world as phenomenon, that is, as subordinated to the principle of causation. It claims to have a word to say on the world regarded as thing-in-itself, as *noumenon.* The immediate investigation into the nature of experience discloses a something which we call *world*, appearing under divers forms, all of which may ultimately be regarded as modes of causation. But what is this thing which appears, which becomes object of consciousness—what is the thing, that is considered apart from its appearance? Schopenhauer's answer is, *that which appears* is not *consciousness*, for the latter, pursue it as far back as you may, still remains only the *form* assumed by the thing itself; this, the *matter* of the world, is not conscious but a-conscious, not Intellect but Will.

"The idea of the soul as a metaphysical being," says Schopenhauer, "in whose absolute simplicity will and intellect were an indissoluble unity, was a great and permanent impediment to all deeper insight into natural phenomena. The cardinal merit of my doctrine, and that which puts it in opposition to all former philosophies, is the perfect separation of the will from the intellect. All former philosophers thought will to be inseparable from intellect; the will was declared to be conditioned by the intellect, or even to be a mere function of it, whilst the intellect was regarded as the fundamental principle of our spiritual existence. I am well aware that to the future alone belongs the recognition of this doctrine, but to the future philosophy the separation, or rather the decomposition of the soul into two heterogeneous elements, will have the same significance as the decomposition of water had to chemistry. Not the soul is the eternal and indestructible principle of life in man, but what I might call the root of the soul, and that is the *Will*. The so-called soul is already a compound; it is the combination of will and *νοῦς*, intellect. The intellect is the secondary, the *posterius* in any organism, and, as a mere function of the brain, dependent upon the organism. The will, on the contrary, is primary, the *prius* of the organism, and the organism consequently is conditioned by it. For the will is the very 'thing-in-itself,' which in conception (that is, in the peculiar function of the brain) exhibits itself as an organic body. Only by virtue of the forms of cognition, that is, by virtue of that function of the brain—hence only in conception—is one's body something extended and organic, and not apart therefrom or immediately in self-consciousness. Just as the various single acts of the body are nothing but the various acts of the will portrayed in the represented world, so is the shape of this body as a totality, the image of its will as a whole. In all organic functions of the body, therefore, just as in its external actions, the will is the '*agens*.' True physiology shows the intellect to be the product of the physical organisation, but true metaphysics show, that physical existence itself is the product, or rather the appearance, of a spiritual *agens*, to wit, the will; nay, that matter itself is conditioned through conception, in which alone it exists. Perception and thought may well be explained by the nature of the organism; the will never can be; the contrary is true, namely, that every organism originates by and from the will." (*Ueber den Willen in der Natur*, 2nd edition, 1854, Frankfort, pp. 19–20.) The foregoing quotation may fairly be taken as a succinct epitome of the more purely metaphysical side of Schopenhauer's philosophy.

Our consciousness of ourself is a consciousness of ourself as object; that which *becomes* consciousness of itself, in other words, the in-itselfness of the world, and *à fortiori*, of ourselves as individuals, is nothing other than that element of our nature which we term Will. By the word Will, in Schopenhauer's sense, is to be understood all impulse whatsoever, mechanical, physical, chemical, no less than organic and psychic. It is the same impulse which is manifested in gravitation, in magnetism, which expresses itself in the growth of the plant, in the reproduction and development of the animal, and in the will of man. Why, then, it may be asked, does Schopenhauer employ the word *will* rather than *force* to designate this in-itselfness, this infinite potentiality of the world? His reply is, that he designates it by the term connoting its highest expression (as it is immediately known to us); *will* is known immediately, *force* mediately only. "The distance," observed Schopenhauer, "the indeed, in appearance, complete diversity between the phenomenon of inorganic nature, and that Will which we perceive to be the inmost nature of our own being, arises mainly from the contrast between the fully determined regularity of the one, and the apparently lawless independence of the other class of phenomena. For in man the individuality comes strongly to the fore; each has a special character, hence the same motive has not the same power over all, and there are thousands of surrounding circumstances having their place in the wide sphere of individual knowledge, but remaining unknown to others, which modify its effect; for this reason the action cannot be predicted from the motive alone, inasmuch as the other factor is wanting, namely, the exact acquaintance with the individual character and the knowledge accompanying it. On the other hand, the phenomena of natural forces exhibits the opposite extreme; they act according to universal laws, without deviation, without individuality, in accordance with obvious circumstances, and are capable of the most precise prevision, the same natural force manifesting itself in millions of phenomena precisely in the same way" (*Welt als Wille*, vol. i. pp. 134–5).

The most immediate objectivation of the will is the organism or body. For the Subject of knowledge the body is given in a twofold way, as an object amongst objects, subject to the laws of matter, and as the direct embodiment of Will. The act of the will and the act of the body are not two things bound together by a causal nexus,—the action of the body does not *follow* the action of the will, as an effect follows a cause—but the two states are the same fact differently viewed, in other words, as above stated, the body is the immediate objectivation of the will. The question as to the existence of the external world resolves itself, when closely viewed, into the question whether the objects known to the individual merely as such, that is, merely as presentations, are, like his own body, manifestations of Will. We are justified, according to Schopenhauer, in applying the analogy of the object, our own body, which, as we have said, is manifested in a double way, to other objects which are not so manifested. They agree with it in that they are phenomena of consciousness. Let us abstract from this aspect of them, and they remain either nothing at all, as the subjective idealist affirms (an assertion which is obviously a *reductio ad absurdum*), or else they must be of the same nature with that which in ourselves we term will. As in man that which determines character is will, so the *quality* which distinguishes things, which gives them their specific character, consists in the particular stage in the objectivation of the will which they represent. The will, as manifested in time and space and subject to cause, appears in an infinity of individuals, for time and space are the principles of individuation. In itself, on the other hand, the Will is absolutely one and indivisible.

Between the will as thing-in-itself, and the will as individualised in space and time, we have to consider the will as expressed in the several stages of its objectivation. These stages of the objectivation of the will correspond to the ideas of Plato. They are the eternal changeless forms, the permanent *entia*, of which the evanescent flux of individuals partakes, and by which they are more or less imperfectly expressed. This doctrine furnishes the basis for Schopenhauer's theory of Art, just as the doctrine of the Will (or as Schopenhauer sometimes terms it the "will-to-live"), as thing-in-itself furnishes the basis for his theory of Ethics.

We have already seen that the will as thing-in-itself is opposed to the Will as phenomenon or object of consciousness, as which it tends to lose its essential character. The essence of will consists in activity, in a striving after something unattained. The essence of intelligence or understanding, as Schopenhauer terms it, that is, of completed consciousness, consists, on the other hand, in passivity—in the contemplation of an object as given. In ordinary Empirical consciousness, however, which takes place under the forms of time and space, the two aspects, that of the world as will, and the world as perception appear, together. It is only in the art-product, in the æsthetic consciousness, that intelligence or perception is to be found pure and undisturbed by the restless striving of Will. First of all let us hear Schopenhauer on the essential nature of Will. "All willing," he says, "arises from desire, that is from want, that is from suffering. Satisfaction makes an end of this; but nevertheless, for every wish that is gratified, there remain at least ten unfulfilled. Furthermore, desire lasts long; its yearnings are infinite, while satisfaction is short, and sparingly measured out. But even the satisfaction is only illusory; the gratified wish at once gives place to a new one; the former is a recognised, the latter a still unrecognised, mistake. Lasting, unfading satisfaction, no desired object of the will can afford; it is like the alms thrown to the beggar, which prolong his life for the day, only to postpone his suffering till the morrow. So long, therefore, as our consciousness is absorbed in our will, so long are we given up to the stress of wishes with its continuous hoping and fearing; so long as we are the subject of will, lasting happiness or rest will never be our lot. Whether we pursue or flee, dread evil or strive after pleasure, is essentially the same, the care for an ever onward urging will, it matters not what be its shape, ceaselessly moves and fills the consciousness; but without rest no true happiness is possible. Thus is the subject of the will bound eternally on the revolving wheel of Ixion, thus does it ceaselessly gather in the sieve of the Danaids, thus, like Tantalus, is it ever languishing" (*Welt als Wille*, vol. i., § 38). In this fine passage the Pessimistic doctrine is admirably expressed. Schopenhauer's pessimism is something more than empirical pessimism. It claims a character of *à priori* certainty. The absolute Will, in sundering itself into I and not I, entered a fiery ordeal which can only be terminated by *the negation of the will to live*, but of this more anon. To the common mind pleasure is positive, and pain negative. For Schopenhauer this is an illusion, the reverse being the truth. Pain is the positive, and pleasure the negative. Pleasure being nothing more than the cessation of a pain, or the satisfaction of a want, consequent on which new pains or new wants obtrude themselves. In short, since all Will implies action, all action want, all want pain, it follows that pain and misery are the essential condition of Will, and of that ordinary empirical consciousness into which Will enters, *i.e.* the consciousness which is subordinated to space, time and cause, and which constitutes the illusory world of multiplicity and individuation—the veil of the Maya, to employ the language of the Upanischads. But as before said, there is another kind of consciousness which is pure and free from any admixture with Will as such.

It is this consciousness which contemplates the stages of the Will's objectivation in their pure form and not as distorted by the time and space world of individual things. In this æsthetic contemplation the Will becomes more or less completely dominated by, or, we may rather say, metamorphosed into, "presentation" (*Vorstellung*), the latter in this case not being, as in ordinary consciousness, merely "the servant of the Will." The third book of Schopenhauer's *Welt als Wille und Vorstellung*, is occupied with a discussion on the place occupied by the several departments of the fine Arts in the presentment of the Will's objectivation. The idea, although not subject to the various forms of the principle of causality, bears nevertheless the most universal characteristic of knowledge or presentment, that of being an object for a subject. As individuals, we have no knowledge but such as is involved in causation, and from the knowledge of individual things we can only raise ourselves to the knowledge of the ideas by virtue of a change in our cognitive nature, by which, from being individual it becomes universal. The natural state wherein consciousness or perception is at the service of the Will is in the case of animals not to be transcended. Man alone can attain to a knowledge of the idea in so far as his consciousness severs itself from its natural obedience to the Will. In the fixed contemplation of the object in its intrinsic nature, the Why, the Wherefore, and the When of things is neglected; their Whatness, their quality, is alone considered, not in discursive thought but in immediate perception. This peculiar mode of cognition is the foundation of Art; in the Art-work the idea seized in this act of contemplation, is reproduced under the forms of empirical consciousness. The aim of Art is the presentment of these ideas, which are the essential and permanent in all the phenomena of the world. What is the process by which the creations of Art are produced? asks Schopenhauer. "It is supposed by the imitation of Nature; but wherein shall the Artist recognise the successful in her and the work which is to be imitated, and pick it out from among her abortive attempts, if he do not anticipate the Beautiful *prior to experience?* Besides, has Nature ever furnished a human being perfectly beautiful in every respect? It has been supposed that the Artist must gather together the beautiful sides of many individual human beings, and out of these piece together a beautiful whole, a false and foolish opinion! For we ask again, How shall we know that precisely these forms are beautiful and those not? * * * Purely *à posteriori* and through mere experience no knowledge of the Beautiful is possible; it is always at least in part *à priori*, although of course, in a different sense to the forms of the principle of cause of which we are also conscious *à priori*."

The idea as such, which the Art-work reproduces, is apart from space, time and individuation, but its reproduction through a sensuous medium shows various gradations represented by the various Arts. In Music we have the purest and most immediate reproduction of the idea; in all the other Arts, notably Sculpture and Painting, this takes place through special archetypal forms, the Platonic ideas proper, but in Music without the intervention of any special form. "After having," says Schopenhauer, "considered in the foregoing all the fine Arts in that universality which our standpoint demands, beginning from Architecture, whose end, as such, is to render clear the objectivation of the Will at the lowest stage of its manifestation, where it appears as dull, unconscious, determinate impulse of the mass—though even here revealing differentiation and struggle, to wit, as between gravity and fixity—and closing our consideration with the tragedy, which, at the highest stage of the objectivation of the Will, exhibits its conflict with itself in fearful magnitude and clearness, we find there is still one of the fine Arts which has of necessity been excluded from our investigation, since there was no place for it in the systematic connection of our exposition; it is *Music*. It stands apart from all others * * * The Ideas are the adequate objectivation of the Will; to excite the knowledge of these through the presentation of individual things is the end of all the Arts. They all objectivise the Will mediately, namely, through the Ideas, our world being nothing but the phenomenon of the Ideas in plurality, by means of the *principium individuationis* which is the only possible form of knowledge for the individual. Music, on the other hand, inasmuch as it transcends the Ideas, is completely independent of the phenomenal world, ignores it entirely, and could, in a sense, exist, even though the world were not, which cannot be said of the other Arts. Music is, therefore, as immediate an objectivation and reflection of the Will as is the World itself; or as are the Ideas, whose manifold phenomenon the world of individual things, is. Music is thus in no wise like the other Arts, the copy of the Ideas, but the copy of the Will itself, whose objectivity the Ideas are. For this reason the effect of Music is so much more powerful and impressive than that of the other Arts, for while *they* speak only of shadows, *it* speaks of substance." (*Welt als Wille*, vol. i., § 52.)

The delight afforded by the Beautiful, the joys of Art, the enthusiasm of the Artist, all turn upon the fact, that in Art the striving of the Will is temporarily stilled. In æsthetic contemplation we cease to will, we become purely passive, we cognise merely. But Art, though a quietude of the Will, does not deliver it for ever, but only during moments of life, and is therefore not the way out of the struggle, but at best, a temporary consolation within it. The final deliverance which constitutes the main problem of the Ethical side of Schopenhauer's philosophy, is dealt with by him in the fourth book of the *Welt als Wille*. The Will-to-live which involves a ceaseless strife, a never-ending effort to attain the unattainable, and therefore an ever-present suffering, may be, according to Schopenhauer, either affirmed or denied. Its affirmation takes place when the individual surrenders himself to the Will which is objectivised in him, by obeying his natural impulses tending to the preservation of himself and the reproduction of the species. It is denied, when the Will-to-live—not necessarily life itself,* but the desires which minister to the preservation and reproduction of life—are extinguished within him. The basis of all practical morality is sympathy with the suffering inseparable from life, a sympathy which is the outcome of the consciousness, vague or clear, of the ultimate identity of our own Will with the Will of all other sentient beings. The Ideal goal of Ethics is the final negation of the Will-to-live, the way to which is to be found in asceticism. Consciousness, the last phase of the Will, must be played out before the end can come. Not until all desire is extinguished in case deliverance finally be accomplished. Schopenhauer naturally found the type of his asceticism in the Buddhist monk, and to a somewhat less extent in the Trappist. "In this way," concludes Schopenhauer, "in the contemplation of the life and career of the saints to meet with whom is seldom granted to one's own experience, but of which their written history assures us with the impress of inner truth that is upon it, and which Art brings before our eyes, we have the dark impression of that nothingness that looms as the final goal behind all virtue and holiness, and which we dread as children dread the darkness. Instead of, like the Hindoos, seeking

* Suicide Schopenhauer regarded as a clumsy solution of the problem, since the will is not thereby destroyed, but only, so to speak, temporarily inverted.

to evade it through myths and meaningless words, such as reabsorption in the world-soul, or the Buddhist Nirvana, let us rather confess freely that after the complete destruction of the Will, what remains is, for all those who are still immersed in the Will, assuredly nothingness. But on the other hand, for those in whom the Will has already turned against and denied itself, this our so very real world, with all its suns and galaxies, is also nothingness." (*Welt als Wille*, vol. i., § 17.)

In spite of the abuse and ridicule which Schopenhauer heaped upon the Guild-philosophers, as he termed Fichte, Schelling and Hegel, there is very little in his system which is not discoverable incidentally at least in the works of the two former thinkers. With Fichte, of course, self-consciousness was a starting-point, but the self-conscious Ego reappears later on in the system as moral impulse, which for Fichte, as for Schopenhauer, consists in the negation of the phenomenal world through Asceticism. Schopenhauer is, of course, far more logical in this respect than even Fichte, who does not carry the principle of asceticism to its final issue of self-starvation, like the pessimist writer. In Schelling, again, the conception of Will as *prius* is clearly traceable. Schopenhauer's chief merit lies in the clearness and consistency with which he carries out positions which had heretofore been either imperfectly developed or thrown out more in the form of suggestion than of positive theory. The prominence Schopenhauer gives to the distinction between the Alogical or Material and the logical or formal element in experience, to which we have already alluded, is the most original feature of the purely metaphysical side of his doctrine, and may be undoubtedly traced to a reaction against the formalism of Hegel. Schopenhauer has the merit of being the first philosopher in modern times, if we except some of the French materialists, who is honest enough to refrain from the usual lip-homage to the dominant creed. His "Free-thought" is, indeed, in some instance, decidedly aggressive. He steadily refused to employ theological terminology in a sense misleading even to the "vulgar." He did not, as many would have done, import the term "God" (innocent little word, the friend in need of speculative time-servers) into his system, well knowing that the notions it implied were foreign thereto. His polemic against Theism extends even to the term "pantheism," which he stigmatises as involving a meaningless use of language.

For a long time Schopenhauer remained entirely unrecognised. Towards the close of his life, however, a circle of devoted admirers began to form around him. Chief among these were his biographer, Dr. Gwinner, and his editor and annotator, Dr. Frauenstädt, both enthusiastic disciples. The subsequent development of the pessimist doctrine in Germany, we shall deal with briefly later on.

HERBART.

Johann Friedrich Herbart was born May 4th, 1776 at Oldenburg, where his father occupied an official position. Originally educated in the Leibnitz-Wolffian school, he soon turned to Kant. In 1794, he attended Fichte's lectures at Jena, and at this period he began to write essays criticizing Fichte and Schelling. On leaving the university he entered a Swiss family, as private tutor, about the same time making the acquaintance of the educationalist Pestalozzi, whose theories he warmly championed. In 1802 Herbart became lecturer in philosophy at the university of Göttingen, where he remained until 1809, when Wilhelm von Humbolt procured him the professorship of philosophy at Königsberg, just then vacant. In Königsberg he instituted a "pedagogic" seminary which he himself directed. Herbart returned in 1833 to Göttingen as professor, remaining there in uninterrupted activity till his death on August 4th, 1841. Herbart's works were published after his death, in twelve volumes, by his pupil Hartenstein (Leipzig, 1850–52).

HERBART'S PHILOSOPHY.

Herbart frequently professes to be a follower of Kant, but adds he is a Kantian of the year 1828, who rejects the entire Idealistic side of the critical doctrine. Under these circumstances it is difficult at the first glance to see how he could have retained anything that was distinctive of the system; nevertheless, the fact remains that he was influenced by Kantism, although rejecting its salient features. Herbart took his stand on Kant's distinction between phenomena and things-in-themselves, between the sense-presentation and the hypothetic cause of the sense-presentation. But while the thing-in-itself, the external cause of the sense-impression, was to Kant unknown, Herbart professed to be able to penetrate the phenomenon and give some account of the producing noumenon. Herbart may thus to a certain extent be regarded as a reaction in favour of the old dogmatism which Kant had expressly combated. All philosophy, according to Herbart, proceeds from a reflection on psychological data. He somewhere calls philosophy "the working out of conceptions," but this working out differs to some extent in method, in the several departments of philosophy. In Logic, which is its vestibule, it is concerned with rendering conceptions *clear and distinct* which is effected in the judgment. The two first figures of the Syllogism correspond to the positive and negative judgment, and may be cast together under the name of the syllogism of subsumption. The third figure is termed by Herbart the syllogism of substitution, inasmuch as it is only valid where a substitution of the minor is admissible. The great result furnished by logic to all the departments of philosophy is the principle of "Identity, contradiction, and excluded middle," in accordance with which, conceptions which are mutually contradictory, must be rejected and their opposite accepted. When we view conceptions from the side of their content, we find that they fall under two classes. The conceptions by virtue of which we comprehend the given world form one class, and the conceptions which do not affect the reality of the thing conceived, inasmuch as they are as capable of application to an imaginary, as to a real fact, those, namely, of which Æsthetics and Ethics treat, constitute the other class. The working out of the first order of conceptions belongs to metaphysics proper, that of the second to "practical philosophy." The two departments are to be kept rigidly asunder. Metaphysics has nothing to do with Ethics, nor Ethics with Metaphysics. Herbart himself in the presentation of his system, contained in his "Introductory Manual of Philosophy" (*Lehrbuch zur Einleitung in die Philosophie*), places the practical side of his system before the theoretical —the Ethics before the Metaphysics—but for the convenience of exposition, we shall in the present sketch follow the usual order in this respect, and give a brief statement of the metaphysics first, more especially as the connection with Kant and the post-Kantians is more easily seen in this way. Under metaphysic, Herbart, like Wolf, includes the whole theoretical side of philosophy. It is easy to see that the influence of his earlier Wolffian training is always uppermost in Herbart. He is essentially a dogmatist with a superficial varnish of criticism. Kant's great service consists to Herbart in the distinction between appearance and thing-in-itself. All appearance points to *being*, of which it is the *appearance*. Every distinction in the phenomenon corresponds to a distinction in the thing-in-itself. The problem of philosophy is to pierce through the given phenomena to the reality of which it is the sign. Physics deals only with the phenomenon, metaphysics, with the entity which the phenomenon denotes. We are driven to investigate this, inasmuch as the phenomenon as given, is seen on closer inspection to involve a contradiction, and hence, by the laws of thought, we are compelled to resolve this contradiction in order to make experience intelligible. Change, for instance, is given in the phenomenal world; but change is a self-contradictory conception, as old Zeno had shown; the problem therefore arises (since, according to Herbart, reality can involve no contradiction), to explain the conditions which create for us the appearance of change. Metaphysics, therefore (and be it remembered, Herbart is speaking here of dogmatic metaphysics, that is, of metaphysics in the pre-Kantian sense of the word) is not to be rejected in the summary manner of the Kantians, but rather to be reformed; the reformation consisting in the recognition of the fact that it is the science of the integration of empirical conceptions, by which the reality at their basis is distinguished from the illusory form they assume in ordinary consciousness.

Herbart retains Wolf's division of the science in the main. He terms the first portion, "General Metaphysics," and the second, "Applied Metaphysics." "General Metaphysics" covers Ontology, the special or "Applied Metaphysics," "Philosophy of Nature," (cosmology), "Rational Psychology" and "Rational Theology." The latter, Herbart, in this respect exhibiting his affiliation to Kant, can only attain to from the "practical" standpoint. The first part of the "General Metaphysics" is closely connected with logic. Herbart here expounds his general method. A contradiction occurs when intelligibility and fact do not coincide; for instance, where two terms are found in combination, which can nevertheless only be conceived in separation. This is the case with the connection of cause and effect where the cause, inasmuch as it precedes the effect, *cannot* be considered as equivalent to the latter, and on the other hand, inasmuch as it implicitly contains the effect *must* be considered as equivalent to it. This contradiction is resolved when the first term, the cause, is conceived as a plurality, which, taken individually, has no resemblance to the second term, the effect, but which, in its totality, produces the effect. What *must* be conceived, in short, but cannot be conceived as one, must be conceived as many. This Herbart calls the method of relations, and compares it to the reduction of a composite direction of motion to its simple components.

The second part of "General Metaphysics," the Ontology, opens with a panegyric on Kant for having shown in his refutation of the "ontological argument," that the conception of being contains no distinct *what*, but only a *that*; in other words, that it is mere *position*, apart from all content. Inasmuch as the conception of being as mere position excludes all negation, so the quality of being also excludes all negation, in other words, all distinction of degree, and all change which necessarily implies negation. To have seen this was the great merit of the Eleatics and their successors the Atomists. It is only by the assumption of a multitude of real essences, or as Herbart terms it, a "Qualitative Atomism" that the contradiction involved in the inherence of many qualities in one substance can be resolved. The conception of substance itself is capable of reduction to that of causality. It is only thus that the notion of substance can be rendered intelligible; just as it is only by the relation of cause and effect that the ordinary mind renders the fact of change intelligible to itself. As we have seen above, the conception of causality itself requires a "working-out" (*Bearbeitung*), but in this process of clarifying conceptions by purging them of the contradictions they contain, we must not rest satisfied with the merely phenomenal or physical, but must continue the process until we arrive at the metaphysical—until we discover the processes of the supersensible-real, itself. We here find that by reason of its absolute simplicity, though no change can take place in the individual essence, yet that this may very easily be the case with the combination of two or more such essences, in each of which a disturbance, and in consequence a resistance, is generated, as is the case with our own mind (the only essence, whose inner processes can be directly known to us) when we feel a *contrast* between colours or tones. Since by these disturbances and resistances or "acts of self-preservation," as Herbart terms them, all the phenomena of physics and empirical psychology may be explained, they may be regarded as the groundwork of the "philosophy of nature," and of psychology.

Herbart gives the name of Synechology to that portion of his doctrine which refers to space and time and matter. According to this, space is indeed appearance, though not as Kant imagined, a subjective merely, but rather an objective appearance, in such wise that where objective multitude is given uncombined, but so that it may be combined, it must assume for every intelligence the form of externality. This intelligible space of Herbart's is not to be considered as a continuum like the "given" space of the phenomenon. The latter involves a contradiction, for the extended object covers many different portions of space lying outside one another, and yet in extension though the one is severed into many it is still thought as one. In intension the same contradiction appears as in extension. In conceiving matter, we begin a division which we must carry on to infinity, because every portion has to be conceived as extended. Each of the dimensions of real or intelligible space is a rigid line differing according to the sum of its tangents. Herbart expounds this idea on geometrical principles with a fulness characteristic of him in matters mathematical, into which exposition we need not enter. As with space so with time; it consists in a sum of points of succession. It appears a continuum because at the close of one series of changes another immediately begins. The conjunction of causality with space and time, gives us the data for the explanation of matter, the attraction and repulsion apparently inherent in which must not be regarded as existent forces, but merely as the appearance resulting from the primary combination of real essences—a view which obviates the absurd assumption of action at a distance. Since space is merely an accident of real entity, it follows that real essences are not necessarily subject to space-relations, and therefore that that which requires explanation is not so much motion, as rest, namely, the particular case, from out of an infinite possibility of cases, in which velocity = 0. Herbart seeks to deduce the phenomena of chemistry and physics from four cases of the opposition of elements. These may be either strong and equal, strong and unequal, weak and equal, or weak and unequal.

The Eidology is, as it were, the vestibule of Psychology, as Synechology is of Cosmology. The conception of the Ego involves the contradiction of the inherence of the many in the one, a circumstance especially noticeable in this case, inasmuch as self-consciousness presents the Ego in perception as a complete unity. Furthermore, it is a contradiction, since the knowledge of the knowing subject seems to demand in its turn a knowledge of this knowledge, and so on to infinity; again, there is a formal contradiction also involved in the identity of the Ego as object with the Ego as subject; this seeming identity remains therefore to be explained. The soul, in common with everything real (in Herbart's sense), is an absolutely simple and indestructible entity, and hence cannot be the substratum of a plurality of faculties. Its quality is like that of every other entity, unknown, although, as above observed, it is the only entity of which we can know immediately the internal processes, namely those disturbances and resistances or "acts of self-preservation," which give rise to sense-presentation. A thorough investigation of the nature of the soul necessarily begins with the primitive impressions of sound, colour, &c. The fact that these are quantitatively distinct, and that "acts of self-preservation" since they are positive cannot destroy, but only limit one another, shows that these latter must be subject to a mathematical regularity, a regularity already acknowledged in one class of these reciprocal limitations, namely, the harmony of musical tones. Herbart therefore claims a mathematical treatment for the investigation. The clue to the whole subsequent exposition is contained in the sentence "every limited perception persists in the soul, as an effort to perceive." This justifies, in the opinion of Herbart, an analogy with the laws of elastic bodies, and, other things being equal, even the assumption of the validity of the same laws in Psychology. In accordance with this, a "static of the mind" is furnished in which the equilibrium of perceptions is discussed. Herbart terms the *sum of limitation* the quantum of perceiving contained in two combined presentments. That which is not limited, or converted into effort, is termed the "perceptive remnant," a mathematical calculation demonstrating that no single perception, however strong, suffices completely to displace another, to effect which it requires at least two such perceptions. The point which constitutes the boundary between entity, as striving or effort, and as conscious perception, is termed the "threshold of consciousness." The union of perceptions of different classes, as, for instance, sound and meaning in the spoken word, Herbart terms *complication;* the union of those of the same class, *blending*. In the "mechanic of the mind," Herbart considers the movement of perceptions, their sinking and rising, memory, association, &c., in the guise of the same mathematical formulæ as before.

In the analytical part of his Psychology he endeavours to show how all given psychological phenomena may be explained by the formulæ without recourse to the hypothesis of special faculties. It is scarcely necessary to say that for Herbart the distinction between the empirical and the pure Ego does not exist. For him, the mind, the psychological object, is the only fact standing in need of explanation. Herbart, on the ground of his ontology, notwithstanding, protests against psychology being confounded with metaphysic or logic. All facts have a psychological side, but this by no means exhausts their whole significance. The confusion of the empirical or psychological space, which is a *continuum*, with the intelligible space, which is an *interruptum*, was, in Herbart's opinion, one of the greatest errors into which Kant fell. The same applies to time as to space. As to the categories, when correctly viewed they are seen to coincide with the forms of language, and a complete system of them presupposes a universal grammar.

Æsthetics is the science treating of that which pleases on account of its beauty apart from any ulterior reason. It has therefore to be distinguished from the desirable and the pleasant, both of which have reference to a subjective interest; after this, the problem, here as in every other department, is to resolve the beautiful as given, into its simplest elements. Such an analysis will show us that these elements consist not of entities but of relations; the problem therefore becomes, to exhibit the simplest relations which can call forth a disinterested sense of pleasure. This has, as yet, only been done in one of the arts, namely, Music. What the theory of harmony and thorough-bass does for Music, remains a desideratum as regards the other Arts. Ethics itself may be regarded as a branch of Æsthetics. In Ethics we have to exhibit the simplest relations of will, or combinations of motives which produce the sense of moral beauty. To ask why such motives please and their contraries displease, is as absurd as to ask why one chord is agreeable to the ear and another not? That these relations, which may be termed *sample-conceptions*, or Ideas, are unconditionally valid, Kant felt, and he is much to be blamed for having mixed them up with metaphysical notions, such as *power* and *being*, with which they have no connection. Herbart is especially severe on Kant's "Transcendental Freedom," an assumption on which neither punishment nor education can be explained, since they both presuppose actions to be the necessary results of character. Duties may be divided into such as concern oneself, such as concern society, and finally such as concern the future of both the individual and society.

There are two points in which the theoretical and practical sides of philosophy meet, and the consideration of which pre-supposes a knowledge of both departments. The combination of "practical philosophy" and "philosophy of nature," furnishes the "theory of religion;" their combination with Psychology the "theory of pedagogic." The former Herbart did not systematically work out, and his utterances respecting it are conveyed in a somewhat detached form. Pedagogic, or the theory of Education, is his great subject outside philosophy proper. Its end is of course the moulding of the moral character. Freewill and Fatalist theories are alike to be rejected. The practical *ideas* and the psychological certainty of the action and reaction of particular perceptions are a true guide for the teacher. Regulation and teaching should be combined. The object of both is *training*, i.e. to give strength to the moral character and to enable the pupil in the end to undertake his own education. Herbart sees in Politics merely an extended Pedagogic. Political forms are for him of little account. His sheet-anchor is the individual character.

Though it is not to be denied that there are suggestive passages and some clever and just criticisms in Herbart's writings, yet as a system his philosophy may not unfairly be described as a grotesque abortion. Its mathematical dress has alone saved it from oblivion. An adept mathematician can always present an idea in a shape to command the attention of the learned world irrespective of its intrinsic value. The attraction a mathematic mode of treatment possesses for the modern "cultured' mind is irresistible, and operates quite independently of any consideration as to the susceptibility of the given subject-matter to such a treatment. To wrap a theory up skilfully in mathematical formulæ, though in itself it may be the baldest nonsense, is the surest passport in the present day to acquiring the reputation of a "serious thinker." Herbart is in this happy position. Although he commits all the errors against which Kant's 'Critique' was directed, although he is essentially a pre-Kantian in his construction, yet the magical charm of his mathematics has sufficed to give him a place in the history of speculative thought he certainly would not otherwise possess. Herbart left behind him a school to which the editor of his completed works, Hartenstein (also the editor of the well-known edition of Kant's works bearing his name), belonged.

HEGEL.

GEORG WILHELM FRIEDRICH HEGEL was born at Stuttgart, August 27th, 1770. His father was an officer in the fiscal service; his mother, whom he lost in his thirteenth year, seems to have been a woman of some little education, and of more than ordinary intelligence. He studied at the University of Tübingen, both in the philosophical and theological faculties. As a student he was the author of one or two essays on philosophical subjects, and he also publicly defended two dissertations. His private reading during this period, of the works of Kant, Jacobi, and other philosophers, in addition to those of Herder, Lessing and Schiller, seems to have powerfully influenced him. Besides this, he carried on at the same time with much enthusiasm his studies in Greek literature and history.

Like Fichte and Herbart, on leaving the university he took a position as private tutor, and to make the parallel more complete, in Switzerland (at Berne). This did not hinder his own studies, which he zealously followed up, engaging at the same time in a correspondence with

Schelling who was still studying at Tübingen. Curiously enough, his first important work was a "Life of Jesus," which was based on the distinction already insisted upon by Lessing, between the doctrines of the founder of Christianity and the dogmas of the Church. The influence of the *Aufklärung* was, however, strong in Hegel at this time, the special form it took being that of Hellenism. In 1797 he entered upon a similar position to that which he had held at Berne, at Frankfort-on-the-Maine; but Hegel was irresistibly drawn to Jena, the philosophical metropolis, whither he repaired in January 1801. It was here that his thoughts began to assume a systematic form, though he deemed himself at this time, in the main, a follower of his younger contemporary Schelling, with whom he subsequently worked in common, for the spread of the "System of Identity," on the *Kritische Journal der Philosophie*, to which he contributed most of the articles.

The differences between the two thinkers soon became apparent on the departure of Schelling from Jena, and with the production of Hegel's first great work, 'The Phenomenology of the Mind' (*Phänomenologie des Geistes*), in 1806, the wide divergence in their intellectual capacities became obvious. In consequence of the Napoleonic war then raging, Hegel left Jena soon after this, and became editor of the *Bamberger Zeitung*, a post he subsequently threw up for the directorship of a public school at Nürnberg. He remained here until the year 1816, and here, among other works, his great "Logic" was written. In the autumn of 1816 Hegel entered the chair of philosophy at Heidelberg, just vacated by Fries. During his stay at Heidelberg he wrote his 'Encyclopedia of the Philosophical Sciences.' Finally, on October 22nd, 1818, Hegel became professor in Berlin. During the Berlin period, the only large work completed by him was 'The Elements of the Philosophy of Right' (*Grundlinien der Philosophie des Rechts*). His disciples, however, after his death, published the lectures delivered during this time on the Philosophy of History, Art, and Religion, as well as on the History of Philosophy. Hegel died at Berlin, of cholera, on the 14th of November, 1831.

The life of Hegel was written by his disciple Rosenkranz. His complete works (including the lectures) occupy eighteen volumes.

THE HEGELIAN SYSTEM.

We now take up again the direct line of thought represented by Kant, Fichte, and Schelling, a line which culminates in the great thinker whose name heads this section. The system of Hegel may be best described as Panlogism. The Real or Concrete is nothing but a synthesis of relations, each of which, taken by itself, and apart from the whole into which it enters, is abstract, and therefore unreal. The ultimate principle of all knowledge is of course the pure form of the unity of the consciousness, the "Synthetic Unity of Apperception" of Kant, the "Pure Ego" of Fichte. This is the "Concept" (*Begriff*) of Hegel. But the synthesis so stated, that is, by itself, is formal; it is a unity of thought, of consciousness as such, and of nothing else but thought or consciousness. But thought or consciousness is in its nature relative. Thinking or knowing implies a striking-out of relations, a fixing of contrasts, a limitation of a conscious state, which is in its turn nothing but the limitation of another conscious state, and so on to infinity. But the infinity is not that of an infinitely produced straight line (to employ an analogy), but rather that of the circle; or, better still, of the spiral. The Concrete or the Real which is Experience-in-general, is the system of all possible momenta or determinations of knowledge, thought, or consciousness. This system, which embraces all possible oppositions and antagonisms, considered as a whole, is the *Logos* or *Idee* in its reality, the "Concrete Idea," as Hegel terms it. Considered abstractly, the "Idea" is the formal unity spoken of above, which embraces all differences, which maintains itself in all these differences, and which is their final principle of explanation. We need hardly repeat what we have already said when treating of Fichte, namely, that this unity, inasmuch as the determinations of thought all and severally presuppose it, can never become itself an object, or, which is the same thing, a determination of thought—that is to say, it can never enter the sphere of the empirical consciousness.

Empiricism and Scepticism in philosophy, in undermining the distinctions of the ordinary consciousness, and of the philosophy which takes its immediate stand upon it, paves the way for the true synthetic view. Thus Scepticism shows that on the ordinary crude dualistic assumption of the absolute independence of subject and object, mind and matter, perceiver and perceived, knowledge would be impossible. It forces us therefore to reconsider the preliminary assumption which we have hitherto received as an unquestionable truth. The same with every fixed distinction, great and small, important and unimportant; every such distinction will be found on examination, when consistently carried out, to refute itself—that is, to contain the germ of its own destruction or negation, or, as Hegel has it, its own "internal dialectic."

In the word Dialectic we have the key to the whole Hegelian system. The method of Hegel is the dialectical method, and to have discovered the full significance of this method, to have struck upon the innermost dynamic principle of the world, gives to Hegel a pre-eminence in a sense above all other thinkers. Herakleitos of Ephesus caught a glimpse of the principle when he said, "all things flow," and "there is nothing that comes into being but it forthwith ceases to be." Zeno of Elea also caught sight of it when he sought to convince the ordinary man, who could not conceive of a world based on contradiction, of the truth of Parmenides' doctrines, by placing him in the dilemma of either admitting the sense-world to be contradictory, or denying its existence altogether, not doubting but that he would accept the latter alternative. The Sophists and Sokrates saw in it respectively, the former the destruction of all certitude, and the latter, a new means for the attainment of truth from the very fact of its potency in undermining the would-be certitudes of current opinion. In Plato, the principle obtained its fullest recognition in the ancient world. Plato's philosophy is essentially an exhibition of the dialectic immanent in all knowledge. Aristotle, although the general bearing of his mind might be supposed to tend in a different direction, nevertheless places it in the fore-front of his system in his distinction of matter and form, and his recognition of all reality as the synthesis of matter and form. In all periods, when the two great thinkers of antiquity have held a foremost place in the higher thought of the world—periods, for instance, such as that of the decline of ancient philosophy and of scholasticism—it has never been left quite out of view however much obscured; but from Descartes and Bacon to Kant it had practically lapsed into oblivion. In Kant's "Transcendental Analytic" and "Transcendental Dialectic," it again appears, though overlaid with much extraneous material. In Fichte it receives a fairly definite expression; but it was reserved for Hegel to recognise its full bearing as the principle of knowledge, and *the* method of philosophic investigation. Among poets, Goethe has best caught the beat of the world-rhythm when he makes the Erdgeist in Faust exclaim

> "In Being's floods, in Action's storm
> I walk and work, above beneath,
> Work and weave in endless motion!
> Birth and Death
> An infinite ocean,
> A seizing and giving
> The fire of Living:
> 'Tis thus at the roaring Loom of Time I ply,
> And weave for God the Garment thou seest Him by."

Hegel claims for his system that all antitheses, all opposing principles, that have ever held sway in philosophy, are therein at once recognised and transcended, that is, shown to be necessary, but incomplete, taken by themselves. The first condition of philosophising, as observed in connection with Plato, is to lift ourselves above the immediate—the *here*, the *this*, and the *now* of things. All intellectual life is more or less an effort to break away from immediate appearances and immediate interests. Kant has said with truth that the Ptolemaic system of Astronomy is the one naturally most intelligible to us, not because it is simpler than the Copernican system, but because, in spite of confusedness and clumsiness, it accounts for astronomical phenomena on the hypothesis of all things revolving round ourselves, viz. our Earth. The superior simplicity and order of the Copernican system did, notwithstanding, in the long run win the victory over common-sense consecrated by tradition. The anthropomorphism and myth of primitive man is an expression of the difficulty man experiences in divesting his view of things of the influence of his immediate surroundings as he conceives them to affect his interests.

There is nothing which presupposes such a revolution in our mental life as the ability to view the world from the synthetic or speculative point of view—as a dialectical movement. All accustomed habits of thought, all the fixed distinctions in which the intellectual wealth of the average man consists, have to be ruthlessly cast into the caldron of an all-consuming Logic. Their hard outlines then begin to alter shape, and finally to lose shape entirely, as they become mixed in a seething mass where one distinction blends into its opposite, the whole acquiring for a moment a new shape only in its turn to give place to another, and yet another. "So strong," says Hegel, speaking of the exposition of his system, "is the sense of the opposition of true and false, that it has accustomed men to expect either agreement with, or contradiction of, some existing philosophical system, and, in explaining such, only to see this or that." If we clarify our conceptions of truth and falsehood—that is, subject them to the purifying fire of dialectic—we shall see that they change their content with our point of view, that their content is not fixed, but fluid. "The bud vanishes with the appearance of the blossom, and one may say that the one is contradicted by the other; the fruit again proclaims the blossom a spurious form of the plant's existence, the truth of the one passes over to the other. These forms are not merely distinct, but crush each other out as being mutually incompatible. But their fluid nature constitutes them none the less momenta of that organic unity wherein they not alone cease to conflict, but to which one is as necessary as the other, which equal necessity makes the life of the whole."

The Hegelian dialectic is based on the recognition of identity in difference, of the fact that all affirmation implies negation, all negation affirmation. In all things there is a capacity unrealised, and a capacity realised; the first is the *material* moment, the second the *formal* moment. The acorn is the unrealised capacity of the oak, it is realised as oak. The realisation of the capacity of a thing is the negation of that thing as actually existent. The possibility or capacity present in the child is realised in the man, but manhood is the negation of childhood—child *quâ* child vanishes in the man, he exists no longer, any more than though he were dead. Every step in the growth or progress of the child is a step towards the negation of childhood. Again, animal life exists only by virtue of the continuous destruction or decomposition of the tissues of which it is actually composed. Arrest this process of destruction or negation, and the animal dies. The fatal effect of many of the mineral poisons is simply due to their action in stopping the natural process of the destruction of the organic tissues, a process which is essential to animal life. Animal life presupposes organic life; but the latter is, as Hegel would term it, the *negative* moment of the former—it is the means only, and not the end. The animal life can only realise or maintain itself in and through the negation of the negative moment; in other words, the continuous destruction of the organic *matter* (the tissue) is essential to the reality of the animal *form* (the living body). This dialectic runs through all things; it is the ultimate expression of all reality, and it may be discovered by analysis on every plane of reality. Its recognition cannot fail to give us a completely new view of the world-order. Our ultimate aim in every science will be henceforward to discover the course of its dialectic, or rather the dialectic of its subject-matter, since this is the key to its mysteries. The significance of formal logic with its laws of thought will be seen to disappear when experience is viewed from this more comprehensive standpoint. So far from its being the case, as the law of contradiction asserts, that a thing cannot both be and not be, we now know that, in a sense, everything is, and at the same time is not, in so far as it expresses a determinate reality at all—*omnis determinatio est negatio.* Since reality, *i.e.* the synthesis of experience, consists alone in the union of contradictories, it necessarily follows that for experience, for consciousness, pure affirmation is precisely on a level with pure negation since they are alike unreal and meaningless. This is all Hegel intends by the, at first sight, astounding proposition with which his Logic opens, that "being and non-being are the same."

In his first great work, the 'Phenomenology of the Mind,' Hegel traces the natural development of the human mind from the naïve consciousness of the ordinary man to the synthetic standpoint of philosophy. The 'Phenomenology' is in fact a kind of philosophical 'Pilgrim's Progress.' "Inasmuch," says Hegel, "as this exposition only has phenomenal knowledge for its subject, it does not exhibit the free movement of knowledge in its scientific form, and must rather be regarded from the present standpoint as the course the natural consciousness takes in its progress towards true knowledge, as the pathway of the soul, passing through the series of forms which its nature prescribes as so many stages of self-purification, until it attains through a complete experience of itself, to a knowledge of that which it is in itself" (*Phänomenologie*, *Einleitung*, p. 61).

The immediate form of our knowledge is the object as *being* or existent thing. In this we occupy a passive attitude, the attitude of naïve sense-perception. In this first attitude of consciousness reality seems to be known in its simplest and purest form. All that knowledge here tells us is of the bare existence of the thing. The object is presented, as *this* thing *here* and *now*. The word *this* itself simply means existence here and now. But what is *now?* "Let us say, for instance, *now* it is night. To our immediate consciousness this is a truth. We note it down as a truth. At noonday we look upon this *ci-devant* truth, and lo, it is a meaningless and palpable absurdity!" The *now*, notwithstanding, remains, but with a totally changed content. It proves itself to be what Hegel terms a "universal negative." The same remarks apply to the other form of the *this*, namely, the *here*. "*Here* is, for instance, a tree. I turn myself round, and this truth has vanished—has transformed itself into its opposite. *Here* is not a tree, but rather a house. The *here* does not vanish, but it is that which remains in the disappearance of the house, the tree, and so forth, and is indifferently house or tree" (*Phänomenologie*, p. 74). "Pure being" is of the essence of this perceptive consciousness; for pure being is its immediateness as abstract form. A comparison between the relation of knowledge to its object, as it immediately presents itself, with the same relation after it has been acted upon by reflection, shows a considerable difference. The universal element, which seemed to belong to the being of the object, is now seen to lie in our knowledge of the object. The perceptive certainty is seen to subsist not in the object, but in us. The *now* and *here* is preserved in the Ego. "What does not vanish is the I, as universal, whose seeing is neither a seeing of the tree nor the house, but a simple seeing, which is brought about by the negation of this house, and so forth, which is absolutely indifferent to anything outside itself, alike to the house and the tree." Thus Hegel begins his 'Phenomenology,' by showing the contradiction of the empirical consciousness with its own prepossessions, to lead up through the discussion of the scientific consciousness, the Understanding—in which the abstract procedure implicit in "common sense," or the ordinary consciousness, becomes explicitly formulated—to the philosophical consciousness, the Reason, which sees the true significance of these various standpoints as parts of an organic whole, as related elements of a synthesis. This is the ladder which, according to Hegel, the ordinary consciousness has a right to demand, to lead it to the absolute knowledge of itself. The task of the 'Phenomenology' is thus to show the progress of knowledge from its lowest to its highest stage; each stage is in its turn shown to involve a contradiction, which necessitates progress to a a higher stage. At each of these stages the immediate certitude or truth of the stage is proved to be illusory, to involve a self-deception. This is corrected in the following stage, the certitude is changed. in its turn to be subjected to the same process, until all these stages are seen to be inadequate in themselves, and to possess meaning and significance only when regarded as the necessary momenta, not of this or that particular limited or individual consciousness, but of consciousness conceived as one absolute all-embracing totality—*Absolute Geist.*

Hegel's dialectic, we must again repeat, is simply the perfecting, as regards its form of Fichte's dialectic. Fichte had shown that the *in-itselfness* of the one plane of consciousness, was the *for-itselfness* of the next plane. Hegel, however, brings out into clear relief a point on which Fichte was somewhat dubious (but which Plato and Aristotle had recognised), to wit, that the negation of the opposite is not absolute, but is rather double-sided—that is, that the opposite or preceding moment is no less preserved than abolished in the succeeding moment. Hegel's aim is to show that the mind is logically compelled, on pain of its own *reductio ad absurdum*, to force its way on and on until it arrives at the standpoint of absolute knowledge. The six stages which the mind has to pass through in its progress to absolute knowledge are from consciousness to self-consciousness, thence to the scientific understanding "the law making and law-finding reason," in the words of Hegel, thence to the moral consciousness (*Geist*), thence to the æsthetic and religious consciousness, and thence to the consciousness of knowledge as absolute. But the world-mind, as exhibited on the plane of History, is, equally with the individual mind, under the necessity, by virtue of its constitution, of passing through the same stages. The 'Phenomenology' shows therefore the stages that humanity has had to pass through, and which the individual must also pass through, before it can attain to absclute knowledge. Knowledge or science in the Hegelian sense consists in the re-reading of experience, in the *comprehending* of experience in the fullest sense of the word.

Before we leave the 'Phenomenology,' the reader may not take it amiss if we give a few extracts illustrative of the style of this, in some respects, greatest work of Hegel. Such extracts, of course, can give but a very imperfect idea of the whole to which they belong, as may be readily imagined from the nature of Hegel's thought. The impossibility, moreover, of rendering many passages adequately in another language, is generally admitted. In the preface (*Phänomenologie*, p. 15) Hegel observes, "The truth is the whole. But the whole is the essence which completes itself in its development. It may be said of the Absolute that it is essentially *result*, that not before the *end* is it that which it is in truth: and herein consists its nature, that of being Reality, Subject, or Self-becoming. However absurd it may appear to regard the Absolute as in essence, *result*, a very little consideration will correct this appearance of absurdity. The beginning, the principle or the Absolute, as it is primarily and immediately spoken of, is only the universal. Just as little as when I say *all animals*, these words can stand in the place of a Zoology, can the words Divine, Absolute, Eternal, &c., express that which is not contained in them. It is true that only such words can express the intuition in its immediate form; but this is not all; a word which is only a passage to a proposition contains within it an otherness of becoming which has to be retraced; it is a mediation (*Vermittlung*)."

The Absolute, although it contains within it the synthesis of all contradictions, considered as Absolute, of course transcends its own immanent contradictions. Absolute knowledge is the resting-point in which all contradictions are at once preserved and abolished, *aufgehoben**, in the language of Hegel. The word mediation (*Vermittlung*) is used by Hegel to denote the negative moment of the Dialectical process, in its purity. This leads us to revert to the question of the concepts true and false. Hegel explains the distinction between them, as viewed from the standpoint of ordinary consciousness, and from that of the philosophical reason. After defining the false as the otherness, the negativity of the substance of the true, as an essential moment in the realisation of the true, and yet as not constituting an element of the true as such, he proceeds: "For the sake of clearness in indicating the moment of *complete otherness* its terminology must no longer be used where the otherness is abolished (*aufgehoben*). Thus the expression, the *unity* of subject and object, of finite and infinite, of being and thought, &c., has the inconvenience that these terms themselves connote what they are outside their unity, and therefore that in their

* Hegel's word *aufheben*, which means both "to preserve" and "to destroy," is a survival of the unity of opposites upon which all primitive language is based. (See Dr. Carl Abel's essay, *Ueber den Gegensinn der Urwörte.*—Leipzig, 1884.)

unity they do not mean what the phrase implies; the false, as false, is no longer a moment of truth. Dogmatism as a mode of thought in Science, and in the study of Philosophy, is nothing but the opinion that the true consists in a proposition which is a fixed result, or in that which is immediately known. To such questions, as when Cæsar was born, or how many toises made a stadium, a concise answer can be given. Similarly it is definitely true that the square of the hypothenuse equals the sum of the squares of both remaining sides of the right-angled triangle. But the nature of such so-called truth is different from the nature of philosophical truth" (*Phänomenologie*, pp. 30-1). A few pages farther on, after the subject of Mathematical truth has been dealt with, and its imperfections shown, we have the following pregnant sentences: "The phenomenon is the coming and going, which yet does not come and go, but *is* in itself, and which constitutes the reality and movement of the life of truth. The true is a Bacchantian revel, in which there is no member that is not drunken; but yet because each, in so far as it severs itself from the whole, is at once dissolved, this revel is none the less transparent and simple repose. In judging the movement, though individual forms of the mind do not obtain as determinate thoughts, they are, notwithstanding, just as much positive and necessary as they are negative and evanescent momenta. In the *totality* of the movement —in the movement conceived as rest—that in it which distinguishes itself and acquires a specific reality, as such, which *recollects*, preserves itself, whose reality is knowledge of itself, is the immediate reality" (*Phänomenologie*, pp. 35-6). "In the nature of that which is," says Hegel, "to realise its conception in its being, consists *logical necessity* generally. This alone is the rational, and the rhythm of the organic whole; it is just as much knowledge of the content, as the content itself is concept and essence —in other words, it alone is *speculative*. The concrete fact, as self-realising, constitutes itself simple determinateness; it thus raises itself to logical form, and is in its nature as essence. In this movement consists its concrete reality which is at the same time logical reality. It is therefore unnecessary to affix to the concrete content a formalism external thereto; the former is itself the transition to the latter, which latter ceases, however, to be external and formal, since the form has become native to the process of the concrete content itself" (*Phänomenologie*, p. 43). One more quotation before we leave the 'Phenomenology.' "Experience," Hegel observes, "is simply this, that the content, that is, consciousness *in itself*, is substance, and therefore object of consciousness. But this substance, which is consciousness, is the process of its becoming what it is in itself; and it is only as this Becoming, reflected into itself, that it is, in truth, consciousness. In itself it is the movement which constitutes knowledge—the transformation of this *in-itselfness* into *for-itselfness*, the substance into the subject, the object of consciousness, into the object of self-consciousness—that is, into the object as in its turn abolished, or in other words into the concept. It is a circle returning in upon itself which presupposes its beginning, and yet only attains it as end. Thus, in so far as consciousness consists necessarily in this distinction within itself, itself as the perceived whole, confronts its simple self-consciousness, and inasmuch as it distinguishes the latter, it is distinguished in its pure perceived concept—that is, in *time*, and in its content, or in-itselfness. Substance has, as subject, the primary inner necessity to display itself, as what it is in itself—as consciousness. The complete objective presentation is primarily its reflection, or its realisation as self" (*Phänomenologie*, p. 585).

We now turn to the Logic of Hegel. In the Logic we have the essential articulations, or momenta of consciousness presented, not in the order in which they disclose themselves to the reflective understanding, as in the 'Phenomenology,' but in the necessary or Logical order of their deduction. The secret of Hegel's method, it will be by this time sufficiently clear to the reader, lies in the triple articulation of each stage or plane of reality. *Matter* or *in-itselfness* becomes negated as *form* or *for-itselfness*. This negation is in its turn negated; but the negation is not absolute in either case, the one form is preserved or, so to speak, held in solution in the succeeding one, notwithstanding its negative character considered *per se*. Thus, in the third term, which is the negation of the negative of the first, we have the completed moment as such. Hegel takes care to observe, what indeed is sufficiently obvious, namely, that his Logic might equally well have been termed Metaphysic or Ontology, since, from the point of view of speculative thought, this distinction of departments can no longer be maintained. The world, reality, experience, consists merely in these logical determinations; the sum total of these determinations is the Absolute. Thus instead of being able to adequately define the Absolute by a single phrase, as Schelling thought he could, Hegel finds it impossible to do this, save in the complete exposition of a science. Logic in Hegel's sense is this science; it is the science of the at once all-embracing, all-determining *Logos* Idea, or Concept, *i.e.* of *consciousness as absolute.*

The categories of which the Hegelian Logic treats, of course entirely traverse the empirical distinctions of mind and matter, subject and object, &c., since they are pre-supposed in these distinctions. Hegel somewhere calls them "the souls of all reality." But taken by themselves, as spread out before the reflective understanding, they are pure abstractions, and the Logic is thus none the less, as Hegel elsewhere calls it, "the realm of shades." It is necessary to effect an entrance into this realm, notwithstanding, nay, to explore its inmost recesses, in order to attain the true speculative insight, for, since the problem of all science is to recognise the reason on the several planes of reality, this problem can only be solved by knowing, first of all, what reason is?—and, secondly, how to find it? The Logic teaches what the Idea or the Reason is, inasmuch as it exhausts the sum of its determinations as they are presented in the forms of abstract thought; it teaches how to find the Idea or the Reason in so far as it is a doctrine of method.

The Hegelian Logic falls into three main divisions: Doctrine of Being, Doctrine of Essence, and Doctrine of Concept. "The Logical has three sides," says Hegel, "the Abstract, or that of the understanding; the Dialectical, or that of the negative reason; and the Speculative, or that of the positive reason. These three sides do not constitute three parts of logic, but are the momenta of every logical real—that is, of every conception or truth . . . thought as *understanding* cleaves to fixed determinateness, and to its distinction from every other determinateness; such a limited abstraction counts with the understanding for an independent existence." "The dialectical moment is the special self-negation of such finite determinations and their transformation into their opposite." Just as the previous abstract or affirmative moment is the classical moment for dogmatism, the mode of thought characterised by hard and fast distinctions and one-sided theories, so the dialectical moment is the classical moment for scepticism, the mode of thought characterised by a criticism of the assumptions made by dogmatism and the common understanding, having as its upshot the special dogma of the illusoriness of Reality and the vanity of Knowledge. These results of course ensue, when the above momenta are isolated and considered apart from their connection in the trichotomy, or system of momenta.

The term Dialectic is often employed, as was the case with the Sophists of old, to denote a mere barren art of confounding an opponent by an appearance of contradiction which does not really exist. In the Hegelian sense, however, Dialectic, "is the true nature of the understanding's determination of things, and of the finite generally. It is the *immanent* externalising, wherein the one-sidedness and limitation of the understanding's determinations presents itself as what it is, namely, as their negation. It is the nature of everything finite to negate itself. Dialectic is therefore the moving soul of the knowing process, the principle, whereby alone *immanent connection and necessity* enters into the constitution of knowledge; and whereby the true, as opposed to the external, transcendence of the finite is possible": "The *speculative* or *positive-rational* comprehends the unity of the determinations in their opposition; the affirmative element, which is contained therein, is their dissolution and their transformation. Dialectic has a positive result, inasmuch as its result has a determinate content; inasmuch, that is, as its actual issue is not empty abstract nothing but the negation of certain determinations, which are nevertheless contained in the result, since the latter is not mere *nothing*, but *result*. This rationality therefore, notwithstanding that it is conceptual and abstract, is at the same time concrete, since it is not mere formal unity, but the unity of determinations, which are clearly distinguished as such. With mere abstractions philosophy has therefore nothing whatever to do; it is concerned only with concrete notions. In speculative Logic, the formal Logic of the understanding is contained, and can easily be separated from it; nothing more is required for this than to eliminate the dialectical and rational element therein; when it becomes what ordinary Logic is, namely, the summary of a variety of coordinated thought-determinations which, although finite, pass for something infinite." (Hegel's *Encyklopädie der Philosophischen Wissenschaften im Grundrisse*, § 79-83.)

The first division of the Logic treats of the doctrine of Being, or Consciousness in its immediateness—the concept in itself—in its various forms. These are quality, quantity, and measure. *Quality* may be variously considered as being, actuality, for-itselfness; *Quantity* as pure quantity, determined quantum, and degree. *Measure* is the synthesis of quality and quantity; it is "a quantum with which is combined an actuality or a quality." This leads to the consideration of the subject-matter of the second division which treats of the doctrine of Essence.

Stated briefly, Essence may be defined as Being translated into appearance. The primary momenta of Essence are *the essence as ground of existence*, which is again determined as "pure reflection" (identity, difference, and cause) "actuality" and "the thing;" the *phenomenon*, which may be reduced to the "world as phenomenon," "content and form," and "relation;" and, lastly, the unity of "reflection" and the "phenomenon," *reality* which is articulated as "substance and accident," "cause and effect" and "reciprocity" (action and reaction). "The manifestation of the real," says Hegel, "is the real itself. This manifestation is, therefore, essential, and is only so far essential as it is in immediate external actuality. Previously *being* and *actuality* have appeared as forms of the immediate; *being* is always unreflected immediateness and *transition* . . . The real is the *positing* of this unity, of this relation that has become identical with itself; it is therefore rescued from *transition*, and its energy manifested as *externality;* in this it is reflected into itself; its actuality is the *manifestation of itself*, not of another." The moment of reality gathers up, so to speak, into itself all previous momenta; it closes the circle. The highest catagory of the Real is that of reciprocity. The category of reciprocity indeed carries us out of the sphere of Essence into that of Concept, with which the third division of the Logic is concerned.

The *concept* is the truth of Being and of Essence, and the system of its momenta constitutes the totality of all determinations of Consciousness. The forms of the concept Hegel terms, "the living spirit of the Real," the truth of the Real being given in and by these forms. The leading momenta of the Concept are the subjective concept, which embraces the forms of Logic, the object, which gives the cosmical notions of Mechanism, Chemistry, and Teleology, and the Idea in its totality and completeness, which sums up the whole of the Logic. The Idea as such may be viewed in its immediate form as life; in its reflected form, as knowledge; and in its absolute form, as unity of subject and object, or rather as the "object," to employ Hegel's language, "in which all determinations are concentrated." The Idea in this sense is absolute truth, the ultimate end of Philosophy. The absolute Idea is the "*pure form* of the Concept which contemplates its content as itself." This content, it is scarcely necessary to say, is nothing other than the system of the momenta of Logic which we have just been considering. The general form of the Idea is expressed in the Dialectical method in accordance with which the momenta are deduced, or rather which is the instrument of their deduction. It may be useful to observe, as bearing on the historical development from Kant to Hegel, that the first division of the Hegelian Logic, the "Doctrine of Being," in which the mere immediateness of Reality is discussed, corresponds, roughly speaking, to Kant's "Transcendental Æsthetic;" the second division, or "Doctrine of Essence" in which the reflected forms which enter into the constitution of Reality are dealt with, corresponds to Kant's "Transcendental Analytic;" while the third division, or Doctrine of Concept, which treats of the categories superimposed upon the synthesis of the immediate Real by the Reason, is represented in the earlier (critical) philosophy, by the Transcendental Dialectic.

The general scheme of Hegel's philosophy of nature will best be understood from the following quotation : " Nature," says Hegel, " is to be conceived as a *system of gradations*, of which one necessarily proceeds from the other, and the immediate truth of which is that from which it results; this is not to be understood as meaning that one is *naturally* generated from the other, the process only taking place in the Idea, which constitutes the innermost ground of nature. The *metamorphosis* applies only to the Concept, as such, since change in the Concept alone constitutes development. The Concept is in its nature partly inward, partly existent as the living individual; hence to the latter only is *existent* metamorphosis limited." (*Encyclopädie*, § 249.) This passage, and the one which immediately follows it, in which the doctrine of evolution conceived as natural process in order of time is combated, exhibits one of the most unfortunate blunders into which Hegel could possibly have fallen. The answer of the Evolutionist, even without departing from Hegelian principles, to Hegel's diatribe is obvious. That the development which Hegel admits to take place in the order of time in the life of the individual takes place on a larger scale in the life of the world's history, is a direct deduction from experience, as real in the one case as in the other, and no amount of arbitrary dicta, for Hegel's attitude in this matter is purely arbitrary, will deprive it of its reality.

Notwithstanding this gratuitously fallacious assumption, Hegel's " Philosophy of Nature " contains some valuable insights, though, on the whole, it is the least original portion of his work, being borrowed largely from Schelling. Following Schelling, Hegel divides " Philosophy of Nature " into Mechanic, Physic, and the synthesis of these, Organic. In nature the Idea or the Absolute, which the Logic has treated of *in itself*, is exhibited in the form of external existence, of a determinate order. Nature is the mediation (*Vermittlung*) by which consciousness comes to a knowledge of itself, and may thus be regarded as *ipso facto* the *out-of-itselfness* of the Idea or the Reason. It stands in direct opposition to the Logic, "the realm of shades," as the region of determinateness, *par excellence*. Hegel allows his impatience at the fact that there are many natural phenomena not yet reduced to law to manifest itself in the frequent assertion, that nature is impotent to display rational order in everything, and that there is much in nature which we must regard as pure chance, and as destitute of any philosophical significance. His general attitude naturally leads him to be unjust to the claims of natural science and its representatives; against Newton he is particularly bitter, though this is perhaps partly attributable to the influence of Goethe. The main momenta of mechanics are, "space and time," "matter and motion," and their synthesis "absolute mechanic," in which matter appears as a completed quantum. This leads us to the second division; qualified matter or Physic, the chief momenta of which are the physic of "universal individuality," of "particular individuality," and of "total individuality," the final determination of the latter, the chemical process, forming the transition to the Organic sphere, the stages of which are "geological nature," "vegetable nature," and the "animal organism." With the consideration of the animal organism we are already on the threshold of the philosophy of mind (*Philosophie des Geistes*), *i.e.* of the philosophy of Consciousness, no longer manifested as *out-of-itself*, but as *returned in upon itself*.

Hegel closes the "Philosophy of Nature" with some observations on the death of the individual. "His incompatibility with the universal," says Hegel, "is his original bane and the innate germ of death. The abolition of this incompatibility is the fulfilment of his destiny. Mind presupposes nature, the truth of which it is. In this truth nature has vanished, and mind has proclaimed itself as the Idea attained to *for itselfness*, for which the *concept* is no less *object* than *subject*. This Identity is *Absolute negativity*, inasmuch as, in nature, the Concept has completely manifested its objectivity, but in mind this its manifestation is abolished, and it has become identical with itself (*Encyclopädie*, § 381).

The triple division of the "Philosophy of Mind," is as follows: first of all, the Subjective Mind, in which mind is related immediately to itself as the ideal totality, whose being is freedom; secondly, the Objective Mind, or mind in the form of reality, a world in which freedom is reduced to necessity; and, lastly, Absolute Mind, which is the unity of the two previous momenta. The first division embraces "Anthropology," "Phenomenology," and "Psychology," Hegel only employing this term for its concluding section. Psychology considers mind theoretically as intelligence, practically as will; and, lastly, as the unity of these, as morality. The intelligence finds itself limited, but posits this very limitation as its own in recognising the all, as realising rational purpose. The essence of morality is, that the will should have a universal rational content for its purpose. The second division, dealing with Objective Mind, shows the realised product of freewill as exhibited in law and right, in a moral code, and in social institutions culminating in the state. The Absolute Mind, with which the third and last division is concerned, is determined in the forms of Art, Religion, and Philosophy. The Idea, as the Philosophic Reason, forms the culmination of the entire system; it is the Reason come to a knowledge of itself. In Art it is presented to sense, in Religion to the reflective understanding, and in Philosophy to the Reason, which presupposes yet transcends both.

Such is a brief outline of the Hegelian system. It remains to notice briefly the working out of the several departments of its last and most practically important division. Hegel's Ethic is apparently based on the doctrine of freedom which had been common to his predecessors. He rehabilitates Kant's separation of the legal from the moral, in admitting a sphere in which the individual subject is completely controlled by the objective mind—in short, in which its freedom is reduced to necessity. This is the second of the cardinal momenta of *mind*. But Hegel does not admit law to be a limitation of freedom; it is merely a limitation of the arbitrariness of the individual will. Nevertheless, it is opposed to the principle on which morality rests, which is conscience, the power wherein good is combined with the possibility of evil; both of these departments are however one-sided, and are united, or find their synthesis in what Hegel terms *Sittlichkeit*, a word generally identical with morality, but which Hegel distinguishes from the latter, and which, employed in his sense, may perhaps best be rendered as Virtue (the ancient civic virtue), the Latin *pietas*. It is a morality with a definite social content. The momenta of this substance or content are, the family, the society, the state. In giving the highest place to social obligation, Hegel shows that he is conscious of the barren and abstract nature of the Ethics of Kant and Fichte, for whom mere subjective freedom was the ultimate goal. By this, he virtually surrenders the standpoint of the "ethics of inwardness," as such, together with its correlate, the "religion of the spirit," although professing to have placed them on an inexpugnable footing. The fact that he finds in the state the culmination and realisation of the family and society, rather than in society the realisation of the family and the state, is, however, one of those strange perversions of view for which, we fear, we must regard governmental patronage as largely responsible. Both logically and historically, the family (or rather the *gens*) is clearly negated in the state, the tendency of which, *quâ* state, must invariably be to abolish the original independence of the family. The complex state-organization is the antithesis of the simple family-organization, which it, so to speak, swallows up. It is plainly then in the negation of the state, in its self-abolition, in which the state (*civitas*) is transformed into a free society, a higher family-organization (*societas*), that the synthesis, the *telos*, of the two previous momenta is discoverable.

Hegel's philosophy of history is in accordance with a point of view founded on the conception of the political moment being the essential one. For the rest, its leading principle, though it may be easily inferred from the general thought of the system, we give in Hegel's own words:—

"The only Thought which Philosophy brings with it to the contemplation of history, is the simple conception of *Reason;* that Reason is the Sovereign of the World;

that the history of the world, therefore, presents us with a rational process. This conviction and intuition is a hypothesis in the domain of history as such. In that of Philosophy it is no hypothesis. It is there proved by speculative cognition that Reason . . . is *Substance* as well as *Infinite Power;* its own *Infinite Material* underlying all the natural and spiritual life which it originates, as also the *Infinite Form*—that which sets this material in motion. On the one hand, Reason is the *substance* of the Universe; viz., that by which and in which all reality has its being and subsistence. On the other hand, it is the *Infinite Energy* of the Universe; since Reason is not so powerless as to be incapable of producing anything but a mere ideal, a mere intention—having its place outside reality, nobody knows where; something separate and abstract, in the heads of certain human beings. It is the *infinite complex of things*, their entire Essence and Truth. It is its own material which it commits to its own Active Energy to work up; not needing, as finite action does, the conditions of an external material of given means from which it may obtain its support, and the objects of its activity. It supplies its own nourishment, and is the object of its own operations. While it is exclusively its own basis of existence, and absolute final aim, it is also the energizing power realising this aim; developing it not only in the phenomena of the natural, but also of the Spiritual Universe—The History of the World. That this "Idea" or "Reason" is the *True*, the *Eternal*, the absolutely *powerful* essence; that it reveals itself in the World . . . is the thesis which, as we have said, has been proved in Philosophy, and is here regarded as demonstrated" * (Hegel's 'Philosophy of History,' Bohn's edition, pp. 9–10).

The lectures on the "Philosophy of History," consist mainly in disquisitions on the various forms the state has assumed in the different historic periods. Social and economic conditions are of course viewed as completely subordinated to political. In his younger days Hegel had subscribed to the revolutionary views of Rousseau and of

* The reader will have no difficulty in reading between the lines of the theistic or pantheistic colouring of this passage.

Fichte, but at this time he had no expectations of patronage from the Prussian Government. For the official philosopher of the great Bureaucratic system which was centred in Berlin—a system the perfection of whose wisdom had shown itself consummated in the choice of its philosophic representative—the state as therein embodied could hardly fail to express the highest incarnation of the Reason. The extent of Hegel's adoration of authority, for its own sake, will be estimated when we inform the reader that he professed to regard marriage as more moral when arranged by parents, than when dictated by the inclinations of "parties" themselves; that, like Schelling, he was prepared to apostrophize the Kaiser, as the political "soul of the world;" that he was the sworn defender (and this on grounds, not of antiquarianism or expediency, but of principle) of monopolies, closed corporations, &c. Erdmann has observed that Hegel's 'Philosophy of History' combines the anthropological view of Herder, according to which humanity passes through four stages, with the political view of Kant, according to which the Oriental state signifies the freedom of one alone (despotism), the Classical state the freedom of some (slave-holding oligarchy), the Germanic state (presumably, as represented by the Prussian system before '48) as the freedom of all (?).

Hegel's lectures on Æsthetic, with the exception of the 'Philosophy of History,' are perhaps the most popular of his works. Hegel felt with Schelling, and in opposition to Kant and Fichte, that the moral consciousness was after all not ultimate; that there was a region in which the individual mind was freed from the restlessness of natural and moral striving, and that this was the region of Art (compare Schopenhauer, *supra*, pp. 296–9). The Art work as the presentment of the Beautiful exhibits the Absolute in sensuous existence; it is an appeal to the heart. It does not merely afford theoretical knowledge or practical satisfaction, but it raises it above these finite forms to a sense of infinite enjoyment.

The chief periods of Art are the Oriental, the Classical, and the Romantic. In Oriental Art the special characteristic of which is symbolism, the matter preponderates over the form; in Classical Art, the characteristic of which is grace, the form and the matter balance each other; in Romantic Art, which is spiritual *par excellence*, sublimity and beauty are combined; the *form* asserts its pre-eminence. In each of the fine Arts these momenta are discoverable no less than in the History of Art as a whole. Thus, in architecture, the art which is first in the order of time, the moment of symbolism or sublimity may be seen in the Monument (*e.g.* the pyramid, the tower, the obelisk, &c.) characteristic of the ancient Oriental civilizations; the classical moment in the Greek Temple; the romantic in the Gothic Cathedral. The peculiarly Romantic Arts of Painting and Music present within themselves the same stages which are all embraced and reduced to unity, in the Art which is the Art of Arts, Art *par excellence*, viz. Poetry. Hegel defines the form of the Beautiful as the unity of multiplicity. The progress of Art, according to Hegel, consists in the gradual elimination of the spacial and material element therein. The beginning of Art Architecture, exhibits, as above stated, an enormous preponderance of the sensuous material. In Sculpture, the peculiarly classical Art, the mere material is less obtrusive; moreover, as embodying a definite form, that of the human body, it is a step towards a higher ideality. Painting, the earlier of the romantic Arts, the perfection of which was reached in the middle ages, inasmuch as it gets rid of the third dimension of matter, implies a further advance towards the ideal, the supremacy of form; it is the objective art of form. Music, of which the material is pure tone, and whose perfection has been reached in the modern world, finally abolishes the element of space altogether; its content is the inner emotional nature, and hence it is the most subjective of all the Arts. Lastly, Poetry dispenses with any specific material whatever, its material being simply language, the medium for the expression of thought in general, and Poetry may be truly termed the Art of universal expression. It comprehends all the other Arts in itself, Painting in the epos, Music in the lyric, and the unity of both in the drama. It is peculiar to no one period of history, but is present in one or more of its forms in all periods.

Hegel showed a far deeper appreciation of the significance of Art than Schelling. The latter could merely regard it as a special department of modern culture, and the artist as a professional man of talent or genius in no special manner the product of his age or race. Hegel, on the contrary, took an historical view; he saw in Art the expression of the life of a period, or of a people; he saw that all true Art, all Art that is worth anything, is essentially *social* and not *individual*. "Each generation hands its beauty on to the next; each has done something to give utterance to the universal thought. Those said to have genius, have merely acquired the particular faculty of expressing the general social forms in their own work, some in this respect, some in the other. Their product is not their invention but that of the whole nation . . . Each adds his stone to the structure, the artist among the rest, only that he happens to have the fortune to come last, and thus when he lays his stone the arch is self-supporting."

The close of Hegel's Philosophy of Æsthetics as usual contains an indication of the next division of the philosophy of Absolute Mind, viz. that of Religion. Religion is the form in which the Absolute is presented, not only to the perceptive consciousness or feeling, but also to the reflective understanding. The historical momenta of Religion are, the nature-religions in which God is regarded as mere natural substance (Fetichism and the lower forms of Polytheism); those Religions in which the Deity is conceived as Subject which comprise the Jewish Religion or the religion of sublimity, the Greek Religion or the religion of beauty, and the Roman Religion or the religion of utility; and, finally, the synthesis of nature-religion, and of subjective-religion, viz. Absolute religion, the ultimate expression of which, it is needless to say, Hegel somehow or other manages to find in the special form of Protestant Christianity established in Prussia. The dexterous evolutions performed to arrive at this end are more curious than instructive; especially the case as regards the manner in which the leading Christian dogmas are twisted into conformity with the Hegelian doctrine.

As Art found its issue in Religion, so Religion finds its culmination in Philosophy. Philosophy is truth in its absoluteness, the thought of the self-thinking Idea, of the self-comprehending Reason. The development of Philosophy shows a progress from the abstract to the concrete; the philosophy of the pre-Socratists, of the Eleatics, of Herakleitos, and of the Atomists represents respectively the momenta of Being, Becoming, and For-itselfness; the philosophy of Plato, the categories of Essence; that of Aristotle, those of the Concept; that of the Neo-Platonists, the totality of the Concrete Idea. Similarly, the philosophy of the middle ages and of modern times, is the philosophy of the Idea as self-conscious, or as mind. The Cartesian philosophy occupies the standpoint of unreflective consciousness; the Kantian, that of self-consciousness; the Hegelian, that of the Reason or Absolute knowledge. Hegel claims therefore that, in his system, all earlier philosophies are implied and embraced as essential momenta, at the same time that they are superseded.

"In the peculiar form of *external history*," he says, "the origin and development of philosophy is presented as the history of this science. This form gives to the Idea's stages of development, the appearance of *accidental* succession, and of mere *diversity* of principles, with their working out in philosophical systems. But the craft-master of this work of ages is the one living spirit whose thinking nature it is to bring what it is, to its consciousness, and immediately this has become object to have already in itself attained a higher stage, a stage which is above and beyond it. The *History of Philosophy* shows us, in apparently diverse philosophies, on the one hand, only a philosophy at different stages of development, and on the other, only the special *principles*, one of which underlies one system, and one another, but which are only *branches* of one and the same whole. The last philosophy in the order of time is the result of all previous philosophies, and must hence contain the principles of them all; it is therefore, in so far as it is philosophy at all, the most developed, the richest, and the most concrete of all philosophies."

Hegelianism had for some years previous to the death of Hegel in 1831, overshadowed the intellectual firmament with its colossal structure. As before with Kantianism, its parent, so now, though even to a greater extent, with Hegelianism, it was the dominant philosophy taught throughout Germany, and asserting its influence in all departments of culture. The term of Hegel's life coincided with the culmination of the authority of his school, and the commencement of its decline, considered as representing a system one and indivisible, as the doctrine of the master, in its orthodox form, claimed to be. Soon after Hegel's death, his disciples published his completed works. But dissensions speedily became apparent. The first crisis in the school occurred about 1835. "The school of Hegel," says Rosenkranz, writing in 1844, "in the sense that others must seek his instruction as that of an immortal master of speculation, not only exists, but will continue to exist in the future, just in the same way as after Aristotle there were still Aristotelians, and after Spinoza, Spinozists. But the school, in the sense of a social union of disciples—in the sense, that is, of a kind of corporate responsibility of one Hegelian for his neighbour, has ceased. The *Berlinerjahrbücher*, its outward meeting-place, can moreover no longer be considered as the expression of the development of the Hegelian philosophy, nor as the organ of its apologetics and polemics. The most violent divergencies of disciples from the master, as well as of disciples from each other, have become notorious."

This break-up of the school, as a school, Rosenkranz, although himself one of the original disciples of Hegel, justly regards as inevitable, and indeed as a hopeful reaction against the worship of phrases, and of the system as a system, towards which there was a tendency in its halcyon days. The collapse of the Hegelian school, he asserts, does not mean the collapse of the Hegelian philosophy, but rather the necessary condition of its continued life and activity.

There is a passage of Hegel's own *à-propos* of this, which is worthy of being inscribed in letters of gold, and which the "man of the world,"—who, strong in his smug ignorance of history and "sound common-sense," jeers at the internal differences accompanying the growth of a movement as signs of decay—would do well to remember: "A party shows itself to have won the victory first when it has broken up into two parties; for then it proves that it contains in itself the principle with which at first it had to conflict, and thus that it has got beyond the onesidedness which was incidental to its earliest expression. The interest which formerly divided itself between it and that to which it was opposed, now falls entirely within itself, and the opposing principle is left behind and forgotten, just because it is represented by one of the sides in the new controversy which now occupies the minds of men. At the same time, it is to be observed that when the old principle thus reappears, it is no longer what it was before, for it is changed and purified by the higher element into which it is now taken up. In this point of view, that discord which appears at first to be a lamentable breach and dissolution of the unity of a party, is really the crowning proof of its success."

The success of Hegelianism as a distinct system was no doubt partly due to its eclectic, and hence to some extent conservative, and even reactionary tendencies. Hegel restored to philosophy in a new form what Kant had demolished in its older form, viz. Metaphysic proper or Ontology. His Logic identified "Theory of Knowledge" and Ontology in seeking to show that existence was only one of the momenta of consciousness, and not *vice versâ*. Again, Hegel had sought to re-establish a *modus vivendi* between Theology and Philosophy (albeit at the cost of the former) in his *Religionsphilosophie*, by an ingenious esoteric interpretation of leading dogmas, and also by taking under his wing the Prussian Church organization. But Hegel differed from his predecessors on a most important point, the practical side of his philosophy, to wit, the virtual surrender of the individualistic Ethics so strongly accentuated by Kant and Fichte, and the rehabilitation of the ancient conception of social virtue, the morality which has for its end the family, the city, and the state. That he was led to this partly by his zeal on behalf of Prussian bureaucracy, does not alter the intrinsic importance of the change of standpoint. With the events consequent on the revolutionary year, 1830, the conservative side, and therewith the system as a system of the Hegelian philosophy became shaken. The political ascendency of the middle class, which was now everywhere the order of the day—the temporary reaction consequent on the French revolution having spent itself—ill accorded with the system which, in a sense, apotheosized class-despotism of a different kind. Hegelianism began to work out in opposite directions; a right and a left wing formed in the school; and the intellectual life of Germany during the seventeen years from the period of Hegel's death to the revolution of 1848, is mainly taken up with the controversies liberated by the dissolution of the original Hegelian school, which resulted in a severe struggle between the various sections of the party. These controversies, religious, social, and political, we shall briefly notice in the following pages.

THE HEGELIAN SCHOOL.

Attacks on the Hegelian system had already begun before the death of Hegel, from standpoints which were not opposed to the speculative method in general. Weisse, professor of Philosophy at Leipzig, in an essay on the "Present Standpoint of Philosophical Science," published in 1829, criticised the Logic in a theistic sense, and subsequently attacked the system in detail in a series of works. The Hegelian right consisted, among others, of Gans, Heinrichs, Göschel, Michelet, Rosenkranz, and Vischer. These men, all pupils of Hegel, adhered to the doctrine, more or less, in its original form, though for the most part emphasising the conservative side. Michelet, who is still living, has recently published a summary of the system. Of these more orthodox and conservative disciples of Hegel, there is little to be said in a work like the present, save that they took an active part in the controversies of the period.

The most remarkable development of the Hegelian doctrine was that accomplished in the left wing, and which is associated with the names of Strauss, Feuerbach, Bruno Bauer, Ruge, &c. Hegelianism, as a system, at once tended to promote and to check the free tendencies of the age in Theology, Politics, &c. Its most noteworthy product in Theology, however, was the celebrated Tübingen school of biblical criticism, the best known names connected with which are Ferdinand Christian Baur, and David Friedrich Strauss. The first actual crisis in the Hegelian party was indeed brought about by the publication of Strauss's *Leben Jesu*, although, considering that the notion of the supernatural in Religion and History had been practically absent from the educated German mind since Kant, it is difficult to understand the sensation produced by the definite working-out of a "mythical theory" as to the origin of Christianity by Strauss. But the main issue in the religious sphere resolved itself into the question of the compatibility of the Hegelian system with theism at all. Hegel himself had of course maintained it to be the only possible form of theism; but this, it must be remembered, was as he understood theism. He also *(vide supra*, p. 334) affirmed its complete accordance with Christian doctrine, as established in Prussia, again with the important reservation, however, that philosophy was to interpret that doctrine, a reservation which effectually "kept the word of promise to the ear," but as effectually broke it the hope of the orthodox. So with the theistic question; it was not long before the more advanced Hegelians made up their minds to expose and disavow what justly seemed to them a merely verbal accommodation. In Strauss's second great work, the 'Christian Dogmatics in their Development, and in their Conflict with Modern Science,' the narrower and the wider issue were brought out into clear relief, and the view insisted on that Christian Religion and Modern Philosophy are opposed to one another as Theism to Pantheism. There is a sly hit at the master where Strauss, playing upon the German word *Grund* (ground or reason), says that a philosopher may have very good *grounds* (*Gründe*) for calling himself a Christian, but he can have no *reason* (*Grund*). To the philosopher, for whom there is no hard and fast distinction between this and the other world, for whom all such distinctions, as mind and matter, subject and object, divine and natural, are at once embraced and transcended in a higher unity there is no greater enemy than a doctrine which affirms and perpetuates this dualism of conception. Inasmuch as the resolution of these oppositions has already accomplished itself, the criticism of dogma becomes identical with its history. The aim of Strauss in the work in question is therefore to point out the precise manner in which the ecclesiastical dogma moulded itself out of the biblical doctrine; how with the Reformation the dissolution began; how the tentative doctrines of the Reformers were in their turn reformed by the Socinians, Spinoza, and the English Deists; how the conclusions of these latter were pushed forward by the French and German *Aufklärung*, till Schelling drew and Hegel formulated the conclusion that there is no other Divinity than the thought in all thinking beings; no Divine attributes other than natural laws; and that the All knows no addition and no diminution, but is continually manifested in the infinity of individuals.

Bruno Bauer, who originally belonged to the extreme right, being bitterly attacked as a representative of this direction by Strauss, and who had been accused of being on the high road to join the then well-known pietist, Hengstenberg, startled every one, when, in 1839, he published his "Herr Doctor Hengstenberg, a contribution to the critique of religious consciousness," in which the artifices of the orthodox apologists were scathingly exposed. In a subsequent work, the notion of a Church organization is treated as a survival, and religion declared to exist only as religiosity—that is, the sentiment of devotion to a higher power; but at present, Bauer declared, there is no power to which the individual can devote himself higher than the state. Between the civil and the antiquated ecclesiastical organization stands Science on the side of the former, and where the State seeks to limit Science in the interest of Theology, it is really fighting against itself.

Bruno Bauer was joined later on by his brother Edgar, who put forward a doctrine, worked out in a metaphysical form by Max Stirner, of whom we shall speak presently, which may be regarded as the prototype of modern Individualism. It proclaimed the individual supreme, and denounced all government and organizations whatever as destructive of the individuality. Thus Bruno's divinity, the state, was rudely swept away. Bruno and Edgar Bauer were alike untiring in proclaiming that in the individual human being was summed up all truth and all reality.

The most prominent name in connection with this movement was that of Ludwig Andreas Feuerbach, who was undoubtedly the most popular exponent of the individualist and empiricist reaction against the Hegelian Monism. It is perhaps hardly fair to call the movement a reaction, for strange as it may at first sight seem, it was the natural working out of one of the sides of Hegel's doctrine. Owing to the very synthetic nature of that doctrine, it only required a very slight change to transform it, on the one hand into pantheism, and on the other into individualism. The moment the fundamental point of view of "Theory of Knowledge" fell out of sight, and to minds which could see in the distinctions it expresses, mere word-jugglery, absolute individualism was the necessary issue. Of course subjective Idealism of the Leibnitzian type must have been the inevitable outcome in a metaphysical point of view, but metaphysic was at a discount just at this time, and in consequence, it was in practical departments rather than in the region of pure speculation, that the new development manifested itself. All Feuerbach's works have a distinctly practical tendency; with pure speculation he concerns himself little. His strength lies in negative criticism. The salient points of Feuerbach's theory will be found in the "Essence of Christianity," the English translation of which, by George Eliot, is well known. Bruno Bauer and Feuerbach were naturally in opposition to Strauss, who held strongly to the Pantheistic side of Hegelianism; for Strauss, the individual mind was the reflection of "the All," the immanent divine principle; for Feuerbach, the divine principle was simply the reflection within itself of the individual mind. On the political side the difference between them was even more accentuated—Strauss was the Tory, Feuerbach and the Brunos were Revolutionists. In a small *brochure*, entitled 'The Holy Family Bauer,' the eminent Socialist writers, Karl Marx and Friedrich Engels, criticised the foregoing writers with characteristic humour.

The most remarkable product albeit the *reductio ad absurdum* of the ex-Hegelian individualists, was the little work of Max Stirner (Dr. Schmidt), entitled the 'Individual and His Possession' (*Der Einzige und sein Eigenthum*), in which the author seeks to show the heresy from their own point of view, even of Feuerbach and Bauer themselves; how, that is, even in their later writings the religious principle still clings to them, as shown in their admission of the Ideal of society or humanity as an object of devotion for the individual. "The Individual and His Property" might serve as a text-book for our modern individualist-anarchists. The principle of Individualism is there pushed to its only logical conclusion. The "self-consciousness" of Bauer, the "humanity" of Feuerbach, the "society" of the Communists, are all stigmatised as relics of superstition, as objects of worship. From these standpoints, all and severally, the individual as such is lost sight of, and yet only the individual is real. He who devotes himself to aught outside himself, without receiving an equivalent for his devotion, surrenders his individuality—he is superstitious. The individual Ego is the only concrete, all else is abstract and unreal. "The Ideal, the Man, is realised when the Christian conception becomes converted into the proposition, 'I this individual am the man.' The conceptual question 'what is the man?' has then resolved itself into the personal one 'who is the man?' with 'what' the conception was sought to be realised; with 'who' there is no longer any more question, but the answer is immediately present in the question, the question answers itself of itself . . . I am the owner of my power, and I it is who know myself as individual. In the individual this owner returns to the creative nothing out of which he was born. Every being that is above me, be it God, be it man, weakens the feeling of my individuality, and pales before the sun of this consciousness. I place my interest in myself, the individual; it stands then on the same footing as its transient mortal creator, who thus feeds upon himself. I may therefore say, 'I have placed my interest in nothing'" (*Der Einzige und sein Eigenthum*, p. 491). This is certainly a novel way of arriving at the Stoic "apathy," for such is practically the result of Max Stirner's reasoning, as will be apparent from the concluding sentences of his book, which we have just quoted. But the preposterous result, and much besides in the work, which is merely paradoxical and *bizarre*, does not detract from the fact of there being much also that is valuable in the shape of criticism scattered up and down the volume. The reply of Feuerbach to this attack was hardly up to his usual standard.

The chief organ of the Hegelian left at this period was the *Halleschen Jahrbücher*, the editor being Arnold Ruge, who was one of the foremost leaders of the German revolutionary movement of 1848. Unlike Strauss, the Bauers, and Feuerbach, who can hardly be regarded as belonging to the Hegelian school at all, Ruge was, at least for a long time, comparatively orthodox in the essentials of his Hegelianism; the *Jahrbücher* nevertheless formed the general meeting-ground for all groups of the party; and indeed it was in their pages that some of the earlier essays of Edgar Bauer appeared. A manifesto, published in the year 1840, by Ruge and his co-editor, Echtermeyer, nominally on "Romanticism and Protestantism," but which was really a thinly veiled political essay, had a wide-reaching influence at the time.

The *Jahrbücher* now began to directly attack the old Hegelians for their superstitious reverence for the master's doctrine, as well as for their political indifferentism. They were accused of treating the Logic as a kind of Veda, while Ruge prophesied the rapidly approaching end of the kingdom of the Hegelian Brahma. Hegel himself was vigorously assailed for his reactionism. In July 1841 the *Halleschen Jahrbücher* appeared as the *Deutschen Jahrbücher*, the change of name being accompanied by a declaration of principles in which the strict Hegelian orthodoxy was formally renounced in its threefold character, philosophic, religious, and political. All the fetters of superstition, which had hitherto clung to the *Jahrbücher*, were henceforward to be discarded. Henceforth it would openly occupy the position of Strauss and Feuerbach in Theology, while a determined war was to be waged against Feudalism in all its surviving forms. The great merit of the Hegelian philosophy would be recognised to consist in its having freed men from traditional prejudice. The time had come, Ruge declared, in a subsequent number, when the Church should become the School, and Liberalism give place to Democracy. The publication of the *Jahrbücher* ceased in 1843, and Ruge repaired to Paris, where, in conjunction with Marx, he brought out a few numbers of another journal, the *Deutschfranzösischen Jahrbücher*. Returning to Saxony, in 1846, he produced his third venture, the *Reform*, and sat for some time in the parliament of Frankfort. On the subsidence of the revolutionary movement, in 1850, Ruge came over to England, where he continued to reside till his death, which occurred at Brighton early in the year 1881. Ruge is unquestionably the leading figure of the Hegelian left on its political side, and, as already observed, on the dissolution of the school practical questions assumed a more and more exclusive importance.

We have only mentioned a few of the more striking names, connected with this period, the interest of which, from a purely speculative point of view, is secondary. With the revolution of 1848 conditions were changed; the Hegelian school was finally dissolved, and those who had constituted it were scattered. Among the surviving academical "monuments" of the older Hegelianism may be mentioned, Erdmann, the author of the well-known 'History of Philosophy,' professor at Halle; Kuno Fischer, professor at Heidelberg, and Michelet of Berlin. Hegel's pupil and biographer, Rosenkranz, died in 1883.

THE DEVELOPMENT FROM KANT TO HEGEL.

RETROSPECT AND CRITICISM.

We have now reached the close of the movement inaugurated by Kant, and therewith the close of the History of Philosophy properly so called. The later speculation, that is, such as is subsequent to the Hegelian movement, belongs to current thought, and cannot as yet be assigned a place in history. Of this we shall treat in the following and concluding division of the present work. Our object in this section is to take a general survey of the Kantian and post-Kantian movement, and to endeavour to extract from it its historical meaning.

Kant, we have seen, was the pioneer of a line of speculative thought, which restored to philosophy the larger basis it had occupied under the ancients, by re-opening those wider issues, which had furnished the themes of the treatises of Plato and Aristotle, issues which form part of one problem—that as to the meaning and constitution of *reality*. We have noted how Kant's simple psychological query, How are synthetic propositions *à priori* possible? directly involved the question, How is experience itself possible? and how this brought us back to the fundamental inquiry of philosophy. The order in which Kant discusses this problem in the 'Critique,' and elsewhere, was immediately determined by the course of his own thought. The key to the whole is however, to be found in the deduction of the categories from the ultimate unity of apperception or consciousness. The question now arises, Is this thought-unity from which Kant starts really ultimate? Is the ultimate form of the category absolute? Is pure thought subject? Does not consciousness presuppose *that which becomes* conscious? In other words, Is not the "I think" itself susceptible of further analysis? Is not this ultimate *I* distinguishable from its *thinking?* * We believe it is, and that the treatment of this principle as final, and as a purely logical or formal unity, is the origin of the tendency in speculation hitherto, even where professing to be most synthetic, to become onesided.

The synthetic unity of the consciousness, the logical element, presupposes the alogical element, the *I*, or the principle, which *becomes* unified. This principle which, considered *per se*, consciousness or knowledge itself presupposes, may hence be regard as the *matter* of which thought or consciousness is the *form*. Now we contend that this ultimate, all-penetrating *material* moment—the subject as such—has been ignored by most of the leaders of speculation from Plato to Hegel, and an appearance of having transcended the distinction been obtained by the hypostasis of *form*. At first sight this may seem a subtlety which can have very little speculative, and certainly no practical, importance; but we shall endeavour to show that it does, as a matter of fact, give a colouring to the whole course of thought, being the general speculative expression of an entire code of ideas; and that the antagonism of Materialism and Idealism, using these terms in their widest sense, is involved in it. In the speculative or generic method, which deals with a process out of relation to time, the starting-point is also the goal, the beginning and the end meet as in a circle. The ultimate principle which involves and includes all others is necessarily the determinant of the entire system of principles. Hence, whether that ultimate principle be formal or material, logical or alogical,† makes a profound difference, and decides indeed the whole character of the system.

In Plato, what we are here contending for, is very plainly

* Descartes, in his famous *Cogito*, gave modern speculation at starting a formalist impulse. (See p. 146, *supra*.)

† The word "alogical," it has been suggested to me is objectionable, as conveying the idea of an "unknowable," a "surd" outside the system of experience rather than an element therein. The terms "positive logical" and "negative logical," might be substituted for "logical" and "alogical," though we venture to think the context will preclude misconception on this head.

exhibited. The unifying *thought-form* the *logos* is abstracted from its alogical *matter*, the *Hyle*, and hypostasized throughout, as the system of Ideas, which reaches its culmination in the all-embracing supreme Idea. Aristotle lights upon the abstraction so glaringly and consistently carried out by Plato and energetically denounces him for it. But, nevertheless, Aristotle himself falls into substantially the same attitude. For him also pure form—in other words, the Ideal, the 'creative intellect,' as *actus purus*—was the determining element—the all-embracing fact—in the constitution of the real. All systems founded on Plato and Aristotle exhibit the same tendency, that namely, to the hypostasis of the pure form of consciousness and *à fortiori* of Thought or the Ideal as such.

We pass over those lines of development, such as the Dogmatic and the Empirical, in which, since they are not based on speculative or transcendental analysis, the abstraction in question is not so obvious, or so easily pointed out in a few words; and coming to Kant, who re-affirmed the analysis of experience or reality as the first problem of philosophy, we find the same abstraction made at starting,* the abstraction namely of the *form* of knowing, or thinking from its *matter*, the alogical subject which it presupposes, and whose self-determination *thought* is. Fichte, at first sight, appears to adopt a more concrete standpoint. This is even confirmed, as it would seem by certain statements and certain portions of his analysis. But when the system is viewed as a whole (not to speak of reiterated assertions to the same effect), it is seen that experience with Fichte, no less than with Kant (in his transcendental deduction), is analysed only into the formal unity of consciousness, that Fichte's "ego" is pure thought, and not *that which* thinks and which is the *possibility* of thought. The moment of actual self-consciousness is the determining moment of the whole. To Schelling the same remarks apply, at least as far as the earlier form of his system is concerned;. the synthetic unity of apperception in Schelling's system appears as the *formal* indifference or identity

* As regards this, it must be remembered, however, that the deduction of the categories, with Kant himself, only concerned one side of his system.

between subject and object. There are modes of statement in Schelling as there are in Fichte, which would seem to indicate that they had a presentiment of the abstraction involved in the procedure which they had inherited from Kant. But these were not strong enough to alter the fundamental character of their systems. Their ultimate principle remained self-consciousness, that is, not the *Ego*, but the Ego's consciousness of itself. They were formal, and abstractly Idealistic.

The principle which Fichte and Schelling were vaguely cognisant of, but the real bearing of which they failed to grasp, was seized by Schopenhauer, and placed in the forefront of his philosophy under the name of Will. We do not of course mean to imply that Schopenhauer was led to his principle by a systematically reasoned-out conception of the defect of his predecessors, or that it adequately supplies those defects. Schopenhauer was more the man of letters than the exact thinker, and his "Will-to-live" was rather a poetical expression than a result arrived at by any strict process of analysis; but his system embodies unmistakably among other things a protest against formalistic Idealism. This explains the favour with which he regards all materialistic views of the universe. Schopenhauer felt that in pure thought, considered *per se*, there was no *dynamic principle;* that the categories of consciousness, even the highest, did not of themselves constitute reality, but presupposed a matter—a subject—of which they were the determinations. Essentially the same revolt against the formalism of the thinkers in the direct line of development from Kant underlies, as we take it, the system of Herbart. The consciousness of the purely formal nature of thought *per se*, it is only fair to remember, also underlies Kant's own distinction between Sense and Understanding. The element of feeling was to Kant as necessary to the constitution of Reality as thought itself. It is also expressed in his distinction between Thing-in-itself and Phenomenon, at least in one of its aspects.

The encyclopedic mind of Hegel, with its Titanic grasp of method, could hardly be oblivious of the fact we are here pointing out, leaving its track, as it does, throughout the whole history of Philosophy. But Hegel evades, in his own case, the obviousness of the formal nature of the standpoint he occupies in common with his predecessors, at least as regards the working-out of his system by his dexterous manipulation of terminology. But it only requires the most cursory glance to see that the taint of Idealistic formalism pervades the whole Hegelian construction. With Hegel, the Concept or the Idea—pure consciousness—is the totality of the Real. This alone is the sharpest and most distinct pronouncement of Thought as the *prius* of the world-order. The way in which Hegel covers up his formalism is ingenious, but hardly convincing. Let us take as an instance, the passages on page 29 of the 'Encyclopedia,' where Hegel defines the Ego as "the universal in and for itself;" and again as "pure self-reference," "the abstract universal" "the abstractly free," &c. Hegel here refers to the synthetic unity of apperception, the universal form—consciousness, which is, as he insists, formal and abstract; but in this he clearly ignores that from which it is abstracted, the "self" of the "reference," the *I* which determines itself as *thinking*.

In his anxiety to grasp the *whatness* of experience, he let go the *thatness*. The Hegelian would, of course, reply that the fact referred to, inasmuch as it represents the *possibility of consciousness*, that its whole positive determination is exhausted in *being* the possibility of consciousness, it is legitimate to regard merely as one of the momenta of consciousness. To this we reply, that such a treatment involves hypostasis, a seizure of the formal instead of the material moment as the primal determinate of the *real*, which although it matters little in pure speculation, amounting to little beyond a difference of emphasis, has important consequences when carried out in more concrete spheres. The difference may be compared to two lines gradually diverging from one starting-point. At first the space between them is scarcely discernible, but the end shows a wide discrepancy.

Mere subtle refinement, as it seems, this distinction between the absoluteness of *the actual*, *formal moment*, or consciousness itself, and of the *possible*, *material moment*, or *that which is* conscious, *that which* thinks, reappears, as already indicated, on another plane in the distinction between the Idealist and Materialist views of the universe. As a natural consequence, the Ethical problem of free-will and necessity, of determination from within or without the empirically-conscious personality, hinges largely upon this. That man is able *consciously* to determine his actions is the theory of free-will; that his empirical consciousness merely registers a determination, of which it is not productive, is the doctrine of necessity as now understood. If the real be simply a system of logical determinations alone, if its totality is exhausted in the Logical; if in its leading momenta, the formal is their determining side; then the philosophical-theistic, and free-will theory of the Hegelians of the right is established: if on the other hand, consciousness is not creative; if the Logical necessarily involves an alogical element, and it is this alogical element which determines, which is the δύναμις in the production of the experienced world, then we have discovered the root-meaning of the protest of the left wing of the Hegelian school against the theistic and idealistic guise in which the doctrine was presented by the conservative side.

Hitherto in all synthetic systems of philosophy it is the moment of *form* of *limitation*, of *for-itselfness* which has dominated the whole; it has been made both *telos* and *dynamis*. For Plato, it was the Ideas which informed the unreal matter of the sense-world. For Aristotle, again the *logos*, the *entelecheia*, was the determining principle of the *Hyle*. For Hegel lastly the formal moment was absolute explicitly; the Concept was self-existent.

But from another point of view, the *matter* may be regarded as self-determining, and the *form* as its self-determination? The hypostasis of the formal moment which has so long dominated the speculative world then disappears. The ultimate principle of "Theory of Knowledge," or philosophy, the science which alone deals with first principles properly so-called, is no longer "Consciousness," or thought as such, but the alogical subject which determines itself as *conscious*, which is the *materia prima* of consciousness. A little reflection, we think, will enable the student to see that this initial change of attitude shifts (so to speak) our point of view throughout every department of thought. The material rather than the formal henceforth becomes the determining moment in the synthesis of all and every *reality*.*

* Thus nature is self-determining and not determined *ab extra* by its mere formal moment which constitutes what we term "natural law."

RECENT AND CURRENT PHILOSOPHY.

IN this concluding portion of the handbook, we propose to consider the state of Philosophy during the second half of the nineteenth century. In doing so we shall pass over lightly those writers whose general influence and importance is secondary in order, to afford more space for the exposition of the views of men who may be regarded as in some sense leaders of contemporary thought.

Since the break up of the Hegelian school, Germany has fallen somewhat into the background in the matter of speculation. Philosophical literature pours forth abundantly from the press, but it represents for the most part merely the survival or the revival of older standpoints, without exhibiting any new development. The views of Herbart and of Schopenhauer have met with amplification and modification at the hands of fluent and able writers. As representative of these may be taken, on the one hand, Von Hartmann, and on the other, Lotze.

Eduard von Hartmann (born 1842, at Berlin) claims to be the reconciler of Hegel and Schopenhauer, but is really in all essentials the follower of the latter. In his leading work, 'The Philosophy of the Unconscious,' Hartmann maintains the Spinozistic thesis of an unconscious Absolute, with the dual attribute of Will and Idea. He rejects the Dialectical method, and claims for his philosophy the inductive basis of physical science. "According to Hegel," says Hartmann, "only the Logical the Idea is ultimate, while according to Schopenhauer, the Alogical, the Will, is ultimate." The conception of the Absolute, the *prius* of all reality, as including both Will and Idea, reconciles the antagonism between them. "It is the great service," as Hartmann thinks of Schelling, "to have shown the possibility of a *modus vivendi* between the two standpoints." Schelling, however, spoilt the fertility of his conception by coquetting with theology, which misled him into fantastic quasi-personifications of these principles. Hartmann will know of no distinction between the method of philosophy and that of physical science: to proceed from the known to its as yet unknown ground of explanation is the true method in both cases. Hartmann's exposition of his philosophy falls into three divisions, headed respectively, "The phenomenon of the Unconscious in corporeality;" "the Unconscious in the human mind;" and "the metaphysic of the Unconscious."

In the first two divisions Hartmann seeks to substantiate and illustrate his fundamental assumption in the regions of physiology and pathology; in the third, in the human mind and in society. The term "Consciousness" with Hartmann, as with Schopenhauer, means the empirical consciousness, and hence, like Schopenhauer, Hartmann properly insists on the correlation of consciousness with cerebral and nervous action. But although conscious activity (in the empirical sense) is inseparable from organic function, this does not preclude us from regarding unconscious activity of a subjective nature from being the *sine quâ non* of brain-function as of every other material process, which may hence be regarded as its product. This "unconscious" principle of Hartmann is not to be identified with Schopenhauer's "Will." Schopenhauer, in proclaiming "Will" the *prius* of the world-order, banished Intelligence, as a primary principle, altogether from his system. This was the weak point, according to Hartmann, in his doctrine, for Will alone, apart from Intelligence, as the basis of the Real can furnish no rational explanation of the experienced world, nor *à fortiori* of the final purpose of such a world. In this particular the Hegelian doctrine of the Idea or the Reason, as the ultimate principle of Reality, has the advantage over the doctrine of Schopenhauer; but Hegel, on his side, is unable to explain the irrational element in the world-order, which he glosses over under the name of chance.

The true inductive method which Hartmann claims to apply to speculation reveals to us, that instinct, *i.e.* unconscious Will in inseparable combination with unconscious Intelligence creates the world: organic and animal functions, arbitrary and reflex motions, sexual love, character, genius, language (in its origin), nay, conscious thought and perception themselves, are all reducible to manifestations of an unconscious Will-Intelligence. The form, the adaptability to its end of the phenomenon, shows us Intelligence; the phenomenon itself in its activity shows us Will. The conjunction of both, Will, which is *per se* unintelligent, and Idea or Intelligence, which is *per se* powerless, as the dual attribute of one substance, suffices as the sole ground of explanation of the phenomenal world. The absence of the principle of Intelligence in Schopenhauer's system prevented his arriving at an explanation of the rationality displayed in the order of the world; the absence of the motive power, Will, prevents Hegel from passing out of the region of the merely logical into that of the real or the existent. The conception of the union of Will and Idea, of the realisation of the logical rational Idea by the alogical non-rational Will, reconciles both systems by supplying the defective element in them. Now, according to Hartmann, the rational is real, and the real is rational.

The rational and intelligent order in the real is expressed in a series of stages. The first is constituted by the simple, attractive and repulsive force-centres, which are the foundation of the corporeal world. They are the first product of the will-impregnated Idea, and form the first rung of the ladder which culminates in the conscious organism. Each successive step expresses a victory of the Idea over the Will, of Intelligence over blind impulse or force, of the Logical over the Alogical. The easiest possible way to the attainment of its immediate end is the one chosen by the Idea. Thus nature prefers to bring about improvement in species by "natural selection," and the "struggle for existence," rather than to attain the same object by a more cumbersome, even though a less wasteful method. The goal of this world-evolution is the complete subjugation of the (non-rational) Will, by the (rational) Intelligence. But the complete victory of the Logical over the Alogical presupposes consciousness, and hence the progressive series of being in the order of evolution gravitates towards one point, to the point, viz., where the organism has the conditions of consciousness complete within itself. This completeness is first attained in the human brain and nerve system. Consciousness may be called the final emancipation of the Intelligence or Reason from its bondage to the Will.

The conscious organism once given, its happiness becomes henceforth the more or less immediate purpose of the world; but this notion of happiness is an illusion which hides from us the higher and ultimate end of consciousness, which is not human happiness, but the emancipation of the world-principle. Here the coincidence of Hartmann with Schopenhauer comes into view. To Hartmann, as to Schopenhauer, existence is a huge blunder. The more intelligence grows, the clearer it becomes that the pleasure of the world is vastly outbalanced by the pain; and this applies alike to the individual life, and to the life of the race. A crucial instance of it is afforded by a comparison of the amount of pleasure present in the animal which eats, as compared to the amount of pain present in the animal which is eaten. In human history the illusion of the possibility of realising human happiness presents itself in three phases. In the classical world happiness was believed to be attainable in the present life of the individual. In the Christian world happiness is believed to be attainable in a future life of the individual. This belief, which modern science has shattered, is now succeeded by the third phase of the illusion, which conceives happiness as possible in the future of the race. Once this illusion has been lived through, the truth will be apparent; there will be no room for any further illusion as to the possible realisation of happiness. The one end will henceforth be Nirvana, though not the Nirvana of Schopenhauer, who takes account of the individual merely, and not of the race. The quietism which Schopenhauer preached is simply a phase of the Christian religious spirit. There is no short cut to Nirvana, such as Schopenhauer imagined, attainable by the individual. The pietistic results of Schopenhauer's philosophy must be given up for a more extended view, which shows us the individual as powerless to arrest the world-process, which exhibits the act of renunciation as brought about through the desire of happiness having been, in the natural order of things, quenched, not in the individual alone, but throughout all conscious beings.

Even the highest of all pleasures, literary and artistic activity, in this third stage of the illusion into which we are now entering begins to wear itself out. All tends to a low level of mediocrity. The combination of selfishness and sympathy, which sees in the future happiness of the whole, a reward for the sacrifice of individual well-being, will have had its day, according to Hartmann, when wealth and comfortable circumstances—in short, all that can be effected alike for the race or the individual—is seen to be of no lasting value in producing happiness, and this experience is being made by increasing numbers (?) in proportion to the spread of civilization. This on the one hand. On the other, the teaching of experience shows us that the sum of actual pain in no wise tends to diminish. Side by side with the advance of medical knowledge, illness, more especially obscure and chronic maladies, increase in greater proportion. Hunger consumes an ever-widening social area with the necessary progress of population. "The most contented peoples are the rude nature races, and of the civilized races, the uneducated classes; with the growing culture of the people, grows, as experience shows us, discontent." We must nevertheless, by the force of an invincible and irresistible destiny, press on along the road which inevitably leads to the dispersion of our most cherished hopes, to the recognition of those hopes as illusions. Nothing will be left then, the last illusion having vanished, than the desire for euthanasia, a painless extinction. "The Logical," says Hartmann, "directs the world-process in the wisest manner towards its goal—the highest possible development of consciousness—which, once attained, consciousness suffices to hurl back the whole actual Will into nothingness, whereby at once the *process* and the world comes to an end without leaving so much as a fragment behind with which a further process could begin. Thus the Logical constitutes the world in the best possible way that it may most readily attain to emancipation, and not in one whereby its pain would be infinitely perpetuated" (*Philosophie des Unbewussten*, 3rd ed., p. 756).

We do not propose to attempt any detailed criticism of Hartmann's system. It is vulnerable at a hundred points. Hartmann, nevertheless, has a significance with relation to the development of German speculation, and this significance consists in his having emphasised the distinction already alluded to between the point of view which analyses all experience into logical or *positive* thought-determinations, and that which sees in the alogical an element of prior necessity to the *logos*. This is the point from which Hartmann's metaphysic starts. But his system exhibits a hopeless confusion between the spheres of "Theory of Knowledge," Physics, and Metaphysics, which inevitably leads to a fantastic semi-theosophical treatment of the problem. His initial rejection of the dialectical method and *naïve* announcement of the attainment of speculative results, according to the method of natural science, many will think, puts the subsequent construction out of court at once, so far as serious criticism is concerned. The "Philosophy of the Unconscious," and indeed, more or less, all Hartmann's works are without doubt suggestive, and apart from their readable style, they will well repay perusal. Hartmann's pessimism, which has descended straight from Schopenhauer, with, however, the not unimportant modification already mentioned, is one of the most natural literary expressions of the effete civilization of an age of transition. This comes out more especially when Hartmann criticises the present order of society with its dull level of mediocrity and growing inequality of social conditions, as though it represented the final stage of human progress. A part at least of his argument in the chapter on the third stage of the illusion, rests upon the assumption that the present basis of society is necessarily permanent. Hartmann sees that things perforce tend from bad to worse, proceeding on current lines, but he ignores the possibility of a fundamental change in the constitution of society, and therefore of human life generally. The all-degrading black coat of the Bourgeois, covering, as it does, a mental and physical constitution, sodden by profit-mongering in its various phases, it does not seem to occur to Hartmann, may possibly account for his pessimism as it does for many other things; and that pessimistic views of the universe may pass away as a tale that is told, together with the aforesaid black-coated creature, whom he justly takes as the sign and symbol of universal mediocrity.

Rudolph Hermann Lotze (born May 21, 1817, died July 1st, 1881) represents another phase of dogmatic reaction against the formalism of Hegel. Just as Hartmann's philosophy is a following out of the doctrines of Schopenhauer, so Lotze's may be considered as related to those of Herbart, though the connection is, perhaps, not so close in the latter as in the former case.

Lotze entirely repudiates the dialectical method and all speculation immediately based on that method, though without on the other hand regarding the methods of physical science as in themselves ultimate. To understand the writings of Lotze, of which 'The Metaphysic' and 'The Logic' were the earliest, though the 'Microcosmos' is the most important, it is necessary to bear in mind that his mind was essentially double-sided. Possessed of a consummate reverence for the methods of physical science, he had an artistic side which could not rest satisfied with those methods considered as final. The following statement of his position is taken from Herr Merz's article "Lotze," in the 'Encyclopædia Britannica,' 9th edition: "Lotze's definition of philosophy is given," says Herr Merz, "after his exposition of logic has established two points, viz. the existence in our mind of certain laws and forms according to which we connect the material supplied to us by our senses, and, secondly, the fact that logical thought cannot be usefully employed without the assumption of a further set of connexions, not logically necessary, but assumed to exist between the data of experience and observation. These connexions of a real, not formal, character are handed to us by the separate sciences, and by the usage and culture of everyday life. Language has crystallized them into certain definite notions and expressions, without which we cannot go a single step, but which we have accepted without knowing their exact meaning, much less their origin. In consequence the special sciences and the wisdom of common life entangle themselves easily and frequently in contradictions. A problem of a purely formal character thus presents itself, viz. this—to try to bring unity and harmony into the scattered thoughts of our general culture; to trace them to their primary assumptions and follow them to their ultimate consequences; to connect them all together; to remodel, curtail, or amplify them, so as to remove their apparent contradictions, and to combine them in the unity of an harmonious view of things, and especially to make those conceptions from which the single sciences start as assumptions the object of research, and fix the limits of their applicability. This is the formal definition of philosophy. Whether an harmonious conception thus gained will represent more than an agreement among our thoughts, whether it will represent the real connexion of things, and thus possess objective not merely subjective value, cannot be decided at the outset. It is also unwarranted to start with the expectation that everything in the world should be explained by one principle, and it is a needless restriction of our means to expect unity of method."

Lotze's metaphysic starts with an examination of causality, and the categories, in accordance with his definition of metaphysics, as the same which has for its objects of investigation those conceptions and propositions which in ordinary life and in the special sciences are applied as principles of investigation. It is divided into Ontology, Cosmology, and Phenomenology.

In entering upon the third division of his Methaphysic, Lotze says (*Grundzüge der Metaphysic*, § 26): "*Ontologically* we have spoken of the 'essence and states of the existent,' without being able to indicate wherein they either of them properly consisted. *Cosmologically*, we have assumed that from these unknown reciprocal effects of things proceeds for us the perceptive world of phenomena. Finally, at the close of the Cosmology, requirements of the mind have made themselves apparent which presumably are only to be satisfied by an insight into the *real nature* of the things which constitutes that which the *formal* conditions of Ontology and Cosmology demand. Now the inner states of all other things are impenetrable by us; only those of *our own soul* which we regard as one of these essences do we immediately *experience*. The hope arises to learn by this example what properly constitutes the *positive essence* of other things. We might therefore term the last section of the Metaphysic as hitherto 'Pyschology,' were it not that the soul is only of essential interest to us *here* in so far as it is the subject of knowledge."

In spite of his repudiation of Herbartianism, there is no thinker from whom Lotze has borrowed more than from Herbart. The method formulated by Lotze, that of the reduction of conceptions to distinctness and consistency, is almost identical with that of Herbart. The extreme pluralism of Herbart is indeed abandoned in favour of what is in essence, a kind of Spinozistic Monism, though it subsequently assumes the regulation theistic guise led up to by "the idea of the Good." As its result Lotze's Metaphysic gives three ultimate ideas, "(1) that of one *infinite essence*, to whose necessity the ontology points; (2) that which we have developed in brief that all *true reality* is possible only in the form of spirituality; (3) the one just indicated, although properly-speaking indemonstrable by metaphysic itself, that the highest ground for the determination of the world and of our metaphysical thoughts thereupon must be sought in the *idea of the highest good*."

"The union of these three propositions," continues Lotze, "gives the result that the substantial ground of the world is an intelligence whose essence our cognition can only indicate as the living actual good. Everything finite is the action of this infinite. Real beings are those of its actions which it continuously maintains as the active and passive centres of out-and-in-going effects; and their 'reality,' that is the relative independence accruing to them, consists not in a 'being outside the infinite' (which no definition can make clear), but only therein that they are *for themselves* as spiritual elements; this for-itselfness is the *real* in that which we inadequately formulate as 'being outside the infinite.' What we ordinarily call 'things' and 'events,' are the sum of those other actions which the highest principle in all minds carries out in so systematic and orderly a connection that this must appear to constitute a spacial world of substantial and active things. But the meaning of the universal laws in accordance with which the infinite mind proceeds in the creation, maintenance, and regulation of this apparent world of things are consequences of the idea of the good in which its nature consists." (*Grundzüge der Metaphysic*, § 94.)

The physiological researches of Lotze it is which have given him his position in the world of thought. There is little that is original in the purely philosophical side of his speculation, which, after all is said, amount to no more in the last resort than a quasi-Leibnitzian Theism, dressed up with results derived from Fichte, Schelling, and Hegel (albeit the speculative method by which those results are obtained, and in the light of which they alone possess meaning is rejected), and last, but not least, of Herbart. The cleverness with which these ideas, derived from different systems, are pieced together and the whole made to acquire plausibility by being dexterously interwoven with the results of the latest scientific research, has sufficed to give the system a certain importance, which it would not otherwise possess, in current philosophical literature. The best short account of Lotze is that given by Erdmann at the close of the second volume of his history.

Among other representatives of current German philosophy may be mentioned EUGEN DÜHRING, whose standpoint, that of a somewhat crude materialism, is worked out in his *Cursus der Philosophie*. Dühring attaches a high value to Comte and Feuerbach as well as to Buckle and the English empirical thinkers, with the exception of Herbert Spencer, for whom he has a profound contempt.

The law of identity is the ultimate law of all reality. (This is of course aimed at the Hegelians.) It is a fallacy to regard the conceptions of universality and law as exchangeable; an individual fact may have the notion of law or necessity attaching to it. Dühring is an Atomist. The atom is the ultimate real. The complementary principle to matter in the construction of reality is that of change and permanence. For the cause of the primal origin of motion or change in material substance, science is at present unable to offer any satisfactory account; this is the task for Mechanics in the future. Antagonistic motion is the sole method of progress. Dühring would explain all phenomena on strictly mechanical principles. Like all other cosmic processes, feeling is reducible to the opposition of forces; all feeling involves a sense of resistance. In sense-perception nature, so to say, repeats herself, hence the natural assumption that perception corresponds to objectivity is justified. What the feelings are for knowledge, the emotions are for action. It is not, however, in his philosophy proper that such importance as Dühring possesses is to be found; but rather in his criticism of society and in his insights into the future, in which he has borrowed largely from Marx and Lasalle, whom he at the same time attacks for their Hegelianism.

We must not omit to notice also the eminent author of the History of Materialism, FRIEDRICH ALBERT LANGE (1828–1875). Lange's great work falls into two divisions, Materialism before Kant, and modern Materialism. The first is divided into four sections, which treat respectively of antiquity, the transition period, the seventeenth century, and the eighteenth century. In the first of these Lange explains how the earliest philosopical attempts necessarily led to a materialism, of which the highest development was in the theory of Demokritos, who undoubtedly gave expression to some of the most important doctrines of modern science. The complementary antithesis to materialism in antiquity Lange finds in the sceptical sensualism of Protagoras. These are alike opposed to the Sokratic-Platonic philosophy. This portion of the work contains much valuable and interesting criticism. The second section, which deals, beside, with the attitude of the three monotheistic religions to Materialism, shows the essentially antipathetic nature of the Aristotelian philosophy, to the pure empiricism of natural science, which latter indeed only became possible, on the fall of Aristotelianism from the supremacy it held during the middle ages. The third section treats of Gassendi and Hobbes as the fathers of modern Materialism, and of their influence on the empiricist movement in England; also of the devleopment of the Cartesian mechanical theory of the universe on the continent, into the thorough-going Materialism of La Mettrie and his successors. This last is dealt with in the fourth section of the first book, which also contains Lange's statement of his own position towards Materialism. While acknowledging the materialistic attitude to be the only one compatible with the true scientific view of the universe, he finds its weak point in the non-recognition of the fact that the scientific aspect of things is not the only one, but that there are other ways of envisaging the universe which if ignored make man one-sided.

The second book treating of the history of Materialism since Kant, is also arranged in four sections, the first dealing with Kant himself and his relation to Materialism, together with the post-Kantian materialists, Feuerbach, Moleschott, Buchner, Czolbe, &c., in the course of which Lange clearly shows Kant to be the dividing line which has cut off the possibility of any return to the old naïve Materialism of the last century. The second section is concerned more particularly with the questions raised by recent scientific research. The result arrived at is that while we have to thank Materialism for the banishment of the notions of miracle and arbitrariness from nature, and for its deliverance of men from the fear of supernatural powers and agencies; that notwithstanding, its central positive dogma of the absoluteness of corporeal substance cannot stand in face of the advances of modern thought alike in physic and metaphysic. The law of the persistence of force is altogether incompatible with the dogmatic side of materialism. Johannes Müller's researches into the physiology of the senses bring us back from a standpoint of physical science to the essentially metaphysical result, that the sense-world, our own body of course included, is only a product of our sense-organisation. The latter portion of the work contains an able criticism of the current political economy. Lange strongly deprecates the tendency to confound truth in the sense of mere theoretical truth with worth or desirability. Man has not only the impulse to attain to truth, but also to the good in the sense of the worthful in-itself. Kant's

Ideas are an instance of confusion between these two essentially disparate things.

Our notice of Lange's book, one which is perhaps more widely read than any other philosophical work in Germany at the present time, and which has been translated into most European languages, aptly closes our brief sketch of current German philosophical literature, since the philosophical activity of Germany at the present time signalises itself rather in the department of historical research than in that of constructive thought. The names of Kuno Fischer, of Erdmann, of Urberweg, of Zeller, and many more, now living or but recently dead, that is well-nigh all the most important German philosophical writers of the present day, illustrate this remark. This tendency of German philosophical thought to turn for its aliment to historical studies is by no means an unmixed evil, if an evil at all. The time has passed, if indeed it ever was, when independent thought was of itself almost sufficient for serious and lasting philosophical work. Henceforward every new departure or development in philosophy must not merely take casual account of, but be consciously based on, the general evolution of philosophy in the past. He who aspires to be a serious thinker and neglects the history of philosophy seals the fate of his work. For this reason the research of the Germans into the history of philosophy is a necessary element in the future progress of philosophy. We now leave Germany to consider the recent and current movement of philosophy in France and England.

The French as a nation have never been remarkable for originality in speculative thought, setting aside one or two noteworthy exceptions, of which Descartes is the most striking. As a result, there is only one modern French thinker who will fall within the scope of the present work, and he not so much because of his originality as on account of his relations to contemporary English thought and of the influence he has exercised directly or indirectly on the average "cultured" Englishman of the present generation. The thinker referred to is AUGUSTE COMTE. Comte was born at Montpellier in 1798, and died at Paris in 1857. Originally a disciple of Saint-Simon, the most learned and original of the Utopian-Socialist thinkers of the first half of the present century, Comte's political and social speculations bear the unmistakable impress of their original, though it may be fairly doubted whether this has been improved by the transformation it has undergone. The philosophical side of "Positivism," as Comte designated his system, consists in a classification of the mathematical and natural sciences and a systematisation of the conclusions of scientific method. The net result is not altogether unlike the system of Hegel inverted. The great polemic of the *Philosophie Positive* is against what Comte terms the metaphysical spirit and metaphysical entities, but which, translated into other language, are simply the hypostasized abstractions proper to the abstract-dogmatic phase of thought. This is all that is meant by the second of the three stages through which Auguste Comte claims the human mind to pass.

The parallel between Comte and Hegel, just referred to, has been noticed elsewhere. "It is worthy of remark," says Mr. Shadworth-Hodgson ('Time and Space,' p. 399 *et seq.*), "that there are many points of resemblance between the Logic of Hegel, the protagonist of Ontology, and the *Philosophie Positive* of Comte, the protagonist of Positivism. There is first the similarity of Hegel's Absolute Mind and Comte's *Vrai Grand Etre*, or Humanity, each of which is the concomitant result, if I may so speak, of the evolution of the world-history; each of which is personified as a single individual; and each of which is the object of divine honours; and these three points of similarity suppose several minor ones. Then again, there is the progression by triplets in Hegel, in which the first member is the *an sich*, the last the *an und für sich*, and the middle the transition between them; while the last stage, when reached, throws back light upon the nature of both the previous stages, not understood before they had produced their results. To this answers Comte's doctrine of a triple stage in the actual history of all development, the middle of which is but a transitional state, which cannot be judged of till the last stage has been reached, for which it was a preparation; for instance, in the fields of the intellectual, the active, and the affective functions of man, three stages may be observed: in the first, the fictive, the abstract, and the positive stage; in the second, the conquering, the defensive, and the industrial; and in the third, the domestic, the civil, and the universal." *Politique Positive*, vol. 4, chap. iii. p. 177. And again ('Time and Space,' pp. 401–2), Mr. Shadworth-Hodgson continues: "Both writers, each from his own point of view, and in his own half of the world, move round the same centre; for the principle which they share is the central truth of their two systems. This truth in Hegel is, that the universe can only be described, analysed, and known within itself. In the *Philosophie Positive*, the ruling thought, as exhibited in the Law of the Three States and elsewhere, is, that the search after causes is vain, and is superseded by the search after laws. In other words, analyse the order of co-existence and the order of sequence of phenomena within the world of phenomena, but seek no cause for any of them that is not itself a phenomenon. Both conceptions are the same, namely, to keep within phenomena, to analyse their order and interdependence, and to abstain from going beyond or seeking the Why of the universe; instead of this, to seek only for the necessary or universal antecedents of particular objects, as parts of the whole. A difference between them there is, and a wide one, namely, that this mode of philosophising is in Comte a renunciation of an attempt as useless, while in Hegel it is a claim to have succeeded in that attempt, the attempt to seize the Absolute. Look only for laws and not for causes, say they both; philosophy is the discovery of laws and not of causes; the absolute is not to be seized, remain within your fixed limits. But why is the absolute not to be seized? With Hegel because it has been seized already, is defined, and contains all causes within it; with Comte, because it cannot be seized at all, and we must content ourselves without causes. Equally however in both cases is the search for cause given up."*

* While quoting the above passages as expressing an undoubted parallel between the two thinkers in question, the present writer must not be understood as accepting every statement contained in them.

To this may be added that even Comte's polemic against what he calls materialism, that is the explanation of the phenomena of a higher plane of nature by those of a lower, *e.g.* the treatment of social phenomena on physiological principles alone, or of vital phenomena on chemical principles, and so on, has its parallel in the *potences* of Schelling and the determinate *momenta* of the *Naturphilosophie* of Hegel.

Comte's law of the three stages with which the Positive Philosophy opens is as follows: "That each of our leading conceptions—each branch of our knowledge—passes successively through three different theoretical conditions: the Theological, or fictitious; the Metaphysical, or abstract; and the Scientific, or positive. In other words, the human mind, by its nature, employs in its progress three methods of philosophising, the character of which is essentially different, and even radically opposed, viz. the theological, the metaphysical, and the positive method. Hence arise three philosophies, or general systems of conceptions on the aggregate of phenomena, each of which excludes the others. The first is the necessary point of departure of the human understanding; and the third is its fixed and definite state. The second is merely a state of transition" (Comte's 'Positive Philosophy,' Martineau, vol. i. pp. 1–2). The employment of the word metaphysical to denote the second of these stages is entirely arbitrary. The originality and importance of the doctrine itself has moreover been greatly exaggerated. Students of Hegel will be familiar with the truth embodied in the conception, although otherwise expressed. In the first of the three stages, the modifications of phenomena are referred to the arbitrary will of a being or beings believed to be present in or ruling over those phenomena; in the second of the three stages, the cause of the phenomena and their modifications is referred to certain properties inherent in bodies, but which are abstracted from the body or whole to which they belong, and conceived as distinct entities or powers acting upon that body independently. The third, the so-called positive or scientific stage, abandons the search for causes which had characterised the two previous stages, and restricts itself to the endeavour to discover the law, that is the order of succession and co-existence obtaining within the various groups or departments of natural phenomena.

According to Auguste Comte, all sciences have reached the positive stage, to a greater or less extent according to the complexity or simplicity of their subject-matter, with the exception of the last and most complex of them all, the science of man considered as a social and a moral being. Of this last science, *as* a science, he claims to have been the founder, and to it he gives the name of *Sociology*. Comte had inherited from Saint-Simon the idea that all mere theoretical knowledge, and indeed all special departments of human activity whatever, should be subordinate to one great practical end; the reorganisation of human life and society. This it is only fair to remember was the goal he set before him from the first, and to this goal, there can be no doubt, he meant all his scientific work to lead. Hence the filiation of the sciences in the form of a hierarchy culminating in Sociology, and hence the importance attached to the elaboration of the latter science. The positive method hitherto had been confined in its application to special groups or orders of phenomena, in other words, the separate sciences, without those sciences ever having been co-ordinated into a whole or complete philosophy in accordance with that method. This co-ordination it is the aim of the Positive Philosophy to accomplish. The key to the arrangement of the sciences Comte finds in the notions, (1) that the order of scientific study follows the order of phenomena; and (2) that the more special and complex phenomena depend upon the more general and simple. The most general facts will therefore be the first that will be studied, and the first to reach perfection as regards their formulation, *i.e.* the positive method. The hierarchy following these principles is arranged thus: Mathematics, Astronomy, Physics, Chemistry, Biology, and Sociology; each step in this arrangement involves something specially its own over and above that involved in the previous step. It should be premised that Comte makes a primary distinction between abstract and concrete sciences; the first (science proper) with which the hierarchy is alone concerned, treats of the abstract relations or general laws of the various groups of phenomena, the second with the history or description of the phenomena themselves, and with the special application of those laws.

The *Philosophie Positive* is comprised in six volumes, of which the first three treat of the simpler or inferior sciences, and the last three of Sociology, which, as we have said, it is the great aim of Auguste Comte to establish on a positive, that is, inductive, basis. The law of the three states and the conception of the hierarchy of the sciences together constitute the framework of the Comtian system. The one shows us the necessary course of human knowledge; the other the necessary dependence of phenomena, and brings the phenomena of human society as much under the domain of law as those of Chemistry or Physics. This does not mean with Comte, that social phenomena can be adequately treated on the methods of any of the lower sciences; on the contrary, he especially insists on each science having its own special logic, terming the non-recognition of this fact—the treatment of a higher science on the methods of a lower—materialism; all he means is that social science is impossible apart from Biology, that this again presupposes Chemistry, while Chemistry presupposes Physics, &c.; the whole series of the sciences resting on the fundamental laws of number, proportion, magnitude, &c., that is, on Mathematics.

Having given a brief view of the general principles on which Positivism rests, we propose to say a few words, first on Comte's view of historic evolution and afterwards on the scheme of social reconstruction, in the elaboration of which the later period of his career was occupied. The fundamental idea of Comte's philosophy of history is the coincidence of the first or theological stage of the human mind with a military state of society. This, on passing into what Comte terms the metaphysical stage, is accompanied by a conflict between the military and the industrial spirit, which last is the social expression of the final stage, the positive or scientific. Briefly expressed, the division is into offensive militaryism, defensive militaryism, and industry. The key to Comte's theory of history is thus to be found in his law of the three stages, from which it is further obvious that he regards the cardinal factor in human development (a point in which the redoubtable founder of Positivism is in full accord with the much decried "metaphysical" thinkers of the eighteenth century) to be man's intellectual side.

"Though the elements of our social evolution are connected and always acting on each other, one must be preponderant, in order to give an impulse to the rest, though they may, in their turn, so act upon it as to cause its further expansion. We must find out this superior element, leaving the lower degrees of subordination to disclose themselves as we proceed; and we have not to search far for this element, as we cannot err in taking that which can be best conceived of apart from the rest, notwithstanding their necessary connection, while the consideration of it would enter into the study of the others. This double characteristic points out the intellectual evolution as the preponderant principle. If the intellectual point of view was the chief in our statical study of the organism, much more must it be so in the dynamical case. If our reason required at the outset the awakening and stimulating influence of the appetites, the passions, and the sentiments, not the less has human progression gone forward under its direction. It is only through the more and more marked influence of the reason over the general conduct of Man and of society, that the gradual march of our race has attained that regularity and persevering continuity which distinguish it so radically from the desultory and barren expansion of even the highest of the animal orders, which share, and with enhanced strength, the appetites, the passions, and even the primary sentiments of Man" (Comte's 'Positive Philosophy,' Martineau, vol. ii. p. 156).

After stating the principles of the new science, Comte proceeds to give a sketch of historic evolution in the light of these principles. The theological and military system already begins with the primitive stage of universal fetichism in which every object is personified or endowed with will. Its immediate development is the ascendency of star-worship (astrolatry) merging into polytheism, the most perfect type of which is to be found in the theocratic civilisations of the East, which represent its first phase, and of which the ancient Egyptian civilisation may be taken as a model. In the second phase presented in the earlier classical civilisation of Greece, we have what Comte terms an intellectual polytheism. No priestly caste exists such as in Egypt. As a consequence, intellectual activity has a free outlet. In the third or Roman period, that of the later classical polytheism, we have a civilisation in which militaryism is supreme, and conquest the all-powerful motive-power, and not as in Greece a mere co-ordinate factor in social life, or as in Egypt subordinate to a sacerdotal class. The old polytheism already undermined by the metaphysical thought of Greece, could now no longer offer any resistance to the incursion of Semitic monotheism. The prevailing conception itself even had come to assume in the popular mind a form somewhat analogous to this. "The popular idea of monotheism," says Comte, "closely resembles the latest polytheistic conception of a multitude of supernatural beings, subjected directly, regularly, and permanently to the sway of a single will, by which their respective offices are appointed; and the popular instinct justly rejects as barren the notion of a god destitute of ministers. Thus regarded, the transition, through the idea of Fate, to the conception of Providence, is clear enough, as effected by the metaphysical spirit in its growth."

The civilisation in which the new monotheism issued was the feudal-catholic organisation of the middle ages. This, the ideal period of Positivism, is characterised first and foremost by the separation of the spiritual and temporal powers, which is accompanied by the conversion of slavery into serfdom, by the institution of chivalry, by the domination of morality over polity, &c. With the decline and break-up of mediæval society commences the transitional era of the "metaphysical spirit" *par excellence*, which reaches its culmination in the revolutionary philosophy of the eighteenth century, and in the ideas, such as "natural religion," "popular sovereignty," "liberty," &c., characteristic of the revolutionary epoch of which the great crisis was the French Revolution, but through which we are still passing. This is destined in its turn to issue in the positive *régime*, social, political, and religious, as described in Comte's work, 'The Positive Polity,' and in a condensed form in the 'Positivist Catechism,' and the 'General View of Positivism.' This, as the reader is doubtless aware, has been described as Catholicism *minus* Christianity; with how much of justice may be gathered from what follows.

Comte's aim in the constructive portion of his work was to reconstitute human life "without God or King"* (*sans Dieu ni Roi*). It has been alleged by a certain section of Comte's disciples that there is a difference of attitude, amounting, indeed, to a change of front, between the earlier and the later sides of Comte's doctrine. An examination of the works themselves will, we think, convince the candid outsider that there is no adequate ground for this assertion. In the later works, it is true, the less pleasing sides of Comte's temper and character assume greater prominence than in the earlier. Views which in the *Philosophie Positive* are expressed with the modesty and reserve of the philosopher, reappear in the *Politique Positive* and other writings, belonging to this period, with all the asperity of dogmas pronounced *ex cathedra* by a pontiff, and to dispute which is impious. Comte's religious disciples would probably defend this attitude as becoming the prophet-priest of a new *cultus;* but that of course is their affair. It must also be remembered that the hypothetical construction of a social order must necessarily involve a play of the imagination which would be altogether out of place in what claims to be a scientific exposition.

Comte divides this portion of his system into the "worship," the "doctrine," and the "*régime*," or "mode of life." The worship has for its object Humanity considered as a corporate being, past, present, and to come. For this worship, public and private, an elaborate ceremonial is mapped out, rivalling the Catholic ritual. The priesthood of the Comtian *cultus* are to be entrusted with the functions of teaching and moral exhortation.

* Not as Mr. Bridges renders it on the titlepage of his translation of the 'General View of Positivism' (presumably with a wholesome dread of the British Philistine before his eyes) *irrespectively of* God or King.

They are to constitute a great spiritual power, resembling the Catholic hierarchy of the middle ages, but possessing neither wealth nor material influence. The doctrine taught, the creed of the new religion, consists of course of the Positive Philosophy. The third part, "the life," embraces a description of the Comtian social and political organization which is to be the material basis of the whole. Politically the Positivist world is to consist of a commonwealth, at first composed of the five western nations of Europe, though ultimately destined to absorb the whole world. Socially, the modern distinction of classes with some modification is to be maintained. The middle classes are to form a hierarchy on an ascending scale, proceeding from the agricultural interest, which is the lowest, to the manufacturing interest, thence to the mercantile interest, and culminating in the banking interest. Outside this hierarchy is the bulk of the people, the proletariat together with the women who are to be rigorously excluded from all industrial as well as public function, and of course the priestly class. The various minute, and to the non-Positivist, exceedingly funny regulations of public and private conduct, may be perused in the works above mentioned.

As regards the philosophical side of Positivism, it may be and has been criticised from a variety of standpoints. The most important *ad hominem* criticism is that of the scientific specialist who declares Comte's treatment of the special sciences in the first three volumes of the *Philosophie Positive* to display inadequate knowledge of the several subjects treated, and a dogmatism as to results, which was not justified by the then state of those sciences, as is proved by the fact that many of them have failed to stand the test of later research. The hierarchy itself, as laid down by Comte, has been severely challenged in various quarters, and the artificial character of any purely linear arrangement has been more than once pointed out.

Turning to what many of his disciples think Comte's greatest title to philosophic fame, the foundation and elaboration of the science of Sociology, we should begin by denying his claim to originality. Kant clearly had the conception of such a science, as already mentioned (see above, p. 251); the same may be said of Herder; while Hegel distinctly formulated a sociological doctrine, besides working out a philosophy of history on its lines. The notion, therefore, of a continuity between the order of nature and that of human society was certainly not new. Just as little original was the notion of the main determinant of human progress being the speculative side of things; this was the view of the French eighteenth-century thinker, of a Turgot and Condorcet, no less than of the German metaphysician. That there are true and valuable suggestions to be found in Comte's philosophy of history, it would be unjust to deny; but it would be vain to deny that alike its fundamental principle and much of its working-out belongs to an antiquated method of dealing with history, and will not stand in face of the light thrown upon social development by later thought, in which, for the first time, we have the clue to a really scientific theory of historical development—a theory which finds the determining factor in progress, to lie in economical and social condition rather than in speculative thought—in short, which treats political, religious and social forms as primarily growing out of material conditions, and not *vice-versâ*, as in all preceding philosophies of history.

Having said thus much in derogation of the exaggerated claims to recognition sometimes made on behalf of Comte as regards Sociology, it remains to notice the real step he undoubtedly effected; this consisted in emphasising the truth that the highest significance of the individual is to be found in Society and *à fortiori* in Humanity. No one before so distinctly seized the fact of the essential unreality of the individual considered *per se*—the fact that his end is social. The travesty of this doctrine furnished in the religious *cultus* of Positivism must not blind us to its intrinsic importance.

There is one claim made by the Positivists on behalf of their master, which we think every non-Comtian acquainted with the information we possess as to his character will be inclined to meet with an unqualified denial. We are asked to admire, and indeed to regard as in effect a paragon of moral excellence, the personality of Comte himself as exhibited in his life. Now we do not hesitate to say that to most persons who have read Littré's biography of Comte, and are tolerably familiar with the later works, Comte's personality will appear as an exceedingly repulsive one, judged by all ordinary standards. Possessed of a personal vanity so offensive in its manifestations and grotesque in its proportions, as to make us almost pardon it on the ground of disease, a superficial reader might be excused for supposing that the one object of the founder of Positivism was its satisfaction. This of course would be an unfair judgment, but the fact remains that before this vanity no relation in life was sacred. After having absorbed the thought of a man of far greater genius, if of less learning and capacity for hard work than himself; a man who had befriended him in his youth, when he most needed friendship, he not only found no difficulty in casting him aside, when he saw the way clear for posing as an independent thinker, but with incredible baseness could stoop to vilify his former friend, lest perchance that friend should carry off a scintilla of the merit there was in his own works. A somewhat similar occurrence took place with regard to John Stuart Mill, on whose generosity he lived for a considerable time. When Mill found it impossible to continue the assistance he, in conjunction with Grote and Molesworth, had been affording, all the recognition received was a rebuke savouring of the worst type of pretentious charlatanry. These may be old charges, but they have never been satisfactorily refuted, and the opinion one unavoidably forms of the moral disposition they indicate is confirmed not only by numberless other small traits (even if we exonerate Comte from all blame in his relations to his wife), but by the tone of many passages in the 'General View,' by almost every page of the 'Catechism,' and by much in the 'Correspondence.' In this particular instance one may be excused noting these things, since it is by way of protest against the attempt that is sometimes made to convert one of the most morally inferior of mortals, into something like an object of adoration.

The quite theological reverence with which Positivists regard the scriptures of their Messiah is well known. Since Auguste Comte wrote, and even since his death, advances have been made in science, which to a great extent have revolutionised conclusions accepted during the earlier half of the century. It is not Comte's fault therefore if there is much in the scientific aspects of his doctrine which is hopelessly obsolete. But the same cannot be said of certain of his followers, when in their zeal for the infallibility of the sacred text they resent advances in science and even denounce those whose names are connected with them. After this it can only excite a smile, that Comte having been gifted with a particularly bad literary style, it should be the mark of the good Positivist to underrate matters of style in general.

Positivism, we may remark in conclusion, partakes of the nature of those systems, the inevitable product of great periods of transition, which are imperfect assimilations of a new principle, and which appear as hybrids between the existing yet decaying order of things and ideas and the new tendencies which are beginning to destroy it, manifesting itself of course in its main strength on the particular side of human affairs on which the progressive movement primarily turns. During the period of the decline of the Roman empire the most prominent aspect of the movement of change was Ethical and Speculative; its expression being in the Christian religion as opposed to Paganism. Hence we have the Semi-Pagan, Semi-Christian, Gnostic systems and subsequently that of Manes, all of which combine elements belonging both to Christianity and Paganism. The dominant aspect of the new tendencies in our present period of transition is more fundamental; it is, that is to say, toward a *material reconstruction* of society on a basis of equality, apart from the theological and ethical sanctions which have hitherto obtained. Positivism in part recognises this; its main interest lies in social renovation, but in this it seeks to preserve the material basis of the present society while rejecting its speculative counterpart. Even its ethics it retains. The change is to be effected on the old principles of individual ethical initiative and regeneration from within, rather than through economic and social reconstruction. Its non-theological attitude, its professed devotion to human progress as the supreme end of all institutions, ill accords with the superstitious reverence attached to certain traditional social forms. The immolation of human happiness before the Comtian Moloch "social order" is in keeping with a *cultus* in which humanity is transformed into a supreme fetich, demanding a drastic asceticism as the highest expression of her worship, and of which the prospective virgin mother is the symbol and ideal.

The contemporary British philosophical movements were until the advent of Herbert Spencer almost exclusively confined to Psychology and formal Logic. In the past generation the main philosophical controversy was that between the Empirical Associationists and Psychological Intuitionists, represented on the one side by the younger Mill, following the footsteps of his father, and on the other, Sir William Hamilton, in conjunction with whom may be mentioned his pupil, Henry Longueville Mansel. The results of Associationism and of the Scotch school of Psychology, generally, have been systematized and presented a form adapted to university students by Alexander Bain.

The philosophy of Mill, and the modern empirical school, generally, is really but little more than a restatement of the principles laid down in the seventeenth and eighteenth centuries by Hobbes, Locke, Berkeley and Hume. The reduction of all mental phenomena to the empirical association of ideas is its characteristic. The intuitional school, of which Hamilton may be regarded as the chief exponent, was a development with modifications along the lines of Reid. Both schools alike reject the tendencies of German speculation, which at this period was represented in this island by one writer only, namely Ferrier, the author of the 'Institutes of Metaphysic,' who, although an original writer, had but imperfectly assimilated its results.

Probably no one, with the exception perhaps of Herbert Spencer, is more connected with philosophical studies in the mind of the average Englishman than John Stuart Mill. During the latter part of his life he was eminently *the* English philosopher. He undoubtedly contributed to popularise the results of the associational school to an extent which no one had done before him. The lucidity of his style was sufficient to place the problems with which he dealt before the minds of persons altogether unused to abstract thought. Nevertheless, Mill cannot be said to have contributed any new development even to psychology, much less to philosophy in general. His father, James Mill, was in the direct line of the Scotch Psychological School, in which the younger Mill in consequence received a thorough training from his earliest years. As a young man Mill met with the works of August Comte, and acknowledges having received a powerful stimulus from them. All Mill's work is essentially critical. Nearly all his independent contributions to Psychology are contained in his 'Examination of Hamilton.' It is here that the dissertation on perception is to be found, the result of which is Mill's well-known definition of the objective-real as "permanent possibility of sensation." The philosophical polemic of Mill's life as expressed in his two great works—the 'System of Logic' and the 'Examination of Sir William Hamilton's Philosophy' above referred to—is with the somewhat crude psychological theory of innate ideas against which Locke had protested. The difference is, however, that whereas in Locke's time nobody had ever conceived such monstrosities, nor would have conceived of them had not Locke found it convenient to set up the theory as a target to attack; Locke having once started the doctrine as the object of his polemic, a school of intuitionists naturally grew up who made it their business to champion this doctrine. Hamilton and his school were the upholders of this rival psychological theory. We believe thinking men will generally agree when we describe the main result of Mill's work as that of a powerful stimulus. He stirred up the minds of many to the consideration of problems which had previously lain outside their range of mental vision.

Alexander Bain is probably the best known and most voluminous of contemporary British writers of the psychological school. His 'Sensations and Intellect,' and 'Emotions and Will,' his 'Mental and Moral Science,' and his 'Logic, are more or less familiar to every student, and any analysis of them will therefore be unnecessary.

We may, however, mention as the chief original result arrived at by Bain his elaborate attempt in the second volume of his 'Logic' to identify the notion of the "persistence of force" with that of causality, or more accurately, to deduce causality from the "persistence of force."

The versatile writer and critic George Henry Lewes (1817-78), although in his earlier years he may be considered simply as an adherent of the 'Philosophic Positive,' towards the close of his life elaborated a system of his own, embodied in a work entitled 'Problems of Life and Mind,' which although not completed in detail at the time of his death, was sufficiently advanced to afford a general view of its leading principles. Lewes's deviations from "Positive" method lie rather in the direction of extending its scope. Problems which his master Comte, and he himself previously, would have declared insoluble, he now claims to treat according to the principles of science. While the first rule of his philosophy is: "no problem to be mooted unless it be presented in terms of experience, and be capable of empirical investigation," he refuses to admit that problems hitherto regarded as essentially metaphysical, such as matter, force, cause, law, soul, &c., cannot be presented in those terms, and solved on the methods of induction. Lewes even retains the name Metaphysics for these problems, inventing the term Metempirics for their treatment on non-empirical methods. Each problem has what Lewes terms an "unexplored remainder," that is to say, an unknowable element which has to be eliminated before the problem can be dealt with on the Positive method. No science is more than symbolical of reality. "Its most absolute conclusions," says Lewes, "are formed from abstractions expressing modes of existence which never were and never could be real; and are very often at variance with sensible experience." Science thus represents a transformed reality, an ideal world of its own. "Science is in no way a plain transcript of Reality, in no respect a picture of the External Order, but wholly an ideal construction, in which the manifold relations of Reals are taken up and assimilated by the mind and then transformed into relations of ideas, so that the world of sense is changed into the world of thought."

The aim of philosophy is not, therefore, to give a magnified picture of the world, as it might appear to enhanced powers of sense, but to reconstruct an ideal world of abstract relations. The difference between the reconstructed ideal world of science and that of the Metaphysicians, or Metempiricists, as Lewes would call them, is, therefore, that the one can be verified and the other not; the one starts from experience and returns to experience, the other altogether leaves the region of experience. The result of Lewes's attempt to treat philosophical problems on scientific methods, can hardly be described as satisfactory, as to some extent indicated in the comparatively small success which, in proportion to the importance of its claims, the work attained. The treatment of the cardinal question of the relation of subject and object, as one might expect from the standpoint occupied, exhibits confusion between the scientific fact of the union of mental and material phenomena in one organism, and the metaphysical fact of all phenomena being determinations of consciousness.

The Monistic position is arrived at in the form of an inference from the parallelism discoverable between physical and psychical processes. This fundamental confusion between the physical and the metaphysical standpoints, naturally pervades the treatment of each of the 'Problems of Life and Mind.' Lewes's accentuation of the distinction between the ideality of science and the reality of "common sense" denotes nevertheless an undoubted abvance on the previous thought of the empirical school.

It remains now to give a somewhat more detailed notice of the system of Herbert Spencer, whose influence has been and still is wide-reaching and considerable. Spencer, like Lewes, Mill, and the other English writers of his generation, has been strongly influenced by the writings of Auguste Comte.

The philosophy of Herbert Spencer starts with the distinction between the knowable and the unknowable, the absolute and the relative. This pronounced demarcation, amounting almost to dualism, is the foundation of Spencer's system. The first and smallest division of his philosophy, which deals with the unknowable, proclaims the existence of the Absolute or the absoluteness of Existence (for the two expressions are in Spencer's case almost interchangeable), outside the phenomenal world, but at the same time Spencer proclaims our nescience of all that concerns this Absolute. Our very recognition of the relativity of knowledge is meaningless except in contradistinction to a non-relative or Absolute. "We have seen," he says in summing up his argument, "how in the very assertion that all our knowledge properly so called is Relative, there is involved the assertion that there exists a Non-relative. We have seen how, in each step of the argument by which this doctrine is established, the same assumption is made. We have seen how, from the very necessity of thinking in relation, it follows that the Relative is itself inconceivable except as related to a Non-relative. We have seen that unless a Non-relative or Absolute be postulated, the Relative itself becomes absolute; and so brings the argument to a contradiction. And on contemplating the process of thought, we have equally seen how impossible it is to get rid of the consciousness of an actuality lying behind appearances; and how, from this impossibility, results our indestructible belief in that actuality." ('First Principles,' pp. 96–7.) In a chapter on "ultimate scientific ideas," Herbert Spencer endeavours to show how all scientific conceptions rest ultimately on the insoluble. Matter, force, space, time on ultimate analysis, abut on incomprehensibility, in other words, they commit us to what Spencer terms "alternative impossibilities of thought." He has already shown this to be the case with ultimate religious ideas. The reconciliation Spencer professes to effect between science and religion consists in the recognition by the former of the existence of an Absolute behind phenomena, and by the latter of the absolutely inscrutable nature of this existence. The relation of philosophy to science is that of the general to the particular; just as the relation of science to ordinary knowledge is that of the general to the particular. "As each widest generalisation of science comprehends and consolidates the narrower generalisations of its own division; so the generalisations of Philosophy comprehend and consolidate the widest generalisations of science. It is therefore a knowledge of the extreme opposite in kind to that which experience first accumulates. It is the final product of that process which begins with a mere colligation of crude observations, goes on establishing propositions that are broader and more separated from particular cases, and ends in universal propositions. Or to bring the definition to its simplest and clearest form:—knowledge of the lowest kind is *un-unified* knowledge; science is *partially-unified* knowledge; philosophy is *completely-unified* knowledge." ('First Principles,' pp. 133–4.)

The positive or constructive side of the Spencerian philosophy is based upon the doctrine of Evolution. The data of science, space, time, matter, motion and force, are treated at the outset from a psychological standpoint. The psychological definition given of reality is interesting and important. "By reality we mean *persistence* in consciousness: a persistence that is either unconditional, as our consciousness of space, or, that is conditional, as our consciousness of a body while grasping it. The real, as we conceive it, is distinguished solely by the test of persistence; for by this test we separate it from what we call the unreal." On the strength of this definition conjoined with what has preceded, the conclusion is once more drawn that we have "an indefinite consciousness of an absolute reality transcending relations, which is produced by the absolute persistence in us of something which survives all changes of relation." Also, that we have a definite reality, which unceasingly persists in us, under one or other of its forms, and under each form so long as the conditions of presentation are fulfilled. The distinction between the two is consequently not one as between greater and less reality, for both are alike real, but between two different kinds of reality.

Spencer's test of truth—the ultimate criterion in philosophy—is the "inconceivability of the opposite;" that is to say, where the opposite of a given proposition is inconceivable, that proposition is true. This, be it observed, is only a roundabout way of affirming that self-consistency of thought on which the speculative or generic method is founded. Reality has already been defined as persistence in consciousness; on the strength of this, Spencer is of course a realist. He terms his doctrine transfigured realism as opposed to the naïve realism of popular conception. The "indestructibility of matter," like the "persistence of force," is deduced from the fundamental postulate of the "inconceivability of the opposite," the contrary of each of these assumptions being shown to involve an impossibility of thought. No less axiomatic is the idea of the continuity of motion. "The first deduction," says Spencer, "to be drawn from the ultimate universal truth that force persists, is that the relations among forces persist. Supposing a given manifestation of force, under a given form and given conditions, be either preceded by, or succeeded by some other manifestation, it must, in all cases where the form and conditions are the same, be preceded by or succeeded by such other manifestation. Every antecedent mode of the Unknowable must have an invariable connection, quantitative and qualitative, with that mode of the Unknowable which we call its consequent. For to say otherwise is to deny the persistence of force. If in any two cases there is exact likeness, not only between those most conspicuous antecedents, which we distinguish as the causes, but also between those accompanying antecedents, which we call the conditions, we cannot affirm that the effects will differ, without affirming either that some force has come into existence or that some force has ceased to exist. If the co-operative forces in the one case are equal to those in the other, each to each, in distribution and amount, then it is impossible to conceive the product of their joint action in the one case as unlike that in the other, without conceiving one or more of the forces to have increased or diminished in quantity; and this is conceiving that force is not persistent." ('First Principles,' p. 193.)

The transformation and equivalence of force, the direction of motion, which is shown to be in the line of least resistance and in the direction of the greatest force; the rhythm of motion, by which is meant the oscillations invariably accompanying motion in every department of phenomena, are deduced from the ultimate principle of the Persistence of force. These things are what Spencer terms the components of phenomena. It now remains, after "having seen that matter is indestructible, motion continuous, and force persistent; having seen that forces are everywhere undergoing transformation, and that motion, always following the line of least resistance, is invariably rhythmic; it remains to discover the similarly invariable formula expressing the combined consequences of the actions thus separately formulated." The formula sought may be defined as the law of the *continuous redistribution of matter and motion.* All objects individually and collectively are undergoing every instant some change of state. In other words they are absorbing motion or losing motion. The question to be answered is therefore what dynamic principle obtaining at once in general and detail, expresses this constant change of relation.

All processes of change may be divided into two classes, those of integration or evolution, and those of disintegration or dissolution. Evolution always means in the last resort the concentration of matter accompanied by the dissipation of motion; while dissolution means the reverse process, that is, the diffusion of matter and the absorption of motion. One or other of these processes is going on in every perceived whole. Evolution may be further described as the progress from an indefinite and homogeneous state to a definite and heterogeneous state.

Evolution may be simple or compound. Where the only forces at work are those directly tending to produce aggregation or diffusion, there will be no more than the approach of the components of the aggregate or whole towards the common centre; in other words, the process of evolution will be simple; such will be the case, moreover, where the forces tending towards the centre are greatly in excess of other forces; or when, on account of the smallness of the mass, or the smallness of the quantity of motion it receives from without, the process proceeds rapidly. But when, on the contrary, from whatever cause, the process proceeds slowly, then the mass will be appreciably modified by other forces. In addition to the chief primary change of integration, secondary and supplementary changes will be produced; the process of evolution will, in other words, be compound. This principle Spencer proceeds to illustrate at length in the course of the discussion, some important facts being brought out, as that the quantity of secondary redistribution in an organism varies according to the contained quantity of the motion we call heat, &c. The principles of evolution are then discussed in detail; first, in their primary aspect of simple evolution, and afterwards more especially with respect to the secondary redistributions constituting compound evolution.

It having been shown that all existences must reach their ultimate shape through processes of concentration. it remains for Spencer to show how different orders of phenomena do actually exhibit the process of the integration of matter, and the dissipation of motion. "Tracing, so far as we may by observation and inference, the objects dealt with by the Astronomer and the Geologist, as well as those which Biology, Psychology and Sociology treat of, we have to consider what direct proof there is that the Cosmos, in general and in detail, conforms to this law." In the course of the ensuing discussion it is shown that the same process is going on in the several parts or members of aggregates, as in the wholes. Thus, while there has been a gradual concentration of the Solar system from its primitive nebulous state, there has been none the less a concentration going on in each planet. The same applies to the geological development of the earth regarded as itself an aggregate; to that of the animal from the embryo; to the differentiation of species and to the development of society. "Alike during the evolution of the Solar system, of a planet, of an organism, of a nation, there is progressive aggregation of the entire mass. This may be shown by the increasing density of the matter already contained in it; or by the drawing into it of matter that was before separate, or by both. But in any case it implies a loss of relative motion. At the same time, the parts into which the mass has divided, severally consolidate in like manner. We see this in that formation of planets and satellites which has gone on along with the concentration of the nebula out of which the Solar system originated; we see it in the growth of separate organs that advances, *pari passu*, with the growth of each organism; we see it in that rise of special industrial centres, and special masses of population, which is associated with the rise of each society. Always more or less of local integration accompanies the general integration. And then, beyond the increased closeness of juxtaposition among the components of the whole, and among the components of each part, there is increased closeness of combination among the parts, producing mutual dependence of them." ('First Principles,' p. 328.)

The secondary process which accompanies the primary in evolution may be formulated as one from the homogeneous and indefinite to the heterogeneous and definite. Spencer shows this exhaustively *à posteriori* in the departments of Astronomy, Geology, Biology, Philology, Psychology, and Sociology, &c. In the chapter on the "instability of the homogeneous," is illustrated with characteristic wealth of examples the tendency of the homogeneous and indefinite towards change; how impossible is the continuance of an aggregate in the state of homogeneity. Another factor in the evolutionary process is the "multiplication of effects," that is, the tendency of the incident force acting upon a uniform aggregate to become itself differentiated in a ratio corresponding with the differentiation of the aggregate. Thus, when one body is struck against another, besides the visible mechanical result, sound, or a vibration in the bodies and in the surrounding air, is produced; the air has moreover had currents raised in it by the passage of the bodies through it; there is a disarrangement of particles of the bodies around their point of collision; heat is disengaged; in some cases a spark or light is produced by the incandescence of a portion, while occasionally this is associated with chemical combination. "Thus," says Spencer, "by the original mechanical force expended in the collision, at least, five and often more different kinds of forces have been produced."

Thus far an explanation has been afforded of the change from homogeneity to heterogeneity, from uniformity to multiformity; but these explanations do not, of themselves, account for the change from indefiniteness to definiteness. The ground of explanation of this is to be found in the principle of "Segregation." This principle of Segregation, by which is meant the union of like with like, and a consequent separation from the unlike, may be variously illustrated; a strong wind in the autumn sweeps the dead leaves in masses to the ground, while the living are left on the trees; a similar process takes place in the separation of dust and sand from small stones, as we may see on any road in March. In every river, again, the materials are deposited in separate layers—boulders, pebbles, sand and mud. The winnowing of chaff from wheat also illustrates this principle, which is of common application in the industrial arts. Spencer as usual traces it through the several orders of phenomena, from the Astronomical to the Social.

With the principle of Segregation, the discussion on the factors constituting Evolution is terminated. The next question is as to the final goal of the evolutionary process. Does this process go on for ever, or is there a point beyond which it can proceed no farther? Spencer replies that there is such a point:—in short, that all evolution tends toward equilibration; that it finally comes to anchor in absolute quiescence or equilibrium. The last point is illustrated, in the usual manner, and it is then shown how all this is a deduction from the primary principle of the persistence of force. "Thus from the persistence of force follows not only the various direct and indirect equilibrations going on around, together with that cosmical equilibration which brings Evolution under all its forms to a close; but also those less manifest equilibrations shown in the readjustments of moving equilibria that have been disturbed. By this ultimate principle is provable the tendency of every organism, disordered by some unusual influence, to return to a balanced state. To it also may be traced the capacity, possessed in a slight degree by individuals, and in a greater degree by species, of becoming adapted to new circumstances. And not less does it afford a basis for the inference, that there is a gradual advance towards harmony between man's mental nature and the conditions of his existence. After finding that from it are deducible the various characteristics of Evolution, we finally draw from it a warrant for the belief, that Evolution can end only in the establishment of the greatest perfection and the most complete happiness." ('First Principles,' p. 517.)

Lastly remains the question of dissolution. The equilibrium once attained, the point having been reached when evolution ceases, the tendency must always be to a reversal of the process. All change henceforth must be in the direction of disintegration, of dissolution. This, which is illustrated in detail by the life and death of planetary systems, of individual animals, of societies, &c., is true no less of the universe as a whole; this also, on the foregoing principles—its evolutionary process having reached its term—must tend to dissolution. This portion of the 'First Principles' recalls to our mind the theories of the early Greek speculators, of Herakleitos, Empedokles, and Anaxagoras, &c., with their eternally alternating processes of world-formation and destruction. For though Herbert Spencer finds Universal Evolution to point to Universal Dissolution, yet this latter itself, none the less, foreshadows a recommencement of the process, on the same reasoning. The summary and conclusion of the 'First Principles' consists of a restatement of the doctrine of the Unknowable in antithesis to the Knowable with which the book opened. "Over and over again it has been shown, in various ways, that the deepest truths we can reach, are simply statements of the widest uniformities in our experience of the relations of Matter, Motion, and Force, and that Matter, Motion, and Force are but symbols of the Unknown Reality."

We refrain from entering on the carrying out of the "first principles" indicated in the foregoing pages, in detail in the departments of Biology, Psychology, Sociology, &c., as embodied in the later works of Herbert Spencer. The 'Principles of Biology' is universally admitted to be a masterpiece of scientific generalization; but we venture to think that Herbert Spencer's most devoted admirers will hardly seriously deny that the

'Principles of Sociology' shows a falling off—a falling off which others might add, that results in an inadequacy of treatment verging at times on the puerile.

Of Herbert Spencer's great powers as a generalizer of the results of modern scientific thought, there can be no doubt. These powers he indeed possesses in an almost unique degree, but side by side with them, we find a total incapacity to appreciate modes of thought foreign to the special grooves in which his way of speculative life has been cast. The most flabby pretences of the *Laissez-faire* economy are argued from as dogmas universally accepted, to dispute which is impious, much in the same way as the Methodist preacher argues from the dogmas of his Calvinistic theology.

Again, his attempted reconciliation of Science and Theology, of Materialism and Idealism, on the basis of a mechanically conceived abstract Monism, betrays a crudity of conception which argues a strange lack of the speculative faculty. This is confirmed by the singular *ignoratio elenchi* involved in his would-be refutations of the Germans. But Spencer is not always consistent with himself in treating of the abstractum he has set up as a receptacle for "religious sentiment," "ultimate facts," &c. The Positivists and the orthodox Empiricists would fling aside the metaphysical problem altogether. Herbert Spencer provides a home for it in the bosom of the Unknowable. We say the Unknowable, since Spencer tells us that the Absolute is unknowable; but, strangely enough, it reappears on occasion in guises not quite so unknowable as they might be. The most usual shape which it assumes in the course of the exposition is Force—the force behind phenomena—which is manifested to us in the phenomena themselves. Yet another time it is insisted upon that it is not to be identified either with the spiritual or material sides of the phenomenal world—the world of relativity—although it is the ground-principle of them both. The Spencerite Unknowable, view it as we may, is a surd entirely cut off from the system of experience, notwithstanding that it is the cause of the phenomena given in experience.

The influence of Herbert Spencer's system has been very

wide. In this country and America he is pre-eminently *the* philosopher. His very failings no less than his merits contribute to his popularity among the English-speaking races; but indeed the importance of the cosmical truths Herbert Spencer has taught might well blind many of his admirers to his defects.

The supremacy of the orthodox British Philosophy, Empiricism, like the orthodox British economy Laissez-faire, has been rudely shaken of late. The one doctrine like the other has been practically driven to adopt the defensive. In philosophy the new movement has been at present chiefly confined to academical circles, but it is already beginning to extend itself beyond this necessarily limited area. The characteristic of this movement is the attempt to rehabilitate in this country philosophy proper, that is the great problem as to the constitution of experience or reality, which occupied the attention of Plato and Aristotle in the ancient world and which was revived in its full meaning by the main line of the German post-Kantian thinkers. Among the names most prominently connected with this movement may be mentioned those of Robert Adamson, Edward Caird, the late T. H. Green, R. B. and J. S. Haldane, Andrew Seth, William and Edwin Wallace, &c. These writers, though differing in some respects among each other, have all made it their task to present in as intelligible a form as possible to the English mind the principle of the speculative method, and to state in clear terms the problem which "speculation" or "theory of knowledge" has to resolve—that namely as to the meaning and constitution of reality. This school is sometimes called the Neo-Hegelian school; and its doctrine may be said to consist in a restatement of the philosophical positions of the Hegelian right. We have already (pp. 345–351) indicated what we conceived to be the shortcoming of this standpoint. This shortcoming we do not think is obviated in the more recent statement of the doctrine. Briefly expressed, it is as follows: In the synthetic unity of consciousness it is said the opposition of the momenta of matter and form, potentiality and actuality, &c., immanent in consciousness—*i.e.* the most ultimate of all oppositions—is transcended. This being admitted, it is contending that the Real consists in a synthesis of positive thought-determinations alone, in other words, the position corresponds to that of Plato—the system of ideas subsumed under the supreme idea; or that of Aristotle —the "creative intellect," the *actus purus* or first principle of pure form which knowledge presupposes. The present writer would suggest that so far from the opposition being transcended in the ultimate unity of the consciousness, it rather finds therein its supreme expression as the distinction between consciousness and its subject, between the *I* of apperception and the *think* of apperception, or, otherwise expressed, between the primal *thatness* and the primal *whatness*.* From this ultimate expression of the antithesis of matter and form all other expressions of the same antithesis are deducible. The final interpretation of the universe is thus pure *potentiality*. One other point. The conception of the world-synthesis as pure *actuality* naturally leads to the dogma of the completed realisation of the world-principle in man as organic individual, in other words, in the individual mind or soul. Nature on this view comes to a complete knowledge of herself in the present human consciousness; but have we any right to make such an assumption? Is such an assumption compatible with a recognition of the social purpose implied in the moral tendency? Does not this imply that the organic synthesis, the human individual, the self-realisation of nature is as yet incomplete, and awaits a higher development? Such a conception as that here hinted at it is difficult to represent to one's self in thought, much more to express in words, but the suggestion will not be an altogether useless one, even though it merely acts as what Kant would have termed a limitative notion in checking the dogmatic assumption above noticed.

It may also possibly have some bearing in connection with an objection which Professor Caird observes (art. "Metaphysic," Encyc. Brit, 9th ed.) is frequently urged against an Hegelian Metaphysic: "The great objection to

* Of course the *thatness* here spoken of is not equivalent to the emptiness of the concept *pure being*, inasmuch as it has a determination, that of constituting the ground-principle or *possibility* of consciousness.

a metaphysic like this, at least an objection which weighs much in the minds of many, is that which springs from the contrast between the claim of absolute knowledge which it seems to involve, and the actual limitations which our intelligence encounters in every direction. If the theory were true, it is felt we ought to be nearer the solution of the problems of our life, practical and speculative, than we are; the riddle of the painful earth ought to vex us less; we ought to find our way more easily through the entanglement of facts, and to be able to deal with practical difficulties in a less tentative manner." This conception of the world-synthesis as form and actuality, and of its final realisation in the psychological unity represented by the organic individual, has, we think, much to do with the apparent opposition of Hegelianism not only to common-sense but also to the scientific intellect. Let us take an instance of the inadequacy of the last-mentioned point of view from the treatment it involves of the problem of liberty and necessity. "Man," says Professor Caird, "is determined' by his desires only so far as he makes their object *his* object, or seeks his own satisfaction in them. We may admit that there is a sense in which the common saying is true that a man's action is the result of his character and circumstances. But this does not make him a necessary agent; for the circumstances are what they are for him by the action of consciousness, and the character is the man as he has framed to himself an idea of good, of a universe of satisfactions, in which he seeks to be realised." ('Mind,' vol. vi. p. 550.) In the argument of which this passage is a sample, the action of the social medium in framing for the man the universe of satisfactions referred to is entirely ignored. The "idea of good" is regarded as framed by the man himself, rather than by the social whole, past and present, into which he enters. The formal principle, consciousness, as such, is moreover treated as *per se* creative.

Now it may with fairness be contended that the man does not identify the desired object with himself, as the late Professor Green would have it, by any *conscious act* of self-determination on his part, but that with his mental concept of the object is already given the notion of it as an "end," which, if not counterbalanced by the presence of other more potent ends, determines his action, a fact which is registered in the empirical consciousness, together with the correlative *possibility* of other ends having under other circumstances become motives, which formal registration we term Freedom! But notwithstanding all criticism, the usefulness of the work done by these writers for English students of philosophy can hardly be overrated.* The Neo-Hegelians, even if they have not said the last word on the speculative problem, are by far the most important school existing at present. The fact that they have introduced the speculative problem at all to the English reading public is of itself a by no means insignificant service. The writings of the school form the best possible introduction to Philosophy, and at least furnish a basis for the discussion of its problems, which did not exist before outside Germany.

* There is one point upon which we would like to hear an explanation from one of the authoritative leaders of the more pronouncedly right wing of the school—that is, as to the theological terminology affected, and especially as to the employment of the word "God!" On the principles admitted by Professor Caird, for example, this word, as popularly used, implies an antithesis to Nature and Man; it is used to express the opposition of finite and infinite. This, we take it, will not be denied. Now we would ask, by what right is a term suggestive of, and associated with, the most decisive aspect of the opposition employed in a connection where the opposition is abolished? A similar line might be taken up as regards the reading of Hegelianism into Christian dogmas.

CONCLUSION.

In the course of the history we have just traversed, the ordinary reader may see little but a chaos of theories. Such a view, however, can only obtain where a superficial glance has been taken of the whole. We have again and again had occasion to point out the continuous reappearance of the same doctrines in thinkers, widely separated in time and intellectual surroundings, and who approached the problem from altogether different and even opposed standpoints. Such indications of what to the superficial reader might appear coincidences could have been almost indefinitely multiplied. This of itself would lead to the suspicion of a central truth around which the most seemingly antagonistic philosophies were revolving. The History of Philosophy is indeed no medley of mere opinions, but represents in various guises, determined immediately by personality, age, surroundings, &c., the several stages through which the human mind must pass in its endeavours to arrive at the complete formulation of the world-problem, together with its solution, which is nothing other than the final rational explanation of the world. By the last expression is meant an explanation which, while it includes all other explanations attained from more limited points of view, yet nevertheless transcends them. Philosophy in the exact sense of the word—philosophy *par excellence*—is, in short, the final and most comprehensive interpretation of Reality. It is not *a* theory of how things may be, but *the* theory of how things are.

Strictly speaking, we have no right to talk of philosophies at all, any more than we have to talk of chemistries or physiologies. The history of Chemistry shows us a series of attempts more or less crude, more or less successful, to treat the problem of chemistry, *i.e.* the constitution of bodies; similarly the history of Biology offers a series of attempts to treat the problem of Biology, *i.e.* to arrive at the theory (the most perfect interpretation or explanation) of organic matter as such. But we do not, nevertheless (nor would it have been fair to do so for that matter, even in the days of "Phlogiston," or of the "animal spirits"), regard Chemistry or Biology as a body of more or less probable or improbable opinion; and this, notwithstanding the divergences of view existing among scientific specialists in many cases on essential points in their respective sciences, even at the present day. We have no more right to regard philosophy as simply made up of a mass of conjectural theories. There is but one Philosophy as there is but one Science; the history of philosophy, we again repeat, is the history of the struggles of the human mind to attain the truth of philosophy, that is the philosophic point of view.

It is important in dealing with the history of philosophy always to distinguish between those systems or parts of systems which mark distinct steps in the analysis of experience and in the recognition of its meaning, and those which are traceable merely to some bias of nationality, religion, or personal temperament; the former alone have any true significance for history. Ordinary electicism or syncretism pretends to find philosophic truth implied or expressed in all systems collectively, forgetful of the fact that philosophic reason or thought is always adulterated more or less with local temporary or personal prejudice, and that the true philosophic insight may quite possibly be wholly absent from any particular system. Emerson's distinction between man thinking and the theologian, the attorney or the scholar thinking, applies here if anywhere. Here, more even than elsewhere in the attainment of truth, it is only where the individual thinker becomes the mere exponent of the universal thought that a genuine insight is obtained. Only in very exceptional cases has such an insight extended even imperfectly over the whole range of the philosophic problem; far oftener it has only been a glimpse of a particular aspect of that problem that has been seized. What is more, such is the difficulty of keeping the true nature of the problem and its interpretation within the intellectual purview, that although it has been disclosed in its main outline more than once in the history of speculation, the effect of such disclosure has been like that of a flash of lightning—it has seemed only to leave a more impenetrable subsequent darkness. Plato, Aristotle, Spinoza, and the post-Kantian thinkers of Germany, of whom it is usual to take Hegel as the type, severally had the solution of the problem within their grasp, but the inner meaning of the systems of these thinkers was imperfectly seized by their successors, and in some cases altogether lost. A crucial instance of this is the treatment of Aristotle by the schoolmen with whom, for the most part, he was whittled down to a mere Psychologist and formal Logician. As regards Spinoza, it must be admitted that the abstract dogmatic mould in which he cast his speculation, almost courted misconception from the first; yet this can be hardly said of Hegel, who is, nevertheless, to the "popular" no less than to the "scientific" mind a kind of subjective idealist who would make his own individual thoughts the criteria of things. The above explains the charge of circularity of movement brought by scientist thinkers against philosophy. While science, it is said, ceaselessly progresses, Philosophy is always returning to the same point. A very obvious explanation of this is, that the difficulty involved in the mind's seizure and retention of the philosophical point of view in its completeness, is so much greater, that in the case of the more limited doctrine of Physical Science, and also that in the case of philosophy where the completeness of the view is lost, the point of vantage gained is itself apt to be lost altogether. Speculation in this case goes stumbling back into the old beaten paths to which it had been accustomed, which lay below and around the true philosophical point of view, and it is not until another speculative genius arises that the lost standpoint is recovered. There is gain of course in this seeming fluctuation; each time that the synthesis of philosophy reappears it is enriched; it is clearer, more explicit, possessed of a fuller content.

The common notion is that Science and Philosophy or metaphysic, represent two rival theories of the universe—two not merely opposed but mutually incompatible methods of approaching one problem. Nothing can be farther from the truth. The problem of philosophy is not identical with the problem of science (although it includes it), and hence the methods are not the same. It is really as absurd for science to rail at philosophy, because philosophy in a sense transforms its conclusions and supersedes its categories, as it would be for "common-sense" to rail at science, because science transforms the notions which common-sense is accustomed to employ. Philosophy, it is true, does not stop at the categories of science, but neither does science stop at the crude reality of sense-perception. We can easily fancy the uncultured man of sense sneering at the scientist as a dreamer, because, forsooth, he declares that the earth moves and not the sun, or because he asserts the rotundity of the earth and the existence of antipodes. The amount of transcendentalism, in the popular sense of that much-abused word—if by it be meant distance from the "solid ground" of sense-perception—in the higher mathematics, is truly something appalling. In a sense, the conclusions of philosophy are not real, but then no more are those of science. Both alike involve a departure from the concrete real of the ordinary consciousness. Each, so to speak, moves in a world of its own, which (according to the relative perfection attained in the formulation of the respective standpoints) is a world more or less perfectly coherent within itself, and with the standpoint or standpoints which fall under it or which it embraces. Science at once embraces and transcends common-sense in the higher unity which constitutes scientific truth; philosophy embraces, while it transcends the standpoints alike of science and common-sense in the ultimate all-comprehensive unity which constitutes philosophic truth. Hence, as it has been justly said, every serious philosophy, that is, every statement of philosophic truth which claims to be even approximately adequate, must *include* materialism—materialism being the final expression of an interpretation of the universe on strictly scientific lines. Any statement or pretended statement of the philosophic position which conflicts with any of the positive doctrines of a scientific materialism may therefore be without hesitation ignored. "Philosophy," as Professor Seth has it, "is ready, accordingly, to accept and patronise any theory which science and history may establish. Idealism accepts all that Physiology has to say about the dependence of thought on the organism, and is not discomfited by the most materialistic statements of the facts. It admits, as a matter of course, the empirical derivation of all our conscious life from feeling or sensation."* From the philosophical standpoint the old antagonisms and controversies lose meaning, or at least their nature is entirely changed; they are sublimated, so to speak, and reappear in a higher atmosphere. Distinctions which under their former aspect appeared sharp, clearly definable and irreconcilably opposed, now resolve themselves into a mere question of emphasis. Such, as we take it, is the case with Materialism and Idealism, Theism and Atheism, &c. A formulation of the philosophic interpretation of the world which shall entirely abolish them remains as yet a desideratum; but from even a more or less inadequate statement of philosophic theory, such as Hegelianism, all their former importance has vanished; neither side is confirmed or refuted, but they are deprived of interest in proportion as their opposition tends to become insignificant.

To attain to a complete view of the world, such is the end of philosophy. Science rationalises the material furnished by common experience; philosophy rationalises the material furnished by science. The rationality of either is not the coinage of our brain, but a part of the nature of things. The categories of science are real, notwithstanding that they may conflict with the cruder notions of common-sense; but, viewed from the standpoint of common-sense, they are, nevertheless, ideal. The same with philosophy; its categories also are real at the same time that they are ideal. From the points of view of common-

* Of course it remains an open question whether current statements of the Hegelian position do not have a formal bias which in effect gives the whole an anti-materialist character. This question has been already discussed.

cientific intellect respectively, they are ideal. es an ultimate identity in the contradictions wer planes of thought are irreconcilable; it in opposition, being in becoming, the poten- ıal, the matter in the form. These distinc- maintained as aspects of a whole, and their ıs opposites consists merely in the generic osteriority of their respective momenta as f the essence of this whole. The meaning of philosophy then consists in its being an ıman mind to attain a view of this Essence— ıe generic order of its deduction, by which meaning of the synthesis as a whole, no less the elements constituting it, is discernible. efore, as we said before, but one philosophy as ıe physical science. Metaphysic like Physic ay of envisaging and transforming the *real* ole experience. Every system of any historical ıs differentiated itself from other systems by some point or aspect which the rest had s defect as a system consists in its having e exclusive prominence to this particular exclusion of others—in its endeavouring to abstracted element a whole in itself.

r necessity of its own nature the mind is through certain successive stages, such as npiricism, scepticism, in one form or another a position to grasp the properly philosophic . It is what we may term a part of the ısonry of things that the mind cannot reach without having previously passed over eps. In the mysteries of the ancient reli- ıring the earlier stages of his initiation, the ine to the reception of which those stages ory, was carefully hidden from the neophyte. , on the other hand, there is no need of alment; the whole of Hegel may be an open ıdent, so-far as paper and print is concerned, l be absolutely sealed lore to him, as regards ıy meaning in it, if he have not passed eliminary stages of his speculative initiation.

In the first blush of youth the mind unhesitatingly accepts all things in their immediateness, be it "common-sense," "morality," or what-not. The period of reflection follows, in which common-sense and naïve moral sentiment are negated in scepticism and cynicism; this phase of thought, which the Germans term the *Aufklärung*, is followed by another which consists in the recognition that these things are not entirely empty of all content as was at first supposed, albeit the content they possess is entirely different from that crudely attributed to them in the naïve stage of innocence.*

Having once come to know the world in the generic order of its articulation as a rational whole, we are irresistibly driven to moot the problem of the end, purpose or *telos* of this world; that whither it—and *à fortiori* man, the highest product up to date of natural revolution—is tending. The only way in which the final aim or ideal of progress can be formulated in a single sentence, is that it consists in the realisation—the bringing to consciousness of the world in its full meaning. This is, of course, only another way of repeating that the end of progress is the actualization of the immanent purpose of the world. But can we discover any adequate formula for this absolute world-telos itself. The thinker who has faced the problem must unhesitatingly answer no. We may, of course, make use of phrases such as the time-honoured "good" of Plato, but without nearer definition they must remain little more than phrases. Further, we are bound to regard, *ex hypothesi*, this *telos* as absolute finality, while we are conscious of

* To take an illustration of this hap-hazard; the unsophisticated mind never doubts the existence of pure disinterestedness in moral action; a follower of Helvetius demonstrates the non-existence of purely disinterested action, the unsophisticated mind resents this demonstration and endeavours to defend its orthodox opinion, but in vain—the cynic triumphs and the unsophisticated mind resigns itself to despair. The philosopher at last appears, and proves the triumph and despair to be alike irrational, since although it is true that the bare abstract and immediate *form* of all motive whatever is self-interest, yet that this does not in any way affect the fact that the *content* of the motive, and therefore the real end of the action, may be wholly without reference, or even opposed to the personal interest of the individual performing the action, and that this is all that is really meant when pure disinterestedness is spoken of.

the fact that finality in this sense—a being in which there is no becoming, a form with no material content—involves an abstraction, and therefore no longer possesses the conditions of a real synthesis.

Let us approach the problem from another point of view. Cannot we regard human happiness, it may be asked, as the purpose of progress? To this it may be answered that pleasure or happiness, be it individual or social, can never be an end in itself, although, it is true, it must form an element of every end, where human action is concerned. It is a triter observation that the search for pleasure *quâ* pleasure invariably defeats its own object. Pleasure or happiness is consequent on the attainment of an end which constitutes, so to speak, the substance or essence of which pleasure is a determination. The immediate pursuit of pleasure, therefore, considered as an end in itself, is the pursuit of an unreal abstraction. The desired object, end, or ideal of action is hence, we repeat, a substance or essence of which pleasure must indeed be a predicate, but which is primarily pursued for its own sake. On the hypothesis of pleasure *per se* exhausting the whole content of the end sought after, the ultimate distinction between higher and lower in taste or in aim remain unaccounted for; the old problem of the pig happy and Sokrates miserable, in spite of all special pleading, is left unresolved. But while contending thus far against the view of Hedonism as commonly formulated, we must not forget that the opposite school ignore the fact that our only criterion of the intrinsic worth of an action can but be as to whether it conflicts or not with the free development of ourselves or others, or of society collectively; and that *à fortiori* the highest end of action consists in the removal of the impediments in the way of that free development—in other words, in that which tends to the greatest possible satisfaction of the immediate wants and aspirations of all men—which, it may be said, is only another way of putting the hedonistic criterion. To argue otherwise is to revert to a dogmatic standpoint which arbitrarily fixes the purpose of Reality. The admission that happiness *per se* cannot rationally be conceived as constituting the *telos* of the world-order does not preclude the conviction that it is logically indissoluble from it in itself, or that it is the primary condition of its realisation. To imagine that this can yield to any *à priori* assumption as to what tends to or is involved in the ultimate realisation of the world-purpose, as is done by the late Thomas Hill Green, and other Neo-Hegelians of his school, can only be regarded as a disastrous attempt to treat a purely regulative conception as constitutive.

The endeavour to formulate the absolute end of consciousness, or the immanent purpose of the world, and to make this the basis of ethics, is the great characteristic of the ethical or quasi-universal religions. These have one and all endeavoured, so to speak, to strike out a short cut by which the *grand dénouement* might be placed within reach of the individual soul. Divers are the methods in the various creeds by which perfection, the perfect good, Nirvana, union with God, or what-not, is to be attained, but they all lie in the severance of the individual from nature and society and the pleasures of the phenomenal world, in the destruction of his natural appetites and affections, and in his complete withdrawal within himself. In the individual soul, the world-principle is believed to realise itself. The primal impulse toward regeneration and the realisation of the world-purpose is hence supposed to come from within. The consciousness is now awakening in men that there is no short cut to perfection or to the Absolute, whether on its speculative side, as first principle, or on its practical side, as final end of the world, and that the attempt of impatient humanity to make one is an illusion, in brief, that it involves an unreal abstraction. The day of the ethical religions is visibly waning, and one can only view with regret the futile efforts of able and earnest men like the late Professor Green, who, following in the steps of Kant and the post-Kantians, would stake their whole intellectual career in the forlorn hope of resuscitating the "ethics of inwardness." With the decline of the religions of introspective individualism, the significance of the individual as such pales, and the consciousness grows, that only in and through a weary course of social development, lies the path of progress, the way of the world-destiny. Freedom, which implies the satisfaction of existent want for each and for all—first and foremost the animal wants the introspectivist disdains—is the first condition of that higher social life which is the farthest visible summit of progress.

This consciousness involves a radical change in our ethical and religious attitude. Morality, as it becomes political and social, loses its exclusively personal character. Sin and Holiness, the supreme ethical categories of "introspection," are superseded henceforth in reality if not in name.

The attempt to formulate the *telos* of the Real, the immanent purpose of the world, is surrendered: much more the vain effort to reach it by the old methods. We expect no longer to attain it as individuals by ecstasy, contemplation, or inward illumination: "Immer höher muss ich streben, Immer weiter mussich schaun," may still be our motto, but our strivings and our constant looks are directed not to possible heights enshrouded in cloudland, but to the limit only of our clear and distinct vision. We know, at all events, that this summit must be reached, whatever may be beyond, before that beyond can become, in its turn, a distinct ideal, much more a reality. This point of view in its own way demands in very truth the sacrifice, the negation, of the individual, but it is not as with the introspective religions, the first step in a circular process which begins with the natural individual, and ends with the apotheosized individual, and hence which, its primary negation of the individual notwithstanding, remains individualistic; but a negation of the individual only in so far as this is essential to the realisation of that higher social whole into which he enters. In short, the abnegation of self becomes on this view a mere accident of morality, and not, as before, a part of its substance.

"Philosophy," says Hegel, "deals only with the universal individual;" the general form of individuation or personality may be deducible, but not the concrete personality determined in a specific time-content. "The individual in this sense," as Fichte has well said, "belongs to the element of the purely contingent;" and we would add its meaning, its reality, is to be found in so.iety; for society represents the highest actual realisation of the world principle, by whatever name we call it, "nenn's Glück, Herz, Liebe, Gott." There is nothing above or beyond society. Society or humanity stands for that universal personality which is permanent and abiding in the flux of the particular, the individuals, constituting it. Whether this larger life manifesting itself on the plane of history as *for-itself* in the individual subjectivities, which are its evanescent components, is destined to attain to *in-and-for-itselfness* in the time order, in other words, to be its own subject, is a question which ever and anon recurs to one, more especially when one reflects on the ruthlessness with which historic evolution sacrifices the individual man on the altar of progress, and above all when one feels that the noblest type of individual character is that which is prepared for this sacrifice when the occasion arises. Such a speculation, if we like to entertain it, is as worthy as any which conceives of a perpetuity of individual existence as such.

A word may be expected in conclusion, as to the immediate future and prospects of philosophy. Since the death of Hegel there has been no great original philosophic genius, no thinker who has thrown any essentially new light on the ultimate problem of philosophy. Dogmatic Pessimism, that product of effete civilization, has had a passing success. Great scientific generalizers like Herbert Spencer have formulated the ultimate principles of Cosmology, in the light of the two great scientific achievements of the age, the doctrines of the "Persistence of force" and of "Evolution." But, save for the recent academic movements of Neo-Hegelianism, there is little noteworthy to record. The immediate future of philosophy, the next formulation of the ultimate world-problem of being and knowledge, which shall appeal to the thinking portion of mankind, to a greater extent than even Plato, Aristotle, or Hegel ever did, must, we believe, be sequent on the realisation of that vast transformation with which the current order of things is big. "The republic has no need of chemists," Lavoisier was told. Thus with brutal frankness was the truth expressed, that in periods of great political and social change, Theory, as such, be it scientific or philosophical, must cede to the all-absorbing questions of Practice. The student as he lays down this little volume, should he by chance take up a newspaper, will inevitably light on accounts of great strikes, of armaments, of the struggle for colonies called imperial expansion, of vast popular revolutionary movements, &c., all of which point to one thing, when followed out in all their bearings, the steady approach of the great class struggle. Let him ponder on this and bethink himself of the part even he, or if not he, his children, may be forced to take in the resolution of that great living contradiction—the contradiction between individual and society—expressed in what we term Modern Civilization.

INDEX.

NOTE.—The names of philosophical works are printed in *italics*.

CATALOGUE OF

BOHN'S LIBRARIES.

N.B.—It is requested that all orders be accompanied by payment. Books are sent carriage free on the receipt of the published price in stamps or otherwise.

The Works to which the letters 'N. S.' (denoting New Style) are appended are kept in neat cloth bindings of various colours, as well as in the regular Library style. All Orders are executed in the New binding, unless the contrary is expressly stated.

Complete Sets or Separate Volumes can be had at short notice, half-bound in calf or morocco.

New Volumes of Standard Works in the various branches of Literature are constantly being added to this Series, which is already unsurpassed in respect to the number, variety, and cheapness of the Works contained in it. The Publishers have to announce the following Volumes as recently issued or now in preparation:—

Boswell's Life of Johnson. New Edition. 6 vols. [*Ready, see p.* 1.

Vasari's Lives of the Painters. Additional Notes by J. P. Richter. *Ready, see p.* 8.

Roger Ascham's Scholemaster. Edited by Prof. Mayor.

Grimm's German Tales. 2 vols. With the Notes of the Original. [*Ready, see p.* 5.

Coleridge's Table-Talk, &c. [*Ready, see p.* 4.

Coleridge's Miscellaneous Works. [*In the press.*

Manual of Philosophy. By E. Belfort Bax. 1 vol.

Goldsmith's Works. Vols. I. and II. [*Ready, see p.* 5.

Fairholt's History of Costume. [*In the press.*

Hoffmann's Stories. Translated by Major Ewing. [*In the press.*

BOHN'S LIBRARIES.

STANDARD LIBRARY.

294 *Vols. at 3s. 6d. each, excepting those marked otherwise.* (51*l.* 10*s.* 6*d. per set.*)

ADDISON'S Works. Notes of Bishop Hurd. Short Memoir, Portrait, and 8 Plates of Medals. 6 vols. *N. S.*

This is the most complete edition of Addison's Works issued.

ALFIERI'S Tragedies. In English Verse. With Notes, Arguments, and Introduction, by E. A. Bowring, C.B. 2 vols. *N. S.*

AMERICAN POETRY.—*See Poetry of America.*

ASCHAM'S Scholemaster. Edit. by by Prof. J. E. B. Mayor. [*In the press.*

BACON'S Moral and Historical Works, including Essays, Apophthegms, Wisdom of the Ancients, New Atlantis, Henry VII., Henry VIII., Elizabeth, Henry Prince of Wales, History of Great Britain, Julius Cæsar, and Augustus Cæsar. With Critical and Biographical Introduction and Notes by J. Devey, M.A. Portrait. *N. S.*

—— *See also Philosophical Library.*

BALLADS AND SONGS of the Peasantry of England, from Oral Recitation, private MSS., Broadsides, &c. Edit. by R. Bell. *N. S.*

BEAUMONT AND FLETCHER. Selections. With Notes and Introduction by Leigh Hunt.

BECKMANN (J.) History of Inventions, Discoveries, and Origins. With Portraits of Beckmann and James Watt. 2 vols. *N. S.*

BELL (Robert).—*See Ballads, Chaucer, Green.*

BOSWELL'S Life of Johnson, with the TOUR in the HEBRIDES and JOHNSONIANA. New Edition, with Notes and Appendices, by the Rev. A. Napier, M.A., Trinity College, Cambridge, Vicar of Holkham, Editor of the Cambridge Edition of the 'Theological Works of Barrow.' With Frontispiece to each vol. 6 vols. *N.S.*

BREMER'S (Frederika) Works. Trans. by M. Howitt. Portrait. 4 vols. *N.S.*

BRINK (B. T.) Early English Literature (to Wiclif). By Bernhard Ten Brink. Trans. by Prof. H. M. Kennedy. *N. S.*

BRITISH POETS, from Milton to Kirke White. Cabinet Edition. With Frontispiece. 4 vols. *N. S.*

BROWNE'S (Sir Thomas) Works. Edit. by S. Wilkin, with Dr. Johnson's Life of Browne. Portrait. 3 vols.

BURKE'S Works. 6 vols. *N. S.*

—— **Speeches on the Impeachment** of Warren Hastings; and Letters. 2 vols. *N. S.*

—— **Life.** By J. Prior. Portrait. *N. S.*

BURNS (Robert). Life of. By J. G. Lockhart, D.C.L. A new and enlarged edition. With Notes and Appendices by W. S. Douglas. Portrait. *N. S.*

BUTLER'S (Bp.) Analogy of Religion; Natural and Revealed, to the Constitution and Course of Nature; with Two Dissertations on Identity and Virtue, and Fifteen Sermons. With Introductions, Notes, and Memoir. Portrait. *N. S.*

CAMOEN'S Lusiad, or the Discovery of India. An Epic Poem. Trans. from the Portuguese, with Dissertation, Historical Sketch, and Life, by W. J. Mickle. 5th edition. *N. S.*

CARAFAS (The) of Maddaloni. Naples under Spanish Dominion. Trans. by Alfred de Reumont. Portrait of Masaniello.

CARREL. The Counter-Revolution in England for the Re-establishment of Popery under Charles II. and James II., by Armand Carrel; with Fox's History of James II. and Lord Lonsdale's Memoir of James II. Portrait of Carrel.

CARRUTHERS.—*See Pope, in Illustrated Library.*

CARY'S Dante. The Vision of Hell, Purgatory, and Paradise. Trans. by Rev. H. F. Cary, M.A. With Life, Chronological View of his Age, Notes, and Index of Proper Names. Portrait. *N. S.*

This is the authentic edition, containing Mr. Cary's last corrections, with additional notes.

CELLINI (Benvenuto). Memoirs of, by himself. With Notes of G. P. Carpani. Trans. by T. Roscoe. Portrait. *N. S.*

CERVANTES' Galatea. A Pastoral Romance. Trans. by G. W. J. Gyll. *N. S.*

—— Exemplary Novels. Trans. by W. K. Kelly. *N. S.*

—— Don Quixote de la Mancha. Motteux's Translation revised. With Lockhart's Life and Notes. 2 vols. *N. S.*

CHAUCER'S Poetical Works. With Poems formerly attributed to him. With a Memoir, Introduction, Notes, and a Glossary, by R. Bell. Improved edition, with Preliminary Essay by Rev. W. W. Skeat, M.A. Portrait. 4 vols. *N. S.*

CLASSIC TALES, containing Rasselas, Vicar of Wakefield, Gulliver's Travels, and The Sentimental Journey. *N. S.*

COLERIDGE'S (S. T.) Friend. A Series of Essays on Morals, Politics, and Religion. Portrait. *N. S.*

—— Confessions of an Inquiring Spirit; and Essays on Faith and the Common Prayer-book. New Edition, revised. *N. S.*

—— Aids to Reflection. *N.S.*

—— Table-Talk and Omniana. By T. Ashe, B.A. *N.S.*

—— Lectures on Shakspere and other Poets. Edit. by T. Ashe, B.A. *N.S.*

Containing the lectures taken down in 1811-12 by J. P. Collier, and those delivered at Bristol in 1813.

—— Biographia Literaria; or, Bio-graphical Sketches of my Literary Life and Opinions; with Two Lay Sermons. *N. S.*

COMMINES.—*See Philip.*

CONDÉ'S History of the Dominion of the Arabs in Spain. Trans. by Mrs. Foster. Portrait of Abderahmen ben Moavia. 3 vols.

COWPER'S Complete Works, Poems, Correspondence, and Translations. Edit. with Memoir by R. Southey. 45 Engravings. 8 vols.

COXE'S Memoirs of the Duke of Marlborough. With his original Correspondence, from family records at Blenheim. Revised edition. Portraits. 3 vols.

*** An Atlas of the plans of Marlborough's campaigns, 4to. 10*s.* 6*d.*

COXE'S History of the House of Aus-tria. From the Foundation of the Monarchy by Rhodolph of Hapsburgh to the Death of Leopold II., 1218-1792. By Archdn. Coxe. With Continuation from the Accession of Francis I. to the Revolution of 1848. 4 Portraits. 4 vols.

CUNNINGHAM'S Lives of the most Eminent British Painters. With Notes and 16 fresh Lives by Mrs. Heaton. 3 vols. *N. S.*

DEFOE'S Novels and Miscellaneous Works. With Prefaces and Notes, including those attributed to Sir W. Scott. Portrait. 7 vols. *N. S.*

DE LOLME'S Constitution of Eng-land, in which it is compared both with the Republican form of Government and the other Monarchies of Europe. Edit., with Life and Notes, by J. Macgregor, M.P.

EMERSON'S Works. 3 vols. Most complete edition published. *N. S.*

Vol. I.—Essays, Lectures, and Poems.

Vol. II.—English Traits, Nature, and Conduct of Life.

Vol. III.—Society and Solitude—Letters and Social Aims—Miscellaneous Papers (hitherto uncollected)—May-Day, &c.

FOSTER'S (John) Life and Corre-spondence. Edit. by J. E. Ryland. Portrait. 2 vols. *N. S.*

—— Lectures at Broadmead Chapel. Edit. by J. E. Ryland. 2 vols. *N. S.*

—— Critical Essays contributed to the 'Eclectic Review.' Edit. by J. E. Ryland. 2 vols. *N. S.*

—— Essays: On Decision of Charac-ter; on a Man's writing Memoirs of Himself; on the epithet Romantic; on the aversion of Men of Taste to Evangelical Religion. *N. S.*

—— Essays on the Evils of Popular Ignorance, and a Discourse on the Propagation of Christianity in India. *N. S.*

—— Fosteriana: selected from periodical papers, edit. by H. G. Bohn. 5*s.* *N. S.*

FOX (Rt. Hon. C. J.)—*See Carrel.*

GIBBON'S Decline and Fall of the Roman Empire. Complete and unabridged, with variorum Notes; including those of Guizot, Wenck, Niebuhr, Hugo, Neander, and others. 7 vols. 2 Maps and Portrait. *N. S.*

GOETHE'S Works. Trans. into English by E. A. Bowring, C.B., Anna Swanwick, Sir Walter Scott, &c. &c. 12 vols. *N. S.*

Vols. I. and II.—Autobiography and Annals. Portrait.

Vol. III.—Faust. Complete.

OETHE'S Works.—*Continued.*

Vol. IV.—Novels and Tales: containing Elective Affinities, Sorrows of Werther, The German Emigrants, The Good Women, and a Nouvelette.

Vol. V.—Wilhelm Meister's Apprenticeship.

Vol. VI.—Conversations with Eckerman and Soret.

Vol. VII.—Poems and Ballads in the original Metres, including Hermann and Dorothea.

Vol. VIII.—Götz von Berlichingen, Torquato Tasso, Egmont, Iphigenia, Clavigo, Wayward Lover, and Fellow Culprits.

Vol. IX.—Wilhelm Meister's Travels. Complete Edition.

Vol. X.—Tour in Italy. Two Parts. And Second Residence in Rome.

Vol. XI.—Miscellaneous Travels, Letters from Switzerland, Campaign in France, Siege of Mainz, and Rhine Tour.

Vol. XII.—Early and Miscellaneous Letters, including Letters to his Mother, with Biography and Notes. Edited by Edw. Bell, M.A.

— Correspondence with Schiller. 2 vols.—*See Schiller.*

OLDSMITH'S Works. 5 vols. *N.S.*

Vol. I.—Life, Vicar of Wakefield, Essays, and Letters.

Vol. II.—Poems, Plays, Bee, Cock Lane Ghost.

[Vols. III. and IV. *in the press.*

REENE, MARLOW, and BEN JONSON (Poems of). With Notes and Memoirs by R. Bell. *N. S.*

REGORY'S (Dr.) The Evidences, Doctrines, and Duties of the Christian Religion.

RIMM'S Household Tales. With the Original Notes. Trans. by Mrs. A. Hunt. Introduction by Andrew Lang, M.A. 2 vols. *N. S.*

UIZOT'S History of Representative Government in Europe. Trans. by A. R. Scoble.

— English Revolution of 1640. From the Accession of Charles I. to his Death. Trans. by W. Hazlitt. Portrait.

— History of Civilisation. From the Roman Empire to the French Revolution. Trans. by W. Hazlitt. Portraits. 3 vols.

[ALL'S (Rev. Robert) Works and Remains. Memoir by Dr. Gregory and Essay by J. Foster. Portrait.

[AWTHORNE'S Tales. 3 vols. *N. S.*

Vol. I.—Twice-told Tales, and the Snow Image.

Vol. II.—Scarlet Letter, and the House with Seven Gables.

Vol. III.—Transformation, and Blithedale Romance.

HAZLITT'S (W.) Works. 6 vols. *N. S.*

— Table-Talk.

— The Literature of the Age of Elizabeth and Characters of Shakespeare's Plays. *N. S.*

— English Poets and English Comic Writers. *N. S.*

HAZLITT'S (W.) Works.—*Continued.*

— The Plain Speaker. Opinions on Books, Men, and Things. *N. S.*

— Round Table. Conversations of James Northcote, R.A.; Characteristics. *N. S.*

— Sketches and Essays, and Winterslow. *N. S.*

HEINE'S Poems. Translated in the original Metres, with Life by E. A. Bowring, C.B. 5*s.* *N. S.*

HUNGARY: its History and Revolution, with Memoir of Kossuth. Portrait.

HUTCHINSON (Colonel). Memoirs of. By his Widow, with her Autobiography, and the Siege of Lathom House. Portrait. *N. S.*

IRVING'S (Washington) Complete Works. 15 vols. *N. S.*

— Life and Letters. By his Nephew, Pierre E. Irving. With Index and a Portrait. 2 vols. *N. S.*

JAMES'S (G. P. R.) Life of Richard Cœur de Lion. Portraits of Richard and Philip Augustus. 2 vols.

— Louis XIV. Portraits. 2 vols.

JAMESON (Mrs.) Shakespeare's Heroines. Characteristics of Women. By Mrs. Jameson. *N. S.*

JEAN PAUL.—*See Richter.*

JONSON (Ben). Poems of.—*See Greene.*

JUNIUS'S Letters. With Woodfall's Notes. An Essay on the Authorship. Facsimiles of Handwriting. 2 vols. *N. S.*

LA FONTAINE'S Fables. In English Verse, with Essay on the Fabulists. By Elizur Wright. *N. S.*

LAMARTINE'S The Girondists, or Personal Memoirs of the Patriots of the French Revolution. Trans. by H. T. Ryde. Portraits of Robespierre, Madame Roland, and Charlotte Corday. 3 vols.

— The Restoration of Monarchy in France (a Sequel to The Girondists). 5 Portraits. 4 vols.

— The French Revolution of 1848. 6 Portraits.

LAMB'S (Charles) Elia and Eliana. Complete Edition. Portrait. *N. S.*

— Specimens of English Dramatic Poets of the time of Elizabeth. Notes, with the Extracts from the Garrick Plays. *N. S.*

LAPPENBERG'S England under the Anglo-Saxon Kings. Trans. by B. Thorpe, F.S.A. 2 vols. *N. S.*

LANZI'S History of Painting in Italy, from the Period of the Revival of the Fine Arts to the End of the 18th Century. With Memoir of the Author. Portraits of Raffaelle, Titian, and Correggio, after the Artists themselves. Trans. by T. Roscoe. 3 vols.

LESSING'S Dramatic Works. Complete. By E. Bell, M.A. With Memoir by H. Zimmern. Portrait. 2 vols. *N. S.*

—— Laokoon, Dramatic Notes, and Representation of Death by the Ancients. Frontispiece. *N. S.*

LOCKE'S Philosophical Works, containing Human Understanding, with Bishop of Worcester, Malebranche's Opinions, Natural Philosophy, Reading and Study. With Preliminary Discourse, Analysis, and Notes, by J. A. St. John. Portrait. 2 vols. *N. S.*

—— Life and Letters, with Extracts from his Common-place Books. By Lord King.

LOCKHART (J. G.)—*See Burns.*

LONSDALE (Lord).—*See Carrel.*

LUTHER'S Table-Talk. Trans. by W. Hazlitt. With Life by A. Chalmers, and LUTHER'S CATECHISM. Portrait after Cranach. *N. S.*

—— Autobiography.—*See Michelet.*

MACHIAVELLI'S History of Flo-rence, THE PRINCE, Savonarola, Historical Tracts, and Memoir. Portrait. *N. S.*

MARLOWE. Poems of.—*See Greene.*

MARTINEAU'S (Harriet) History of England (including History of the Peace) from 1800-1846. 5 vols. *N. S.*

MENZEL'S History of Germany, from the Earliest Period to the Crimean War. 3 Portraits. 3 vols.

MICHELET'S Autobiography of Luther. Trans. by W. Hazlitt. With Notes. *N. S.*

—— The French Revolution to the Flight of the King in 1791. *N. S.*

MIGNET'S The French Revolution, from 1789 to 1814. Portrait of Napoleon. *N. S.*

MILTON'S Prose Works. With Preface, Preliminary Remarks by J. A. St. John, and Index. 5 vols.

MITFORD'S (Miss) Our Village. Sketches of Rural Character and Scenery. 2 Engravings. 2 vols. *N. S.*

MOLIÈRE'S Dramatic Works. In English Prose, by C. H. Wall. With a Life and a Portrait. 3 vols. *N. S.*

'It is not too much to say that we have here probably as good a translation of Molière as can be given.'—*Academy.*

MONTESQUIEU'S
Revised Edition, with
sis, Notes, and Memo

NEANDER (Dr. A.)
Christian Religion and
J. Torrey. With Sho

—— Life of Jesus C
torical Connexion and

—— The Planting
the Christian Churc
With the Antignostic
tullian. Trans. by J.

—— Lectures on
Christian Dogmas.
land. 2 vols.

—— Memorials of
the Early and Midd
Light in Dark Place
Ryland.

OCKLEY (S.) Hist
cens and their Conqu
and Egypt. Comp
Mohammed and his
Death of Abdalmelik,
By Simon Ockley, B
in Univ. of Cambrid
hammed.

PERCY'S Reliques
lish Poetry, consistin
and other Pieces of ou
some few of later d
Ancient Minstrels, a
N. S.

PHILIP DE COMM
of. Containing the H
and Charles VIII., a
Duke of Burgundy.
Louis XI., by J. de
and Notes by A. R
2 vols.

PLUTARCH'S LIV
lated, with Notes
Stewart, M.A., late
College, Cambridge,
4 vols. *N. S.*

POETRY OF AME
from One Hundred
1876. With Introd
Specimens of Negro
Linton. Portrait of

RANKE (L.) Hist
their Church and Sta
with Protestantism i
Centuries. Trans. by
of Julius II. (after R
(after Velasquez), an
Titian). 3 vols. *N.*

—— History of Ser
Kerr. To which is a
vinces of Turkey, by C

REUMONT (Alfred

REYNOLDS' (Sir J.) Literary Works. With Memoir and Remarks by H. W. Beechy. 2 vols. *N. S.*

RICHTER (Jean Paul). Levana, a Treatise on Education; together with the Autobiography, and a short Memoir. *N. S.*

— **Flower, Fruit, and Thorn Pieces,** or the Wedded Life, Death, and Marriage of Siebenkaes. Translated by Alex. Ewing. *N. S.*

The only complete English translation.

ROSCOE'S (W.) Life of Leo X., with Notes, Historical Documents, and Dissertation on Lucretia Borgia. 3 Portraits. 2 vols.

— **Lorenzo de' Medici,** called 'The Magnificent,' with Copyright Notes, Poems, Letters, &c. With Memoir of Roscoe and Portrait of Lorenzo.

RUSSIA, History of, from the earliest Period to the Crimean War. By W. K. Kelly. 3 Portraits. 2 vols.

SCHILLER'S Works. 6 vols. *N. S.*

Vol. I.—Thirty Years' War—Revolt in the Netherlands. Rev. A. J. W. Morrison, M.A. Portrait.

Vol. II.—Revolt in the Netherlands, *completed*—Wallenstein. By J. Churchill and S. T. Coleridge.—William Tell. Sir Theodore Martin. Engraving (after Vandyck).

Vol. III.—Don Carlos. R. D. Boylan —Mary Stuart. Mellish — Maid of Orleans. Anna Swanwick—Bride of Messina. A. Lodge, M.A. Together with the Use of the Chorus in Tragedy (a short Essay). Engravings.

These Dramas are all translated in metre.

Vol. IV.—Robbers—Fiesco—Love and Intrigue—Demetrius—Ghost Seer—Sport of Divinity.

The Dramas in this volume are in prose.

Vol. V.—Poems. E. A. Bowring, C.B.

Vol. VI.—Essays, Æsthetical and Philosophical, including the Dissertation on the Connexion between the Animal and Spiritual in Man.

SCHILLER and GOETHE. Correspondence between, from A.D. 1794-1805. With Short Notes by L. Dora Schmitz. 2 vols. *N. S.*

SCHLEGEL'S (F.) Lectures on the Philosophy of Life and the Philosophy of Language. By A. J. W. Morrison.

— **The History of Literature,** Ancient and Modern.

— **The Philosophy of History.** With Memoir and Portrait.

SCHLEGEL'S Works.—*Continued.*

— **Modern History,** with the Lectures entitled Cæsar and Alexander, and The Beginning of our History. By L. Purcell and R. H. Whitelock.

— **Æsthetic and Miscellaneous** Works, containing Letters on Christian Art, Essay on Gothic Architecture, Remarks on the Romance Poetry of the Middle Ages, on Shakspeare, the Limits of the Beautiful, and on the Language and Wisdom of the Indians. By E. J. Millington.

SCHLEGEL (A. W.) Dramatic Art and Literature. By J. Black. With Memoir by A. J. W. Morrison. Portrait.

SHAKESPEARE'S Dramatic Art. The History and Character of Shakspeare's Plays. By Dr. H. Ulrici. Trans. by L. Dora Schmitz. 2 vols. *N. S.*

SHERIDAN'S Dramatic Works. With Memoir. Portrait (after Reynolds). *N. S.*

SKEAT (Rev. W. W.)—*See Chaucer.*

SISMONDI'S History of the Literature of the South of Europe. With Notes and Memoir by T. Roscoe. Portraits of Sismondi and Dante. 2 vols.

The specimens of early French, Italian, Spanish, and Portugese Poetry, in English Verse, by Cary and others.

SMITH'S (Adam) Theory of Moral Sentiments; with Essay on the First Formation of Languages, and Critical Memoir by Dugald Stewart.

SMYTH'S (Professor) Lectures on Modern History; from the Irruption of the Northern Nations to the close of the American Revolution. 2 vols.

— **Lectures on the French Revolu**tion. With Index. 2 vols.

SOUTHEY.—*See Cowper, Wesley, and (Illustrated Library) Nelson.*

STURM'S Morning Communings with God, or Devotional Meditations for Every Day. Trans. by W. Johnstone, M.A.

SULLY. Memoirs of the Duke of, Prime Minister to Henry the Great. With Notes and Historical Introduction. 4 Portraits. 4 vols.

TAYLOR'S (Bishop Jeremy) Holy Living and Dying, with Prayers, containing the Whole Duty of a Christian and the parts of Devotion fitted to all Occasions. Portrait. *N. S.*

THIERRY'S Conquest of England by the Normans; its Causes, and its Consequences in England and the Continent. By W. Hazlitt. With short Memoir. 2 Portraits. 2 vols. *N. S.*

TROYE'S (Jean de).—*See Philip de Commines.*

ULRICI (Dr.)—*See Shakespeare.*

VASARI. Lives of the most Eminent Painters, Sculptors, and Architects. By Mrs. J. Foster, with selected Notes. Portrait. 6 vols., Vol. VI. being an additional Volume of Notes by J. P. Richter. *N. S.*

WESLEY, the Life and Progress of Meth Southey. Portrait. 5

WHEATLEY. A R tion of the Book of Co the Substance of ever all former Ritualist Co subject. Frontispiece.

HISTORICAL LIBRARY.

21 Volumes at 5s. each. (*5l. 5s. per set.*)

EVELYN'S Diary and Correspondence, with the Private Correspondence of Charles I. and Sir Edward Nicholas, and between Sir Edward Hyde (Earl of Clarendon) and Sir Richard Browne. Edited from the Original MSS. by W. Bray, F.A.S. 4 vols. *N. S.* 45 Engravings (after Vandyke, Lely, Kneller, and Jamieson, &c.).

N.B.—This edition contains 130 letters from Evelyn and his wife, contained in no other edition.

PEPYS' Diary and Correspondence. With Life and Notes, by Lord Braybrooke. 4 vols. *N. S.* With Appendix containing additional Letters, an Index, and 31 Engravings (after Vandyke, Sir P. Lely, Holbein, Kneller, &c.).

JESSE'S Memoirs England under the St Protectorate. 3 vols. Portraits (after Vandyl

—— **Memoirs of the** their Adherents. 7 Po

NUGENT'S (Lord) Hampden, his Party Memoir. 12 Portra and others). *N. S.*

STRICKLAND'S (Ag Queens of England Conquest. From au public and private. (*N. S.*

—— **Life of Mary** 2 Portraits. 2 vols.

PHILOSOPHICAL LIBRARY

15 *Vols. at 5s. each, excepting those marked otherwise.* (3*l.*

BACON'S Novum Organum and Advancement of Learning. With Notes by J. Devey, M.A.

COMTE'S Philosophy of the Sciences. An Exposition of the Principles of the *Cours de Philosophie Positive.* By G. H. Lewes, Author of 'The Life of Goethe.'

DRAPER (Dr. J. W.) A History of the Intellectual Development of Europe. 2 vols. *N. S.*

HEGEL'S Philosophy of History. By J. Sibree, M.A.

KANT'S Critique of Pure Reason. By J. M. D. Meiklejohn. *N. S.*

—— **Prolegomena and Metaphysical** Foundations of Natural Science, with Biography and Memoir by E. Belfort Bax. Portrait. *N. S.*

LOGIC, or the Scie A Popular Manual. I

MILLER (Professor) sophically Illustrated, Roman Empire to the With Memoir. 4 vols

SPINOZA'S Chief W Introduction by R. H *N.S.*

Vol. I.—Tractatus —Political Treatise.

Vol. II.—Improve standing—Ethics.—Le

TENNEMANN'S Ma tory of Philosophy. Johnson, M.A.

THEOLOGICAL LIBRARY.

15 *Vols. at* 5*s. each, excepting those marked otherwise.* (3*l.* 13*s.* 6*d. per set.*)

BLEEK. Introduction to the Old Testament. By Friedrich Bleek. Trans. under the supervision of Rev. E. Venables, Residentiary Canon of Lincoln. 2 vols. *N. S.*

CHILLINGWORTH'S Religion of Protestants. 3*s.* 6*d.*

EUSEBIUS. Ecclesiastical History of Eusebius Pamphilius, Bishop of Cæsarea. Trans. by Rev. C. F. Cruse, M.A. With Notes, Life, and Chronological Tables.

EVAGRIUS. History of the Church. —*See Theodoret.*

HARDWICK. History of the Articles of Religion; to which is added a Series of Documents from A.D. 1536 to A.D. 1615. Ed. by Rev. F. Proctor. *N. S.*

HENRY'S (Matthew) Exposition of the Book of Psalms. Numerous Woodcuts.

PEARSON (John, D.D.) Exposition of the Creed. Edit. by E. Walford, M.A. With Notes, Analysis, and Indexes. *N. S.*

PHILO-JUDÆUS, Works of. The Contemporary of Josephus. Trans. by C. D. Yonge. 4 vols.

PHILOSTORGIUS. Ecclesiastical History of.—*See Sozomen.*

SOCRATES' Ecclesiastical History. Comprising a History of the Church from Constantine, A.D. 305, to the 38th year of Theodosius II. With Short Account of the Author, and selected Notes.

SOZOMEN'S Ecclesiastical History. A.D. 324-440. With Notes, Prefatory Remarks by Valesius, and Short Memoir. Together with the ECCLESIASTICAL HISTORY OF PHILOSTORGIUS, as epitomised by Photius. Trans. by Rev. E. Walford, M.A. With Notes and brief Life.

THEODORET and EVAGRIUS. Histories of the Church from A.D. 332 to the Death of Theodore of Mopsuestia, A.D. 427; and from A.D. 431 to A.D. 544. With Memoirs.

WIESELER'S (Karl) Chronological Synopsis of the Four Gospels. Trans. by Rev. Canon Venables. *N. S.*

ANTIQUARIAN LIBRARY.

35 *Vols. at* 5*s. each.* (8*l.* 15*s. per set.*)

ANGLO-SAXON CHRONICLE. —*See Bede.*

ASSER'S Life of Alfred.—*See Six O. E. Chronicles.*

BEDE'S (Venerable) Ecclesiastical History of England. Together with the ANGLO-SAXON CHRONICLE. With Notes, Short Life, Analysis, and Map. Edit. by J. A. Giles, D.C.L.

BOETHIUS'S Consolation of Philosophy. King Alfred's Anglo-Saxon Version of. With an English Translation on opposite pages, Notes, Introduction, and Glossary, by Rev. S. Fox, M.A. To which is added the Anglo-Saxon Version of the METRES OF BOETHIUS, with a free Translation by Martin F. Tupper, D.C.L.

BRAND'S Popular Antiquities of England, Scotland, and Ireland. Illustrating the Origin of our Vulgar and Provincial Customs, Ceremonies, and Superstitions. By Sir Henry Ellis, K.H., F.R.S. Frontispiece. 3 vols.

CHRONICLES of the CRUSADES. Contemporary Narratives of Richard Cœur de Lion, by Richard of Devizes and Geoffrey de Vinsauf; and of the Crusade at Saint Louis, by Lord John de Joinville. With Short Notes. Illuminated Frontispiece from an old MS.

DYER'S (T. F. T.) British Popular Customs, Present and Past. An Account of the various Games and Customs associated with different Days of the Year in the British Isles, arranged according to the Calendar. By the Rev. T. F. Thiselton Dyer, M.A.

EARLY TRAVELS IN PALESTINE. Comprising the Narratives of Arculf, Willibald, Bernard, Sæwulf, Sigurd, Benjamin of Tudela, Sir John Maundeville, De la Brocquière, and Maundrell; all unabridged. With Introduction and Notes by Thomas Wright. Map of Jerusalem.

ELLIS (G.) Specimens of Early English Metrical Romances, relating to Arthur, Merlin, Guy of Warwick, Richard Cœur de Lion, Charlemagne, Roland, &c. &c. With Historical Introduction by J. O. Halliwell, F.R.S. Illuminated Frontispiece from an old MS.

ETHELWERD. Chronicle of.—*See Six O. E. Chronicles.*

FLORENCE OF WORCESTER'S Chronicle, with the Two Continuations: comprising Annals of English History from the Departure of the Romans to the Reign of Edward I. Trans., with Notes, by Thomas Forester, M.A.

GESTA ROMANORUM, or Entertaining Moral Stories invented by the Monks. Trans. with Notes by the Rev. Charles Swan. Edit. by W. Hooper, M.A.

GIRALDUS CAMBRENSIS' Historical Works. Containing Topography of Ireland, and History of the Conquest of Ireland, by Th. Forester, M.A. Itinerary through Wales, and Description of Wales, by Sir R. Colt Hoare.

GEOFFREY OF MONMOUTH. Chronicle of.—*See Six O. E. Chronicles.*

GILDAS. Chronicle of.—*See Six O. E. Chronicles.*

HENRY OF HUNTINGDON'S History of the English, from the Roman Invasion to the Accession of Henry II.: with the Acts of King Stephen, and the Letter to Walter. By T. Forester, M.A. Frontispiece from an old MS.

INGULPH'S Chronicles of the Abbey of Croyland, with the CONTINUATION by Peter of Blois and others. Trans. with Notes by H. T. Riley, B.A.

KEIGHTLEY'S (Thomas) Fairy Mythology, illustrative of the Romance and Superstition of Various Countries. Frontispiece by Cruikshank. *N. S.*

LEPSIUS'S Letters from Egypt, Ethiopia, and the Peninsula of Sinai; to which are added, Extracts from his Chronology of the Egyptians, with reference to the Exodus of the Israelites. By L. and J. B. Horner. Maps and Coloured View of Mount Barkal.

MALLET'S Northern Antiquities, or an Historical Account of the Manners, Customs, Religions, and Literature of the Ancient Scandinavians. Trans. by Bishop Percy. With Translation of the PROSE EDDA, and Notes by J. A. Blackwell. Also an Abstract of the 'Eyrbyggia Saga' by Sir Walter Scott. With Glossary and Coloured Frontispiece.

MARCO POLO'S Travels; with Notes and Introduction. Edit. by T. Wright.

MATTHEW PARIS'S English History, from 1235 to 1273. By Rev. J. A. Giles, D.C.L. With Frontispiece. 3 vols.—*See also Roger of Wendover.*

MATTHEW OF WESTMINSTER'S Flowers of History, especially such as relate to the affairs of Britain, from the beginning of the World to A.D. 1307. By C. D. Yonge. 2 vols.

NENNIUS. Chronicle of.—*See Six O. E. Chronicles.*

ORDERICUS VITALIS' Ecclesiastical History of England and Normandy. With Notes, Introduction of Guizot, and the Critical Notice of M. Delille, by T. Forester, M.A. To which is added the CHRONICLE OF St. EVROULT. With General and Chronological Indexes. 4 vols.

PAULI'S (Dr. R.) Life of Alfred the Great. To which is appended Alfred's ANGLO-SAXON VERSION OF OROSIUS. With literal Translation interpaged, Notes, and an ANGLO-SAXON GRAMMAR and Glossary, by B. Thorpe, Esq. Frontispiece.

RICHARD OF CIRENCESTER. Chronicle of.—*See Six O. E. Chronicles.*

ROGER DE HOVEDEN'S Annals of English History, comprising the History of England and of other Countries of Europe from A.D. 732 to A.D. 1201. With Notes by H. T. Riley, B.A. 2 vols.

ROGER OF WENDOVER'S Flowers of History, comprising the History of England from the Descent of the Saxons to A.D. 1235, formerly ascribed to Matthew Paris. With Notes and Index by J. A. Giles, D.C.L. 2 vols.

SIX OLD ENGLISH CHRONICLES: viz., Asser's Life of Alfred and the Chronicles of Ethelwerd, Gildas, Nennius, Geoffrey of Monmouth, and Richard of Cirencester. Edit., with Notes, by J. A. Giles, D.C.L. Portrait of Alfred.

WILLIAM OF MALMESBURY'S Chronicle of the Kings of England, from the Earliest Period to King Stephen. By Rev. J. Sharpe. With Notes by J. A. Giles, D.C.L. Frontispiece.

YULE-TIDE STORIES. A Collection of Scandinavian and North-German Popular Tales and Traditions, from the Swedish, Danish, and German. Edit. by B. Thorpe.

ILLUSTRATED LIBRARY.

ach, excepting those marked otherwise. (23*l.* 2*s.* 6*d.* *per set.*)

h, R.N.) Battles of Revised edition, with and Events, and 57 Por- 2 vols.

anish Fairy Tales. hey. With Short Life gravings.

ando Furioso. In V. S. Rose. With Notes . Portrait after Titian, ivings. 2 vols.

age and Chamber ral History, Habits, &c. VEET'S BRITISH WAR- and Woodcuts. *N. S.*

tes Coloured, 7*s.* 6*d.*

veh and its Palaces. of Botta and Layard icidation of Holy Writ. Woodcuts. *N. S.*

ibras, with Variorum iphy. Portrait and 28

Evenings at Had- ntic Tales of the Olden Steel Engravings after

il, Descriptive, and me account of Ava and i, and Anam. Map, and tions.

Pursuit of Know- culties. Illustrated by noirs. Numerous Wood- *S.*

Three Courses and sing three Sets of Tales, ish, and Legal; and a o Illustrations by Cruik-

Tudy. The Dialogue of an Account of its Origin, s by Cruikshank. *N. S.*

Plates. 7*s.* 6*d.*

i Verse, by I. C. Wright, oduction and Memoir. Steel Engravings after

itian Iconography; stian Art in the Middle E. J. Millington. 150 s.

DYER (Dr. T. H.) Pompeii: its Buildings and Antiquities. An Account of the City, with full Description of the Remains and Recent Excavations, and an Itinerary for Visitors. By T. H. Dyer, LL.D. Nearly 300 Wood Engravings, Map, and Plan. 7*s.* 6*d.* *N. S.*

— **Rome:** History of the City, with Introduction on recent Excavations. 8 Engravings, Frontispiece, and 2 Maps.

GIL BLAS. The Adventures of. From the French of Lesage by Smollett. 24 Engravings after Smirke, and 10 Etchings by Cruikshank. 612 pages. 6*s.*

GRIMM'S Gammer Grethel; or, German Fairy Tales and Popular Stories, containing 42 Fairy Tales. By Edgar Taylor. Numerous Woodcuts after Cruikshank and Ludwig Grimm. 3*s.* 6*d.*

HOLBEIN'S Dance of Death and Bible Cuts. Upwards of 150 Subjects, engraved in facsimile, with Introduction and Descriptions by the late Francis Douce and Dr. Dibdin. 7*s.* 6*d.*

HOWITT'S (Mary) Pictorial Calendar of the Seasons; embodying AIKIN'S CALENDAR OF NATURE. Upwards of 100 Woodcuts.

INDIA, Pictorial, Descriptive, and Historical, from the Earliest Times. 100 Engravings on Wood and Map.

JESSE'S Anecdotes of Dogs. With 40 Woodcuts after Harvey, Bewick, and others. *N. S.*

— With 34 additional Steel Engravings after Cooper, Landseer, &c. 7*s.* 6*d.* *N. S.*

KING'S (C. W.) Natural History of Gems or Decorative Stones. Illustrations. 6*s.*

— **Natural History of Precious** Stones and Metals. Illustrations. 6*s.*

— **Handbook of Engraved Gems.** Numerous Illustrations. 6*s.*

KITTO'S Scripture Lands. Described in a series of Historical, Geographical, and Topographical Sketches. 42 Maps.

— With the Maps coloured, 7*s.* 6*d.*

KRUMMACHER'S Parables. 40 Illustrations.

LINDSAY'S (Lord) Letters on Egypt, Edom, and the Holy Land. 36 Wood Engravings and 2 Maps.

LODGE'S Portraits of Illustrious Personages of Great Britain, with Biographical and Historical Memoirs. 240 Portraits engraved on Steel, with the respective Biographies unabridged. Complete in 8 vols.

LONGFELLOW'S Poetical Works, including his Translations and Notes. 24 full-page Woodcuts by Birket Foster and others, and a Portrait. *N. S.*

—— Without the Illustrations, 3*s.* 6*d.* *N. S.*

—— **Prose Works.** With 16 full-page Woodcuts by Birket Foster and others.

LOUDON'S (Mrs.) Entertaining Naturalist. Popular Descriptions, Tales, and Anecdotes, of more than 500 Animals. Numerous Woodcuts. *N. S.*

MARRYAT'S (Capt., R.N.) Masterman Ready; or, the Wreck of the *Pacific*. (Written for Young People.) With 93 Woodcuts. 3*s.* 6*d.* *N. S.*

—— **Mission; or, Scenes in Africa.** (Written for Young People.) Illustrated by Gilbert and Dalziel. 3*s.* 6*d.* *N. S.*

—— **Pirate and Three Cutters.** (Written for Young People.) With a Memoir. 8 Steel Engravings after Clarkson Stanfield, R.A. 3*s.* 6*d.* *N. S.*

—— **Privateersman.** Adventures by Sea and Land One Hundred Years Ago. (Written for Young People.) 8 Steel Engravings. 3*s.* 6*d.* *N. S.*

—— **Settlers in Canada.** (Written for Young People.) 10 Engravings by Gilbert and Dalziel. 3*s.* 6*d.* *N. S.*

—— **Poor Jack.** (Written for Young People.) With 16 Illustrations after Clarkson Stanfield, R.A. 3*s.* 6*d.* *N. S.*

MAXWELL'S Victories of Wellington and the British Armies. Frontispiece and 4 Portraits.

MICHAEL ANGELO and RAPHAEL, Their Lives and Works. By Duppa and Quatremère de Quincy. Portraits and Engravings, including the Last Judgment, and Cartoons. *N. S.*

MILLER'S History of the Anglo-Saxons, from the Earliest Period to the Norman Conquest. Portrait of Alfred, Map of Saxon Britain, and 12 Steel Engravings.

MILTON'S Poetical Works, with a Memoir and Notes by J. Montgomery, an Index to Paradise Lost, Todd's Verbal Index to all the Poems, and Notes. 120 Wood Engravings. 2 vols. *N. S.*

MUDIE'S History of British Birds. Revised by W. C. L. Martin. 52 Figures of Birds and 7 Plates of Eggs. 2 vols. *N.S.*

—— With the Plates coloured, 7*s.* 6*d.* per vol.

NAVAL and MILITARY HEROES of Great Britain; a Record of British Valour on every Day in the year, from William the Conqueror to the Battle of Inkermann. By Major Johns, R.M., and Lieut. P. H. Nicolas, R.M. Indexes. 24 Portraits after Holbein, Reynolds, &c. 6*s.*

NICOLINI'S History of the Jesuits: their Origin, Progress, Doctrines, and Designs. 8 Portraits.

PETRARCH'S Sonnets, Triumphs, and other Poems, in English Verse. With Life by Thomas Campbell. Portrait and 15 Steel Engravings.

PICKERING'S History of the Races of Man, and their Geographical Distribution; with AN ANALYTICAL SYNOPSIS OF THE NATURAL HISTORY OF MAN. By Dr. Hall. Map of the World and 12 Plates.

—— With the Plates coloured, 7*s.* 6*d.*

PICTORIAL HANDBOOK OF Modern Geography on a Popular Plan. Compiled from the best Authorities, English and Foreign, by H. G. Bohn. 150 Woodcuts and 51 Maps. 6*s.*

—— With the Maps coloured, 7*s.* 6*d.*

—— Without the Maps, 3*s.* 6*d.*

POPE'S Poetical Works, including Translations. Edit., with Notes, by R. Carruthers. 2 vols.

—— **Homer's Iliad,** with Introduction and Notes by Rev. J. S. Watson, M.A. With Flaxman's Designs. *N. S.*

—— **Homer's Odyssey,** with the BATTLE OF FROGS AND MICE, Hymns, &c., by other translators, including Chapman. Introduction and Notes by J. S. Watson, M.A. With Flaxman's Designs. *N. S.*

—— **Life,** including many of his Letters. By R. Carruthers. Numerous Illustrations.

POTTERY AND PORCELAIN, and other objects of Vertu. Comprising an Illustrated Catalogue of the Bernal Collection, with the prices and names of the Possessors. Also an Introductory Lecture on Pottery and Porcelain, and an Engraved List of all Marks and Monograms. By H. G. Bohn. Numerous Woodcuts.

—— With coloured Illustrations, 10*s.* 6*d.*

PROUT'S (Father) Reliques. Edited by Rev. F. Mahony. Copyright edition, with the Author's last corrections and additions. 21 Etchings by D. Maclise, R.A. Nearly 600 pages. 5*s.* *N. S.*

RECREATIONS IN SHOOTING. With some Account of the Game found in the British Isles, and Directions for the Management of Dog and Gun. By 'Craven.' 62 Woodcuts and 9 Steel Engravings after A. Cooper, R.A.

REDDING'S History and Descriptions of Wines, Ancient and Modern. 20 Woodcuts.

RENNIE. Insect Architecture. Revised by Rev. J. G. Wood, M.A. 186 Woodcuts. *N. S.*

ROBINSON CRUSOE. With Memoir of Defoe, 12 Steel Engravings and 74 Woodcuts after Stothard and Harvey.

—— Without the Engravings, 3*s.* 6*d.*

ROME IN THE NINETEENTH CENTURY. An Account in 1817 of the Ruins of the Ancient City, and Monuments of Modern Times. By C. A. Eaton. 34 Steel Engravings. 2 vols.

SHARPE (S.) The History of Egypt, from the Earliest Times till the Conquest by the Arabs, A.D. 640. 2 Maps and upwards of 400 Woodcuts. 2 vols. *N. S.*

SOUTHEY'S Life of Nelson. With Additional Notes, Facsimiles of Nelson's Writing, Portraits, Plans, and 50 Engravings, after Birket Foster, &c. *N. S.*

STARLING'S (Miss) Noble Deeds of Women; or, Examples of Female Courage, Fortitude, and Virtue. With 14 Steel Portraits. *N. S.*

STUART and REVETT'S Antiquities of Athens, and other Monuments of Greece; with Glossary of Terms used in Grecian Architecture. 71 Steel Plates and numerous Woodcuts.

SWEET'S British Warblers. 5*s.*—*See Bechstein.*

TALES OF THE GENII; or, the Delightful Lessons of Horam, the Son of Asmar. Trans. by Sir C. Morrell. Numerous Woodcuts.

TASSO'S Jerusalem Delivered. In English Spenserian Verse, with Life, by J. H. Wiffen. With 8 Engravings and 24 Woodcuts. *N. S.*

WALKER'S Manly Exercises; containing Skating, Riding, Driving, Hunting, Shooting, Sailing, Rowing, Swimming, &c. 44 Engravings and numerous Woodcuts.

WALTON'S Complete Angler, or the Contemplative Man's Recreation, by Izaak Walton and Charles Cotton. With Memoirs and Notes by E. Jesse. Also an Account of Fishing Stations, Tackle, &c., by H. G. Bohn. Portrait and 203 Woodcuts. *N. S.*

—— With 26 additional Engravings on Steel, 7*s.* 6*d.*

—— **Lives of Donne, Wotton, Hooker,** &c., with Notes. A New Edition, re-revised by A. H. Bullen, with a Memoir of Izaak Walton by William Dowling. 6 Portraits, 6 Autograph Signatures, &c. *N.S.*

WELLINGTON, Life of. From the Materials of Maxwell. 18 Steel Engravings.

—— **Victories of.**—*See Maxwell.*

WESTROPP (H. M.) A Handbook of Archæology, Egyptian, Greek, Etruscan, Roman. By H. M. Westropp. Numerous Illustrations. 7*s.* 6*d.* *N. S.*

WHITE'S Natural History of Selborne, with Observations on various Parts of Nature, and the Naturalists' Calendar. Sir W. Jardine. Edit., with Notes and Memoir, by E. Jesse. 40 Portraits. *N. S.*

—— With the Plates coloured, 7*s.* 6*d.* *N. S.*

YOUNG LADY'S BOOK, The. A Manual of Recreations, Arts, Sciences, and Accomplishments. 1200 Woodcut Illustrations. 7*s.* 6*d.*

—— cloth gilt, gilt edges, 9*s.*

CLASSICAL LIBRARY.

TRANSLATIONS FROM THE GREEK AND LATIN.

95 *Vols. at* 5*s. each, excepting those marked otherwise.* (23*l.* 7*s. per set.*)

ÆSCHYLUS, The Dramas of. In English Verse by Anna Swanwick. 3rd edition. *N. S.*

—— **The Tragedies of.** In Prose, with Notes and Introduction, by T. A. Buckley, B.A. Portrait. 3*s.* 6*d.*

AMMIANUS MARCELLINUS. History of Rome during the Reigns of Constantius, Julian, Jovianus, Valentinian, and Valens, by C. D. Yonge, B.A. Double volume. 7*s.* 6*d.*

ANTONINUS (M. Aurelius), The Thoughts of. Translated literally, with Notes, Biographical Sketch, and Essay on the Philosophy, by George Long, M.A. 3*s.* 6*d.* *N. S.*

APULEIUS, The Works of. Comprising the Golden Ass, God of Socrates, Florida, and Discourse of Magic. With a Metrical Version of Cupid and Psyche, and Mrs. Tighe's Psyche. Frontispiece.

ARISTOPHANES' Comedies. Trans., with Notes and Extracts from Frere's and other Metrical Versions, by W. J. Hickie. Portrait. 2 vols.

ARISTOTLE'S Nicomachean Ethics. Trans., with Notes, Analytical Introduction, and Questions for Students, by Ven. Archdn. Browne.

—— **Politics and Economics.** Trans., with Notes, Analyses, and Index, by E. Walford, M.A., and an Essay and Life by Dr. Gillies.

—— **Metaphysics.** Trans., with Notes, Analysis, and Examination Questions, by Rev. John H. M'Mahon, M.A.

—— **History of Animals.** In Ten Books. Trans., with Notes and Index, by R. Cresswell, M.A.

—— **Organon;** or, Logical Treatises, and the Introduction of Porphyry. With Notes, Analysis, and Introduction, by Rev. O. F. Owen, M.A. 2 vols. 3*s.* 6*d.* each.

—— **Rhetoric and Poetics.** Trans., with Hobbes' Analysis, Exam. Questions, and Notes, by T. Buckley, B.A. Portrait.

ATHENÆUS. The Deipnosophists; or, the Banquet of the Learned. By C. D. Yonge, B.A. With an Appendix of Poetical Fragments. 3 vols.

ATLAS of Classical Geography. 22 large Coloured Maps. With a complete Index. Imp. 8vo. 7*s.* 6*d.*

BION.—*See Theocritus.*

CÆSAR. Commentaries on the Gallic and Civil Wars, with the Supplementary Books attributed to Hirtius, including the complete Alexandrian, African, and Spanish Wars. Trans. with Notes. Portrait.

CATULLUS, Tibullus, and the Vigil of Venus. Trans. with Notes and Biographical Introduction. To which are added, Metrical Versions by Lamb, Grainger, and others. Frontispiece.

CICERO'S Orations. Trans. by C. D. Yonge, B.A. 4 vols.

—— **On Oratory and Orators.** With Letters to Quintus and Brutus. Trans., with Notes, by Rev. J. S. Watson, M.A.

—— **On the Nature of the Gods,** Divination, Fate, Laws, a Republic, Consulship. Trans., with Notes, by C. D. Yonge, B.A.

—— **Academics,** De Finibus, and Tusculan Questions. By C. D. Yonge, B.A. With Sketch of the Greek Philosophers mentioned by Cicero.

CICERO'S Orations.—*Continued.*

—— **Offices;** or, Moral Duties. Cato Major, an Essay on Old Age; Lælius, an Essay on Friendship; Scipio's Dream; Paradoxes; Letter to Quintus on Magistrates. Trans., with Notes, by C. R. Edmonds. Portrait. 3*s.* 6*d.*

DEMOSTHENES' Orations. Trans., with Notes, Arguments, a Chronological Abstract, and Appendices, by C. Rann Kennedy. 5 vols.

DICTIONARY of LATIN and GREEK Quotations; including Proverbs, Maxims, Mottoes, Law Terms and Phrases. With the Quantities marked, and English Translations.

—— With Index Verborum (622 pages). 6*s.*

—— Index Verborum to the above, with the *Quantities* and Accents marked (56 pages), limp cloth. 1*s.*

DIOGENES LAERTIUS. Lives and Opinions of the Ancient Philosophers. Trans., with Notes, by C. D. Yonge, B.A.

EPICTETUS. The Discourses of. With the Encheiridion and Fragments. With Notes, Life, and View of his Philosophy, by George Long, M.A. *N. S.*

EURIPIDES. Trans., with Notes and Introduction, by T. A. Buckley, B.A. Portrait. 2 vols.

GREEK ANTHOLOGY. In English Prose by G. Burges, M.A. With Metrical Versions by Bland, Merivale, Lord Denman, &c.

GREEK ROMANCES of Heliodorus, Longus, and Achilles Tatius; viz., The Adventures of Theagenes and Chariclea; Amours of Daphnis and Chloe; and Loves of Clitopho and Leucippe. Trans., with Notes, by Rev R. Smith, M.A.

HERODOTUS. Literally trans. by Rev. Henry Cary, M.A. Portrait.

HESIOD, CALLIMACHUS, and Theognis. In Prose, with Notes and Biographical Notices by Rev. J. Banks, M.A. Together with the Metrical Versions of Hesiod, by Elton; Callimachus, by Tytler; and Theognis, by Frere.

HOMER'S Iliad. In English Prose, with Notes by T. A. Buckley, B.A. Portrait.

—— **Odyssey,** Hymns, Epigrams, and Battle of the Frogs and Mice. In English Prose, with Notes and Memoir by T. A. Buckley, B.A.

HORACE. In Prose by Smart, with Notes selected by T. A. Buckley, B.A. Portrait. 3*s.* 6*d.*

JUSTIN, CORNELIUS NEPOS, and Eutropius. Trans., with Notes, by Rev. J. S. Watson, M.A.

JUVENAL, PERSIUS, SULPICIA, and Lucilius. In Prose, with Notes, Chronological Tables, Arguments, by L. Evans, M.A. To which is added the Metrical Version of Juvenal and Persius by Gifford. Frontispiece.

LIVY. The History of Rome. Trans. by Dr. Spillan and others. 4 vols. Portrait.

LUCAN'S Pharsalia. In Prose, with Notes by H. T. Riley.

LUCRETIUS. In Prose, with Notes and Biographical Introduction by Rev. J. S. Watson, M.A. To which is added the Metrical Version by J. M. Good.

MARTIAL'S Epigrams, complete. In Prose, with Verse Translations selected from English Poets, and other sources. Dble. vol. (670 pages). *7s. 6d.*

MOSCHUS.—*See Theocritus.*

OVID'S Works, complete. In Prose, with Notes and Introduction. 3 vols.

PHALARIS. Bentley's Dissertations upon the Epistles of Phalaris, Themistocles, Socrates, Euripides, and the Fables of Æsop. With Introduction and Notes by Prof. W. Wagner, Ph.D.

PINDAR. In Prose, with Introduction and Notes by Dawson W. Turner. Together with the Metrical Version by Abraham Moore. Portrait.

PLATO'S Works. Trans., with Introduction and Notes. 6 vols.

—— **Dialogues.** A Summary and Analysis of. With Analytical Index to the Greek text of modern editions and to the above translations, by A. Day, LL.D.

PLAUTUS'S Comedies. In Prose, with Notes and Index by H. T. Riley, B.A. 2 vols.

PLINY'S Natural History. Trans., with Notes, by J. Bostock, M.D., F.R.S., and H. T. Riley, B.A. 6 vols.

PLINY. The Letters of Pliny the Younger. Melmoth's Translation, revised, with Notes and short Life, by Rev. F. C. T. Bosanquet, M.A.

PLUTARCH'S Morals. Theosophical Essays. Trans. by C. W. King, M.A. *N. S.*

—— **Lives.** *See page 6.*

PROPERTIUS, The Elegies of. With Notes, Literally translated by the Rev. P. J. F. Gantillon, M.A., with metrical versions of Select Elegies by Nott and Elton. *3s. 6d.*

QUINTILIAN'S Institutes of Oratory. Trans., with Notes and Biographical Notice, by Rev. J. S. Watson, M.A. 2 vols.

SALLUST, FLORUS, and VELLEIUS Paterculus. Trans., with Notes and Biographical Notices, by J. S. Watson, M.A.

SENECA. [*Preparing.*

SOPHOCLES. The Tragedies of. In Prose, with Notes, Arguments, and Introduction. Portrait.

STRABO'S Geography. Trans., with Notes, by W. Falconer, M.A., and H. C. Hamilton. Copious Index, giving Ancient and Modern Names. 3 vols.

SUETONIUS' Lives of the Twelve Cæsars and Lives of the Grammarians. The Translation of Thomson, revised, with Notes, by T. Forester.

TACITUS. The Works of. Trans., with Notes. 2 vols.

TERENCE and PHÆDRUS. In English Prose, with Notes and Arguments, by H. T. Riley, B.A. To which is added Smart's Metrical Version of Phædrus. With Frontispiece.

THEOCRITUS, BION, MOSCHUS, and Tyrtæus. In Prose, with Notes and Arguments, by Rev. J. Banks, M.A. To which are appended the METRICAL VERSIONS of Chapman. Portrait of Theocritus.

THUCYDIDES. The Peloponnesian War. Trans., with Notes, by Rev. H. Dale. Portrait. 2 vols. *3s. 6d.* each.

TYRTÆUS.—*See Theocritus.*

VIRGIL. The Works of. In Prose, with Notes by Davidson. Revised, with additional Notes and Biographical Notice, by T. A. Buckley, B.A. Portrait. *3s. 6d.*

XENOPHON'S Works. Trans., with Notes, by J. S. Watson, M.A., and others. Portrait. In 3 vols.

COLLEGIATE SERIES.

10 *Vols. at 5s. each.* (*2l. 10s. per set.*)

DANTE. The Inferno. Prose Trans., with the Text of the Original on the same page, and Explanatory Notes, by John A. Carlyle, M.D. Portrait. *N. S.*

—— **The Purgatorio.** Prose Trans., with the Original on the same page, and Explanatory Notes, by W. S. Dugdale. *N. S.*

NEW TESTAMENT (The) in Greek. Griesbach's Text, with the Readings of Mill and Scholz at the foot of the page, and Parallel References in the margin. Also a Critical Introduction and Chronological Tables. Two Fac-similes of Greek Manuscripts. 650 pages. 3*s.* 6*d.*

—— or bound up with a Greek and English Lexicon to the New Testament (250 pages additional, making in all 900). 5*s.*

The Lexicon may be had separately, price 2*s.*

DOBREE'S Adversaria. (Notes on the Greek and Latin Classics.) Edited by the late Prof. Wagner. 2 vols.

DONALDSON (Dr.) The Theatre of the Greeks. With Supplementary Treatise on the Language, Metres, and Prosody of the Greek Dramatists. Numerous Illustrations and 3 Plans. By J. W. Donaldson, D.D. *N. S.*

KEIGHTLEY'S (Thomas) Mythology of Ancient Greece and Italy. Revised by Leonhard Schmitz, Ph.D., LL.D. 12 Plates. *N. S.*

HERODOTUS, Notes on. Original and Selected from the best Commentators. By D. W. Turner, M.A. Coloured Map.

—— **Analysis and Summary of,** with a Synchronistical Table of Events—Tables of Weights, Measures, Money, and Distances—an Outline of the History and Geography—and the Dates completed from Gaisford, Baehr, &c. By J. T. Wheeler.

THUCYDIDES. An Analysis and Summary of. With Chronological Table of Events, &c., by J. T. Wheeler.

SCIENTIFIC LIBRARY.

57 *Vols. at 5s. each, excepting those marked otherwise.* (*15l. 2s. per set.*)

AGASSIZ and GOULD. Outline of Comparative Physiology touching the Structure and Development of the Races of Animals living and extinct. For Schools and Colleges. Enlarged by Dr. Wright. With Index and 300 Illustrative Woodcuts.

BOLLEY'S Manual of Technical Analysis; a Guide for the Testing and Valuation of the various Natural and Artificial Substances employed in the Arts and Domestic Economy, founded on the work of Dr. Bolley. Edit. by Dr. Paul. 100 Woodcuts.

BRIDGEWATER TREATISES.

—— **Bell (Sir Charles) on the Hand;** its Mechanism and Vital Endowments, as evincing Design. Preceded by an Account of the Author's Discoveries in the Nervous System by A. Shaw. Numerous Woodcuts.

—— **Kirby on the History, Habits,** and Instincts of Animals. With Notes by T. Rymer Jones. 100 Woodcuts. 2 vols.

—— **Kidd on the Adaptation of External** Nature to the Physical Condition of Man, principally with reference to the Supply of his Wants and the Exercises of his Intellectual Faculties. 3*s.* 6*d.*

BRIDGEWATER TREATISES.—*Continued.*

—— **Whewell's Astronomy and** General Physics, considered with reference to Natural Theology. Portrait of the Earl of Bridgewater. 3*s.* 6*d.*

—— **Chalmers on the Adaptation of** External Nature to the Moral and Intellectual Constitution of Man. With Memoir by Rev. Dr. Cumming. Portrait.

—— **Prout's Treatise on Chemistry,** Meteorology, and the Function of Digestion, with reference to Natural Theology. Edit. by Dr. J. W. Griffith. 2 Maps.

—— **Buckland's Geology and Mineralogy.** With Additions by Prof. Owen, Prof. Phillips, and R. Brown. Memoir of Buckland. Portrait. 2 vols. 15*s.* Vol. I. Text. Vol. II. 90 large plates with letterpress.

—— **Roget's Animal and Vegetable** Physiology. 463 Woodcuts. 2 vols. 6*s.* each.

BROWNE. Manual of Geology. By A. J. Jukes Browne. With numerous Diagrams and Illustrations, 6*s.*

CARPENTER'S (Dr. W. B.) Zoology. A Systematic View of the Structure, Habits, Instincts, and Uses of the principal Families of the Animal Kingdom, and of the chief Forms of Fossil Remains. Revised by W. S. Dallas, F.L.S. Numerous Woodcuts. 2 vols. *6s.* each.

—— **Mechanical Philosophy, Astronomy,** and Horology. A Popular Exposition. 181 Woodcuts.

—— **Vegetable Physiology and Systematic** Botany. A complete Introduction to the Knowledge of Plants. Revised by E. Lankester, M.D., &c. Numerous Woodcuts. *6s.*

—— **Animal Physiology.** Revised Edition. 300 Woodcuts. *6s.*

CHEVREUL on Colour. Containing the Principles of Harmony and Contrast of Colours, and their Application to the Arts; including Painting, Decoration, Tapestries, Carpets, Mosaics, Glazing, Staining, Calico Printing, Letterpress Printing, Map Colouring, Dress, Landscape and Flower Gardening, &c. Trans. by C. Martel. Several Plates.

—— With an additional series of 16 Plates in Colours, *7s. 6d.*

ENNEMOSER'S History of Magic. Trans. by W. Howitt. With an Appendix of the most remarkable and best authenticated Stories of Apparitions, Dreams, Second Sight, Table-Turning, and Spirit-Rapping, &c. 2 vols.

HIND'S Introduction to Astronomy. With Vocabulary of the Terms in present use. Numerous Woodcuts. *3s. 6d. N.S.*

HOGG'S (Jabez) Elements of Experimental and Natural Philosophy. Being an Easy Introduction to the Study of Mechanics, Pneumatics, Hydrostatics, Hydraulics, Acoustics, Optics, Caloric, Electricity, Voltaism, and Magnetism. 400 Woodcuts.

HUMBOLDT'S Cosmos; or, Sketch of a Physical Description of the Universe. Trans. by E. C. Otté, B. H. Paul, and W. S. Dallas, F.L.S. Portrait. 5 vols. *3s. 6d.* each, excepting vol. v., *5s.*

—— **Personal Narrative of his Travels** in America during the years 1799-1804. Trans., with Notes, by T. Ross. 3 vols.

—— **Views of Nature; or, Contemplations** of the Sublime Phenomena of Creation, with Scientific Illustrations. Trans. by E. C. Otté.

HUNT'S (Robert) Poetry of Science; or, Studies of the Physical Phenomena of Nature. By Robert Hunt, Professor at the School of Mines.

JOYCE'S Scientific Dialogues. A Familiar Introduction to the Arts and Sciences. For Schools and Young People. Numerous Woodcuts.

—— **Introduction to the Arts and** Sciences, for Schools and Young People. Divided into Lessons with Examination Questions. Woodcuts. *3s. 6d.*

JUKES-BROWNE'S Student's Handbook of Physical Geology. By A. J. Jukes-Browne, of the Geological Survey of England. With numerous Diagrams and Illustrations, *6s. N.S.*

KNIGHT'S (Charles) Knowledge is Power. A Popular Manual of Political Economy.

LECTURES ON PAINTING by the Royal Academicians, Barry, Opie, Fuseli. With Introductory Essay and Notes by R. Wornum. Portrait of Fuseli.

LILLY. Introduction to Astrology. With a Grammar of Astrology and Tables for calculating Nativities, by Zadkiel.

MANTELL'S (Dr.) Geological Excursions through the Isle of Wight and along the Dorset Coast. Numerous Woodcuts and Geological Map.

—— **Medals of Creation; or, First** Lessons in Geology: including Geological Excursions. Coloured Plates and several hundred Woodcuts. 2 vols. *7s. 6d.* each.

—— **Petrifactions and their Teach**ings. Handbook to the Organic Remains in the British Museum. Numerous Woodcuts. *6s.*

—— **Wonders of Geology; or, a** Familiar Exposition of Geological Phenomena. A coloured Geological Map of England, Plates, and 200 Woodcuts. 2 vols. *7s. 6d.* each.

MORPHY'S Games of Chess, being the Matches and best Games played by the American Champion, with explanatory and analytical Notes by J. Löwenthal. With short Memoir and Portrait of Morphy.

SCHOUW'S Earth, Plants, and Man. Popular Pictures of Nature. And Kobell's Sketches from the Mineral Kingdom. Trans. by A. Henfrey, F.R.S. Coloured Map of the Geography of Plants.

SMITH'S (Pye) Geology and Scripture; or, the Relation between the Scriptures and Geological Science. With Memoir.

STANLEY'S Classified Synopsis of the Principal Painters of the Dutch and Flemish Schools, including an Account of some of the early German Masters. By George Stanley.

STAUNTON'S Chess-Player's Handbook. A Popular and Scientific Introduction to the Game, with numerous Diagrams and Coloured Frontispiece. *N.S.*

STAUNTON.—*Continued.*

—— **Chess Praxis.** A Supplement to the Chess-player's Handbook. Containing the most important modern Improvements in the Openings; Code of Chess Laws; and a Selection of Morphy's Games. Annotated. 636 pages. Diagrams. 6*s.*

—— **Chess-Player's Companion.** Comprising a Treatise on Odds, Collection of Match Games, including the French Match with M. St. Amant, and a Selection of Original Problems. Diagrams and Coloured Frontispiece.

—— **Chess Tournament of 1851.** A Collection of Games played at this celebrated assemblage. With Introduction and Notes. Numerous Diagrams.

STOCKHARDT'S Experimental Chemistry. A Handbook for the Study of the Science by simple Experiments. Edit. by C. W. Heaton, F.C.S. Numerous Woodcuts. *N. S.*

URE'S (Dr. A.) Cotton Manufacture of Great Britain, systematically investigated; with an Introductory View of its Comparative State in Foreign Countries. Revised by P. L. Simmonds. 150 Illustrations. 2 vols.

—— **Philosophy of Manufactures,** or an Exposition of the Scientific, Moral and Commercial Economy of the Factory System of Great Britain. Revised by P. L. Simmonds. Numerous Figures. 800 pages. 7*s.* 6*d.*

ECONOMICS AND FINANCE.

GILBART'S History, Principles, and Practice of Banking. Revised to 1881 by A. S. Michie, of the Royal Bank of Scotland. Portrait of Gilbart. 2 vols. 10*s.* *N. S.*

REFERENCE LIBRARY.

27 *Volumes at Various Prices.* (8*l.* 4*s.* *per set.*)

BOHN'S Dictionary of Poetical Quotations. Fourth Edition. 6*s.*

BUCHANAN'S Dictionary of Science and Technical Terms used in Philosophy, Literature, Professions, Commerce, Arts, and Trades. By W. H. Buchanan, with Supplement. Edited by Jas. A. Smith. 6*s.*

BLAIR'S Chronological Tables. Comprehending the Chronology and History of the World, from the Earliest Times to the Russian Treaty of Peace, April 1856. By J. W. Rosse. 800 pages. 10*s.*

—— **Index of Dates.** Comprehending the principal Facts in the Chronology and History of the World, from the Earliest to the Present, alphabetically arranged; being a complete Index to the foregoing. By J. W. Rosse. 2 vols. 5*s.* each.

BOHN'S Dictionary of Quotations from the English Poets. 4th and cheaper Edition. 6*s.*

BUCHANAN'S Dictionary of Science and Technical Terms. With Supplement. 820 pp. 6*s.*

CLARK'S (Hugh) Introduction to Heraldry. Revised by J. R. Planché. 5*s.* 950 Illustrations.

—— *With the Illustrations coloured,* 15*s.* *N. S.*

CHRONICLES OF THE TOMBS. A Select Collection of Epitaphs, with Essay on Epitaphs and Observations on Sepulchral Antiquities. By T. J. Pettigrew, F.R.S., F.S.A. 5*s.*

COINS, Manual of.—*See Humphreys.*

DATES, Index of.—*See Blair.*

DICTIONARY of Obsolete and Provincial English. Containing Words from English Writers previous to the 19th Century. By Thomas Wright, M.A., F.S.A., &c. 2 vols. 5*s.* each.

EPIGRAMMATISTS (The). A Selection from the Epigrammatic Literature of Ancient, Mediæval, and Modern Times. With Introduction, Notes, Observations, Illustrations, an Appendix on Works connected with Epigrammatic Literature, by Rev. H. Dodd, M.A. 6*s.* *N. S.*

GAMES, Handbook of. Comprising Treatises on above 40 Games of Chance, Skill, and Manual Dexterity, including Whist, Billiards, &c. Edit. by Henry G. Bohn. Numerous Diagrams. 5*s.* *N. S.*

HUMPHREYS' Coin Collectors' Manual. An Historical Account of the Progress of Coinage from the Earliest Time, by H. N. Humphreys. 140 Illustrations. 2 vols. 5*s.* each. *N. S.*

LOWNDES' Bibliographer's Manual of English Literature. Containing an Account of Rare and Curious Books published in or relating to Great Britain and Ireland, from the Invention of Printing, with Biographical Notices and Prices, by W. T. Lowndes. Parts I.–X. (A to Z), 3*s*. 6*d*. each. Part XI. (Appendix Vol.), 5*s*. Or the 11 parts in 4 vols., half morocco, 2*l*. 2*s*.

MEDICINE, Handbook of Domestic, Popularly Arranged. By Dr. H. Davies. 700 pages. 5*s*.

NOTED NAMES OF FICTION. Dictionary of. Including also Familiar Pseudonyms, Surnames bestowed on Eminent Men, &c. By W. A. Wheeler, M.A. 5*s*. *N. S.*

POLITICAL CYCLOPÆDIA. A Dictionary of Political, Constitutional, Statistical, and Forensic Knowledge; forming a Work of Reference on subjects of Civil Administration, Political Economy, Finance, Commerce, Laws, and Social Relations. 4 vols. 3*s*. 6*d*. each.

PROVERBS, Handbook of. Containing an entire Republication of Ray's Collection, with Additions from Foreign Languages and Sayings, Sentences, Maxims, and Phrases, collected by H. G. Bohn. 5*s*.

—— **A Polyglot of Foreign.** Comprising French, Italian, German, Dutch, Spanish, Portuguese, and Danish. With English Translations. 5*s*.

SYNONYMS and ANTONYMS; or, Kindred Words and their Opposites, Collected and Contrasted by Ven. C. J. Smith, M.A. 5*s*. *N. S.*

WRIGHT (Th.)—*See Dictionary.*

NOVELISTS' LIBRARY.

10 *Volumes at 3s. 6d. each, excepting those marked otherwise.* (1*l*. 18*s*. *per set.*)

BURNEY'S Evelina; or, a Young Lady's Entrance into the World. By F. Burney (Mme. D'Arblay). With Introduction and Notes by A. R. Ellis, Author of 'Sylvestra,' &c. *N. S.*

—— **Cecilia.** With Introduction and Notes by A. R. Ellis. 2 vols. *N. S.*

FIELDING'S Joseph Andrews and his Friend Mr. Abraham Adams. With Roscoe's Biography. *Cruikshank's Illustrations.* *N. S.*

—— **History of Tom Jones, a Foundling.** Roscoe's Edition. *Cruikshank's Illustrations.* 2 vols. *N. S.*

FIELDING.—*Continued.*

—— **Amelia.** Roscoe's Edition, revised. *Cruikshank's Illustrations.* 5*s*. *N. S.*

GROSSI'S Marco Visconti. Trans. by A. F. D. *N. S.*

MANZONI. The Betrothed: being a Translation of 'I Promessi Sposi.' Numerous Woodcuts. 1 vol. (732 pages), 5*s*. *N. S.*

STOWE (Mrs. H. B.) Uncle Tom's Cabin; or, Life among the Lowly. 8 full-page Illustrations. *N. S.*

ARTISTS' LIBRARY.

5 *Volumes at Various Prices.* (1*l*. 8*s*. 6*d*. *per set.*)

BELL (Sir Charles). The Anatomy and Philosophy of Expression, as Connected with the Fine Arts. 5*s*. *N. S.*

DEMMIN. History of Arms and Armour from the Earliest Period. By Auguste Demmin. Trans. by C. C. Black, M.A., Assistant Keeper, S. K. Museum. 1900 Illustrations. 7*s*. 6*d*. *N. S.*

FLAXMAN. Lectures on Sculpture. With Three Addresses to the R.A. by Sir R. Westmacott, R.A., and Memoir of Flaxman. Portrait and 53 Plates. 6*s*. *N. S.*

LEONARDO DA VINCI'S Treatise on Painting. Trans. by J. F. Rigaud, R.A. With a Life and an Account of his Works by J. W. Brown. Numerous Plates. 5*s*. *N. S.*

PLANCHÉ'S History of British Costume, from the Earliest Time to the 19th Century. By J. R. Planché. 400 Illustrations. *s*. *N. S.*

BOHN'S CHEAP SERIES.

PRICE ONE SHILLING EACH.

A Series of Complete Stories or Essays, mostly reprinted from Vols. in Bohn's Libraries, and neatly bound in stiff paper cover, with cut edges, suitable for Railway Reading.

ASCHAM (ROGER).—

SCHOLEMASTER. By PROFESSOR MAYOR.

CARPENTER (DR. W. B.).—

PHYSIOLOGY OF TEMPERANCE AND TOTAL ABSTINENCE.

EMERSON.—

ENGLAND AND ENGLISH CHARACTERISTICS. Lectures on the Race, Ability, Manners, Truth, Character, Wealth, Religion, &c. &c.

NATURE: An Essay. To which are added Orations, Lectures, and Addresses.

REPRESENTATIVE MEN: Seven Lectures on PLATO, SWEDENBORG, MONTAIGNE, SHAKESPEARE, NAPOLEON, and GOETHE.

TWENTY ESSAYS on Various Subjects.

THE CONDUCT OF LIFE.

FRANKLIN (BENJAMIN).—

AUTOBIOGRAPHY. Edited by J. SPARKS.

HAWTHORNE (NATHANIEL).—

TWICE-TOLD TALES. Two Vols. in One.

SNOW IMAGE, and other Tales.

SCARLET LETTER.

HOUSE WITH THE SEVEN GABLES.

TRANSFORMATION; or the Marble Fawn. Two Parts.

HAZLITT (W.).—

TABLE-TALK: Essays on Men and Manners. Three Parts.

PLAIN SPEAKER: Opinions on Books, Men, and Things. Three Parts.

LECTURES ON THE ENGLISH COMIC WRITERS.

LECTURES ON THE ENGLISH POETS.

HAZLITT (W.).—Continued.

LECTURES ON THE CHARACTERS OF SHAKESPEARE'S PLAYS.

LECTURES ON THE LITERATURE OF THE AGE OF ELIZABETH, chiefly Dramatic.

IRVING (WASHINGTON).—

LIFE OF MOHAMMED. With Portrait.

LIVES OF SUCCESSORS OF MOHAMMED.

LIFE OF GOLDSMITH.

SKETCH-BOOK.

TALES OF A TRAVELLER.

TOUR ON THE PRAIRIES.

CONQUESTS OF GRANADA AND SPAIN. Two Parts.

LIFE AND VOYAGES OF COLUMBUS. Two Parts.

COMPANIONS OF COLUMBUS: Their Voyages and Discoveries.

ADVENTURES OF CAPTAIN BONNEVILLE in the Rocky Mountains and the Far West.

KNICKERBOCKER'S HISTORY OF NEW YORK, from the Beginning of the World to the End of the Dutch Dynasty.

TALES OF THE ALHAMBRA.

CONQUEST OF FLORIDA UNDER HERNANDO DE SOTO.

ABBOTSFORD AND NEWSTEAD ABBEY.

SALMAGUNDI; or, The Whim-Whams and Opinions of LAUNCELOT LANGSTAFF, Esq.

BRACEBRIDGE HALL; or, The Humourists.

ASTORIA; or, Anecdotes of an Enterprise beyond the Rocky Mountains.

WOLFERT'S ROOST, and Other Tsles.

LAMB (CHARLES).—

ESSAYS OF ELIA. With a Portrait.

LAST ESSAYS OF ELIA.

ELIANA. With Biographical Sketch.

MARRYAT (CAPTAIN).

PIRATE AND THE THREE CUTTERS. With a Memoir of the Author.

WEBSTER'S DICTIONARY.

'SEVENTY years passed before Johnson was followed by Webster, an American writer, who faced the task of the English Dictionary with a full appreciation of its requirements, leading to better practical results.' . . .

'His laborious comparison of twenty languages, though never published, bore fruit in his own mind, and his training placed him both in knowledge and judgment far in advance of Johnson as a philologist. Webster's *American Dictionary of the English Language* was published in 1828, and of course appeared at once in England, where successive re-editing *has yet kept it in the highest place as a practical Dictionary*.'

'The acceptance of an American Dictionary in England has itself had immense effect in keeping up the community of speech, to break which would be a grievous harm, not to English-speaking nations alone, but to mankind. The result of this has been that the common Dictionary must suit both sides of the Atlantic.' . . .

'The good average business-like character of Webster's Dictionary, both in style and matter, made it as distinctly suited as Johnson's was distinctly unsuited to be expanded and re-edited by other hands. Professor Goodrich's edition of 1847 is not much more than enlarged and amended; but other revisions since have so much novelty of plan as to be described as distinct works.' . . .

'The American revised Webster's Dictionary of 1864, published in America and England, is of an altogether higher order than these last [The London Imperial and Student's]. It bears on its title-page the names of Drs. Goodrich and Porter, but inasmuch as its especial improvement is in the etymological department, the care of which was committed to Dr. Mahn of Berlin, we prefer to describe it in short as the Webster-Mahn Dictionary. Many other literary men, among them Professors Whitney and Dana, aided in the task of compilation and revision. On consideration it seems that the editors and contributors have gone far toward improving Webster to the utmost that he will bear improvement. The *vocabulary has become almost complete as regards usual words, while the definitions keep throughout to Webster's simple careful style, and the derivations are assigned with the aid of good modern authorities*.'

'On the whole, the Webster-Mahn Dictionary as it stands is most respectable, and **certainly the best Practical English Dictionary extant**.'—From the *Quarterly Review*, Oct. 1873.

LONDON:

Printed by STRANGEWAYS AND SONS, Tower Street, Upper St. Martin's Lane.

www.ingramcontent.com/pod-product-compliance
Lightning Source LLC
Chambersburg PA
CBHW031826270326
41932CB00008B/564

* 9 7 8 3 3 3 7 2 3 8 4 4 5 *